YOUNG PEOPLE IN RURAL AREAS OF EUROPE

Perspectives on Rural Policy and Planning

Series Editors:
Andrew Gilg
University of Exeter, UK
Keith Hoggart
King's College, London, UK
Henry Buller
Cheltenham College of Higher Education, UK
Owen Furuseth
University of North Carolina, USA
Mark Lapping
University of South Maine, USA

Young People in Rural Areas of Europe

Edited by

BIRGIT JENTSCH and MARK SHUCKSMITH
The Arkleton Centre for Rural Development Research

ASHGATE

Published by
Ashgate Publishing Limited
Gower House
Croft Road
Aldershot
Hants GU11 3HR
England

Ashgate Publishing Company
Suite 420
101 Cherry Street
Burlington, VT 05401-4405
USA

Ashgate website: http://www.ashgate.com

British Library Cataloguing in Publication Data
Young people in rural areas of Europe. - (Perspectives on
   rural policy and planning)
   1. Rural youth - Europe - Economic conditions 2. Rural youth
   - Europe - Social conditions 3. Rural youth - Employment -
   Europe 4. Rural development - Europe 5. Marginality, Social -
   Europe 6. Rural unemployment - Europe 7. Europe - Social
   policy
   I. Jentsch, Birgit II. Shucksmith, Mark
   307.1'412'083'094

Library of Congress Cataloging-in-Publication Data
Young people in rural areas of Europe / edited by Birgit Jentsch and Mark Shucksmith.
      p. cm. -- (Perspectives on rural policy and planning)
   Includes bibliographical references and index.
   ISBN 0-7546-3478-7
   1. Rural youth--Europe. 2. Rural youth--Employment--Europe. 3. Rural
development--Europe. 4. Europe--Rural conditions. I. Jentsch, Birgit. II. Shucksmith,
Mark. III. Series.

HQ799.E9Y65 2003
305.235'094'091734--dc21

2002043979

ISBN 0 7546 3478 7

Printed and bound in Great Britain by Athenaeum Press Ltd.,
Gateshead, Tyne & Wear

Contents

List of Tables

Appendices

List of Figures

List of Contributors

Co-ordinating Team:
Professor Mark Shucksmith, Dr Birgit Jentsch, Dr John A. Burnett

Scientific Consultants:
Dr Euan Phimister and Dr Alana Gilbert
Arkleton Centre for Rural Development Research
University of Aberdeen, Scotland

Partners:
Dr Toivo Muilu
Department of Geography
University of Oulu
Finland

Elizabeth Auclair and Didier Vanoni
Fors Recherche Sociale, Paris
France

Gerhard Dietz and Dr Gerhard Christe
Institute fur Arbeitsmarktforschung and Jugendberufshilfe (IA)
Oldenberg, Germany

Brian McGrath, Dr John Canavan and Professor Chris Curtin
Dept of Political Science and Sociology
National University of Ireland, Galway
Ireland

Dr Thomas Dax, Ingrid Machold and Christine Meisinger
Bundesanstalt fur Bergbauernfragen – BABF, Vienna
Austria

Dr Jose Portela, Dr Chris Gerry, Patrícia António, Carlos Marques
and Vasco Rebelo
Departamento de Economia e Sociologia
Universidade de Tras-os-Montes e Alto Douro, Vila Real
Portugal

Acknowledgements

During the course of this project many people have volunteered their time and energies to assist us in this research on Policies and Young People in Rural Development (PaYPiRD). Thanks are due to those who participated in the piloting of the project, both interviewees and 'local actors', as well as the various 'gatekeepers' who helped us identify potential interviewees and, in some cases, provide facilities for that purpose. We would also like to acknowledge the help given by various people in the process of obtaining relevant secondary and background material, including national data sets, during the different stages of the research. Thanks are especially due to Janet Shucksmith for pointing us towards the literature of youth research, and commenting on a draft of the conclusions.

Our grateful thanks are also due to Rona Kennedy, Rob Burton and Jane Atterton for their excellent work in producing the camera-ready copy and liaising with the publishers. We also wish to acknowledge the important contribution of our colleague, John Burnett.

Finally, and fittingly, our main debt of gratitude is to the young people themselves, who by agreeing to share their thoughts and opinions with us, gave a sophisticated and heartfelt account of the experiences of European youth in the participant rural areas. This international comparative dimension was facilitated by the exchange of information between the different partner countries. Hopefully, the recommendations on which this research is based will make young people's transition to the labour market a less troubled and uncertain journey.

Please note that the following companion volume is also available: "Voices of Rural Youth – A Break with Traditional Patterns" PaYPiRD Volume 2, edited by Thomas Dax and Ingrid Machold, published by Bundesanstalt fur Bergbauernfragen, Vienna, Austria. Orders: Bundesanstalt fur Bergbauernfragen, Mollwaldplatz 5, A-1040 Wein. Fax +43 (1) 504 88 69 39 email: office@babf.bmlf.gv.at.

Chapter 1

Introduction

Birgit Jentsch and Mark Shucksmith

1. Rural Youth and Social Inclusion in the New Europe

Unemployment, especially of young people is a central concern of the European Union, in rural areas as elsewhere. This is not surprising, given that youth unemployment in the EU affects 6% of the total population aged 15-19, and 13.7% of those aged 20-24. There are, however, wide variations across member states. For example, Germany and Austria have rates below 6%, whereas Finland's unemployment rate for the 20-24 age group is 17% (http://europa.eu.int/comm.dg05/empl&esf/naps/naps_en.htm). While labour markets are not the only important dimension of social inclusion, they are the primary focus of this project.

It is clear that high priority is accorded to these issues of social cohesion and exclusion in the Treaty of European Union agreed at Maastricht and in the objectives of the structural funds. The theme of combating unemployment and reinsertion into work, in particular, is further developed in the Commission's papers on Growth, Competitiveness and Unemployment and on Social Policy, and is referred to in the Cork Declaration which proposed "an integrated approach", aimed at "reversing out-migration, combating poverty, stimulating employment and equality of opportunity, and improved rural well-being" among other objectives.

Perhaps most significantly in practical terms, national action for employment has been shaped by the Employment Guidelines for 1998, which were adopted by the European Council in December 1997, following the Luxembourg Job Summit the month before. A common structure for National Action Plans (NAPs) was negotiated, and the Member States agreed to submit their plans by mid-April. The aim of the NAPs is to implement the EU employment guidelines, fight against unemployment, and the harmonisation of basic objectives. The Commission reviewed the actions proposed under the Employment Guidelines 1998, and assessed how Member States have endorsed the policy objectives and targets included in each of the nineteen guidelines. One aim is "to increase the effectiveness of labour market policies in fighting youth unemployment, by shifting towards an increasingly preventive approach underpinned by early identification of individual needs".

Notwithstanding such significant activities at European and national level aiming at social inclusion, the processes of European integration themselves are likely to generate opportunities as well as social exclusion for some groups of people (for example, through the convergence disciplines of the EMU requiring fiscal restraint and reduced social expenditure). Apart from the overarching concerns with promoting an 'active society' rather than a 'dual society', these changes are likely to have uneven impacts upon different areas of Europe, and one crucial dimension here might be whether these areas are rural or urban. However, most research on social exclusion focuses on urban areas in spite of the fact that social exclusion is also an issue in rural development, the more so as sectoral policies give way to territorial policies, as envisaged in the Cork Declaration (1996) and in the Hyland Report to the European Parliament. The Maastricht Treaty identifies the development of the EU's rural areas as one of the objectives of cohesion policy, and at Lisbon European leaders subsequently confirmed that rural development should be one of the priorities of Community structural policies. This has been further emphasised in Agenda 2000.

Yet, despite this commitment, we are very poorly informed about rural society across Europe beyond the agricultural industry, and little attention is paid to social exclusion and integration in rural Europe. The few studies of rural labour markets which exist have tended to be concerned mainly with the 'demand' side, and pay little attention to employees and their skills. Even less is known about how young people live in rural areas of Europe, their incomes and quality of life, their perceptions of how policies impact upon them, and how they are affected by the dynamics of social and economic change. There has been no comparative study across EU member states of the experience of living in rural society, least of all for young people, although the rural projects in the Poverty 3 programme met for a series of cross-national seminars to analyse issues arising from their own immediate experiences. Notwithstanding these seminars, which inevitably focused on local concerns, the lack of information remains and continues to hamper attempts to formulate effective rural policies.

Rural Europe is subject to major structural changes, both as a result of changes in rural economies and societies and as a consequence of the Maastricht Treaty, the Single European Act, CAP reform, the GATT agreement, the disciplines of the ERM, and the further enlargement of the EU. Mernagh and Commins (1992) have pointed to:

- transition to an era of production limitations in agriculture;
- decoupling of income supports from food production programmes;
- reorganisation of industrial production to the possible disadvantage of rural areas;
- growth of the services sector in urban areas;
- centralisation tendencies as a consequence of the single market;
- continuing depopulation from many rural areas;
- the expansion of information technologies, tourism and leisure industries.

To this list might be added:

- counter-urbanisation tendencies in several northern European states;
- the impacts of political changes in Eastern Europe on eastern EU states;
- increasing environmental demands placed on the countryside;
- the effects of European regional policy (the structural funds);
- ageing rural populations;
- declining service provision and fiscal constraints on public provision;
- changing conceptions of countryside itself.

Mernagh and Commins indicate that these trends have different implications for differently situated rural areas (for example, remote or accessible) and that they will have uneven impacts on different social groups. "Several groups face the risk of economic and social exclusion...", yet at this crucial juncture we still know very little about the specific causes of young people's exclusion from rural labour markets, still less how these will be modified by the macro-trends listed above and by the meso-level of institutions between the state and the individual. In order to develop effective policies both for achieving rural development objectives (for example, through LEADER and through the Structural Funds), and for tackling young people's economic and social exclusion in rural areas, the EU needs information about the effects of existing policies on young people's rural labour market opportunities, the causes of their exclusion or inclusion, how these are changing, and how young people themselves respond. This study is in part based on the recognition that it is crucial at the present time to gain such knowledge and to devise effective strategies for rural development policies that broaden and deepen the labour market opportunities of young people in rural areas. Of course, in order to achieve such an objective, we need to concern ourselves also with conceptual and theoretical considerations, and these are explored in Chapter 2.

In Chapter 3 we review existing knowledge of these issues and provide such contextual information as we can, drawing primarily on Eurostat data and the Luxembourg Expenditure Survey. We will argue that this data is inadequate, and that our knowledge of rural social exclusion and its causes is still rudimentary. We do have some knowledge from studies in Britain, Ireland and Austria, and a major new French study by INRA, CNRS and SEGESA, but these findings may not reflect circumstances in other rural areas of Europe, particularly given its diversity. Neither do they focus on the specific situation of young people and the effects of policies upon them. More research is required to explore how the systemic failures set out above are related to pathways to exclusion and insertion, and to policies in different rural areas, especially for young people. Until then, it will be hard to frame policies which address the underlying causes of young people's social exclusion in rural areas of Europe.

This study seeks to answer the questions: How do policies at various levels impact on the 'pathways' to young people's exclusion and integration in rural areas, and how do these differ between social groups (especially by class and gender) and between rural areas? What role can policies play in ensuring the active participation of young people in rural labour markets?

2.   Research Objectives

The specific objectives of this research are as follows:

- to analyse in a bottom-up approach in seven study areas (in UK, Ireland, Germany, Portugal, France, Finland, and Austria) the effects of policies and operational programmes at various levels on young people's integration into rural labour markets, and therefore on social cohesion in rural areas;
- to explore how changes in labour markets, labour market policies and welfare regimes, at various levels, interact with changes in the nature and duration of the youth transition to include or exclude young people from rural employment opportunities;
- to consider appropriate means and levels of policy implementation.

The emphasis is on comparative case studies of how policies impact on real-life conditions and experiences, and on linking these narratives with macro processes of economic, social and institutional change. Consequently, the methodology is mainly qualitative, supplemented by quantitative contextual enquiry and secondary data analysis.

3.   The Study Areas and Research Design

The research is being carried out in case study areas in seven EU member states, selected to include a range of labour market policies, welfare regimes, and types of rural area, following the typology proposed by the EC's document "The Future of Rural Society" (1988). This identified three standard problems facing rural areas: ·

- accessible rural areas, particularly in the centre-north of the Community, facing pressures on land use from competing interests, and undergoing social and economic transformation and threats to the environment;
- areas of rural decline, particularly in the outlying Mediterranean parts of the Community, where the need is perceived in the book to be for development and economic diversification;
- very marginal areas remote from the mainstream of Community life, such as mountain areas and islands, where rural decline, depopulation and abandonment of the land are characteristic and the need is perceived to be to maintain a minimum population to protect the fragile environment.

As noted above, the countries included in the study are Scotland, Ireland, Germany, Portugal, France, Finland, and Austria. It is intended that a study area within each of these countries will allow the inclusion of each of these three types of standard rural problem, while also allowing for sufficient variation for analysis. This is not to say that these study areas are representative of each country. Within each country, case study areas were selected in relation to remoteness, population density, strength of local labour market, and other social and cultural variables. While a classification of the study areas can be seen in the table below, summary information about each study area with regard to their population, economy, education, employment and unemployment is provided in Appendix 1. Of course, each of the study areas might be seen as overlapping different categories in the CEC's typology, and more nuanced differences emerged in the course of the study.

Table 1.1 The PaYPiRD Study Areas

Study Area	Country	Type 1	Type 2	Type 3
Angus, NE Scotland	UK	√		
Suomussalmi	Finland			√
Murau, Upper Styria	Austria			√
NE Mayenne	France		√	
Wesermarsch	Germany	√		
NW Connemara	Ireland			√
Santa Maria di Penaguiao (SMP)	Portugal		√	

A common research design has been developed and applied in all study areas, which is elaborated in Chapter 4. In summary, this can be divided into three crucial stages.

- Stage one consisted of an audit of policies affecting young people in rural areas, especially those policies pertaining to labour markets. It also includes a review of literature and other secondary sources on changing labour markets.
- Stage two comprised empirical surveys and the preparation of national reports. This also included the international comparative analysis of secondary data sets. At the same time, each national team conducted in-depth, semi-structured interviews with 30 to 40 young people in each study area. The interviews were based on a commonly agreed interview schedule and a short questionnaire, and were followed by focus group interviews.
- Stage three consisted of the preparation of the final book, involving the development of six themes by the national teams, one of which will be jointly dealt with by two partners.

As is argued in the next Chapter, from the outset we have found it helpful to focus on the different systems through which resources, including knowledge and information, are allocated in society. These four systems (market, state, civil society, and social networks) are crucial in structuring the life-chances of young people in rural areas as well as in forming the arenas in which young people themselves can engage and act. From this conceptualisation we developed a number of themes for analysis which seek to investigate the operation of each of these systems and their interactions. These are as follows:

- how far can state policies addressing integration of young people into employment tackle social exclusion?
- what characteristics make rural areas attractive to young people, and what are the implications of this for rural development? ("The attractiveness of rural areas: a crucial issue for local development policies")
- an analysis of rural labour markets in Europe and young people's role in them ("Rural young people and labour market indicators")
- what can be learnt from projects involving youth in local community development? ("Rural Youth in Local Community Development – Lessons through 'Partnership'")
- the effect of rural development policies on young people's integration into the social and economic life in rural areas? ("Rural development programmes and their impact on youth integration")
- the role of social networks in finding employment ("Social networks, labour market and policy impact in Santa Marta de Penaguiao")
- the interface between school and the labour market as one dimension of youth transition ("Experiences of rural youth in the 'risk society': transitions from education to the labour market")

4.   The Structure of the Book

Following this introductory chapter, Chapter 2 summarises the conceptual and theoretical context for this work, touching on labour markets, social exclusion, and the youth transition.

In Chapter 3 we review existing knowledge of these issues and provide such contextual information as we can, drawing primarily on Eurostat data and the Luxembourg Expenditure Survey. One section explores the feasibility of developing indicators of rural labour market strength, given the available data sources. Another substantial section explores the use of household panel micro-data.

Chapter 4 describes the methodology in more detail, explaining how the research was undertaken and discussing the issues which arise in comparative international studies of this type.

Chapters 5 to 10 then investigate, in turn, each of the themes listed above, except for the theme of strength of local labour markets which is included within Chapter 3. Each of these chapters is written by one of the partners but seeks to integrate findings from all of the study areas, drawing on the reports produced by each national team concerning their own study area. These 'national' reports are not included in this volume but are available separately, either in full or in summary form.

Finally, we draw conclusions from the research and make recommendations for policy.

Chapter 2

Conceptual Framework and Literature Review

Mark Shucksmith

This chapter reviews the existing literature on a number of key concepts for this study and seeks to ascertain what is already known about policies and rural development in relation to young people. It also seeks to clarify the use of these concepts (rural development; social exclusion; youth transitions; local labour markets) to assist with later analysis.

1. Rural Development

There have been many attempts to define rural development. According to the OECD (1990), quoted by Kearney, Boyle and Walsh (1995):

> A view is emerging that it is constructive to view rural development as a broad notion, encompassing all important issues pertinent to the individual and collective vitality of rural people and places. It encompasses such concerns as education, environment, individual and public health, housing, public services and facilities, capacity for leadership and governance, and cultural heritage as well as sectional and general economic issues.

Over the 1990s many countries were re-orienting their approaches and recognising the necessity of framing a comprehensive rural policy in the interest of society as well as rural people. At the international level the debate centred on increasing understanding for the complex framework and changes in the patterns of sectoral and territorial inter-relations between and among rural and urban areas (OECD 1993b). This perception has been adopted by most OECD countries and has been included both in territorial development (Bryden 1999) and sector policies, e.g. agricultural policy reform (OECD 1998). The EU Commission has particularly looked in its preparatory studies for Agenda 2000 on the scope of enlarging the Common Agricultural Policy (CAP) towards a Common Agricultural and Rural Policy for Europe (CARPE) (Buckwell et al., 1997). As a result of this all-embracing perspective, an integrated or holistic approach to rural development now tends to be seen as desirable, if difficult to achieve.

Kulkarni and Rajan (1991) placed a particular emphasis on community empowerment and the reduction of inequalities in their definition. For them, rural development is a social and political process through which to:

- increase the standard of living of all citizens, reduce inequality of incomes, expand employment opportunities, and improve the supply of services;
- enhance the self-esteem of individuals and groups by ensuring they have the opportunity to participate in the development process, rather than being alienated through a variety of exclusion processes;
- expand the range of economic and social choices available to individuals and groups, so reducing dependency; and
- ensure the development process is both economically and environmentally sustainable.

It is notable that this conception of rural development refers not only to reducing income inequality and expanding employment opportunities, but also to other dimensions of exclusion, dependency and choice. These have been and will be central elements in our study, and it is our understanding also that these should be regarded as integral concerns of rural development. Rural development may therefore be about building prosperity but it is also about inequality. While it promotes access, participation and cohesion, it must also be concerned with exclusion and empowerment.

Whether rural development policies, in practice, can also help to combat poverty, inequality and exclusion is an empirical question, but one that is often obscured. As Curtin et al. (1997) point out:

> Traditional 'rural development' perspectives have generally taken for granted that rural poverty, in the sense of economic and social peripherality, is identical with or a result of geographical peripherality, and have sought interventions that would make rural *areas* less marginal or less 'spatially excluded'.

Moreover, the territorial approach favoured by integrated rural development initiatives tends to obscure inequalities and power relations between social groups within 'a community', by employing a consensus perspective (Curtin et al., 1997). It is for this reason that many previous integrated rural development initiatives have failed in their attempts to reduce inequalities and exclusion, instead merely reinforcing the power and wealth of existing elites (Shortall 1994). The discussion on rural research has been driven by an elaboration from a predominantly territorial approach to a concept which largely incorporates social dimensions as crucial issues within rural research. The critics of a simple juxtaposition of rural and urban areas (e.g. Hoggart 1990, Pratt 1996) have been addressed by increasing the importance in research of issues like social exclusion and giving greater attention to spatial and societal inter-relation and inter-action. Recently focus has therefore been placed on the challenge of understanding rural diversity through incorporating social and political analysis within a multidisciplinary approach (Lowe 1997). This is a crucial question for both European and national policy, which currently presents LEADER, for example, as serving both rural economic development and social policy objectives (see the Green Paper on Social Policy, and the Cork Declaration). The crucial point, for our purposes, is that rural development is closely bound up with issues of social exclusion, particularly from labour markets, and it is to social exclusion that we now turn.

In Europe, rural development policies have particularly been developed since the late 1980s. This policy shift has been influenced by the publication the EC's document "The Future of Rural Society" (1988) and the reform of Structural Funds since 1988. The framework of the Structural Funds and the development of regional programmes and policies for rural areas are presented in more depth in Chapter 8 (Rural Development Programmes and their Impact on Youth Integration).

2.   Social Exclusion

At the outset it is important to distinguish between social exclusion and poverty, and secondly between process and outcome. Poverty was the focus of the EU's Poverty 1 and Poverty 2 programmes, and indeed the Council of Ministers in 1984, following Townsend (1979), defined "the poor" as "persons, families and groups of persons whose resources (material, cultural and social) are so limited as to exclude them from the minimum acceptable way of life in the member states in which they live". In contrast, the Poverty 3 programme was concerned with the integration of the "least privileged" and by the time the programme was actually launched, the focus had shifted to "social exclusion". According to Room (1994), the distinction between poverty and social exclusion represents a three-fold change in perspective: (i) the shift from a focus on income or expenditure to multi-dimensional disadvantage; (ii) the shift from a static account of states of disadvantage to a dynamic analysis of processes; and (iii) the shift from a focus on the individual or household to a recognition of the importance of the local context. The focus of research is now therefore "on multi-dimensional, dynamic processes of social exclusion, within the context of local communities".

The rapporteurs of the Poverty 3 programme in turn suggested that we should consider the distinction between poverty and social exclusion as a distinction between outcome and process. Berghman (1995) points out that each term could have a double connotation as both process and outcome, and he suggests clarifying matters by using "poverty and deprivation to denote the outcome,... and pauperisation and social exclusion to refer to the process". In accordance with this, the focus of current research is on dynamic processes, and the identification of "pathways" of exclusion and inclusion in the "risk society" (Beck 1992) of late modernity. Berghman argues that this necessitates a research emphasis on social mobility and social differentiation, and this point will be returned to below as one important means by which research on social exclusion may be founded more securely on social theory (see also Shucksmith and Chapman 1998).

It is clear, however, that social exclusion and inclusion are processes which amount to more than social mobility, and indeed there are a number of contrasting perspectives on these concepts. As Lee and Murie (1999) have noted, "the concept of social exclusion is contested, and there is no one single accepted definition". Lee and Murie follow Levitas[1] (1998) in identifying three competing ways, corresponding to different intellectual traditions in which the term social exclusion has been used:

- a European "integrationist" approach in which the excluded have no jobs and need to be reintegrated through paid employment, such as through 'welfare to work' initiatives. Employment is seen as an integrating force, both through income, identity and sense of self-worth, and networks. A link is often made with the concept of "active citizenship";
- an Anglo-Saxon "poverty" approach in which the causes of exclusion are related to low income and a lack of material resources, as discussed above;
- an "underclass" approach, deriving from US writers, in which the excluded are viewed as deviants from the moral and cultural norms of society, exhibit a "culture of poverty" or a "dependency culture" and are blamed for their own poverty and its intergenerational transmission. This approach has been vigorously contested.

If one's purpose is to develop and apply the concept of social exclusion then it is the first (integrationist) approach which offers promise for the reasons already discussed. However, even this approach may be criticised as unduly narrow, with its exclusive emphasis on integration through paid employment. As Lee and Murie (1999) observe, households access resources in many other ways than through the labour market. Accordingly, it will be argued in this book that processes of social exclusion, in both rural and urban areas, extend far beyond the labour market and indeed are multi-dimensional.

A similarly broad framework has been proposed by the Belgian researchers, Duffy (1995), Kesteloot (1998) and Meert (1999), in which the processes of social exclusion and inclusion are related to overlapping spheres of integration.

> This refers to different ways in which households access resources – through the market and payment for work; through transfer payments and services provided by the state...; and through reciprocal and other non-market transactions based on family, community and other affiliation. (Lee and Murie 1999).

This approach echoes that of Commins (1993), who in a report on Combating Exclusion in Ireland 1990-1994, suggested that social exclusion should be defined in terms of the failure of one or more of the following four systems, of which the second and third are especially relevant to this research:

- the democratic and legal system, which promotes civic integration;
- the labour market, which promotes economic integration;

---

[1] It should be noted that Levitas is tracing the evolution and appropriation of the term social exclusion, particularly in policy debates in the UK, rather than trying to use the concept.

- the welfare state system, promoting social integration;
- the family and community system, which promotes interpersonal integration.

One's sense of belonging in society depends on all four systems. Civic integration means being an equal, empowered citizen in a democratic system, with a sense of access to policymakers and centres of political power. Economic integration means having a job, having a valued economic function, and being able to pay your way. Social integration means being able to access the social services provided by the state, without stigma. Interpersonal integration means having family and friends, neighbours and social networks to provide care and companionship and moral support when these are needed. Distinctions are made between a "dual society", in which a large proportion are excluded and forced to rely on transfer payments, and an "active society" in which all enjoy opportunities for participation in all four systems.

The conceptual distinction is now clear. Poverty is an outcome, denoting an inability to share in the everyday lifestyles of the majority because of a lack of resources (often taken to be disposable income). Social exclusion is a multi-dimensional, dynamic concept which refers to a breakdown or malfunctioning of the major societal systems that should guarantee the social integration of the individual or household. Room (1994) argues that such recent conceptual shifts open the way towards a redirection of the research agenda, from a "mundane and atheoretical tradition of counting and comparing the poor", towards wider issues of social stratification and political order, affording closer links with mainstream sociological analyses of class and social mobility, and discussion of European welfare regimes. This is possible because very different theoretical paradigms underpin the two concepts of poverty and social exclusion: while the notion of poverty is primarily focussed upon distributional issues (the lack of resources at the disposal of an individual or household), the notion of social exclusion focuses primarily on relational issues (inadequate social participation, lack of social integration, powerlessness).

Accordingly it has been identified as an important part of the research to develop adequate theoretical accounts of the links between policies at various levels, social and economic change at macro, meso and micro scales, and processes of social exclusion and integration affecting young people in rural Europe. These processes must be analysed in relation to the institutional context of rural societies: the labour market, the family, the social security system, the educational system, and others (Hingel and Fridberg 1994).

Further conceptual development of the concept of social exclusion, and its application to rural Britain, has recently been undertaken by Shucksmith and Philip (2000). They argue that it is helpful to view processes of social exclusion and inclusion in terms of a series of overlapping spheres of integration, as suggested above, according to the means through which resources and status are allocated in modern society, and that this may also be related to various social theories.

In accordance with such ideas, and drawing on the theories of Polanyi (1944) and others, Reimer (1998) has recently suggested modifications to Commins' proposed set of systems. Valuable as they are in helping to conceptualise social exclusion, Commins' systems had no consistent logical basis, and omitted important arenas (such as housing markets, financial markets, and states' agricultural, rural and regional policies). Reimer addresses these defects, providing both a consistent logical basis, and a comprehensive set of systems. In a similar approach to Kesteloot (1998) and Duffy (1995), he argues that it is helpful to distinguish the dimensions of social exclusion according to the different means through which resources are allocated in society. He identifies four means of allocation, though, and therefore proposes four systems. They are as follows:

- **Private systems**, representing market processes.
- **State systems**, incorporating authority structures with bureaucratic and legal processes.
- **Voluntary systems**, encompassing collective action processes.
- **Family and friends networks**, based on reciprocity associated with cultural processes.

These four systems are illustrated in Figure 2.1 (page 15), and are further elaborated by Shucksmith and Philip (2000). It is this typology which is employed in this study.

3. The Youth Transition and Social Exclusion

Within the broad area of enquiry of rural development and social exclusion, there are particular theoretical and conceptual developments in relation to young people's situations. As Chisholm and DuBois-Reymond (1993) have noted, "theoretical analyses have predominantly understood 'youth' as a developmental stage, one in which new kinds of roles, relationships and competences must be practised and mastered in order to pass from the social status of childhood to adulthood" (Coleman 1990; Kräger 1988). While "these institutionalised transitions are generally ordered and experienced in ways which reproduce existing patterns of social differentiation (and inequality), in particular, by gender, ethnicity and class", recent work notes that youth transitions are changing and, arguably, losing their internally structured differentiated quality.

It is generally accepted that across Europe there has been a lengthening of **the youth transition** from childhood to adulthood, from school to work, from dependency to independence, which may last now until the mid- to late-20s (DuBois-Reymond and Van der Zande 1993) or even longer, and that this in itself has had major consequences for young people and for society (OECD 2000). And at the same time as rural society is undergoing rapid changes which generate uncertainty and uncontrollability of outcome, as noted above, the **individualisation** thesis (Fuchs 1983; Zinneker 1990) suggests that transformation of production processes in large areas of work and changes in many areas of leisure and domestic life have changed the relationship of individuals to their social reference groups.

Thus young people's lives today are less structured by their class origins and gender, giving young people greater freedom to construct their own biographies.

Figure 2.1 Means Through Which Resources are Allocated in Society

State Systems
Authority structures with bureaucratic and legal processes

Likely to be status related; integration requires deference to a person or to a position, individuals must meet the requirements of particular roles for integration
Exclusion from the distribution of resources or services occurs when individuals cannot meet the formal or informal requirements of those roles.

Private Systems
Market processes

Favours tradable skills, profitable commodities, contractual arrangements, and mobility
Individuals without the above qualities are likely to be excluded from such a system.

RESOURCES
SERVICES
INFORMATION

Voluntary Systems
Collective action processes

Equality matching relationships based upon shared interests
Exclusion is likely where one person does not share the goal of others, where the symbols of commitment to the goal are inadequate, or where there is insufficient contribution to the goals on the part of a member.

Family and Friends
Reciprocal processes

Communal sharing, inclusion requires common origins or significant commitment to the group
Stigmatisation, secrecy, and racism are the mechanisms whereby people or groups are excluded

"The socially standardised life course (*Normalbiographie*) of the past is gradually changing into a socially individualised life course" (Chisholm and DuBois-Reymond 1993), with an associated shift of power between the sexes and social classes, according to this thesis. Despite this, Chisholm and DuBois-Reymond (1993) conclude that while youth aspirations and expectations have indeed become individualised, the outcomes of youth transitions continue to be marked by the effects of systematic social inequalities, especially in relation to gender and social class. Young people's freedom to construct their own biographies is differentially constrained according to structures of class, gender and ethnicity, among others (Furlong and Cartmel 1997). This thesis is returned to specifically in Chapter Ten, and in the Conclusion.

Another key concept relating strongly to social exclusion is that of youth citizenship, with its concomitant, youth rights (Jones and Wallace 1992). "Contemporary youth policies are typically a rather uneasy mixture of social control measures and citizenship rights" (Chisholm 1993; Chisholm and Bergeret 1991). On the one hand, young people may be regarded as family dependants, with a need for care and protection on the basis of their immaturity, while, on the other, children and young people have acquired many rights of their own in society, for example, as a consequence of the expansion of the welfare state. To what extent then do young people in rural areas of different countries enjoy rights to further education or training, to work, to welfare payments, to housing, to political expression? The presence or absence of such rights will be important in structuring exclusion.

Finally, there is an emphasis in recent research on the value of a **holistic** approach. As Jones (1992) has argued:

> When social policies affecting young people so obviously fail to take a holistic view of young people and their needs, it is timely to indicate through empirical study the futility of trying to understand young people through focusing on one aspect of their complex lives... Transitions into the labour market, household formation, housing, career and family formation interact with one another. Thus, changing marital and parental status affects employment careers, and these in turn affect household composition and thus housing and income needs.

Chisholm (1993) agrees that "a productive European youth research tradition must place inter-relatedness and multidimensionality at the core of the analysis". This necessity has informed our research design in this project.

4.   Labour Markets

The concept of a local labour market is important to this research since it enables attention to be focussed on a specific rural locality within which young people seek employment and employers seek to recruit workers. However, this concept is by no means simple, as we will see.

Vera-Toscano (2000) has summarised theories of labour market behaviour, including *Classical and neo-Classical theories*, the *American Institutionalist School*, and *Labour Market Segmentation theory*. Each of these three approaches is reviewed briefly here, drawing heavily on Vera-Toscano's work.

Classical and Neo-Classical Theories assume maximising behaviour on the part of individuals and firms. Wage rates arise from the interaction of the forces of supply and demand within a single, universal labour market, although it is recognised that labour markets are segmented due to geographical and biological factors, especially age, which cause labour inputs to be imperfect substitutes for each other. Unfortunately, these theories leave unexplained many major labour market policy issues, such as the dispersion of wages, income distribution, unemployment and discrimination. The principal weaknesses are:

- the atomistic approach, equilibrium framework, and rigid and unrealistic assumptions;
- inadequate treatment of collective bargaining and trade union activities;
- the assumption that frictionless labour markets eliminate persistent spatial differences.

The American Institutionalist School of the 1940s and 1950s argued instead that labour markets are determined primarily by the formal and informal rules of contemporary institutional structures. Kerr (1954, 93) sees a labour market to be "merely an area of indistinct geographical and occupational limits within which certain workers customarily seek to offer their services and certain employers to hire them". The result is a "balkanised" labour market where institutional rules allow mobility among sub-markets according to well-defined boundaries between internal and external components.

More recent Labour Market Segmentation Theories (Edwards et al., 2000) seek to explain why certain industries, localities, and occupational and social groups have fared better than others. The focus is on institutional constraints in relation to pay formation, and on the endogeneity of individual tastes. Labour market segmentation corresponds not only to skill differentials, they argue, but also to the substitution of institutional rules for market processes. Thus, one main aspect of segmentation is that between a "structured" sector, characterised by employment security and stability, career progression and incremental pay increases (the primary sector), and a "structureless", casualised sector where jobs are insecure, low-skilled and low-paid (the secondary sector).

Labour market segmentation theories may be helpful in understanding spatial differences, according to Vera-Toscano. Thus, the characteristics of local people in rural areas, together with social and ideological factors that shape their experience, may be important in explaining the dominance of secondary labour market employment in rural areas. "For example, the small-scale nature of many rural workplaces may encourage a particular type of personal relationship between workers and their employers, which may be related to low levels of unionisation and low wages, and the greater proportion of secondary jobs in rural areas" (Vera-Toscano 2000, 13).

For some researchers, the geographical subdivision of labour markets is largely a consequence of the pecuniary and psychological costs of extensive daily travel to work, and the similar costs of migration. "These costs spatially subdivide a labour force already stratified occupationally... [since] those with particularly scarce occupational skills see their moving expenses covered by their employers, but such a provision is less common for manual workers" (Vera-Toscano 2000, 14). The interaction between travel costs and housing costs may also be relevant here. The consequence is that the labour market is much more spatially restricted for low-skilled groups.

Communication, especially through social networks, is another important factor in the geographical segmentation of labour markets. For some, often in lower skill occupations, the information network is unlikely to extend beyond the immediate neighbourhood, whereas for others broader social networks and information networks are the norm.

Vera-Toscano (2000, 15) argues that:

> The concept of local labour market faces particular difficulties when applied to rural areas. The spatial dispersion of the working population, the diversity of firms, the high level of self-employment means that any rural area selected is likely to actually include a wide range of sub-markets.

The main problem is the definition of a relevant 'labour market'. Monk and Hodge (1995) argue that it is inappropriate to view rural labour markets in a purely spatial sense. Rather we should focus on the particular opportunities and constraints experienced by specific groups in specific areas. The important question is how the attributes of rural areas constrain the abilities of the target section of the population (e.g. young people) in relation to employment.

However, there may also be other factors at work, which limit young people's employment opportunities and pay, and which the segmented labour market theory cannot account for. Looking at the suggested 'skills differentials' between the segments from a perspective which recognises gender inequality could be instructive here. It can be argued that in evaluations of 'male' and 'female' skills, it has been the job components of typically male employment which has been associated with skills. By contrast, the skill content of female jobs has tended to be downgraded, reflecting women's inferior socio-economic status in society. But cultural values or prejudice have not been included as possible roots for the structure of the segmented labour market. However, 'prejudice' may also affect young people, whose characteristics could be constructed in a way, which portrays them as unreliable, with few skills, and as being able to depend on their parents for an income, thereby enabling employers to pay low wages.

Recent work by Monk et al., and others, has been summarised by Shucksmith (2000) in terms of the following "barriers and bridges" facing those in rural areas:

Barriers to Finding Employment

Structure of Local Labour Markets – Mismatches Between Jobs and Skills. A lack of qualifications or skills relevant to jobs available in the locality was an important barrier to gaining employment in rural areas. Often people's skills and experience related to agriculture or other manual work, and when they lost their jobs they had no formal qualifications.

Employers' Behaviour and Attitudes. Frequently, jobs are found through word of mouth and employers rarely advertise vacancies formally. This advantages those from the locality who are perceived to be good workers and who are well connected to local networks, but presents barriers to those moving from outside, or those who have transgressed in some way within these typically small communities (or who are associated with others 'labelled' in this way).

Accessibility Between Home and Workplace. Transport was found in all rural areas to be a major barrier in gaining access to labour markets.

The Costs of Participating in the Labour Market. The low level of wages on offer presented problems for those who faced significant costs in participating, notably in relation to childcare and transport. They would have to earn significantly more than offered by any local job in order to afford formal childcare.

Bridges to Labour Market Participation

Formal Job Search Strategies or Linking into Local Networks. Most people attributed successful job search to local contacts and networks, rather than to formal job search strategies.

Self-Employment. Some sought to escape unemployment through self-employment. This strategy was often associated with low income, and with substantial risk of failure.

Transport Solutions. Some firms provided a works bus, which helped women and young people to get to work, but this offered only a limited choice of jobs and usually led to dependence on one employer.

Training. Training was considered by some to be an important way to improve their position in the labour market by updating their skills or retraining. However, training was not always available nearby, and many mentioned a mismatch between the training available and the jobs in the locality.

Childcare Solutions. While it was mostly women who found childcare a barrier to finding work, the solutions often involved men. Typically these included finding shift-work or part-time work to fit around a partner's hours (i.e. in the evenings or at night), informal arrangements with friends or relatives, and home-working.

Support Networks and the Informal Economy. Several mentioned the importance of support networks, family and friends, who helped out when times were hard, either with payment or help in kind. But even with such support, living on a low income was difficult and some people attempted to supplement their resources in different ways, including benefit fraud, or jobs 'on the side', such as gardening, cleaning and childminding.

Hidden Unemployment

Eliminating low pay, for example by raising the Minimum Wage, is important for those in work, but this will not in itself assist most low income households. For some, integration into paid employment can resolve their poverty, perhaps with help from active employment policies, together with related policy initiatives directed at transport, childcare provision and care services. For others it is the level and take-up of welfare benefits which offers the only prospect of escaping low income.

Work by Beatty and Fothergill (1997, 1999) has found evidence of substantial hidden unemployment in rural areas, especially among men. Much of this took the form of premature early retirement and (in particular) a diversion from unemployment to long-term sickness. Distinctively rural dimensions to the problem of joblessness included the difficulties of 'getting to work', the narrow range of jobs available, the low level of wages on offer, and ageism among employers.

More recently these authors (Breeze et al., 2000) have investigated in what ways the UK's active employment programme (the New Deal) needs to be adapted to rural circumstances. Their principal conclusion is that while New Deal addresses the supply side, it is demand-side problems which remain deeply entrenched in rural labour markets. "Put simply, the main reason why so many men remain out-of-work is that there aren't enough jobs to go to." What is needed most in rural areas is job creation. Moreover, the jobs which are available offer low wages which provide no incentive to come off benefit, even with Working Families Tax Credit. The other distinctively rural barrier to finding work is transport, experienced by those without regular access to a car and especially by those without a driving licence.

5.   Existing Knowledge of Rural Social Exclusion of Young People

Rural Poverty

Exclusion, as we have seen, is a much broader concept than poverty, and social exclusion may not be poverty-based. Nevertheless, poor households are likely to face many forms of exclusion, and so knowledge of rural poverty is a starting point. Little information is available on the extent of rural poverty in Europe. Such systematic information as there is tends to relate to average incomes rather than to the income distribution, and is available at too large a scale (see Chapter 3 below), telling us little about the characteristics or the causes of rural poverty and exclusion.

In this respect, a 1979 study of rural deprivation in England (McLaughlin 1986a, b, c; Bradley 1987) and a follow-up study of rural lifestyles in 1990 (Cloke et al., 1994), are more illuminating. In terms of absolute poverty, these found 25% of rural households to be living in or on the margins of poverty. The study found that rural incomes are highly polarised with richer as well as more poor households, so emphasising the degree of relative poverty, with clear implications for social exclusion. The disparity between male and female earnings is also greater.

Comparable survey data have recently been collected for Scotland (Shucksmith et al., 1996), using a combination of in-depth qualitative and large-sample quantitative methods. Indications from this, and from previous desk-studies, confirm that in rural Scotland the main elements of rural poverty are elderly people and those in low-paid occupations. Agriculture and tourism are particularly notable in this respect. A third element of rural poverty in Scotland, not found in the English study, derives from local concentrations of unemployment. The study did not specifically address young people's exclusion, but found that poverty was widespread, with 65% of heads of households earning below £200 per week (the Low Pay Unit's poverty threshold). Half had incomes below half the median Scottish wage. Yet people's subjective assessment of their welfare tended to contradict such externally determined criteria: they compared their situation with the harsher conditions of the past rather than with current lifestyles of the majority, and therefore did not see themselves as poor.

In Austria, similar results have emerged from the country-wide study of Lutz et al. (1993) which found that "rural regions are affected more strongly" by poverty and exclusion, with farmers one of the groups at greatest risk. As in Scotland, their study also found that subjective assessments denied the presence of poverty, because the comparison was made with much earlier times. The study did not enquire into the dynamics or processes of exclusion, however. A more recent qualitative study focused on the different "faces of rural poverty" and pointed to the need of raising awareness and local community work (Wiesinger 2001). In Finland, some work has enquired into the difficulties of reinsertion into labour markets (Mannila 1993) and of the position of young people in particular (Nyyssola 1994; Virtanen 1995) but the studies are not concerned with rural localities. In Ireland, work conducted in NW Connemara as part of a Poverty 3 project also revealed high levels of rural poverty (Byrne 1991). The study found that many disadvantaged people not only have the least resources but also have poor access to public services. Housing was sub-standard, transport was lacking, educational opportunities were restricted and health care services were distant. Dependency on unemployment pay and other social welfare payments was high, despite the inappropriateness of these to rural labour market strategies. The study concluded that "on virtually every key variable, NW Connemara is in a much worse position than the rest of Ireland". According to Harvey (1994), the Poverty 3 programme in this area identified ways in which services might be delivered more appropriately and ways to enhance the capacities of small, remote communities to effect change.

In Germany, Struff (1992) researched regional living conditions in urban and rural areas at the level of administrative districts using official statistics. Although this analysed data for all regions of the former West Germany, including measurement of the dimensions of inequality, the reliance on secondary sources precluded any insights into the experience of rural life or the dynamics of social exclusion in a rural context. Pfaffenberger and Chasse (1993) examined the living conditions of people in a rural area of West Germany using a combination of qualitative and quantitative methods, but despite many virtues the findings were mostly descriptive and mainly addressed to social workers. Since reunification, many studies have contrasted living conditions in West and East Germany, using official statistics and panel data to document the manifold dimensions of exclusion (e.g. Glatzer and Noll 1995). Hanesch (1995) has also used qualitative interviews to explore subjective dimensions of poverty in the new landau. Yet despite all these studies there is little knowledge of rural poverty and exclusion.

Rural Social Exclusion

Very little survey work has been conducted on rural exclusion in Europe, and even where surveys have been conducted these have not addressed either the effects of interacting policies, the 'pathways' to social exclusion and integration, the causes of social exclusion, or the ways in which exclusion is subjectively experienced. Nevertheless, there has been a recent tendency away from 'area-specific' research and towards 'people-specific' research.

It has already been noted that social exclusion may be regarded as a breakdown or malfunctioning of the major societal systems (democratic and legal; labour market; welfare state; and family and community) that should guarantee social integration. However, little research has sought to transcend the crude "arithmetic of woe" to explore the processes and system failures lying behind social exclusion in a rural context. Evidence from the Scottish study (Shucksmith et al., 1996) identified failures in each of the first three systems, with important consequences for the last. In terms of civic integration, interviewees spoke consistently about a huge gap between people and policy-makers: in the remoter communities a sense of powerlessness was universal, especially in relation to dramatic social changes over which people felt they had no control; in more accessible areas people's sense of powerlessness was closely bound up with social stratification and inequality. Labour market and housing market issues were also crucial, with a majority of respondents perceiving employment opportunities and housing opportunities to be very restricted. Young people and women tended to have the fewest options, and generally jobs tended to be low-paid and insecure. These impediments to economic integration were closely bound up with transport and childcare services, both of which were deficient. The welfare state system was patently failing to reach potential recipients and the take-up of benefits was low: less than half received any state benefits. Access to advice in urban centres was problematic, and respondents were often confused about the benefits available and their entitlement. Moreover, their denial of their poverty together with a culture of independence also militated against the receipt of entitlements. Clearly policy innovation is required if civic, economic and social integration is to be achieved in rural Scotland. All of these impacted upon the family and community system, both through a loss of young people which was seen as inhibiting the social reproduction of the community and damaging informal support networks, and through material and social changes which led to loss of a distinctive rural culture, of the Gaelic language and dialects and of a myriad of other intangible qualities. Such empirical accounts of social exclusion, in the rare instances where they do exist, have still to be connected to the broader forces operating at macro and meso levels (for example, economic restructuring, CAP reform), but this study in Scotland points a way forward.

6.   Youth and Work in Rural Areas

The OECD Employment Outlook (1996) points to worsening social exclusion in many OECD countries as a result of poor labour-market performance. The OECD Jobs Strategy (1996) identifies as a core issue the need to improve young people's ability to make a better transition into the world of work. (This is only one element of the youth transition, of course.) Problems appear especially severe for male school-leavers who, the OECD report suggests, are likely to have the least educational qualifications among the youth population and are particularly adversely affected by "the shift in the composition of labour demand towards more experienced and skilled workers". They conclude that "policies that contribute to reducing early school-leaving are critical since anything less than a sound upper-secondary education or its equivalent vocational qualification may be associated with low earnings-capacity and is insufficient preparation for getting into the job market and for access to further learning". This study provides a useful context for our concern with young people in rural areas, suggesting the need to focus on the interface between changing rural labour market requirements (such as credentialism and new concepts of skill, and reflecting rural restructuring) and changes in the nature and duration of the youth transition in its broadest sense.

We are fortunate that there exist a small number of studies of young people in rural areas, most notably in Scotland and in France. Jones (1992) studied young people leaving home in rural Scotland and found that young people in rural areas are likely to lead a qualitatively different kind of youth from those in towns, especially in their patterns of residence and migration. Their experience of growing up is affected by the lack of local provision for leisure, education, training and employment, by the unavailability of a local peer group, and by the difficulty of travelling to centres where facilities and peers exist. Young people in rural communities were obliged to leave home earlier than those in towns for their education, for jobs, and for housing, "leaving a community impoverished by their absence". By the age of 19, young people in rural areas are twice as likely to have left home, mainly because of lack of employment and educational opportunities in the rural area. Some, of course, find ways of remaining in the locality and adapting to their different circumstances, e.g. by staying on at school, by modifying their ambitions, or, among women, by marrying locally. Education was found to act as an "escape route" for young people, especially women who tended to stay longer in education because of the lack of local job opportunities for women and the need for marketable skills. Very few training opportunities were available because of the predominance of small firms in rural areas. Access to job information was problematic, and difficulties of transport restricted job opportunities for young people still further.

In France, Durand and Auclair (1994) have also studied the difficulties of young people in finding employment in rural areas. Their research identified several factors which limited young people's access to their first job in rural areas, including the changing structures of local economies, weaknesses of the training system, isolation and low population densities, cultural and social characteristics, and an absence of partnerships. Moreover, the importance of these factors differed according to the characteristics of the area, suggesting a need to structure future research around a number of localities. In Germany, research on young people in rural areas had traditionally focused on the situation of young farming population Only about a decade ago concern for youth in rural areas reached a peak and has been extended to adopt a more general view on young people. However, most studies took a rather pessimistic note on young people's perspective (Böhnisch and Funk 1989; Böhnisch et al., 1991). Given the strong labour segregation gender issues have been particularly important here and the particular situation of young women has been investigated (Funk 1993).

A recent study by Rugg and Jones (1999) explores the experiences of 60 young people, aged 22, growing up in rural England, and shows how difficult it is for them to find both a job and somewhere to live in the countryside. Many wished to stay in their home area, and by the time they reached their late teens and twenties they were happier there than when they had been reliant on their parents and public transport for mobility. Most needed their own transport to hold down work. Almost all said that the limited availability of affordable housing was acute, forcing them to stay longer in the parental home and ultimately forcing them to move away to urban areas even though they had jobs. Furthermore, although few were unemployed, most felt that the work available in the countryside was low paid and offered limited prospects for career development. Those who went into higher education considered it unlikely that they would find graduate status work in the countryside. "At the age of 22, only one or two of the 60 had actually succeeded in achieving any level of independence whilst staying in a rural location. For the great majority, the only long-term solution to their housing and employment problems was to leave the countryside."

It is clear from these studies that an appropriate starting point for our research is the thesis that social exclusion of young people derives from the interaction of changes in labour markets and welfare regimes with changes in the nature and duration of the youth transition. Furthermore, because rural labour markets differ from those in urban areas, while welfare assistance may be less available or acceptable, and because the youth transition is qualitatively different in a rural context, it follows that the causes of social exclusion of young people in rural areas may well differ from those identified in urban research. If confirmed, this conclusion will have important policy implications.

The conclusion of this section, however, is that our knowledge of young people's social exclusion in rural areas and its causes is still rudimentary. We do have some knowledge from studies in Britain, Ireland and Austria, and a major French study by INRA, CNRS and SEGESA, but these findings may not reflect circumstances in other rural areas of Europe, particularly given the diversity identified by the CEC in its document *The Future of Rural Society* (1988) and the increasing evidence of rural diversity provided through a range of case studies and shifting policy focus during the 1990s (CEC 1997). Few of these focus on the specific situation of young people and the effects of policies upon them. How exactly the systemic failures set out above are related to pathways to exclusion and insertion and contrasting policies in different rural areas of Europe, and especially for young people, requires further research: until this is completed, it will be hard to frame policies which address the underlying causes of young people's social exclusion in rural areas of Europe. This study seeks to answer the questions: How do policies at various levels impact on the 'pathways' to young people's exclusion and integration in rural areas, and how do these differ between social groups (especially by class and gender) and between rural areas? What role can policies play in ensuring the active participation of young people in rural labour markets?

Chapter 3

The Changing Rural Context

Toivo Muilu, Alana Gilbert, Euan Phimister and Mark Shucksmith

1. Forces for Change in Rural Areas of Europe

The economies and societies of rural areas of Europe are changing rapidly in the face of globalisation, economic restructuring, migration, and other social and policy changes, including EU enlargement. These forces have different implications for different areas and different social groups, including young people in a wide diversity of rural contexts.

Market and Economic Forces

Many rural areas (for example, in Scotland) are now growing faster than urban districts, while many others experience decline: the economic and social processes underlying these diverse trends are not always well understood. One key element is the increasingly global penetration of local markets. International capital may seek to exploit those rural areas characterised by low wages, a compliant, non-unionised workforce, and lower levels of regulation, leading to increased dependency and peripherality. On the other hand, many rural areas and firms seek to protect themselves from global competition by creating local products which depend upon a local identity for their market niche, so 'selling the local to the global'.

According to the European Commission (1997, 15), "agriculture and forestry no longer form the backbone of rural economies throughout the EU". Agriculture still employed 16 million people in Europe in 1993, but this constituted only 5.5% of total EU employment, and even in the most rural regions its share in 1990-91 was only 12%. Less than one quarter of these jobs were full-time, and an increasing proportion is part-time or casual. The Commission forecast a further fall of 15% in the number of farm holdings in Europe over the period 1993-2003, from 7.3m to 6.2m Employment has declined even more steeply in other primary sectors, such as coal mining. In terms of output, agriculture contributes a declining share to GDP (e.g. in UK this has fallen from 3% in 1973 to 1%), and this long-term decline is reflected in people leaving the industry and, during the late 1990s, in falling farm incomes. The structural force underlying this decline is continuing technological change which increases farmers' ability to supply while demand remains static. To some extent farmers have been protected from such global forces by subsidies, with EU expenditure on agricultural support currently amounting to some 42.5 billion Euros per annum (2000-2006), and through trade protectionism.

The declining importance of agriculture and other primary activities has been more than offset in many rural areas by the growth of the service sector. The EC (1997, 16) highlights some rural areas as the most dynamic in the EU, including Tyrol in Austria, East Bavaria, East-Central Ireland, the Alps and Atlantic-Arc departements in France, and several areas of Spain and Italy. Around 73% of jobs in rural Britain are now in services, compared to 60% in 1981, notably in public administration, education, health, distribution, tourism, and the financial services. In Sweden, every third job in the most rural areas is in public services. Rural areas have shared in a general shift to a service-based economy in which the information and knowledge-based industries play an increasing role, bringing both opportunities and threats. The impact of new information and communication technologies on rural areas has increased particularly rapidly over the last years and analysis has stressed its potential for changing local labour structures and the attractiveness of rural regions. Due to the high speed of the technological developments, diversity between and among regions has risen and is subject to rather short-term influences. Case studies on European best practices (AEIDL 2000a) and current activities of OECD (2000) reveal the importance which has recently been attached to the issue at the international debate.

The EC (1997, 16) concludes that "rurality is not itself an obstacle to job creation which cannot be overcome: it is not synonymous with decline". Most rural areas in the UK, for example, have coped well with the need for structural economic change. "Employment in rural areas has increased more rapidly than in other areas,... [and] unemployment in rural areas is generally lower than in the rest of the country (4.2% for rural districts compared to 6.1% in England in 1998)" (Cabinet Office 2000). This may be misleading, however, in so far as research by Beatty and Fothergill (1997) shows that unemployment is systematically under-reported in rural Britain, and this is likely to be the case throughout Europe. In addition, both part-time employment and self-employment are more common in rural areas. Moreover, some areas have found it harder to adjust to rapid restructuring, notably those which are remote and have a high dependence on agriculture or other primary activity. Even where new jobs have appeared, some people have found it hard to adjust, as made clear in the previous chapter's discussion of labour-market segmentation, casualisation, flexible accumulation and social exclusion.

A particular feature of rural employment throughout Europe is the prevalence of small firms. Over 90% of all rural firms in Britain are micro-businesses, employing fewer than ten people, and 99% employ fewer than fifty. The rate of small-firm formation in accessible rural areas of the UK is well above the national average, and most of these are set up by people who have earlier moved into these areas for a better quality of life, in contrast to urban start-ups (PIU 1999). However, in the remoter rural areas the rate of small-firm formation is below the national average, partly because fewer people move there.

The European Commission (1997, 14) notes that, "over the coming years, the capacity of rural areas to maintain or create jobs will have a major impact on the unemployment rate and/or migration flows". Given that these are not likely to be in agriculture, that report goes on to suggest (p. 16) that the creation of rural employment results from a specifically territorial dynamic which may not yet have been systematically analysed at EU level, but which seems to include such features as:

- a sense of regional identity and social cohesion;
- an entrepreneurial climate, a capacity to link up with the economic mainstream, public and private networks;
- a good educational level;
- an attractive cultural and natural environment.

These may be summarised as cultural, social, human and natural capital. Their role in rural development is discussed further in Shucksmith (2000).

Demographic and Social Changes

Fundamental demographic, social and cultural changes also characterise rural areas. Migration flows are critical in determining rural population levels and, while some rural areas in Europe continue to lose population, in many parts people are moving into rural areas because of the new values placed on rural space (e.g. clean environment, healthy lifestyles, community life). The consequences of the imposition of such values on rural societies may be far reaching. Between 1971-1996, for example, the population of rural England grew by 24%, compared to 6% nationally. Across the EU, 46% of predominantly rural regions are growing, while 42% experience population decline; and of significantly rural regions 57% are growing, while only 34% decline (EC 1997, 10).[1]

This migration tends to be highly socially selective. Gentrification has been evident in many accessible or touristic areas of rural Europe, in so far as the affluent middle classes have migrated into the countryside, perhaps displacing less affluent groups (cf. Phillips 1993 for evidence of this process in Britain) through competition for scarce housing. Much has been written about the rise of a rural professional and managerial 'service class' such that certain regions, notably the Southeast of England, may be colonised by knowledge-workers at a distance from production activities. Even in some attractive remoter areas, retirement migration and distance-working may produce similar effects, though in less attractive (or ex-industrial) rural areas, with low wages and low rents, low-grade jobs may be all that can be attracted. The migration also tends to be age-specific, with young people often leaving rural areas, as discussed later in this chapter, and older families moving in.

Social relations are also changing in other ways with the rise of individualist values and the decline of established institutions, such as the churches, and the family. Higher divorce rates, delays in the age at which people get married and

---

[1] This classification of rural regions (OECD 1994) is defined in the section *Data Issues and Indicators Employed in this Study* on page 33.

have children, and increasing life expectancies all tend to lead to a decline in the average size of households and to a greater demand for houses. Moreover, changes in the age structure of the rural population, together with the economic restructuring described above, are tending towards increased dependency ratios, casualisation, part-time working, and less job security. The interactions between these changes, in the family and in employment, are not well understood in rural contexts.

Housing markets are crucial in understanding the social changes taking place in rural Britain and in parts of Ireland, but their operation is less well researched in the rest of rural Europe. Social housing accounts for only 14% of the stock in rural areas of Britain, compared to 23% in urban areas. For most people, their housing opportunities depend upon being able to afford one of the owner-occupied houses which constitutes three-quarters of the stock. And yet there is often a strong demand for these houses from relatively affluent households who aspire to rural life while at the same time the supply of houses is tightly constrained by the planning process and the opposition of middle-class home owners to new building. This tends to raise house prices and often restricts who can live in rural areas.

Changing Policy Contexts

Rural policies are changing in response to these forces, and many wider policies (especially macroeconomic policies and social policies) also have pervasive impacts upon rural areas. For example, many countries in Europe recently experienced protests about the impact of high fuel taxes on those living in more isolated locations and in heightening social exclusion more generally in rural areas. Again, the Minimum Wage might be expected to have made a special impact on the typically low-wage labour markets of rural Europe (Gilbert and Phimister 2000). Planning and housing policies have already been mentioned above.

Social policy and welfare reforms are particularly important in addressing inequalities and in offering support and opportunities to the most disadvantaged. In Britain, the social chapter of the Maastricht Treaty has been introduced, and the Labour government's welfare reforms have sought to provide both incentives and pathways towards labour market integration, facilitated by the expansion of the economy and an associated increase in the aggregate demand for labour. Throughout the EU National Employment Action Plans (NAPs) have sought to address, in the first instance, the integration of young people into work and in the UK this has faced particular obstacles and challenges in rural areas, notably arising from the small size of rural firms, the distances involved, and the low levels of skills required. A number of other measures have sought to address child poverty, and to offer improvements in early education and childcare. Unfortunately, there is strong evidence that awareness of welfare entitlements, and take-up rates, are lower in rural areas (Bramley et al., 2000). Similar national policies operate in most of the countries of the EU, as discussed later.

European policies are particularly important in relation to agriculture and rural development. Farmers receive very large subsidies from the EU, as noted above, and indeed agricultural spending dominates the EU's expenditure. A reform of the

EU's Common Agricultural Policy (CAP) has recently been agreed and this will reduce price support, tariffs on imports and export subsidies while partially compensating farmers for these through enhanced direct payments. Increasingly these will become linked to environmentally sensitive farming and to areas facing particular hardship (e.g. less favoured areas). Further reforms appear inevitable, in the context of EU enlargement and World Trade Organisation (WTO) negotiations, with declining support to farmers unless linked with rural development or environmental goals.

Agreement has also been reached on reforms to the EU structural funds, which will now be focused on fewer areas of the EU-15. The most generously funded areas (Objective 1) with 69% of the funds are those lagging behind economically, and include a number of rural areas. The former 5b areas of rural decline, however, have been reduced both in area and in budget under the new Objective 2 (11.5% of the budget). In both types of designated area, delivery is typically through a partnership structure and an integrated programming document. A new development is the Rural Development Regulation, which will apply to all rural areas, and is intended to become "a second pillar of the CAP" promoting rural diversification and capacity building, as well as more competitive and environmentally friendly agriculture. This will be implemented in different ways in different member states.

2. Indicators of Labour Market Change

This section explores the concept of indicators and their use in regional analysis. The main aims are to gauge what possibilities exist for creating indicators for the analysis of rural labour markets, and to make empirical comparisons of such indicators between PaYPiRD partner countries and regions. This helps to provide a context for the analysis as well as identifying avenues for future work.

For most indicators annual data only became available on a comparable basis from the early 1990s. Moreover, the spatial comparisons are made within regional hierarchies so that it is possible to compare each study area with both the EU15 and national averages, capital regions and other study areas whenever the data is available.

What Are Indicators?

An indicator is a 'pointer' to some phenomenon of interest. The indicator consists of data, which produce significant information on the quality of the phenomenon through interpretation. Indicators may differ from statistics in that sense that they are indirect and need interpretation. They are often used where there is so much data that the essential information could otherwise be lost. Another aim in using indicators is simplification. In practical terms indicators are relative statistical variables like GDP, unemployment rate etc. (see e.g. European Commission

1999a) which are based on commonly used classifications. Also in this book the terms "indicator" and "variable" are used more or less synonymously.

Previous Studies on Rural and Employment Indicators

There have been some international attempts to create indicators for rural development. Perhaps the most extensive has been the OECD Project on Rural Employment Indicators which took place in 1994-1996. In the European Union, indicators are also widely used in regional analysis. In Finland a study of Rural Indicators started in 1997. It should be noted, that the aim here is not to give a comprehensive picture of all the indicators which are included in those projects, but to concentrate on labour market indicators especially from the viewpoint of young people.

OECD projects on rural indicators. In the OECD's report *What Future for Our Countryside* (1993) it was stated (p. 20), that:

> Rural development is a complex and challenging concern on the agenda of decision makers in most OECD countries. Many countries are re-orienting their approaches and recognising the necessity of framing a comprehensive rural policy in the interest of the society as well as rural people. However, many governments still operate with limited quantitative and qualitative information on rural trends in economic and societal conditions.

According to this report, most OECD member countries suffered similar problematic trends in rural areas, such as a loss of jobs in primary production and declining and ageing rural populations. This formed the basis for a Project on Rural Indicators in which one aim was to "identify a set of basic rural indicators that covers the relevant dimensions of rural development and rural policy" (OECD 1994, 10).

The OECD report sets out some basic principles (1994, 14) which will be important for any attempt to develop and operationalise a set of rural indicators:

- relevance: indicators must serve a clearly defined purpose.
- reliability: indicators must have a sound scientific basis.
- realisability: indicators must be built on available statistical data.

The report defines also three concrete basic dimensions of rural development, which any reasonable assessment of rural conditions and trends must take into account (OECD 1994, 15):

territory: rural development is a **spatial concept**;
themes: rural development is a **multi-sectoral concept**;
time: rural development is a **dynamic concept**.

All of these principles are important in any statistical analysis, and especially in international comparative projects like PaYPiRD. We will come back some of these issues later in this section. The four general subjects covered in the OECD project were population and migration, economic structure and performance, social well being and equity, and environment and sustainability.

Subsequently, OECD published a report of the results of its *Project on Rural Employment Indicators* (REMI) concentrating specifically on rural employment and labour markets. REMI's aim was to build up a comprehensive territorial database for rural indicators, to support the OECD Rural Development programme with quantitative information on employment conditions and trends, so raising awareness of the economic and social importance of territorial diversity and disparities, and encouraging OECD member countries to have a closer look at the problems and potentials of rural development and employment creation (OECD 1996c, 15). This OECD study used a large data set concerning the key sectors of rural labour markets, which include unemployment, labour force participation, sectoral employment structures, changes in employment and sectoral mix and territorial dynamics. Most of these indicators will be analysed in this study as well.

One proposal made in the OECD report on rural indicators was that this could serve as a possible field for improved future co-operation between the OECD and other international organisations, such as Eurostat and UN-ECE. In the field of spatially differentiated information, co-operation is seen as particularly important because the costs of data collection and processing can be significantly reduced if there is an international consensus about appropriate territorial units and hierarchies, classification systems and typologies (OECD 1994, 10-11).

Statistical and regional indicators in EU. The EU's statistical information is co-ordinated by Eurostat. It publishes an annual statistical yearbook on regions of the EU (see e.g. Eurostat 1997). The EU also follows up the development of regions in member countries at NUTS 2 level in a series of periodic reports, in which several regional indicators are used for analysing the changes and disparities in the EU regions. The labour market is just one issue in those reports, and indicators like unemployment (total, young people, women) and participation and employment rates are presented (see European Commission 1994, 1999a).

Labour market indicators are also used in the National Action Plans for Employment (NAP) which each member country has been committed to produce since 1998, as noted in Chapter 1 above. Each NAP employs several indicators on labour markets, and once again unemployment is central to the monitoring of progress in all member countries. However, regional issues and indicators are not widely employed in NAPs, although some of their recommendations may have regional aspects (see, for example: http://europa.eu.int/comm/employment_social/empl&esf/naps/commen.pdf).

Finnish projects on indicators. The Finnish Project for Indicators on rural Development was commissioned in 1997 by the Rural Policy Committee and the Finnish Ministry of Agriculture and Forestry, and implemented by Statistics Finland. The basis of the project was the OECD Rural Development Programme mentioned above. An indicator database was developed for the project which is largely based on Statistics Finland's registers and statistics. The project covers four main rural phenomenon areas:

- population and migration;
- structure and function of the economy;
- living conditions and welfare; and
- environment.

Labour market issues are included in the second of these, and several indicators on the labour force, unemployment and workplaces are analysed in the study (Palttila and Niemi 1999).

There are also many other Finnish projects in which indicators have been developed and used for different purposes. The Association of Finnish Local and Regional Authorities established a project in 1997 for developing indicators for planning sustainable development in municipalities (Suomen kuntaliitto 1998). The Committee for Urban Policy carried out a pilot project on Urban Indicators in 21 different Finnish cities (Kaupunkipolitiikan yhteistyöryhmä 1998) and in 1999 they published a final report in which all the 38 urban districts of Finland were analysed with indicators (Committee for Urban Policy 1999). A local example about the indicators is the project on Fast Indicators (nopeat indikaattorit) in the capital region of Helsinki which aimed to create an up-to-date system of indicators which would serve local planners as a versatile and predictable tool on different fields of society (Helsingin seudun nopeat indikaattorit 1996). Indicators have also been used in developing evaluation methods for assessing ESF-projects in Finland (Silander & Välimaa 1999).

In all the Finnish projects on indicators there are similar background factors: they seem all to be aiming to serve as a tool for regional planning and they are based on the effective regional statistical system of Statistics Finland. Compared to international indicators both of these factors have advantages. Firstly, when indicators are formulated for national or regional/local purposes, they are probably more applicable for concrete planning situations than the internationally standardised indicators which may not include all the possible information useful for the local conditions. Secondly, national statistics are naturally more comparable than international statistics.

Data Issues and Indicators Employed in this Study

Eurostat regional data. The key question in using regional indicators is the availability of regional data. In all the EU countries there are many national sources of data and they could be employed as a primary source in international projects like PaYPiRD, but there is huge variation in the validity and classifications used in different countries. So it was decided that the major source for the indicators must be Eurostat, the Statistical Office of European Communities, which aims to harmonise statistics used in the Union.

The second question after choosing Eurostat as the data source was the regional level employed in analysis. Eurostat uses NUTS regions (Nomenclature of territorial units for statistics), which is a five-level hierarchical classification (three regional levels and two local levels). Some of the study areas (like Suomussalmi in Finland) accord with the most local category, which is NUTS5 and refers to municipality level. Unfortunately this level is not used in published Eurostat statistics in which NUTS2 form the units for the socio-economic analyses of regions. The best that can be achieved is therefore to use the NUTS3 level, which refers to provinces or counties, in this study whenever possible. The data source used was Eurostat's NewCronos REGIO database (Eurostat 2000).

Types of rural areas. One problem in rural and regional analysis is the definition of rural areas, as OECD (1994, 17) states, "an official definition of 'rural' does not always exist (in Member countries)". Several attempts at a single and common international definition of rural areas or rurality have been made, without success, since national conditions and interests are very different. For example, the use of population density in defining rural areas is problematic, since densities which might be appropriate to England or France (e.g. below 100 or 150 inh./km^2 for rural regions) include even most of the larger cities in sparsely populated countries like Finland and Sweden.

The typology from the European Commission's "The Future of Rural Society" has already been noted above: *remote areas, intermediate areas* and *economically integrated areas*. This classification was used in selecting the PaYPiRD project's study areas, so that the UK and German study areas belong to type 1 (economically integrated areas), the French and Portuguese areas are type 2 (intermediate areas) and the Finnish, Austrian and Irish study areas are type 3 (remote areas).

In its "Project on Rural Indicators", OECD developed a territorial scheme for the collection and presentation of sub-national data at the international level, and this has been adopted in more recent European Commission work (1997). The typology of regions was based on 50,000 communities in 24 OECD Member countries and the basic idea was the use of population thresholds; a region is:

- predominantly rural, if more than 50 percent of the population lives in rural communities;
- significantly rural, is the share of rural population is between 15 and 50 percent; and
- predominantly urbanised, if less than 15 percent of the population is classified rural.

(OECD 1994, 20-25).

Finally, in NewCronos REGIO database there is a variable called "degree of urbanisation". This has been introduced in order to indicate the features of the area where the interviewed person lives. This variable is not employed in this study, however, since data for this variable is available only at NUTS2 level and there is too much missing data from most of the regions for comparisons to be achieved.

Indicators selected for this study. The following themes have been selected both on the basis of previous studies, especially OECD studies described above, and depending on the availability of data:

- unemployment;
- labour force participation (activity rate);
- sectoral employment structures;
- farming;
- purchasing power parity.

There are many other indicators which are related to labour markets and are widely used in rural policy analysis, such as demographic variables and GDP, but they are less appropriate here where the aim is not to make comprehensive statistical comparisons but to illuminate this research. These also fail to take account of the complexity of rural labour markets, noted above in Chapter 2, and so may not reflect the opportunities open to Young People in these rural areas.

Applying These Indicators of Rural Labour Markets to the Study Areas

Unemployment indicators. Unemployment is probably the most important and most widely used theme in analysing the strength of labour markets. Unemployment relates both to demographic and socio-economic factors and to geographical locations e.g. a peripheral location may mean limited possibilities for innovations which could produce new jobs. OECD (1996c, 9-10), for example, states that in the OECD area, not only are there large differences between national unemployment rates, but also that within countries territorial disparities are significant. In most OECD Member countries (but not the UK), unemployment rates are higher in rural than in urban regions.

The NewCronos REGIO database includes both absolute and relative variables on unemployment. Here only unemployment rates are compared since the study areas differ so greatly by population figures that it is not reasonable to use absolute data. The estimations of the number of unemployed and of the working population in REGIO are based on the results of the Community Labour Force Survey (LFS). The LFS is carried out every spring (2nd quarter) in each Member State. The definition of unemployment used in the LFS corresponds to that of the International Labour Office (ILO). According to this definition, which can differ significantly from those used by national administrations, unemployed persons are those who, during the reference period, were aged 15 years or over, without work, available for work within the next two weeks and had used an active method of seeking work at some time during the previous four weeks.[2] The updating of the

---

[2] It should be noted that the above definition is a more restrictive application of the ILO guidelines than that used by Eurostat up to December 1994. Together with the national statistical offices and the OECD, Eurostat undertook a revision of the method of calculating the unemployment rates with effect from the beginning of 1995, the aim being the

number of unemployed provided by the LFS is done according to the trend of the number of persons registered at unemployment offices. For Italy, Spain, Portugal and the UK, the figures are updated with the results of the quarterly national labour force survey in conjunction with data on those registered at unemployment offices. For Finland and Sweden the number of unemployed in the monthly labour force survey is used. The LFS results are not updated for Greece. The working population is calculated by adding the estimated unemployment figures to the employment data that are provided by the LFS (Eurostat 2000).

The estimated unemployment data for April for each category and for each Member State are subsequently regionalised on the basis of the number of persons registered at unemployment offices in April of the reference year. Exceptions stand: for Greece, Spain, Italy, Portugal, Finland and Sweden where the regional unemployment structures are taken from the LFS. The regional unemployment rates are obtained by dividing the estimated number of unemployed by the corresponding figures of the working population. These rates are subject to revision when the results of the LFS for the reference year become available. (Eurostat 2000).

In Tables 1-4 (see Appendix 1) total and young people's unemployment rates are compared by EU15, PaYPiRD partner countries and some NUTS2 and NUTS3 level regions in 1991-1998. In total unemployment rates, only Finland and France were above EU15 in 1998. Finland experienced the widest fluctuations in unemployment figures, and Kainuu region where our study area is located (NUTS3) had the highest rate of all in 1998. In Austria and Portugal the development fluctuated least, but the downward development of unemployment in Ireland is perhaps the most impressive finding in Table 1. This may be at least partly due to the effective use of EU structural funds in Ireland.

---

improvement of the degree of international comparability. From 1992, in some Member States, this revision introduces a break in the series.

**Figure 3.1 Relative Unemployment in PaYPiRD Countries and some
Sub-regions in 1991-1998**

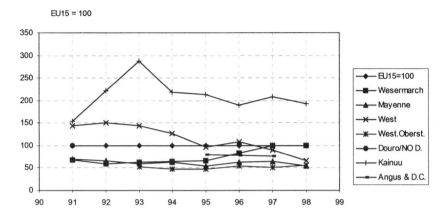

Source: Eurostat New Cronos, REGIO database

Attempting to analyse youth unemployment rates illustrates the major problem in using international statistical information: the more elaborated the data, the more there is missing data. This is especially true in Tables 3 and 4 (Appendix 1) in which youth unemployment rates are compared by sex. Nevertheless the figures reveal very big differences between the reference areas. In the Finnish study area of Kainuu almost every second young person was unemployed in 1998, while in Austria in Westliche Obersteiermark "only" 8.6% were in the same situation. Young females' unemployment rates were generally at least 3% higher than those for young males. Finland's figures by gender were missing and France's situation was the worst in this respect. The most remarkable finding may be that in many NUTS3 "rural" reference areas the gap between the unemployment rates of young females and males was much higher than the average gender gap in the EU. This was especially true in Austria and France, which indicates unfavourable labour markets for young females (Tables 2-4, Appendix 1).

In Figures 3.1 and 3.2 the NUTS3 level reference regions from each partner country are compared to the EU15 average of 100 in each year in order to visualise the regional figures from Tables 3.1 and 3.2. The total relative unemployment has been clearly above the average only in the Kainuu region in Finland during the whole period of 1991-1998 and it was almost three times higher than EU15 average in the worst year of recession in 1993. The development in the West region of Ireland shows an improvement in employment there while all the other regions besides Wesermarsch in Germany are below the average (Figure 3.1). Young people in Kainuu are clearly in the worst position among their counterparts in other regions where all the curves are below the EU15 average in 1998 (Figure 3.2).

**Figure 3.2   Young People's (<25 years) Relative Unemployment in PaYPiRD
Countries and Sub-regions, 1991-1998**

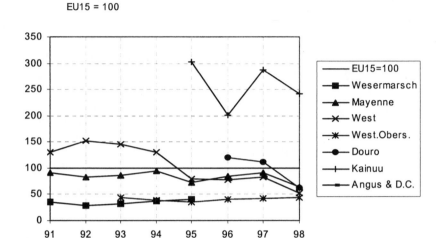

Source: Eurostat New Cronos, REGIO database

One problem in using unemployment figures in international comparisons should
be already mentioned: the figures of Eurostat do not totally correspond to national
figures. In Finland, for example, the difference between total unemployment rates
of Eurostat and Statistics Finland is more or less one percent. It is assumed here,
however, that these differences do not have any remarkable effects for comparisons
between regions.

Labour force participation (activity rate). The activity rate is the percentage of
people of working age (15 years and above) who belong to the labour force. In the
NewChronos REGIO database, activity rates by age and sex are based on the
Community Labour Force Survey (LFS). From 1983 onwards, the definitions in
LFS conform with the International Labour Office (ILO) recommendations. The
results of the survey refer exclusively to private households, since persons living in
institutional households make up only a small fraction of the population (the
Community average is around 2%). The Community survey is carried out in
spring, but the precise period during which it takes place varies somewhat from
one country to another. As the survey is conducted on a sample basis, results
relating to small numbers of persons in some regions must be treated with caution.
Great care must be taken when comparing the results with those of earlier surveys.
This is mainly because the sample and the basis for grossing up the results may
change from one survey to the next. In addition, the Community coding system has
been slightly modified in order to increase the precision of the results and certain
countries have modified their national questionnaires (Eurostat 2000).

Both total and young people's activity rates are presented in Tables 5-8 (see Appendix 1). Unfortunately the figures were available at NUTS2 level only since the figures are based on a sample study (LFS). No PaYPiRD partner country stayed below the EU15 average in 1997 and the highest rates were measured in UK and Finland. Portugal enjoyed a rapid rise until 1998 and also the Norte region had a high activity rate. However, the highest rate was in Eastern Scotland (Table 5, Appendix 1). Young people's activity rates were in most regions around 10% lower than that for all people over 15 years. Youth activity rates varied much more than the total figures, which points to big differences in young people's activities other than employment, i.e. education and unemployment. While in Pays de la Loire region the young people's activity rate was only 40.4% in 1998, in Steiermark, Austria it was 58.5%. In those countries where there was data available from the capital region, the activity rates there were clearly lower than in more rural areas (Table 6, Appendix 1). Finally young males' labour force participation was higher than that of young females, largely because the latter are more active in education (Tables 7-8, Appendix 1). No comparative graphs on activity rates will be presented here since the changes between different years were quite small.

Sectoral employment structures.   The regional accounts on the structure of employment are compiled in accordance with the European System of Integrated Economic Accounts (ESA). They form a whole designated by the abbreviation ESA-Reg (regional), which is a simplified version of the ESA. At branch level the ESA-Reg covers only a part of the aggregates defined by the ESA. The sum of regions may be different from the country total because of the "out of regional territory" classification (Eurostat 2000).

In the NewCronos REGIO database so called NACE-CLIO branch nomenclatures are used for dividing the employment into categories. At NUTS3 level the database employs NACE-CLIO R3 nomenclature which divides the branches into three main categories. In Tables 9-11 (see Appendix 1) those branches are presented by PaYPiRD countries and regions. In the tables the time series begins from the end of the 1980s and the final year available was 1995. Each major sector is discussed in turn.

Agriculture, forestry and fisheries form the primary production sector. This has suffered a steady decrease in the EU and in all the comparative regions. Portugal and Ireland could still be classified as agricultural countries in 1995 and also Finland was above the EU15 average. All the other study regions except Angus and Dundee City[3] were above both the national and EU15 figures in 1995. Douro in Portugal was in its own category as an agriculture-dominated region, since in 1995 almost 43% of its working population were in the primary sector (Table 9, Appendix 1).

In manufacturing, which includes also fuel and power production and building and construction, the changes have not been as dramatic as in primary production. There is a lot of variation between countries and regions, since the range of

---

[3] This aberration is entirely due to the inclusion of Dundee City in this NUTS3 area.

proportions in manufacturing varied from only 13.8 % in Douro, Portugal to 44.0% in Wesermarsch, Germany in 1995 (Table 10, Appendix 1).

Services include both market and non-market services and they comprised two thirds of total EU15 employment in 1995. The service sector is an increasing branch and all the regions seem also to be on a way towards the future "service society" in spite of the fact that in most countries the study areas were below the national average in 1995 (Table 11, Appendix 1).

There is probably no straightforward connection between the structural development of regional economies and the strength of local labour markets since the local conditions are so different. It may be, however, that one should concentrate on developing indicators that could point to the emergence of growth sectors, when comparing local labour markets to European and national averages. Unfortunately the sector figures are not classified by age categories at regional level, and so it is impossible to say anything from this data about the possible growth sectors for young people.

Farming. It was noted above from Table 9 (see Appendix 1), that primary production is a decreasing sector of employment. Since NewCronos REGIO database includes some NUTS2 level data on farmers also by age categories, some indicators on farming will be presented here as one of the few 'rural-like' indicators on young people's labour market.

The figures presented in Table 12 (Appendix 1) are from several Community surveys on the structure of agricultural holdings between 1979-1995 (see Eurostat 2000 for details on different countries) and there is a lot of missing data and so the figures should be treated with caution. There is no data available from the newest member countries, Austria and Finland, so no EU15 averages were calculated either. Only a few regional figures were available.

The proportion of young (under 35 years) farmers is highest in Ireland and France and lowest in Portugal. In Weser-Ems NUTS2 region in Germany the proportion was almost one fifth, but the general age structure of farmers is tending towards the older age groups. In Douro region in Portugal nearly 57% of the farmers were more than 55 years old. Table 12 (see Appendix 1) shows the proportion of farm holdings situated in less favourable and mountain areas which seems to be very high (even 100%) in many areas, and this may partly explain the lack of young farmers. The relatively high proportion of part-time farms also points to the difficulty of making a living from agriculture in these areas, and more positively to the availability of labour market alternatives through which farm families can supplement their incomes (Table 12, Appendix 1). On this subject see also Bryden et al. (1992).

Purchasing power parity. Purchasing Power Parities (PPPs) are currency conversion rates that convert to a common currency and equalise the purchasing power of different currencies. In other words, PPPs are both price deflators and currency converters; they eliminate the differences in price levels between countries in the process of conversion. This means that a given sum of money, when converted into different currencies by means of PPPs, will buy the same volume of goods and services in all countries. Conversely, the sums of national currency needed to purchase a given volume of goods and services in different countries will all equal the same amount of common currency when PPPs are used as conversion rates. Gross Domestic Products (GDPs) of countries expressed in a common currency using PPPs reflect only differences in the volume of goods and services purchased. As such they are valued at international prices and are called 'real measures'. This is because they are like a time series of GDP for a single country at constant prices (http://www.oecd.fr/std/nahome.htm).

PPP per inhabitant is used mostly in national level comparisons but not widely as a regional indicator, since the most common economic indicator in this sense is GDP which is also the key indicator in defining EU regional policies (see e.g. EC 1999). PPP was chosen here, however, as the only economic indicator as an example to tell something on the economic situation of the people in study areas. The idea is then that PPPs would reveal more than GDP about the 'results' of the workers action in labour market, i.e. what they actually can afford to buy with their salaries (or subsidies).

Table 13 (see Appendix 1) shows that there are remarkable differences between the PaYPiRD countries and regions in terms of PPP. Portugal fell more than 25% under the EU15 average in 1997 and also Finland and France were slightly under the average, while the other countries were above it. All the NUTS3 regions were far below EU15 and national averages. In this indicator the differences between capital regions and study areas were huge, since in most countries the PPPs of study areas were less than a half (or even a third in France) of the capital region. It should be noted, however, that PPPs do not take into account the regional differences in living costs which are much higher in capital regions, but in every case the people in rural areas have less purchasing power than their urban counterparts (Table 13, Appendix 1).

Summary of Indicators. A visual summary of the indicators presented in this section is shown in Figure 3.3. NUTS2 as a regional level and the year 1998 were selected for comparison (see exceptions from figure text). It is of course to some extent a subjective matter which indicators are chosen, but unemployment is definitely the single indicator that explains most the strength of the labour market. On the basis of Figure 3.3 it may be concluded that the labour market situation was best in Eastern Scotland and worst in Eastern Finland. No straightforward connection between accessibility and remoteness can be seen, however, since NUTS2 level is too rough for reliable regional conclusions.

Figure 3.3 Summary of Labour Market Indicators on NUTS Level Regions

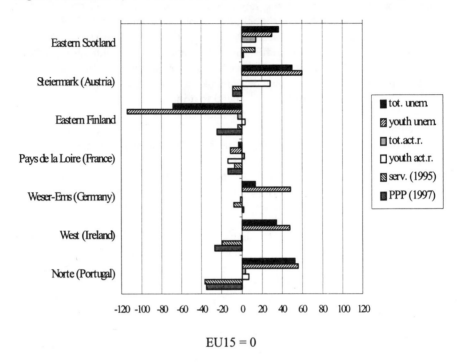

EU15 = 0

Source: Eurostat New Cronos, REGIO database

Figures are from 1998, with the following exceptions: (1) Figures for activity rates
(series 3-4) are from 1997. The Irish data of activity rates is for the whole country
since the data for West was missing. Also the data for Eastern Scotland from 1997
is missing and the total activity rate is from 1998 (youth activity rate for Eastern
Scotland is also missing from 1998). (2) Figures for service branch are from 1995.
(3). Figures for Purchasing Power Parity (PPP) are from 1997.

3.   Analysis of Household Panel Micro-data

A further approach is to analyse micro-data at the household level, rather than rely
on Eurostat data. In this section we provide aggregate descriptive information on
work and opportunity for young people in four of the countries in the PaYPiRD
project, namely, France, Austria, Finland and the UK. As such it represents part of
the quantitative work undertaken within the project. It aims to provide – for the
four countries – some information on the national context for the rural young to
complement the other qualitative and quantitative information available. It also
illustrates some of the benefits and limitations of attempting to use national
datasets for analysis of rural issues.

More specifically, the book provides a basic picture of the extent to which work and opportunity for young people in rural areas differs from that for their urban counterparts, particularly with respect to the structure of employment, unemployment and job search, employment mobility and – for two of the countries – earnings. Ideally, the use of datasets of this type would facilitate cross-country (particular cross-country rural) comparisons. Although in principle three of the national datasets used have been harmonised, in practice the rural definitions available for each country are very different so that cross-country comparisons are extremely difficult to make in general and can only be made with strong reservations.

The structure of this section is as follows. First, the datasets and the particular rural definitions used are briefly discussed. Following this, there is a detailed descriptive analysis for each of the four countries of general sample characteristics, unemployment and job search, employment mobility and earnings. In so far as is possible, identical information is presented for all countries. However, in a number of cases, e.g. earnings for Austria and Finland, the data are missing for certain countries.

Data and Rural Definitions

The data used for France, Austria and Finland were from the National Employment Surveys available from the Luxembourg Employment Study (LES) at CEPS/INSEAD, while the UK data was drawn from the British Household Panel Survey (BHPS). The LES is a databank containing Labour Force Surveys from the early 1990s from a number of countries including Austria, Poland, Slovak Republic, Czech Republic, Slovenia, Finland, Spain, France, Sweden, Hungary, Switzerland, Luxembourg, United Kingdom and Norway. These surveys provide information on areas such as individual characteristics, employment characteristics, job search, education, and earnings and income. The sample sizes of the Labour Force Surveys, and therefore of the LES files, are large compared with other surveys and thus allows statistically significant results to be obtained for small sub-population groups. While the LES is an attractive source of information, for the countries included in PaYPiRD only Austria, Finland and France have an explicit 'rural identifier' variable. Therefore, initial analysis was limited to three countries. In addition, for the UK the availability of the British Household Panel Survey provided an alternative source of information on young people in rural areas. However, this was an exception and it did not prove possible to include information from any of the other countries from the PaYPiRD study.

In principle, the LES is an attractive source of data because efforts have been made to harmonise some of the data for all of the countries covered making many of the variables in the data sets more directly comparable across countries.[4] However, not all the data has been treated in this way. In particular, the rural definitions are country specific. Further, factors which determine whether an

---

[4] It should be noted that in Austria and Germany those in vocational training may be counted as employed.

individual is deemed to be living in a rural or a urban area have proved difficult to determine precisely. Hence, in some cases they reflect population densities but in others economic structure also plays a role in the definition.

The French data are derived from the Enquête sur l'emploi of 1997, and covers the entire population aged 15 and over. The rural identifier variable is identified as rural municipalities, which are not urban where the 'least' urban district is defined as urban areas with less than 5000 inhabitants. The Austrian data are derived from the Mikrozensus of September 1991, covering all persons in private households. Rural areas are defined as 'rural with over 10% of farmers'. The Finnish data are derived from Tyoevoiman vuosihaastattelu sysky in autumn of 1990 with additional information on activity in the previous year derived from the monthly LFS of autumn 1989. This survey covers the entire population between the ages of 15 and 74. Identifying rural areas in Finland was less straightforward. The rural identifier distinguishes between 'towns' and 'other municipalities'. Information obtained from the Finnish CSO indicates that this is an essentially administrative classification and that currently any municipality can apply to the government authorities to become a town. However, prior to 1995 this was difficult to achieve and the categorisation more reflected population size, density and economic structure of the municipality, with most urban areas defined as towns and most rural areas defined as other municipalities.

As mentioned previously the UK data are derived from the British Household Panel Survey. This is a national representative sample of approximately 5,500 households recruited in 1991, containing a total of around 10,000 individuals. These same individuals are re-interviewed each year or wave. The rural sub-sample is identified using the Local Authority District information that is available within the sample. Unfortunately at present only a consistent rural definition is available for England. This is based upon the one used by Tarling et al (1993) which classifies Local Authority Districts into Remote Rural, Accessible Rural, Coalfield areas, Urban and Metropolitan. In the tables presented below the rural sample are those individuals living in LADs classified as both remote rural and accessible rural.

Table 3.1 reports the basic samples available using the rural definitions for the various countries. Two further potential sources of cross-county variability should be noted from this table, namely, that rural sample sizes vary considerably across countries and that the time period considered is not consistent.

Table 3.1 Sample Size

country	year	whole sample		those aged 16 to 25	
		total	living in rural areas	total	living in rural areas
Austria	1991	56510	15277	8491	2504
Finland	1990	36274	13872	6362	2329
France	1997	148891	43137	24771	6182
UK	1998	12392	3426	1643	422

The sample sizes given in Table 3.1 are the raw numbers of individuals. However, in subsequent tables the data shown the results are weighted so that the figures presented represent estimates of population values as opposed to the raw sample statistics. In most of the subsequent tables figures are given for rural young sample, the urban young sample, and as a comparator group, the relevant national average of all young people.

France

General characteristics. Tables 3.2 and 3.3 provide a general picture of the structure of economic activity and employment by young people in France. From Table 3.2 as might be expected, a higher proportion of young people in the rural sample work and a lower proportion are students.

Table 3.2 Usual or Main Economic Activity (France)

	urban	rural	all young people
worker	0.241	0.272	0.248
unemployed	0.103	0.098	0.102
student	0.605	0.580	0.599
conscript	0.024	0.026	0.024
other inactive	0.028	0.024	0.027
sample size			24771

For those engaged in the labour force, Table 3.3 provides a breakdown of the sector of employment. The industry codes for each of the countries differed, and so were recoded into the divisions of the Standard Industrial Classification 1980 (SIC) to facilitate cross-country comparison. As expected, a higher proportion of the rural sample work in agriculture. Further, more of the young worked in the manufacturing and construction sector and fewer in services than in the urban case.

Table 3.3 Industry (France)

	urban	rural	all young people
agriculture, forestry and fishing	0.014	0.115	0.038
energy and water supply industries	0.006	0.002	0.005
extraction of minerals and ores other than fuels; manufacture of metals, mineral products and chemicals	0.016	0.015	0.016
metal goods, engineering and vehicles industries	0.098	0.120	0.104
other manufacturing industries	0.097	0.153	0.111
construction	0.061	0.111	0.073
distribution, hotels and catering, repairs	0.247	0.195	0.235
transport and communication	0.042	0.037	0.041
banking, finance, insurance, business services and leasing	0.042	0.015	0.035
other services	0.377	0.237	0.343
sample size			6339

Tables 3.4 and 3.5 provide an overview of hours worked and number of jobs held by young people in the rural and urban samples. Table 3.4 indicates that a higher proportion of rural young workers are employed full-time (79.3%) perhaps also reflecting the lower proportion of students in the rural sample. However, in contrast to what is observed elsewhere there is no apparent difference in the number of rural individuals holding down more than one job.

Table 3.4 Full-time or Part-time Employment (France)

	urban	rural	all young people
full-time	0.721	0.793	0.739
part time	0.279	0.207	0.261
sample size			6014

Table 3.5 Existence of Second Job (France)

	urban	rural	all young people
one job	0.978	0.978	0.978
more than one job	0.022	0.022	0.022
sample size			6340

Finally, in terms of the characteristics of the rural and urban samples of young people, Table 3.6 reports the highest level of education attained by each of the two groups. In passing, it should be noted that the interpretation of these results is complicated somewhat by the inclusion in the survey of those who did not answer the question in the "no degree" group. Nevertheless, it can be seen that a greater proportion of those living in rural areas than those living in urban areas cite the lower levels of education as the highest completed level. Obviously, for young people any such differences may not be permanent but these results do suggest that lower education levels in the general rural population are likely to be maintained in the future.

Table 3.6 Highest Completed Level of General Education (France)

	urban	rural	all young people
no degree/no answer	0.283	0.316	0.290
degree primary education, compulsory education completed	0.008	0.011	0.009
degree 1st cycle educ.	0.397	0.501	0.420
1st part bacc., secondary education completed	0.003	0.005	0.003
A-E bacc., 2nd part bacc.	0.308	0.166	0.276
elementary, primary high, or high degree	0.001	0.001	0.001
sample size			24361

Unemployment. Table 3.2 indicated that in the two samples 9.8% of the rural young and 10.3% of the urban young were unemployed. In this section we consider the unemployment experience in a little more detail. Table 3.7 describes the employment experience of the unemployed, i.e. have they ever been employed while Table 3.8 gives a breakdown of the length of the unemployment spell.

Table 3.7 Previous Employment Status of Unemployed Respondents (France)

	urban	rural	all young people
never been employed	0.873	0.859	0.870
already been employed	0.127	0.141	0.130
sample size			18431

From Table 3.7 there is a slight difference in the previous employment experience of the rural unemployed with 14.1% of the rural unemployed having already had some work experience relative to 12.7% in the urban sample. Slight rural-urban differences are also apparent in the length of time individuals have been unemployed with a somewhat higher proportion of urban young unemployed for more than six months.

Table 3.8 Time Since Last Worked (France)

	urban	rural	all young people
less than a month	0.023	0.013	0.021
1-6 months	0.400	0.430	0.407
7-12 months	0.214	0.197	0.210
over a year	0.363	0.359	0.362
sample size			2373

Job search. Table 3.9 and 3.10 provide an indication of how young people search for work in France. The sample here includes all individuals looking for work, i.e. unemployed, those in work, and out of the labour force. Table 3.9 indicates that there are few differences in the methods used to search for a new job by rural and urban young people. In so far as differences are apparent, fewer of the rural sample appear to have applied to employers directly, while more were likely not to have used any method of job search within the past four weeks.

Table 3.9 Main Method Used to Find a Job in the Last Four Weeks (France)

	urban	rural	all young people
contacted public employment office	0.188	0.178	0.186
contacted private employment agency	0.120	0.138	0.124
applied to employers directly	0.237	0.200	0.229
asked friends, relatives, TU etc.	0.138	0.146	0.140
inserted or answered ads in newspaper	0.084	0.072	0.081
studied adverts in newspapers	0.082	0.082	0.082
other methods	0.025	0.032	0.027
no method used	0.126	0.154	0.132
sample size			3395

Table 3.10 reports the reason why the individuals were seeking work. With the exception of the higher proportion of individuals having left the military, again the rural and urban samples seem broadly comparable.

Table 3.10 Reason for Seeking Work (France)

	urban	rural	all young people
lost job	0.076	0.073	0.075
quit job	0.029	0.020	0.027
gave up own business	0.021	0.011	0.019
seasonal work ended	0.314	0.333	0.318
left school	0.379	0.385	0.380
left military	0.098	0.124	0.104
other	0.083	0.054	0.076
sample size			2585

Employment mobility. In general the previous tables provide a snapshot of what individuals were doing at a point in time or during a given period. While the French data is cross sectional, i.e. it is collected at a given point in time, it has limited information about labour markets status in a previous period. Hence, some analysis of the dynamics of labour market states is possible. Table 3.11 uses this historical information to construct a partial transition matrix for those who were working or unemployed in the previous period.

For example, of the sample of rural young people who said they were working one year ago, 80.4% were still working, 13.1% had become unemployed and 6.5% were now out of the labour force, e.g. conscripted, full-time childcare.

Table 3.11 Transition Matrix (France)

status last year	status this year	urban	rural	all young people
working	working	0.789	0.804	0.793
	unemployed	0.145	0.131	0.141
	other	0.066	0.065	0.066
			sample size: 4624	
unemployed	working	0.388	0.415	0.394
	unemployed	0.518	0.494	0.513
	other	0.094	0.091	0.093
			sample size: 1857	

In terms of destinations of both those employed and unemployed a year ago, only slight differences are apparent between the rural and urban samples, with slightly more rural young people remaining in employment, i.e. 80.4% versus 78.9% and more moving from unemployment to employment.

Earnings. Finally for France, Tables 3.12 and 3.13 present simple statistics on the earnings in the samples of rural and urban young. Average hourly earnings figures were not available for the French survey, and hence were calculated from net monthly earnings. Table 3.12 reports this basic information with the average hourly earnings of young people in rural and urban apparently rather similar, at 34.20 FF for those in urban areas, against 35.27 FF in the rural sample.

Table 3.12 Average Earnings (France)

	urban	rural
average earnings	35.27	34.20

However, this similarity masks differences in the distribution of earnings between the two groups. Table 3.13 considers the proportion of young people whose can be classified as 'low paid'. Low pay is defined here as being earning in the bottom third of the distribution, calculated for all age groups. From the above table it can be seen that 82.5% of young people living in rural areas were low paid, while a much smaller proportion, 71.0%, of young people living in urban areas were low paid.

Table 3.13 Proportion in Low Pay (France)

		urban	rural	all young people
young	not in low pay	0.290	0.175	0.263
	in low pay	0.710	0.825	0.737
				sample total: 4919
25 plus	not in low pay	0.723	0.646	0.705
	in low pay	0.277	0.354	0.295
				sample total: 4863

For comparison, those who were 25 and over are also examined here. We see a similar pattern, with 27.7% of urban dwellers being in low pay compared to 35.4% of rural dwellers. As expected for both age groups, there were significantly more young people in low pay than older people.

These differences may in part reflect the differences in education levels between the rural and urban samples, but there may also be differences in terms of real wages which are not accounted for here.

Austria

General characteristics. Tables 3.14 and 3.15 provide a general picture of the structure of economic activity and employment by young people in Austria. In comparison to the French sample the striking difference is in the significantly greater proportion of young people who are classified as working. In terms of the rural urban difference there is also a significantly higher proportion of the rural sample who work (73.9%) – this difference is explained by the lower proportion of students in rural areas.

Table 3.14 Usual or Main Economic Activity (Austria)

	urban	rural	all young people
worker	0.599	0.739	0.638
unemployed	0.024	0.017	0.022
student	0.294	0.168	0.259
conscript	0.032	0.037	0.033
other inactive	0.051	0.040	0.048
sample size			8491

In terms of the industrial sectors of those employed, again a greater proportion of young people in rural areas work in the agriculture, forestry and fishing industries, while fewer work in services.

Table 3.15 Industry (Austria)

	urban	rural	all young people
agriculture, forestry and fishing	0.017	0.091	0.041
energy and water supply industries	0.008	0.006	0.007
extraction of minerals and ores other than fuels; manufacture of metals, mineral products and chemicals	0.052	0.034	0.046
metal goods, engineering and vehicles industries	0.174	0.177	0.175
other manufacturing industries	0.085	0.145	0.105
construction	0.108	0.110	0.109
distribution, hotels and catering, repairs	0.238	0.219	0.232
transport and communication	0.054	0.042	0.050
banking, finance, insurance, business services and leasing	0.075	0.043	0.065
other services	0.190	0.133	0.172
sample size			5623

In interpreting Table 3.16 some caution needs to be exercised as the full-time/part-time distinction is based upon a cut off point of 35 hours per week (for other countries this is 30 hours). There are few apparent differences in the proportions of young people who work full-time in the rural and urban samples.

Table 3.16 Full-time or Part-time Employment (Austria)

	urban	rural	all young people
full-time	0.876	0.866	0.873
part time	0.124	0.134	0.127
sample size			5820

In contrast, Table 3.17 illustrates that significantly greater number of the rural sample of young people held two jobs. Although the question is phrased differently, this also contrasts with the French sample where no rural-urban differences were apparent. In the Austrian LES, those with two jobs are explicitly divided up into farmers and non-farmers, with everyone else labelled as not applicable. Amalgamating the two "in a second job" categories, we see that 73.7% of those in rural areas had a second job, while 57.7% of those in urban areas had a second job.

Table 3.17 Existence of Second Job (Austria)

	urban	rural	all young people
is farmer in second job	0.005	0.022	0.009
is not farmer in second job	0.572	0.715	0.611
"inapplicable"	0.423	0.263	0.380
sample size			6853

Finally, in terms of general characteristics, Table 3.18 reports the pattern of educational attainment in the two samples This is similar to that for France with the attainment of the rural sample significantly lower than that for the urban sample.

Table 3.18 Highest Completed Level of General Education (Austria)

	urban	rural	all young people
compulsory school	0.663	0.807	0.703
vocational middle school	0.088	0.088	0.088
general high school	0.156	0.052	0.127
vocational higher school	0.078	0.049	0.070
university	0.015	0.004	0.012
sample size			8491

Unemployment. Table 3.14 indicated that in the two samples 1.7% of the rural young and 2.43% of the urban young were unemployed. Unfortunately, there is little information available in the Austrian LES to give more substance to these figures.[5] The limited information available on the previous work experience of the unemployed is reported in Table 3.19. This does indicates some rural-urban differences with 16.9% of young rural unemployed having had previous employment experience against only 9.8% for the urban unemployed.

Table 3.19 Previous Employment Status of Unemployed Respondents (Austria)

	urban	rural	all young people
never been employed	0.902	0.831	0.889
already been employed	0.098	0.169	0.111
sample size			2543

Employment mobility. As for France, the Austrian LES has limited information about labour market status in a previous period. Hence, Table 3.20 reports the partial transition matrix for those who were working or unemployed in the previous period. For example, of the sample of rural young people who said they were working one year ago, 99.1% were still working in the current period.

Table 3.20 Transition Matrix (Austria)

status over the last year	status this year	urban	rural	all young people
working	working	0.990	0.991	0.990
	unemployed	0.003	0.002	0.003
	other	0.007	0.007	0.007
			sample size: 3862	
unemployed	working	0.668	0.775	0.697
	unemployed	0.257	0.160	0.230
	other	0.075	0.065	0.072
			sample size: 452	

The large differences between the French and Austrian data in terms of the proportion of individuals remaining in work (around 80% as against 99%) may be partially explained by the different way in which work status is coded in the data. It is clear however, that there are no differences in the Austrian case between the rural and urban samples in the proportions that remain in work. However, in terms of exit from unemployment, higher proportions enter employment in the rural sample.

---

[5] In addition, questions on the reason for seeking new job were not asked in the Austrian LES nor were any comparable earnings data available.

Finland

General characteristics. Tables 3.21 and 3.22 provide a general picture of the structure of economic activity and employment by young people in Finland. In contrast to both the French and Austrian samples fewer young people in the rural sample were employed and more were students than in the urban case. As discussed above this may reflect some problems with the definition of rural districts, or it may derive from the much higher unemployment in Finnish rural areas during this period.

Table 3.21 Usual or Main Economic Activity (Finland)

	urban	rural	all young people
worker	0.530	0.490	0.515
unemployed	0.042	0.043	0.043
student	0.356	0.394	0.370
conscript	0.033	0.036	0.034
other inactive	0.039	0.037	0.038
sample size			6362

While Table 3.21 casts some doubt on the rural definition used, Table 3.22 shows that – as one would expect – that of those young people who are employed a considerably greater proportion are engaged in agriculture in the rural sample, i.e. 11.2% against 1.6% in the urban sample. However, perhaps fewer differences are apparent in the proportion of those employed in industry and services across the two samples than is evident in the French and Austrian cases.

Table 3.22 Industry (Finland)

	urban	rural	all young people
agriculture, forestry and fishing	0.016	0.112	0.049
energy and water supply industries	0.011	0.010	0.010
extraction of minerals and ores other than fuels; manufacture of metals, mineral products and chemicals	0.019	0.029	0.022
metal goods, engineering and vehicles industries	0.065	0.077	0.069
other manufacturing industries	0.109	0.109	0.109
construction	0.091	0.118	0.100
distribution, hotels and catering, repairs	0.259	0.195	0.237
transport and communication	0.080	0.061	0.073
banking, finance, insurance, business services and leasing	0.126	0.061	0.103
other services	0.224	0.227	0.225

The proportions of those in full-time and part-time employment reported in Table 3.23 are based on a variable reporting usual weekly hours. Here, an individual working 30 hours or more a week is classified as working full time, and one working less than 30 hours is classified as working part time.

Table 3.23 Full-time or Part-time Employment (Finland)

	urban	rural	all young people
full-time	0.850	0.875	0.858
part-time	0.150	0.125	0.142
sample size			3234

Table 3.24 Existence of Second Job (Finland)

	urban	rural	all young people
one job	0.944	0.931	0.940
more than one job	0.056	0.069	0.060
sample size			3234

In terms of proportion of those working full-time or in the numbers with more than one job there are no apparent differences between the rural and urban samples.

Unemployment. Table 3.21 indicated that in the two samples 4.3% of the rural young and 4.2% of the urban young were unemployed in Finland. Unfortunately as for Austria there is little further information available on unemployment experience to give more substance to these figures. Table 3.25 illustrates the previous work experience of those currently unemployed with no clear difference apparent between the rural and urban samples.

Table 3.25 Previous Employment Status of Unemployed Respondents (Finland)

	urban	rural	all young people
never been employed	0.926	0.934	0.929
already been employed	0.074	0.066	0.071
sample size			3128

Of the young people who were unemployed at the time of the survey, the majority had never been employed. Of those resident in rural areas 93.4% had not previously been employed, while 92.6 of those resident in urban areas had never been employed. A greater proportion of those resident in urban areas than those resident in rural areas had previously worked, the percentages being 7.4% and 6.6% respectively.

In common with the Austrian LES, the Finnish LES does not contain the questions that would have been required to look at time since last worked, and reason for seeking new job. Also, in common with the Austrian LES, there are no earnings data recorded for the Finnish LES that would have enabled comparison of mean earnings or low pay status of youths in urban and rural areas.

Job search. For Finland, only those not in employment were asked about their job search methods. The methods used by unemployed job seekers are recorded in Table 3.26. Clearly given the small sample sizes, the figures need to be treated with some caution. Notably 90.6% of the young people were actively seeking work. The most common method for both urban and rural dwellers was to contact the public employment office. However, a somewhat greater percentage of those living in urban areas asked friends, relatives or trade unions etc. while those in rural areas appear to apply more to employers directly.

Table 3.26 Main Method Used to Find a Job in the Last Four Weeks (Finland)

	urban	rural	all young people
contacted public employment office	0.822	0.822	0.822
applied to employers directly	0.066	0.096	0.077
asked friends, relatives, TradeUnion etc.	0.012	0.000	0.008
studied adverts in newspapers	0.028	0.000	0.018
other methods	0.072	0.083	0.076
sample size			268

Employment mobility. Unlike the Austrian and French surveys, the Finnish Labour Force Survey contains no information about the situation of the respondents in the year prior to the interview. In order to obtain this information, the monthly LFS for autumn 1990 was matched to the monthly LFS from autumn 1989. According to Forster, Helliesen and Kolberg (1996) only around 1/6 of the respondents in 1990 were also interviewed in 1989. Thus, only 15.7% of the observations in this Finnish LES have valid information on the employment status in the previous year. In Table 3.27 this limited information is used to construct the transitions from employment in the previous period. Because of the limited sample size available, the calculations for transitions from employment are not reported.

Table 3.27 Transition Matrix (Finland)

status last year	status this year	urban	rural	all young people
working	working	0.739	0.791	0.755
	unemployed	0.039	0.036	0.038
	other	0.222	0.174	0.206
				sample size: 529

From this restricted information, there does seem to be possible differences in the proportion of young people who remain in employment in consecutive periods with the rural proportion over 5% greater than that for the urban sample.

United Kingdom

General characteristics. Tables 3.28 and 3.29 repeat the information on the structure of economic activity and employment by young people in the United Kingdom. Consistent with other sources, what is noticeable in both tables is the degree to which the rural and urban samples are similar. Not only do similar proportions work, but also Table 3.29 illustrates, the extent to which employment structure in terms of the division between manufacturing and services is broadly comparable across the two samples.

Table 3.28 Usual or Main Economic Activity (UK)

	urban	rural	all young people
worker	0.572	0.574	0.572
unemployed	0.083	0.060	0.078
student	0.289	0.304	0.292
other inactive	0.056	0.061	0.058
sample size			1523

Taking those in employment first, it can be seen from the above table that 57.2% of young people in urban areas were in employment, while 57.4% of young people in rural areas were in employment. Thus, in the UK in 1998, young people in rural areas were more likely to be in employment than young people in urban areas. Young people in rural areas, compared with their urban counterparts, were less likely to be unemployed and more likely to be a student.

Table 3.29 Industry (UK)

	urban	rural	all young people
agriculture, forestry and fishing	0.009	0.042	0.017
energy and water supply industries	0.010	0.000	0.008
extraction of minerals and ores other than fuels; manufacture of metals, mineral products and chemicals	0.020	0.038	0.025
metal goods, engineering and vehicles industries	0.070	0.086	0.074
other manufacturing industries	0.080	0.077	0.079
construction	0.054	0.042	0.051
distribution, hotels and catering, repairs	0.380	0.351	0.373
transport and communication	0.052	0.050	0.051
banking, finance, insurance, business services and leasing	0.145	0.096	0.133
other services	0.179	0.218	0.189
sample size			1096

Some differences are apparent in terms of the division between full-time and part employment with somewhat higher proportions in full-time employment in the rural sample.

Table 3.30 Full-time or Part-time Employment (UK)

	urban	rural	all young people
full-time	0.745	0.768	0.751
part time	0.255	0.232	0.249
sample size			1076

Further, in terms of number of jobs held Table 3.31 indicates that the proportion of those in the rural sample with more than one job is almost twice that for the urban sample.

Table 3.31 Existence of Second Job (UK)

	urban	rural	all young people
one job	0.868	0.780	0.847
more than one job	0.132	0.220	0.153
sample size			1499

Table 3.32 reports the highest education level attained for the rural and urban samples of young people. In marked contrast to the other countries there is no clear

education gap in the UK sample, with rural individuals being at least as well educated as their urban counterparts.

Table 3.32 Highest Completed Level of General Education (UK)

	urban	rural	all young people
no qualifications	0.048	0.037	0.046
O-levels and equivalent	0.404	0.408	0.405
A-levels and equivalent	0.279	0.262	0.275
nursing and other higher qualifications	0.162	0.193	0.169
first degree, teaching qualification	0.097	0.092	0.096
higher degree	0.009	0.008	0.009
sample size			1432

Job search.[6] The analysis of the other countries above used information on the most common method of job search over the past four weeks. While there was no equivalent question in the BHPS those who were not in employment and who had actively sought paid work were asked whether they had employed five different methods of job search. The proportions using these methods are reported in table 3.33 but as individuals may have used multiple methods and no ranking of importance was given the column sums do not add to one in this case. Rather, each number in the main body of the table shows the proportion of young respondents who did employ that particular method of job search.

Table 3.33 Methods Used to Find a Job in the Last Four Weeks (UK)

	urban	rural	all young people
used a job centre or employment agency	0.496	0.454	0.489
applied to employers directly	0.574	0.663	0.590
asked friends, relatives, TU etc.	0.465	0.685	0.505
studied/answered ads in newspaper	0.686	0.671	0.683
taken steps to start own business	0.028	0.037	0.029
sample size			129-132

While caution needs to be exercised given the small sample sizes, there are some indications of differences between rural and urban samples, with higher proportions in the rural sample applying to employers directly and especially using social networks than for the urban case.

Employment mobility. As for Finland, the BHPS did not ask about historical labour status in 1998. However as it is longitudinal in nature, information on what an individual was doing in the previous year was merged using the BHPS from

---

[6] It did not prove possible to construct comparable unemployment data for the UK.

1997. For those working in the previous year, in both rural and urban sample over 90% were still working in the next year with the urban proportion slightly higher than the rural case. For the unemployed, although the sample size is small, the proportion of the rural sample gaining employment was significantly greater than for the urban case.

Table 3.34 Transition Matrix (UK)

status last year	status this year	urban	rural	all young people
working	working	0.938	0.919	0.934
	unemployed	0.029	0.058	0.036
	other	0.032	0.024	0.030
				sample size=629
unemployed	working	0.494	0.609	0.515
	unemployed	0.438	0.337	0.420
	other	0.068	0.054	0.066
				sample size=104

Earnings. Finally, Tables 3.35 and 3.36 present simple statistics on the earnings in the samples of rural and urban young. The BHPS has a number of earnings questions that allows usual hourly earnings including overtime to be calculated.[7]

Table 3.35 Average Earnings (UK)

	urban	rural
average earnings	5.035	5.440

Contrary to what was found in the case of France, young people in rural areas appear to be slightly better paid than their urban contemporaries. The average hourly wage of young people in rural areas was £5.44 while young people in urban areas earned just £5.04 an hour. In so far as earnings are related to education level, this may reflect the fact that in contrast to the French case, there was no obvious difference in education levels between the rural and urban samples in the UK.

---

[7] Usual as opposed to actual hourly earnings gives a more accurate indication of earnings, as the figures will not be distorted by unusual payments such as sickness benefit, or bonuses. Overtime is assumed to be paid at a rate of time and a half.

Table 3.36 Proportion in Low Pay (UK)

		urban	rural	all young people
young	not in low pay	0.422	0.329	0.399
	in low pay	0.578	0.671	0.601
				sample size: 721
25 plus	not in low pay	0.726	0.702	0.720
	in low pay	0.274	0.298	0.280
				sample size: 3235

Again the apparent similarity in the mean wage between the rural and urban samples masks differences in the distribution of wages. Table 3.36 reports the proportion of young workers classified as low paid. As for France, it is the case that the majority of young people are in low pay and significantly more young people in rural areas are low paid than their urban counterparts.

4. Conclusions and Policy Implications

Rural and labour market indicators are useful and necessary if the aim is, for example, to verify and analyse findings, such as the OECD's (1996c, 10) statements that "some rural regions belong to the most dynamic areas within OECD Member countries" and that "rurality in itself is not an obstacle to job creation". One finding of the OECD on the factors lying behind successful rural regions is that they are not yet properly understood, but probably include aspects such as regional identity and entrepreneurial climate, public and private networks, or the attractiveness of the cultural and natural environment. Muilu et al. (1999) found evidence for this in a case study from Northern Finland. They compared the municipalities of Suomussalmi (also the Finnish study area in the PaYPiRD project) and Sievi, the former being a declining rural area and the latter a rural 'success story'. It turned out that the reasons for the success of Sievi region were mostly those proposed by OECD.

Although the statistical indicators analysed in this study did bring out many national and regional differences between labour markets, they can not give direct information on background factors of the local labour market, such as the entrepreneurial climate or the social and cultural environment. This is of course a task for qualitative analysis, since the aim here was only to analyse the concept of indicators and to present some empirical examples on labour market indicators.

The extent to which general conclusions are possible based upon the descriptive analysis of micro-data is hampered by the difficulties caused by differences in definitions and information across the four countries. In particular, the differences in the rural definitions used need to be borne in mind when any comparisons are attempted.

Nevertheless, the results of the analysis of micro-data do suggest some common qualitative differences between rural and urban areas across counties, e.g.

lower education level of rural young people, the higher proportion of low paid young people in rural areas than urban, differences in the proportions moving from unemployment. Despite these apparent regularities, it should be noted that in general any rural-urban differences tend to be significantly less than the overall differences between countries. For example, in each of the countries considered the proportion of rural young people who work is much closer to the respective national average than to any of the figures from the other counties. Thus, while there are apparent rural–urban differences, the differences between countries generally seem more significant.

Some problems and policy implications can be identified on the basis of this analysis:

- *The problems of international statistics.* In multinational statistics like Eurostat the basic aim is to achieve as high reliability and comparability as possible. In spite of the efforts made in harmonising the statistics, the different statistical systems in different countries can still cause problems related to, for example, different dates and methods of data collection. This may cause problems like missing data. It will take a long time to resolve these problems and in the foreseeable future there are new problems to be faced, like the enlargement of EU and its effects on the international comparability of statistics.

- *The problems of regional units.* There are still no Eurostat statistics available at a more accurate level than NUTS3, and even this level is moderately rare in regional statistics. NUTS4 or even NUTS5 level would be very useful for the international analysis of labour markets, and many other phenomena. It would also be interesting to compare NAPs of different countries at a regional level if more localised regional units were used in them.

- *The problems of classifications.* In some indicators, like sectors of employees, it would be useful to have more accurate categories. Classification into only three main sectors is insufficient to analyse which individual fields of the economy are actually increasing in a region.

- *The problem of age analysis.* The main indicators like unemployment and activity rates are classified both by sex and age, but, for example, young employee's employment by sector can not be analysed at all since no age grouping is used.

The different national definitions of rurality frustrate attempts at international analysis even where the datasets have been carefully harmonised, as in the Luxembourg Employment Study. It would be very useful if the OECD's rurality variable were applied consistently to each country's data.

Notwithstanding all these problems, an overall picture of labour market strength did emerge from the use of a range of indicators shown in Figure 3.3, and a broad context has been established for this study.

Chapter 4

Methodology

Birgit Jentsch

1. Overall Objectives

The project set out to analyse the effects of policies on young people (aged 16-25) across rural areas of Europe, focusing in particular on their integration with or exclusion from labour markets. For this purpose, a methodology was employed which was based on the recognition that little information exists on young people's attitudes towards economic and social issues. It thus seemed an ethical as well as pragmatic imperative to shed light on the youngsters' views through interviews and focus group discussions, and to take a 'bottom up' approach when considering policy options. Since it is young people themselves who have most expertise in the conditions, which contribute towards shaping their lives, their accounts can clearly make valuable contributions to the formulation of policies and to practice development.

The research project aimed to consider policies at various levels, including the EC, national, regional and local. The impact of such policies on the 'pathways' to young people's inclusion or exclusion and integration in rural areas was to be examined, and the variation in the impacts between social groups (especially by class and gender) and between rural areas be analysed. In addition, the research was to explore the role of policies in ensuring the active participation of young people in rural labour markets. The specific objectives of the research were as follows:

- To analyse in a bottom-up approach in seven study areas (UK, IE, DE, PT, FR, FI, AT) the effects of policies and operational programmes at various levels on young people's integration into rural labour markets, and therefore on social cohesion in rural areas;
- To explore how changes in labour markets, labour market policies and welfare regimes, at various levels, interact with changes in the nature and duration of the youth transition to include or exclude young people from rural employment opportunities;
- To consider appropriate means and levels of policy implementation.

In addition, each partner developed a theme, which was to be examined taking a comparative perspective, as outlined in Chapter 1. A thematic framework was developed to ensure that the seven themes would contribute comprehensively to different aspects of our research questions. Considering the overarching objectives of the project, as outlined above, it became clear that the conceptual framework for such analysis would have to have at its heart the youth transition from education to secure fulfilling employment (which is interwoven with other aspects of the youth transition to independence and adulthood). Beginning with a young person, aged 16, we can already characterise that person in terms of their resources (skills, etc) and values and attitudes, situated within a local, national and global context. This context is provided by the systems of socialisation and the systems that allocate resources, status and honour in society. These will continue to form the context for agency during the youth transition, although the ways in which these operate will change in nature and significance through that transition.

We can then conceive of this youth transition as a path towards integration into the labour market, and of a series of bridges and barriers in between, some of which are acted upon by policies. Amongst these barriers and bridges we are likely to find:

- Personal attributes and their valency (eg. Education and qualifications; presentation and 'labelling' within small communities; soft skills; work experience and reliability; social class, age and gender).
- Social networks (personal contacts and word of mouth may be important not only in finding employment, but also housing, transport and recreation).
- Parental support (not only financial – giving money, buying driving lessons and a car, providing free accommodation and laundry, etc – but also through use of the parents' social networks to find employment for their children, among other aspects).
- Access to transport – reliance on parents or others for lifts, public transport, own car.
- Training availability within reach.
- Range of employment opportunities within reach, and their quality.
- Childcare and other support services may be necessary for some.
- Local cultures – for example of hard work and independence (perhaps pressure to take whatever work is available), and in relation to gender roles.
- State support, for example for training, housing, transport, and including welfare to work and similar youth employment schemes; state intervention, perhaps in partnership with private and voluntary sectors, to develop employment opportunities and to increase the quality of jobs and wage rates.
- Young people's perceptions of the rural area itself, which may change radically through the youth transition (for example, when a car has been acquired), and of the urban-rural duality.

Most of the thematic reports investigated one or more of these bridges and barriers, and the ways in which they assisted or hindered young people in their transition into employment, either narrowing or broadening their choices and opportunities.

2. The Selection of the Partners and Study Areas

It has been an unfortunate experience of cross-national research projects that reliable collaborators are not always easily identifiable and available, as a consequence of which "the quality of contributions to multinational projects is all too often depressingly uneven" (Hantrais and Mangen 1996, 10-11). As a consequence, there may be a trade off between partners that are known to the co-ordinator of a project, and those whose particular research expertise, as well as national or regional location may seem particular suitable for the research question and design. The PaYPiRD research seemed to have benefited from a situation where both advantageous factors could be combined. The partners were known to the co-ordinator for their experience in European rural research, their reliability in delivering the required, high quality contributions, and their enthusiasm. Moreover, they were located in countries whose inclusion in the research could certainly be justified. The seven case study areas in seven EU member states were

> selected to include a range of labour market policies, welfare regimes and types of rural areas, following the typology proposed by the EC's document 'The Future of Rural Society' [(EC 1988)]. These will allow the inclusion of each of these three types of standard rural problem, while also allowing for sufficient variation for analysis. Within each country, case study areas have been selected in relation to strength of local labour market, while also taking account of remoteness, population density, and other social and cultural variables. (FAIR Project nr: 4171, Proposal)

The following table elaborates on these dimensions for the study areas, going beyond the uni-dimensional typology of rural areas used, using national and local data to go beyond Figure 3.3's NUTS data from Eurostat.

Table 4.1 Characteristics of the PaYPiRD Study Areas

	Strength of labour market (see also Table 3)	Remoteness	Social and cultural variables
Angus, Scotland	Unemployment amongst young people moderate	Accessible area; close to major Scottish cities	Strong dependence on nearby urban centre for employment leading to relatively high number of commuters and culture of mobility; attempts to rejuvenate the traditional agricultural sector subject to pressures operating at a macro level; recent initiative to increase youth participation in local politics
Suomussalmi, Finland	Unemployment amongst young people very high	Very marginal area	Several projects aiming to improve young people's lives; close social relations; general negative perceptions of the future of Suomussalmi; high living costs due to climate and remoteness
Murau, Upper Styria, Austria	Unemployment amongst young people low/moderate	Remote area	common experience of dependence on other regions, leading to commuting and out-migration; against traditional value system some youth pilot actions are emerging
NE Mayenne, France	Unemployment amongst young people low	Remote area	Several development projects based on local industries and services are piloted
Wesermarsch, Germany	Unemployment amongst young people moderate	Accessible area	Several organisations/agencies providing advice, skills training and active labour market measures
Santa Marta de Peniguao, Portugal	Unemployment amongst young people moderate	Remote area	Scarcity of social and cultural facilities; culturally negative perception of agriculture's future; close social relations
NW Connemara, Ireland	Unemployment amongst young people moderate	Remote area	Strong history of local community development

Contact amongst the partners took place through co-ordination meetings from month one of the project, and then every six months until the end of the research. In total, five meetings were held, which lasted for around three days each. More regular contact amongst the partners was maintained through e-mail. This included very intense communication prior to the meetings, when drafts of documents, which were to be discussed, were circulated and commented upon. As a result, the meetings were characterised by efficiency and high level discussions.

3. The Sampling Frame and Access

The first two co-ordination meetings with all partners included discussions and decisions on the research target groups. It was agreed that an accidental quota sampling procedure should be used: three groups of young people were to be part of the research, capturing some important steps in the transition process. The groups included first, those in education/training; second, those in employment; third, the unemployed. The total target number for individual interviews was agreed to be around 35. Flexibility was granted in the composition of the sub-groups, allowing the partners to research groups who seemed to be especially relevant in their contexts (for example, participants in a particular training scheme). Practical constraints were encountered in some study areas, which led to an overrepresentation of one particular group at the expense of another. The distribution of the 254 interviewees in the different occupational categories is provided in Appendix 2. It can be seen, for example, that the number of unemployed represented in the samples range from three young people in the Scottish study area to 14 in the Finnish, to some extent reflecting differences in the prevalence of unemployment in the study areas. Variations in the composition combined with the different sizes of the samples, which ranged from 32 to 46 (see Appendix 2) meant that caution had to be taken to interpret findings cross-nationally in a way which took account of the differences in the composition and size of the samples. To some degree, this qualification can also apply to the way in which the sample members were accessed. Here, several techniques were used, which ranged from a very informal process in Portugal that mainly relied on approaching youngsters in public spaces as well as snowballing, to a rather formalised approach taken in France, where youth organisations assisted in identifying potential sample members. Other study areas used a combination of those two approaches. It can be imagined that studies which are based on a more formalised approach are likely to have a greater number of young people included who already benefit to varying degrees from supporting social institutions. Those without such contacts – conceivably the most vulnerable – will not be captured.

4. The Interview Schedule and Questionnaire

Discussions at the two initial co-ordination meetings also covered the design of the interview schedule and the questionnaire. The interview schedule had to take account of data required for those themes, which were relying on primary data collection. The schedule covered six areas which were regarded as integral to the transition from education to employment, namely young people's experiences and expectations in education, training, employment, housing, social networks, and young people's participation. At the end of the interview, the research participants were asked to sum up the advantages and disadvantages of living in the study area, to review their decision making processes up to the date of the interview, and to comment on the future of their area.

The interview schedule was piloted in the different study areas, and issues which arose were discussed electronically. Those included problems, which had occurred in relation to the notion of 'participation', which evoked different connotations in different areas, and sometimes left interviewees altogether with a lack of ideas of what could be meant. For example, while in the UK context, the concept is often used to refer to activities at some political level at a time when youth congresses have been established across the country, in the Portuguese case, the notion was more associated with societal participation. It was agreed that the different possible aspects of 'participation' should be explored as appropriate in each study area.

All interviews were taped, and later transcribed. It was initially decided that each team would circulate half a page of notes on an evaluation and the main findings of an interview, including brief biographical details, but this turned out to be an impractical decision. It was agreed that a more useful and graphic 'summary' would be a diagram of interviewees' work history. An example of such a diagram was presented by the Portuguese team at the third co-ordination meeting, and all partners regarded the diagrams as helpful, not least for their data analysis.

5. The Questionnaire

In addition to the qualitative data, quantitative data was collected by means of a questionnaire with closed questions. It was hoped that this 'triangulation' of methods could help to compensate for the weaknesses of one method with the strengths of another, and provide some quantitative measure, which could be more easily compared. The questionnaire was to be administered at the end of the interview either by the interviewee him or herself, or by the interviewer. OECD educational categories were referred to for standardising purposes. In relation to employment, EUROBAROMETER's occupation grid was used.

6. Focus Group Discussions

Once the process of interviewing was completed, a preliminary analysis of the data took place, allowing the research teams to get an overview of the total data collected, and helping to detect those subject areas, which were thought to especially benefit from further data collection. Hence, the focus groups could serve as a tool to expand data in particular areas, as well as adding the extra dynamics a group discussion entails. Focus groups were also helpful in being able to compensate for the under-representation of those research target groups who – often due to practical reasons – were difficult to recruit for the individual interviews. The content of the topic guide for the focus group discussion was derived from the context report and the feedback from the individual interviews as well as e-mail discussion amongst the partners.

In addition, in all study areas bar the German, one focus group interview was carried out with key personnel working with and for youth. In Germany, eight members of local key personnel were interviewed individually.[1] As far as it was possible, the sample of young people in each study area comprised similar proportions of pupils, students and trainees, employed, and unemployed youths. In most cases, similar numbers of men and women were included.

7. Analysis of Data

Qualitative

Different approaches to qualitative data analysis were considered at the third co-ordination meeting, one of which comprised three stages of coding the data (see for example, Strauss and Corbin 1990; Neuman 1994, 407). The first stage involves 'open coding', where code labels are assigned to the data; this is followed by the second stage, 'axial coding', where the initial coded themes are reviewed and examined, and attempts are made to identify an axis of key themes. This process includes the search for causes and consequences, strategies and processes, and for connected categories and concepts. Last, 'selective coding' takes place after attempts have been made to identify all major themes. Here, data and previous codes are scanned. Cases are looked for 'selectively' in order to illustrate themes, and comparisons and contrasts can be made. Another, four stage model of qualitative data analysis was discussed, where in the first reading of the transcript, the researcher is looking for 'the story' in a person's account of their history and experiences; in the second reading, the search is for 'I's. The third passing through focuses on 'social relations', and the final, fourth reading on wider structures and general linkages which may exist. While all partners considered the use of (aspects of) either or both of these models, it was agreed that as long as there was clarity about the objectives of the qualitative data analysis, the actual process could be left to the discretion of the partners. The general objectives were defined as follows: there should be an analysis of the impact of policies on pathways; an examination of the variations of the impact; and an exploration of the underlying policies and active participation. It was emphasised that the dimension of time may be of particular importance, and the work history diagram which was to be designed by all partners to illustrate this dimension was agreed to be of good use here. It was agreed that the qualitative data analysis for each theme was to be carried out by each partner, and then forwarded to each team to compile the comparative report.

---

[1] The interview with key personnel gave us the opportunity to feed back some preliminary findings to those with some power in decision-making processes, as well as informing us about their insights into the barriers and enabling factors young people may experience during transitions leading towards adulthood.

Quantitative

As to the quantitative data analysis, a coding scheme and SPSS command file was devised by the Portuguese team, and distributed for discussion to all partners. The scheme was modified, and agreed at the third co-ordination meeting in Vila Real. As expected, the need for further refinements occurred when partners started to input their data using SPSS, and arrangements by e-mail were made to guarantee the same use of codes for the same data. Once partners had completed this process, the files were sent to the co-ordinator to compile, and an SPSS file containing the data from all study areas was distributed to all partners for their own use. The data was mainly used for cross tabulations (see Scottish thematic report) as well as multivariate analysis (see Portuguese thematic report).

8. The Comparative Dimension of the Research

Rationales Behind Cross-national Research

A number of principal benefits have been claimed for international comparative studies. First, it has been argued that comparative analysis can help to provide a tool to explain common trends and account for national differences, and possibly to predict developments. Second, and more related to policy and practice development, it has been suggested that we can learn from the experiences, successful and otherwise, of other countries. This notion is rooted in the fact that countries often develop different policies in response to apparently similar problems. As a consequence, 'policy borrowing' may occur where certain provisions have been successful (May 1998). Similarly, we may be able to identify 'best practice' models, the suitability of which can be considered in different national contexts (O'Reilly 1996). This is especially relevant within the framework of the EU. Third, cross-national comparisons may provide us with new perspectives, suggesting fresh approaches to a research problem. Fourth, it is possible that through cross-national research, we can identify those gaps in knowledge which prevent effective comparative studies, so that new research can be formulated (Hantrais and Mangen 1996, 3). Finally, there are the benefits for theory development, as in this example.

> Relationships once assumed to be universal have been shattered on the proving ground of the non-western world. As a result, there is now a more cautious and less grandiose attitude in theory construction and a renewed quest for explanations that will stand the test of varying socio-cultural conditions. (Warwick and Osherson 1973, 6 in: O'Reilly 1996, 2)

As to the approaches to comparative research, they have differed, not least in the degree in which the comparison is made explicit. Sometimes, while country-specific ranges and types of policies and delivery systems are detailed, a direct comparative assessment is then left to the reader. Other studies are more explicit in their comparisons, but then may vary in their foci.

> Some, especially those undertaking government-sponsored studies or concerned to inform policy-making, concentrate on programmes, usually with broad socio-economic and political structures. (May 1998, 22)

The type of approach taken may have implications for the way research teams are formed and operate. Individual researchers or research teams can investigate their own national contexts, and the information can be pooled and analysed from a centre. Alternatively, a researcher or team of researchers develop the research problem and hypotheses, and conduct the study in more than one country. The latter method seems to presuppose a small number of countries involved in the research (Hantrais and Mangen 1996, 4-5).

PaYPiRD's Cross-national Dimension in Retrospect

As to the rationale behind PaYPiRD's comparative research dimension, such an approach promised useful outcomes for policy recommendations, allowing researchers to question their own culture and institutions, which they are often likely to take for granted (Rainbird 1996, 110).

> The research methodology has to take account of distinctive national institutions, the articulation of different policy debates and perceptions of significant issues, and the reference of distinct intellectual traditions. (Rainbird 1996, 110)

Bearing this imperative for cross-national research in mind, the first task of all research teams was to compose a 'context report'. The report comprised the following elements: a profile of the study area, including demographic developments; key characteristics of the local economy; levels of educational attainment, employment and unemployment, as well as an overview of the housing situation. This was followed by an account of policies and programmes at different levels, which may have had an impact on young people's opportunities with regard to education, training, employment and related issues. Those reports, together with introductions given in the thematic reports, provided the main context in which the empirical research could be placed. Due to the research project's objectives the methodologies mainly applied qualitative approaches (Strauss 1987) though also some quantitative data has been collected for illustration of the assessments and distribution of different groups of young people.

On the positive side, the considerable breadth of this research design did facilitate the examination of the multi-dimensional problems young people face in rural areas – the most important of the objectives of our research. On the other hand, a corollary of this was an ambitious analytical framework, which covered many areas of the transition process as well as a whole range of policies, programmes and services, and this meant that the national analyses could not delve into great depth. As a result, apart from the substantive findings reported in the chapters which follow, one of the main benefits of the study in comparative terms could be its ability to contribute significantly to future research agendas, and to provide the basis for more narrowly focused research. For example, it was a surprising result found by all partners that very little information exists on the experiences of young people in rural areas. It became clear that the particular needs young people have due to their geographic location is rarely considered by policy makers, let alone taken into account in policy making. Where rural youth is a subject area, this often derives from a mixed and somewhat conflated agenda concerned about the sustainability of rural areas, for which rural youth are regarded as a means to an end, rather than looking at young people as an object of policy in their own right.

Some language issues also merit our attention, since these will necessarily be experienced in other cross-national projects funded by the EU. It is often emphasised that interview data should be collected by native speakers or by bilingual researchers in order to minimise translation problems at the data collection and analysis stage (Ungerson 1996, 64). This approach was followed by this project, where the national teams carried out the fieldwork and analysed their own data. The national reports were written in a common language (English), however, and thus included translated quotes from the young people. This may detract from the authenticity of young people's voices, although the illustrative power of the quotes remained and of course the national analyses themselves remained undistorted. Further issues inevitably arise at the next stage of writing comparative reports, which necessarily rely on data collected in other countries. Thus, the thematic reports were based on the national reports, which included translated interview excerpts. Although partners could be asked to provide extra-information, there is a danger that particular meanings might be attributed to words deriving from the researchers' own cultural background, rather than from the interviewee.

> Where qualitative methods, leading to grounded theory, are used, the loss of meaning and nuance arising from the translation of direct quotation can be an insuperable difficulty. ... [Translation] will lock the culturally loaded meanings of interview material from many languages into a single language which can only provide a very partial key. (Ungerson 1996, 64)

In addition, since it is necessary to be selective in translation and circulation, one must be aware of the 'filters' at work. In collecting the data and passing it on, each team selects and translates only those aspects of the data which they perceive would meet the needs of their partners. The partner in turn selects data for interpretation from that pool. There is thus a loss of information and the potential for bias, which we were keen to guard against.

In order to minimise the danger of such effects, the reports were fed back to the fieldworkers in each country, and their views on the accuracy of the findings, including the interpretation, were sought. It is believed that this will have ensured the validity of the comparative analysis as far as possible. Nonetheless, given these translation issues, it is worth considering for future research whether the advantages of including several countries in a project outweigh the disadvantages arising from the number of languages involved. Ungerson (1996) suggests as a possible solution the use of multi-lingual teams of researchers who are involved throughout the research process. Of course, this means that qualitative methods in comparative research more require generous and long-term funding than is usually available, and may present practical problems.

What, then, have been the main strengths of this project in methodological terms? This project was designed to look at the totality of young people's lives, from their own perspectives, and this was necessarily broad in scope. The methodology was well suited to this task, with both the in-depth interviews and the focus groups providing a rich source of information on how young people perceive their lives and the choices open to them in these rural localities. Subsequently, more narrowly focused studies each limited to particular aspects of the transition in a smaller number of countries will be able to build on this contribution and deepen our understanding of individual elements.

The methodology has also allowed the identification of 'models' of policies, programmes and services, which were well liked by young people in these rural areas. Components of such provisions could certainly be considered for adoption in other countries, although this will require careful consideration of the conditions in which they currently operate and the context into which they are to be 'imported'.

A particular strength of this project's methodological approach has been the understanding gained of young people's circumstances in each of the diverse study areas, and these can serve as useful reference case studies for young people's policy involvement in other European regions. Beyond this, a surprisingly high and complex degree of commonality (as well as many differences) emerged between young people's experiences in these diverse study areas, which might be explored further in subsequent analyses. The detailed findings are reported in the remaining chapters of this book.

Chapter 5

The Attractiveness of Rural Areas for Young People

Elizabeth Auclair and Didier Vanoni

1. Introduction

The object of the PaYPiRD research is to analyse young people's perceptions concerning the transition between education and employment. The aim is to evaluate the impact of policies on the social and professional integration of young people living in rural areas. This transition is a complex phenomenon, which has many different dimensions. In order to study this transition and to examine the individual pathways, it is necessary to have a precise knowledge of the employment and education systems. Various other elements that condition this transition must also be analysed, such as the role of local networks, the efficiency of local structures or the impact of local development programmes.

First, though, it seems important to place these elements in their local contexts. Thus, to understand the perceptions and representations of rural youth, we must analyse the characteristics of rural areas as they are described by young people themselves. The object of this chapter is therefore to examine the attractiveness of rural areas, highlighting key issues for young people which have examined in detail in subsequent chapters. What characteristics make rural areas attractive (or not) to young people, at different stages of the youth transition?

The attractiveness of a region is partly due to its "natural" or "objective" features, but also to the policies which have been conducted locally. In fact, rural development policies concern, on the one hand, the rural territories and, on the other hand, the populations that live there. The policies are supposed to enhance the articulation between these populations and their local environment. Therefore, local development projects cannot be undertaken without taking into account the characteristics of the population, as well as those of the territory itself. But a territory does not only present objective conditions of life and opportunities. The inhabitants, and the young people in particular in our case studies, develop their own perception of the region in which they live.

This raises many questions, such as:

- According to today's rural youth, what are the place and functions of rural areas today in a rapidly changing economic context?

- How does the increase of mobility influence the ways of life in rural areas?
- Do the changes in urban patterns modify the perception of "rurality"?
- What are the values that influence the way young people perceive rural areas?
- What makes some areas more attractive than others for young people?

These questions related to crucial choices and policy issues, within each country, *viz.*:

- What is the future for rural areas?
- Do the populations who live there, and the young people in particular, want to stay or do they want to leave?
- Will these areas attract new populations, and, if so, under what conditions?

These are important questions and a greater understanding of the attractiveness and what it means for young people should help to define recommendations concerning rural development policies.

2. The Situation of Rural Areas in Europe

In order to analyse young people's perceptions, we will, first of all, refer to the local contexts and present the general situation and perceptions concerning rural areas today. Many studies and debates during the last few decades have focused on the decline of rural areas and on the problems related to rural depopulation. In fact, there have been many changes in rural areas over the last fifty years, though not all of this transformation has been negative.

The modernisation of agriculture during the 1950s and 1960s – sometimes called the "agriculture revolution" – enabled many European countries to develop a modern and competitive agriculture sector. But though the agriculture sector gained a dominant position in some areas, it declined in others. In the 1970s, several movements emerged, based on various ideologies and objectives, but with the principal goals of arresting decline and promoting rural areas. But some of these movements were controversial, particularly when the countryside was only considered as a place to live in by "urbanites" wanting to leave the cities. Moreover, this promotion of the countryside was partly based, at least in France, on traditional or old-fashioned values and a nostalgic way of thinking about the advantages of nature.[1]

Some changes also came from the shift in the Common Agriculture Policy. These changes were characterised by a modification of the intensive production strategies and the promotion of a better integration of farm activities into a wider process of rural development. But these new policies were not able to prevent an

---

[1] The description of the countryside by the French philosopher JJ Rousseau, when he speaks of "l'ordre éternel des champs", is still a strong reference point in France.

increase in the disparities inside the countries themselves, with many rural regions continuing to face major difficulties despite the reforms.

However, it seems that in the last decade, several countries have seen an important evolution. This has encompassed "concrete" or visible transformations in the villages themselves such as the increase in the rural population, more housing construction, and the creation of jobs and services, but there has also been a shift in the way these rural territories are communicated to a wider audience. This valorisation of the countryside is mainly related to the development of new functions.

Many studies confirm this revival; a revival which is partly due to the spreading of ideas concerning sustainable development. Thus, the promotion of the countryside is no longer based on an idealistic vision of something that is disappearing – or even lost for ever – but is linked to real uses and practices by the inhabitants of these areas, and by tourists. In France, the last census (1999) shows that many rural villages are gaining population and the studies undertaken for the LEADER program confirm this phenomenon in other European countries also.[2] The most important changes are observed in the local communities situated close to the cities, that is to say under the influence of urban areas, but even in more remote regions, positive changes can be seen.

Several objective reasons can explain this "revival". First of all, the new forms of urban development, which spread from the outskirts of the cities into the countryside, induced new ways of life in which mobility became one of the main components.[3] The traditional patterns of cities, where activities are concentrated in the centre, are becoming obsolete. There are now several 'centres' within the city, not just one, and sometimes they are quite distant from one another. Therefore, today, life in these new urban districts is not so different from the rural areas. One lives in a place, works in another, goes shopping elsewhere and chooses various places for cultural or leisure activities. Thus, the countryside can present several advantages (peacefulness, proximity to nature, low cost of housing). These evolutions induce questions on the meaning of concepts such as rural or "rurality".

A second reason for the 'rural revival' is related to the situation of the rural economy, which is in fact quite dynamic in certain regions. Agriculture does still occupy a central place, if not in terms of jobs at least in terms of structuring rural areas. Environmental issues can be seen as a new incentive, especially for the young generation of farmers. In some cases, like in Austria, forestry plays an important part in the economic activities. It also must be stressed that some rural areas, such as Mayenne (in France) benefit from the existence of local industries that are an important economic element. In Ireland and Scotland, there have been clear changes in recent years, resulting in an increased availability of employment in different sectors, such as services.

---

[2] LEADER magazine, n°22, spring 2000.
[3] The concepts of "ville émergente", discontinuous urbanisation, or "cita diffusa" that we find in different countries express these changes in the urban patterns.

Moreover, numerous policies, procedures and actions have been undertaken at different levels (European, national or local) in order to diversify the economy, and to valorise the natural, cultural, architectural or traditional heritage for tourism projects. In Portugal, the production of Port wine, which is the main economic activity of the study area, constitutes a growing potential as a tourist attraction. In Germany, the Wesermarsch district is already a touristic area which offers several museums, art galleries, historic buildings, cycle paths. Hotels, coffee shops and various entertainments have emerged to cater for the demand (600 000 overnight stays are booked each year on the peninsula). Important communication strategies have also been undertaken such as the campaign to popularise a new name for the area and the promotion of specific food products. Nevertheless, in many regions, such as in Mayenne (France) or in Murau (Austria), the results of these policies are still weak, and tourism is considered as a strategy that has to be developed.

Thus, in spite of the important differences, and even increased inequalities in some cases, it no longer seems possible to speak of a general decline of rural areas.[4] Several studies, mediated by French magazines and newspaper articles, analyse and comment on these new trends.[5] Across the European Union, many rural areas are exhibiting growth (CEC 1997), as noted in Chapter 2. It seems that an increasing number of people are leaving the cities in order to settle in the countryside. Though the number of people concerned is not yet that high, what seems important is the change in the discourse. The attractiveness of rural areas, at least for urban populations, now seems an obvious fact, acknowledged in many countries.[6]

A recent survey conducted in France presented the expressions people use in order to describe the countryside.[7] Several words were used, out of which we can mention "peacefulness" (for 92% of the interviewees), "liberty" (65%), "health" (64%), "solidarity" (62%) and "beauty" (57%). Similar results have been found in Scotland (Shucksmith 1999). These terms illustrate the changes that have occurred in the image of the countryside. It must be stressed that for many decades it was the cities that were supposed to represent liberty and upward social mobility, whereas the countryside, on the contrary, meant hard work, domination, oppression, and backwardness.

Nevertheless, this positive evolution does not concern all rural areas to the same extent and most of the European countries are still characterised by a certain fragility of their rural territories.[8] In fact, for our research, we intentionally decided to select, in the seven countries, different categories of areas, as explained in Chapter 3.

---

[4] That does not mean, however, that rural areas do not meet crucial difficulties, and many research outcomes do emphasise the social exclusion phenomenon.

[5] See list of articles in references.

[6] "The new values placed on rural spaces" Shucksmith 2000.

[7] Sondage CSA pour la DATAR, 1995.

[8] Kurikka, Paiva (2000), *Suomen kuntaliitto*, ACTA nro 127, Helsinki, Finland.

In all the cases, the main difficulties are related to the lack of jobs, or at least the lack of choices and qualified jobs. In spite of a rapidly increasing commuting phenomenon, many young people have to leave their home area and go to the cities in order to find a job. But on the other hand, new populations are also moving in. It is therefore important to compare the situations, and to analyse the attractiveness of these different rural areas.

All these transformations raise several questions:

- Is attractiveness only related to efficient communication strategies and to the creation of a new image of rural areas?
- How do the new residents adapt to their new life?
- And how do the villages react to the arrival of these newcomers?

Several difficulties have been often mentioned concerning the opposition between the expectations of these new populations and the realities of life in the countryside. One issue concerns the specific characteristics of the people who move into the countryside. In France, several studies showed that an increasing number of disadvantaged people, who face important problems in the cities, decide to settle in rural areas. Thus, the question of their difficult social integration arises. In Scotland and Ireland however, some difficulties seem related to the fact that the newcomers are considered as being "well off" or "money people", a perception that can induce a kind of rancour towards them from sections of the local population. Several interviewees believed that the increase of this phenomenon could even lead to tensions in the locality, and previous research (Jedrej and Nuttall 1996; Burnett 1998) have explored these tensions in depth.

But a major question concerns the attractiveness for the rural population itself. Do the inhabitants want to stay or to leave? And what about the young people? What are their expectations and opinions? These are some of the questions we propose to analyse in this report.

3.   A General Frame for the Concept of Attractiveness

Many typologies have been elaborated in order to classify rural areas according to different criteria.[9] These various typologies are useful to study population movements or to foresee new changes. However, they are not sufficient to analyse the complex concept of attractiveness. Three different dimensions contribute in defining the attractiveness of rural areas:

---

[9] We can mention, for instance, the EC typology presented in the document *The Future of Rural Society*, or the typology which is often used in France and which was elaborated by the SEGESA in order to appreciate the fragility of the French rural cantons (an administrative level between the municipality and the Departement).

- The measured attractiveness
  This is defined by what can be actually observed, locally, in terms of demographic movements or economic changes. Several indicators can be used such as population trends (increase rate, migration), construction data and/or housing market situation, number of new firms and jobs created in the last years, number of tourists (and general or specific data on tourism), and the number of events in the area (scientific or cultural).
- The constructed attractiveness
  This covers actions or projects undertaken at different levels, the aim of all the measures being to make rural areas more attractive. Various strategies exist such as communication strategies (concerning the image of the area), branding or labelling of spaces and products, and creation of new infrastructures (in order to attract population or jobs).
- The perceived attractiveness
  This is composed of a series of elements mentioned by the population, and by the young people in particular in the case of this research. It includes the importance of nature and landscapes, the impact and role of family, friends and networks, the rural/urban differences, the childhood/native attachment to the area, the quality of life versus professional career issues, and the leaving or staying issues.

The two first dimensions have been already partly described in the interim report, where the local contexts of the seven case studies were presented. We will therefore focus here on the third dimension of attractiveness.

Attractiveness is not a simple, one-dimensional characteristic. It must be thought of as a multidimensional scale on which a cursor moves, and indicates different levels of attractiveness depending on a series of elements. These elements associate together into different combinations, according to the areas. Rural areas can therefore be regarded as "more or less" attractive.

We will consider the term attractiveness, in this chapter, as the result of the way young people, according to their individual characteristics, perceive the objective characteristics of rural areas. These characteristics are partly determined by the policies and programmes implemented at European, national or local levels. On the other hand, the representations and perceptions of the young people are also influenced by the systems of values of the present society.

Figure 5.1 Factors Influencing Young People's Perception of Rural Areas

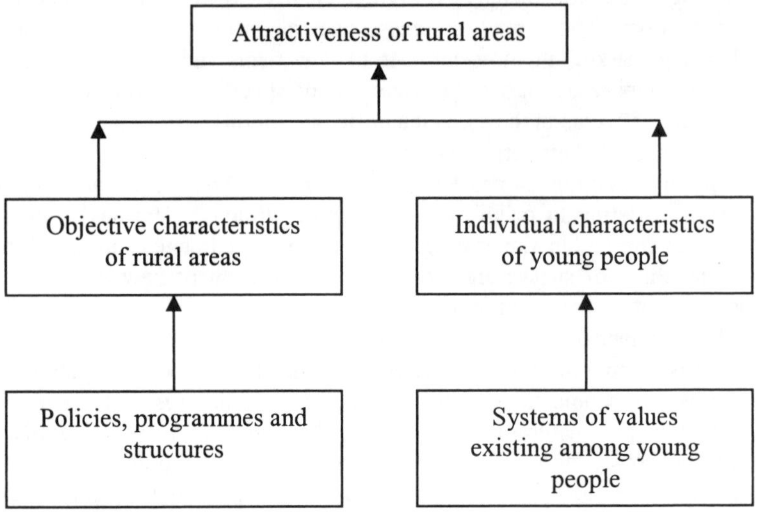

```
                    ┌─────────────────────────────────┐
                    │  Attractiveness of rural areas  │
                    └─────────────────────────────────┘
                                    ▲
              ┌─────────────────────┴─────────────────────┐
              │                                            │
┌───────────────────────────────┐    ┌───────────────────────────────┐
│    Objective characteristics   │    │    Individual characteristics  │
│         of rural areas         │    │        of young people         │
└───────────────────────────────┘    └───────────────────────────────┘
              ▲                                            ▲
┌───────────────────────────────┐    ┌───────────────────────────────┐
│    Policies, programmes and    │    │       Systems of values        │
│           structures           │    │      existing among young      │
│                                │    │            people              │
└───────────────────────────────┘    └───────────────────────────────┘
```

The following section is based on the interviews and focus groups conducted in seven European countries. We will therefore be analysing the young people's perceptions and opinions, as they were expressed during these interviews and meetings. Following the common topic guide and questionnaire, all the interviewees were invited to answer a certain number of questions and to talk about various themes related to training and employment issues, and more generally about the social integration of young people in rural areas.

The analysis of these various opinions enabled us to identify a certain number of elements which appear as being the principal components of the attractiveness of rural areas. Seven elements compose the general discourse held by the young people concerning their home regions. Through this discourse, the main values, representations, expectations, strategies and ways of life of today's rural youth are highlighted. The understanding of this discourse is therefore crucial for the implementation of local development policies addressing young people.

4.   Young People's Perceptions Concerning their Home Region

One of the interests of this international comparison is to study the variations that exist between rural areas among different European countries. This includes identifying the way these rural areas are perceived by young people and to analyse the eventual differences of opinion. In a schematic way, we can make the hypothesis that there are elements which usually contribute to the attractiveness of rural areas, while others can be considered as handicaps. The second hypothesis is that the appreciation of these elements varies both according to the local contexts, and also according to the characteristics of the young people themselves.

The following table presents, as an example, a series of characteristics that can be considered as positive elements and another series of characteristics that can be considered as negative elements.

Table 5.1 Positive and Negative Characteristics of Rural Areas

+	-
- rural landscapes, natural environment	- difficulties of access, remoteness
- calm, peacefulness, security	- lack of activities, isolation
- existence of attractive towns, nearby	- no public transport
- existence of strong networks	- ageing population, social pressure
- good housing conditions	- weak offer or high cost housing
- many job opportunities	- restricted job market
- large offer of sport activities	- lack of activities for young women

We must stress the fact that in spite of the differences of the local contexts, we have identified many common opinions, and that there is a general appreciation of rural areas that is shared by many young people all over the countries.

Geographical Elements: Landscapes, Natural Environment, Climate

One of the reasons for the attachment to the area, which is often given by the interviewees, is related to the geographical context of rural areas. For example, the landscapes, the existence of forests, wildlife and beautiful scenery were mentioned by a great number of people.

They are attractive places to live. Just look outside: you have a nice view, nice clean air. Generally, it's lovely. (interview 13, Ireland)

Fresh air, a beautiful landscape – what else could you wish for? (interview 12, Germany)

Many interviews mentioned the "fresh air" and other "environmental" elements as important factors, a phenomenon that can probably be related to the importance attached to the discourse of 'protecting the countryside':

Well, one advantage of living here: we have unpolluted air, unpolluted water, and it's fun. (interview 12, Germany)

Also, several interviewees explained how they enjoyed living in the countryside because it enabled them to have animals and to go walking, cycling or horse riding. This sense of freedom is often appreciated:

We don't go out much. We don't really like going to town. It's not much my thing to go out shopping. We're not too attracted by cities. We enjoy the countryside. We have three dogs and we go out for long walks. (interview 8, France)

Here, I can just peacefully walk around with my dog; without anybody making trouble, I can let him run without a leash and stuff like that. (interview 11, Germany)

However, the geographical context can also be a source of difficulties for the inhabitants, when the hilly (in Portugal) or mountainous topography (in Austria), or the climate (in Finland or Germany) makes accessibility, transport or communication uneasy:

I'd prefer moving away to commuting... The streets can be icy in the winter or you're stuck in a traffic jam and stuff like that and then it gets hard to be in time for work. (interview 2, Germany)

These elements also induce low densities of population, small communities, and therefore very often a lack of job opportunities and leisure activities for the young:

That is it, Santa Marta de Penaguiao has nothing. It is a very close milieu. We have not got places to wander, nothing. All we have got are hills and hills. There is not a pub, nothing. (interview 29, Portugal)

The remoteness is not only seen as a disadvantage related to the lack of activities for the young but also in terms of security or heath problems:

The worst thing about living here would be, say, you broke your arm in the morning, you would have to travel 50 miles to Galway into casualty. You'd be sitting there, I don't know how long. We're a bit out of the way in that sense. (interview 2, Ireland)

The case of Suomussalmi, in Finland, is in that regard, quite representative. Finland can be regarded as a marginal country in Europe, and the study area is in a particularly remote region with harsh natural conditions. The cold and wet climate and the vegetation (three-quarters of the region is covered with forest) do not contribute in making the area very attractive, especially for young people,[10] despite a cultural life which is diverse and rich in tradition. Yet, even then, the natural conditions can be considered as advantages for some categories of persons.

It's obvious that if you live in Hossa... or somewhere which is 100 kilometres or so from here, there are wonderful opportunities for hunting or fishing. I know a couple of fellows who are not registered as looking for work, although they've been at home since they finished secondary school. They just enjoy living there and do whatever it seems reasonable to do at home. Chopping wood, and the forest and the nature, these are riches that they appreciate. (focus group, Finland)

---

[10] The data shows a sharp decrease in the population over the last years, combined with an ageing of the population.

Also, many respondents did express their satisfaction of living in rural areas, pointing out the beautiful nature that surrounded them as justification.

Calm, Peacefulness, Security

The very positive characteristics of rural areas, such as the calm and peacefulness, can also be viewed in a different way that emphasises the lack of activities and services for the young. Undoubtedly, this is a double-edged feature which also constitutes one of the main disadvantages of the countryside. Many students who live in town, for example, expressed their eagerness to come home at weekends, and said that they enjoyed being back in the countryside. A majority of interviewees contrasted the calm and peacefulness of the rural area, to the busyness, high population densities and the stress levels that exist in towns:

> I suppose it's quiet and you haven't a thousand people running past you, roaring every few minutes. You can walk outside and sit down and have a cup of tea and listen to the birds or whatever. The peace and quiet more than anything else. (interview 11, Ireland)

Thus, the opposition between a relatively negative image of urban life and the positive image of the countryside life was often emphasised. However, there seem to be different opinions according to the size of towns. For instance, a great majority of the interviewees explained that they did not want to live in very large towns, but that they would be satisfied to live in smaller size ones. One young woman living in Mayenne (France) explained that she often went to Paris to visit friends and that she enjoyed being there for a few days, but she would never want to live there all the time.

The proximity of an urban centre, within commuting distance, was also mentioned in Scotland as an element which makes some young people satisfied to remain in the rural villages, or at least which reduces the pressures to move away. That can partly explain why in some areas, such as Suomussalmi (Finland), the remoteness, both geographically and psychologically, is one of the most severe problems for the young: "The regions where things really happen are elsewhere". The comparison with the big urban centres was sometimes drawn to show the kind of inequality the young people from rural areas were confronted with. Some interviewees projected a negative image of rural areas because of the lack of activities:

> In Porto, there is everything and even more. Here we have nothing, that's the way it is. We have nothing, we are poor fellows…This is why they say that we are "mocotos". (interview 9, Portugal)

However, several interviewees mentioned the absence of violence, insecurity and social problems as being one of the great advantages of living in the countryside.

> It's a little town, it's really calm, especially compared to big cities. There aren't any problems of violence, here you can park your car without locking it. (interview 1, France)

> Here, it isn't like it is in Hanover, where people are really violent, and Nordenham is a pretty calm place. We don't have that many fights and stuff like that. (interview 15, Germany)

The increasing problems of certain disadvantaged urban neighbourhoods which affect most of the European cities today, and which are very present in the general discourse and in the media, seem to be an important element in the comparison between rural and urban areas:

> A positive element: the tranquillity. We are in security here. When you see what's going on in the big cities, it's sure that we don't have all that here. (interview 15, France)

Many young people underlined the advantages of living in small villages, in particular for raising children.

> The most positive side is the small town. A little bit of warmth and security. More security than in a city, let's say, with a child. With a child, it's easier in a small town. (interview 8, Austria)

> My son can ride to the playground or the sports without me worrying that someone might pull him into a corner and do him any harm, and that is one of the small bits that are important to me. (interview 11, Germany)

Nevertheless, in some countries (Scotland, Finland and Germany) the interviewees did mention an increase in the youth crime level in rural areas. The lack of activities offered to the young was often presented as one of the reasons for this phenomenon, characterised mainly by drug-taking, petty vandalism, violence and under-age drinking:

> I don't know if it's outside influence or just the fact that they're bored with their life here, you know, whether it's escapism they get into the drink and drugs which then get you into trouble, yeah I don't know. I think that could be a factor rather that outside influences the fact that they're stuck here you know. (interview 12, Scotland)

The problem of drinking was also mentioned in Ireland and Germany, where many interviewees criticised the dominance of pub culture in the area, directly related to the lack of activity and to the boredom of the local youth:

> The pub has a really big influence around here. Everyone drinks around. That's where everyone goes. They should try and get some activities going something to keep them away from the pubs. (interview 10, Ireland)

> Well, here in Brake, nothing is done for young people. One shouldn't wonder about them hanging around the streets or getting drunk on the weekends and beating their heads off. (interview 28, Germany)

However, although this phenomenon is acknowledged by most of the young, a majority of the interviewees are not directly involved. It was also suggested that those from 'traditional' backgrounds such as farming, including those who have strong family connections in the area, had more stability and were less likely to indulge in those types of behaviour.

5. Services and Activities for Young People

In spite of the different contexts, the situation regarding young people's occupations seems quite similar from one area to another, and the criticisms made against the general lack of activities were observed in all the countries:

> There are no activities here, it doesn't move much. People have to go here or there to do things. Even in Laval, its doesn't move much, so here in the north it's even worse. People must think it's really a godforsaken hole here. (interview 1, France)

Many interviewees, in France and in Germany for example, explained that most of the activities concern sports, and even so, they are often quite distant and that means taking the car:

> Well, it's boring for young people up here. If you'd like to join a course or anything else, you don't have the opportunity. There aren't any clubs and happenings interesting for young people. I'd like to attend a course of self-defence, but I'd have to drive several miles to get there. And if you rely on public transport... forget about it. (interview 18, Austria)

Thus, many interviewees complained about the lack of cultural activities. These opinions were expressed in practically all the countries:

> There are no cultural things in Murau... regarding theatre or something like that, there's nothing. There is one cinema in S. 40, 50 kilometres away. For example, I like to go to the cinema, but during winter-time, when the weather is really bad, you have to think about it, if you want to drive a car for 50 km in bad road conditions. (interview 28, Austria)

Several persons, in Germany and in Ireland in particular, expressed dissatisfaction about the high costs of the existing activities (swimming pools, movies, etc.), and the excessive fees charged for membership of certain clubs:

> It would be nice if there was a pool or a gym. They have one but you have to be a member and not everyone can afford to be a member. (interview 7, Ireland)

The lack of shopping opportunities added to the concerns of rural youth. Several interviewees disliked the fact that only a small range of shops were situated in the region. In order to buy furniture or clothes, or to have a larger choice, people have to travel to a bigger city nearby:

> If you really want to do some shopping, clothes or any other stuff, you just have to go to a city. Though we have some shops here, you won't get everything, and sometimes you just want to stroll along in the city, and you just can't do that here. (interview 23, Germany)

However, with the development of new technologies, some people said that this situation could change and there could be new shopping or information facilities. In fact, one German interviewee did explain that with the internet he felt connected to every possibility. He also said that internet-commerce enabled him to buy anything he needed without leaving the Wesermarsch. This advantage of the internet for young people in remote regions, despite the problem of the high cost of a computer and internet access, was also mentioned by interviewees who expressed the wish for an internet-café.

In the French and German case study areas, the youngest interviewees seemed quite satisfied with the offer of activities, while the older categories and especially the females expressed more dissatisfaction. In fact, in many villages, there were activities for children, but as the young people grow progressively older, there are fewer opportunities and their expectations change:

> It's not a very dynamic region. There aren't many activities, not enough culture, concerts, etc. But also a lack of communication maybe. There are many sport activities, but you have to like football, that's the only thing that works here. There should be more choice, for everyone. (interview 32, France)

But in Finland, the situation seems quite the opposite, with the interviewees complaining about the lack of opportunities for the youngest:

> It's quite a nice little place, really. Well, perhaps I'm not entirely satisfied with it...There's no work here, nor anything very much for young people. There's nowhere you can spend the evening's if you're under 18. (interview, Finland)

Moreover, in the Austrian region, the traditional activities are still dynamic and attract some categories of young people:

> Traditional activities like folkdance and Schuhplattln. It's simply fun and that's it. As long as I have fun, and I can do it together with my friends. That's what we can do by ourselves for example in the rural youth group. (interview 31, Austria)

Many young people said it was necessary to develop specific 'places' or activities for the local youth, otherwise the tendency for the young would be to socialise away from their local area, and then, with no friends around, decide to leave the region. Another advantage of promoting youth clubs, which was mentioned by some interviewees (such as in Scotland), was that it allowed young people from different backgrounds to mix.

In Portugal, it appears that local organisations play a very important part in the social integration of young people. The majority of the interviewees had current or previous connections with local organisations or local initiatives, such as the village's feast, the Carnival, the church parish, the fire brigade or the hunting or fishing club. In some cases the young people are 'managed' by the adults, but for other projects, the young people are the 'actors'.

Accessibility and Mobility: The Transport Question

Opinions concerning the transport conditions seem quite diverse. One focus group discussion, held in France, showed that transport issues were, for many young people, completely integrated in their perception of life in rural areas. In many areas, in fact, children and young people are used to travel – for school, to study or to work:

> In the village where I live, there is nothing at all. Just to buy a loaf of bread, it means driving 12 kilometres, so it seems to me quite normal to have to drive much more to study or for a job! (focus group 1, France)

Also, part of the population seems to have adapted to this situation by passing the driving licence and buying a car. The lack of public transport is then no longer mentioned as a handicap:

> Now and then we go to Klagenfurt. We go to cinemas and out in pubs. But we have to drive one hour minimum to get there. However, it's not too bad. You get used to it. It usually takes 20 minutes to get somewhere. If it takes you double time, it doesn't really matter, does it? (interview 14, Austria)

These appreciations must be placed in a wider context. The general changes in society, and the new ways of life which promote mobility and freedom, encourage young people to be independent as soon as possible. The increase in the number of cars in all the European countries confirms this evolution. So quite naturally in rural areas, even more so maybe than in cities, young people consider that they must have a car to accede to this mobility.

Nevertheless, some people do consider that the lack of public transport is a real problem, and that things should be done for people living in the countryside:

> I have a car. For me it is essential, it enables [me] to find a job. Without a car one cannot move around, one cannot go to work. There's just one bus to go into the big towns, and that's it. Everyone has a car. (focus group 2, France)

The lack of public transport makes accessing the difficult labour market even harder:

> There are several advantages about Murau. But there are also severe disadvantages. For example, local job opportunities are terrible. Furthermore, you have to have a car, which is quite expensive too. Without a car, you're lost. If you rely on public transport, you're lost. (interview 15, Austria)

Recent research in England (Storey and Brannen 2000) has shown that both passing the driving test and obtaining the use of a car are heavily influenced by parent's social class, as well as by gender. Those whose parents were wealthy enough to meet the costs of driving lessons and of purchasing a car on average passed their driving tests two years earlier and gained access to a car two years earlier than those from the working class. A further two years differential existed between sons and daughters.

However, many interviewees explained how they got organised with their family or with friends before they became independent, that is to say before the age of 17 or 18, or before they had enough money to have their own car:

> Before I had my car, I managed, as I could. I hitch hiked for two months when I had my first job. In rural areas, a car is necessary. There should be a bus that goes into the small villages. It is hard for people who want to move around. (interview 27, France)

In most countries, being 17 or 18, passing the driving test and having access to a vehicle seems to mean freedom. Therefore it does change the way the young people perceive their home village, consider the advantages of the countryside, and are also able to enjoy the activities offered in the cities around. This raises important policy questions, discussed in the final chapter.

6.   The Labour Market

The influence of the labour market is usually presented as one of the main factors with regard to leaving or staying in the region. Some study areas, such as Mayenne (France), or Connemara (Ireland) benefit from relatively numerous job opportunities, while others, such as Suomussalmi (Finland) are still characterised by very high unemployment rates. The attractiveness of the area seems therefore strongly related to the possibility of finding a job.

In Ireland, there was a general consensus among the interviewees that work was available, though some efforts were needed to find a job:

> There are loads of jobs out there. It's just up to yourself to go and look. Jobs don't come to you. (interview 3, Ireland)

In France also, a number of respondents explained how easy it was to get a job, either through a temporary job agency, or with the recommendation of parents or members of the family.

> In general, young people always manage to find work here, if they are a little resourceful. I know two persons who work in a factory: it's clear that they don't like the job, but it's to earn some money. I don't know anyone who's having a hard time, being unemployed. One doesn't need to leave the region to find a job. (interview 11, France)

But this situation can also have negative effects. The hypothesis is that some young people can be reluctant to pursue their studies, as they know that they can easily find a job, and some can even be tempted to interrupt their studies in order to work. One young woman explained the impact of a local job offer on her own pathway:

> I know I should never have started this job. Once you have started, it is very hard to get out of it, because you earn money. Before I was a dynamic girl, full of desires. Since I went into the factory, I kind of fell asleep. To change means to have a lot of courage, and to take a risk. It's a hard step to take. (interview 1, France)

A Lack of Choice in the Offer and Many Unsatisfactory Jobs

In many countries, a number of respondents suggested the lack of choice as being the main problem for young people.

> The young who come from farmers or unskilled workers backgrounds, and who have no qualification[s], they can manage to find temporary jobs in some of the local factories, under the condition they have a means of transport. But they'll never be able to do anything else than production jobs. Those who have vocational degrees in agriculture, they also can find something. But for people like me, highly qualified, it's not even worth trying. One mustn't dream. I think that in Mayenne the majority of the income comes from agriculture. There are still some young farmers who settle here. But if you're neither a farmer, nor a factory worker, nor a service worker, you haven't a chance. (interview 18, France)

According to the countries, the lack of choice means very different situations. In some cases, such as in Mayenne (France) most of the job opportunities are factory jobs, while in other areas such as in Santa Marta de Penaguiao (Portugal), most of the employment offers concern viticulture. These contexts which induce an absence of professional choice for young people, are often perceived very negatively:

> Santa Marta is a hole. We are surrounded by vines. Vineyards, vineyards and more vineyards. There are very few employment opportunities here, and those that do become available are somehow already taken. (interview 20, Portugal)

The problem of the lack of choice is generally articulated with other problems related to the characteristics of the jobs offered locally (tourism, construction, manufacturing), which are often quite hard, unpleasant, underpaid, or with inconvenient time schedules. Moreover, all the interviewees emphasised the increasing number of part-time, temporary, seasonal or intermittent jobs. In most countries, the interviewees criticised the jobs offered in the tourist sector (in hotels and restaurants, bed and breakfasts). In Ireland for example, several young people talked about the exploitative strategies of some tourism businesses, and the bad work conditions offered primarily to females (low pay, long hours). This can lead to difficulties with recruiting local staff. But young people are also more demanding nowadays:

I just know it's getting harder and harder to get local people to work. They have to go out and get recruitment agencies in to get people. It's their own fault though; they are not paying proper wages. There is minimum wage now. I don't see a huge amount of them actually sticking to it. (focus group, Ireland)

A Lack of 'Qualified' Jobs

Several people also mentioned the lack of employment that related to their qualifications. This led young people either to leave the region (or even the country, such as in Portugal, where many people emigrate to other European countries), or to accept a job that did not correspond with their qualification:

We were lucky. But I know many people, who have some kind of vocational degree and who work in factories. They are obliged to accept what there is, because there are not enough qualified jobs. You just have to go and see in the factories, they are full of overqualified people. (interview 6, France)

A number of interviewees mentioned the fact that it was impossible to do the kind of work that they were interested in within their local area. It therefore always induces a difficult choice between staying in the home area with an unsatisfactory job, or leaving the region for professional reasons:

I always wanted to do something like sound engineering or work with television or music. Living around here, it's not the easiest job because there is no places that you could apply to do it. The only job you could get around here is bar tending, building sites. There are other jobs, but they are the main areas. (interview 14, Ireland)

Finally, many interviewees expressed a general feeling of dissatisfaction concerning the local labour market, and a kind of pressure, probably related to the fear of unemployment, that leads young people to take up jobs they would not normally want:

All my friends work. I don't know anyone unemployed. But there are big problems here. Many people have taken the first job that was offered, but now they are not satisfied at all. When I talk with my friends, out of twenty, a large majority want to change and are looking for something else. I think it is the same everywhere: it is linked to unemployment problems. (interview 27, France)

The question of emigration seems a particularly important issue in Portugal, as it has characterised the country for several decades. Emigration strategies seem to be a kind of 'cultural' element, however strong the fondness of young people for their home area:

The young do think a lot about emigrating. As it happened with their uncles as well as with their cousins, as it happened with their parents, they think over it. (interview, Portugal)

The Specificity of the Farming Jobs

The respondents seem to have various opinions concerning the jobs offered by the agriculture sector, but most of them, however, emphasise the difficulties of the farmer's life, which can diminish the desires of young people to work in that field:

> I think there will be an important decline in the region. Young people don't want to settle as farmers anymore. The only young who settle are farmer's children, there are no newcomers, and there are families where nobody is going to stay. They cannot be forced. And, to see the hard living conditions of their parents does not encourage them either. (interview 16, France)

In Portugal, where viticulture appears as the main sector of the local economy, the local youth do not consider it to be a source of attractive job opportunities:

> You may perhaps work a few days to earn some pocket money, or to purchase something you really want. Today, nobody likes farm work. Nobody wants to do this type of work. There's no future for anyone in vineyards. (interview 15, Portugal)

In Ireland too, in the areas characterised by small-scale non-viable farms, young people are increasingly moving away from farming as an occupation. It must be stressed that farm work and rural life in general did mean, until recently, difficult conditions of life. Either the children, considering the hard life of their parents, decided to go for different professions, or the parents themselves encouraged their children to do something else, with higher social prestige. The traditional image of the farmer was for many decades generally devalued, and the phenomenon of "educating out" has been observed in almost all studies of farmer's children in EU countries.

However agriculture is not universally disparaged as a means of employment, and appears in some countries as an interesting opportunity. In particular, the new values related to sustainable development and the new demands concerning "quality food" production, a crucial issue nowadays, will probably induce new orientations in farming:

> I know young people who want to work in that sector. I don't know if it's a question of generation, but they want to take over the parents' farm and orient it towards biological agriculture. I have a friend who's doing that. I think it's interesting. But it seems quite hard if you're not organised. Family life doesn't seem to be that easy, especially for the wife. (interview 11, France)

The arrival of young people in farming is sometimes seen as a chance for the regions who need some changes:

> There have to be people coming into the industry with fresh ideas and fresh initiatives, with new enthusiasm. And with those people, the industry can go on, there will always be an agriculture industry where there is green pasture. And I want to be there when it happens. (interview 17, Scotland)

Family, Friends and Networks

A number of young people mentioned ties with family and friends as one of the main reasons for their attachment to the region:

> I don't want to move anywhere else. Well, my family lives here, my friends and my fiancé. It's impossible for me to move away. I just can't. (interview 1, Germany)

A number of interviewees talked of the good relations they had with their parents, and of the importance the family meant for them. They often mentioned the strong support, financial as well as moral, given by their parents. Many interviewees still live with their parents and seem satisfied with that arrangement. Some parents also help their children to settle in the area, by helping them buy a house.

In some countries, such as Portugal, the family bonds seem particularly strong and there is often a reciprocal aid between parents and young people. Quite often, the young help their parents, financially, and also, more generally, when they get old. The increased life expectancy of the elderly and the instability of the labour market seem to reinforce this inter-dependency, and therefore the wish or necessity to stay in the home area increases:

> I do not depend only on my parents, I also depend on myself. I receive my salary, I give half of it to my parents and the rest is for me. (interview16, Portugal)

The existence of friends is also mentioned by many interviewees as contributing to the attachment to the area. It can even sometimes be considered as a tie that makes individual decisions harder:

> I have some very good friends here, there is a strong friendship, but I try not to get too attached to them, otherwise it will be even more difficult to leave. (interview 1, France)

The small size of the communities makes it easy to know the neighbours and also to meet with friends frequently on an informal basis:

> Everybody knows everybody. If I was going out, I wouldn't have to arrange to meet someone out, because I could just walk into a pub and I could start talking to someone anyway, 'cause I just know them... (interview 8, Ireland)

> It's just the people themselves. They are much more open, everybody knows everyone. In Bremen, it was like that, you probably only know your neighbour next door and that's it. It wasn't very nice. (interview 5, Germany)

However, many young people talked of the difficulties of living in small communities, where people have little intimacy:

> It can be positive at times, but you always have the impression you are being spied upon by the population. There's a lot of gossip. You have to live with it, but it's sometimes

hard to fight against all that. Generally it's not nasty, it doesn't go very far. (focus group 1, France)

Several persons emphasised this lack of privacy, an opinion which can be related to important values of today's society, such as individualism and independence:

People here like to know what the others are doing, they know at what time you come home, how many people were with you... Sometimes it can really be annoying. (interview 6, France)

In the German and Irish case study areas, the interviewees complained about the labelling and stigmatisation that derives from gossip, rumour, and the exchange of information among employers (after dismissal from a company for example). All of this makes it difficult to find a new job or apprenticeship elsewhere:

Let's put it this way. Brake is a town that spreads rumours very quickly. Once you've got a bad reputation and you're grown up here, people soon start telling that boy's lazy and stuff like that. When something goes wrong, half the town knows. (interview 33, Germany)

But, that does not mean young people don't appreciate the friendly relations that seem to exist in the villages:

I love the fact that you can go in and have a chat with everyone, if you go into the pub or shop. You could have a chat with people in Galway, but it wouldn't be to the same extent. (interview 7, Ireland)

Several interviewees felt quite positive about the close relations that usually exist in rural areas, and even admitted fearing the anonymity of towns:

In towns, living is more difficult than in the countryside. There are many people whom you know and who will help you. (interview 11, Austria)

Some young people suggested that this proximity can sometimes be very useful and that people in rural areas needed mutual aid. The strength of the networks in rural areas was often highlighted:

In a farmers circle, we have permanent exchanges with the neighbours. In spite of the differences, the neighbours are always there when you're in trouble. They accepted us as we are, even though there is gossip. We are all part of a whole thing, which is indestructible because we all need one another. In urban areas we don't need so much to create these social links. (focus group 1, France)

In Portugal and Ireland for example, the usefulness of local networks was mentioned by a majority of interviewees, particularly for finding jobs. These networks involve parents, the wider family, as well as friends, neighbours and acquaintances in the community. Several interviewees described the advantages of this kind of "sense of community":

> The thing is if you are living in a city and things are going wrong, you are really on your own. But if you are out in a rural area where people know you, there is a nice sense of community I think. Here, they look out for each other a bit. If someone knows you are interested in something and they hear, they tell you and they help you out like that. (interview 7, Ireland)

Nevertheless, some problems were mentioned concerning the existence of conflicts between the generations and also concerning the difficulty of introducing change in the villages:

> Murau is a more like a traditional town, everything is very quiet, everything carries on as usual, and nothing unusual is likely to be introduced. Nobody wants that. All the people, all the inhabitants are against it, they don't want anything new. They like it as it is. (interview 16, Austria)

It must be stressed that there are often different opinions concerning the area, depending on whether the young people are from the area or whether they are newcomers. Many interviewees suggested that the local population was not very sociable, nor very open minded towards newcomers:

> I would say that the people here are unsociable. Where I used to live before, it wasn't at all the same. It was much more welcoming, more hearty. Everybody knew each other, and we often met. Here it's very cold. (interview 4, France)

That kind of reaction from the newcomers did not seem to surprise the "natives". In one focus groups held in France, the young people confirmed the fact that the local population was not very welcoming, and they appreciated that it must be hard for people who are not 'native' to the region. The main reasons are related to the population itself, but also to the geographical context:

> I don't know any person coming from outside who's happy to live here, in Mayenne. I even wonder if to be able to live in Mayenne, you don't have to be born here. You need a strong-minded character to live here, it's an environment which is quite rough. The countryside, it's very very beautiful in the summer, when there's nice weather, but in December, in the middle of the cows, and in the mist, it's quite hard. One has to appreciate isolation. (focus group 1, France)

Some people suggested that part of the difficulties come from the demographic situation, that is to say the existence of a large number of old people living in the area and a corresponding lack of young people:

> There are some part of Mayenne where the population is really behind the times, especially in the north east part. The Departement is known for that. One has the impression of a jump fifty years back into the past. There are holes where there's nothing but old people, so it's normal if it's like that. But it's not only the old people.

There are also people who are forty and who are still in the atmosphere of the villages of the past. But when there are young people, the mentalities do change all the same. (focus group 1, France)

7. The Housing Conditions

The housing conditions also seem to be an important element in what makes rural areas 'attractive' to young people. In the French, Austrian, German and Finnish case study areas, the interviewees mentioned good quality housing at affordable prices as facilitating factors for settlement in the villages.[11] Several interviewees suggested that it was relatively easy to find a dwelling, either through advertisements or through relations:

I first found a room in a private house, it's quite easy, there are advertisements everywhere. (interview 31, France)

We lived in a flat before, with many other families, there was always something going on. Now, we have a house of our own, you can do what you want, that's much better. (interview 23, Germany)

In Ireland and Scotland, the interviewees complained about the lack of accommodation in the countryside, the high prices and the difficulty of obtaining planning permissions for new houses. The high prices are perceived as being caused by residential development being concentrated in the cities or tourism development and the purchase of properties for use as holiday homes:

That's really an issue, trying to rent out a house long term in Connemara is impossible. I know from personal experience, myself and my boyfriend were looking for some place to live, and we were turned out of everywhere for the summer. By May, there would be 200 pounds put on the rent. (focus group, Ireland)

Moreover, the interviewees explained that this phenomenon induces an unpleasant atmosphere in the villages. It leads to a general rejection of these newcomers because they are considered as responsible for the price raising. Consequently, the newcomers do not always integrate into the community:

It's nearly a ghost town because you have all these empty shells of houses all over the countryside. I'm sort of angry at the way it's turning out because we are all from Connemara. Connemara is our home but yet it is being changed by people who are not from here. (focus group, Ireland)

But it also must be stressed that in rural areas, as well as in urban areas, according to recent studies, young people tend to stay on for longer in the parental home. In

---

[11] In Austria, for example, the construction and housing policies undertaken for the last 30 years have led to an increase in the quality of the housing facilities.

some cases this phenomenon can be caused by the lack of affordable housing, but it can also be related to general changes in the society and the emphasis on "family" values. Many interviewees expressed their satisfaction with their living arrangements. Living with the parents is becoming a common situation – again – and particular relations have developed where young people can have both freedom and financial comfort:

> Whenever I'm coming home from work, dinner is already prepared and ready to eat on the table. (interview 8, Austria)

In the countryside, parents often have large farms or big houses with enough room to keep the children as long as necessary. In Portugal for example, many young people stay at the parent's home until they get married and it is very rare for young people to live alone. This phenomenon is due to employment issues, and house prices, but also to cultural traditions. However, several interviewees mentioned a desire to become independent and distance themselves from their parents. If they do not manage to find appropriate housing in the area, this can result in them leaving the region for the town:

> Well, I'd like to have my own flat as soon as possible, just to become more independent from my parents. (interview 10, Austria)

However, the satisfactory housing conditions offered in the villages seem to contribute to the attachment to the countryside:

> It's a choice, we could live in Alençon. But here, I am in my own place. We're in the countryside, we're happy. My husband says that even if he has to do fifty km to go to work, it's better to be here than to live in social housing. It's a choice, we like our area, and it's good for our children. Here, it's silent, we don't hear the noise of machines, of cars. (interview 3, France)

Some explained that living in the countryside, with its distinctive physical environment, enabled them to keep animals, such as dogs or horses, and enjoy all the possibilities offered locally:

> We used to live in an apartment. We moved two years ago. We now have a house. It's very quiet, peaceful and nice. We have a little courtyard, we have a little dog, for him it's much better. For us, too, we can eat outside, in the summer it's better. (interview 4, France)

Several interviewees mentioned the satisfaction of being alone, far from other people, which living in the countryside offered:

> We live in a little house that we rent. It's not exactly what we wanted, we are just at the limit of the town. We wanted to be really in the countryside. We will look for something else later. The ideal is to be completely isolated. I love being all alone, I don't like

having people around me. I would like to be in the middle of a big field, with no one around, that would be great. (interview 8, France)

8.   A Real Attractiveness of Rural Areas?

A Strong Concern about the Future of the Home Region

A clear indicator of the real attractiveness of rural areas seems to be the strong concern expressed by many interviewees concerning the future of their home region. Many mentioned the fears they had and suggested some orientations for local development policies. Sustainable development and environmental issues were frequently cited as being important values for the interviewees. There was a precise knowledge of the different economic trends, and many interviewees seemed conscious of the difficult balance between strong economic development on one hand and the protection of the local resources and of the specific rural identity, on the other.

Several young people are already active members of various local structures and movements. Others suggested that more considerations should be given to those of them who want to act for the development of the area. The way young people want to participate has changed during the last decades however, with less emphasis on formal political structures but still a desire among young people to participate at the local level in some form or another.

Many young people are quite pessimistic concerning the future of rural areas. They think the local economy is gradually declining and that it will have negative consequences for the social and demographic structure of their home region:

There's a firm that closed down, and many people had to leave, it did a lot of harm to the area. In ten or fifteen years, there won't be much left here, there's already not much today... We must get firms back in this area, because people go where the jobs are. (interview 1, France)

In Austria and Finland, the interviewees fear that the decline of rural activities might increase depopulation movements:

One day everyone will have left... the whole region will then be just a holiday area for people who come back for the week ends. (interview 18, Austria)

The rural areas might therefore lose their permanent residents, or be confronted with a rapid ageing of the population:

If the age structure, as they call it, gets to the point where there are only old people here, how drastically will services in the area be cut back? When there are no wage-earners any longer, only pensioners, there will be no purchasing power left in the district. (focus group, Finland)

The strong attachment of many interviewees to their home region makes them quite conscious about the resources that exist and the potential to develop them. Several young people mentioned a possible revival of the rural areas through the development of tourism.

> I would be quite optimistic concerning the future of the region, if things could be done to valorise the region and its assets. It's a region that is not very urbanised, so there is a real attractiveness for rural tourism. It could be complementary with what exists already, but you mustn't do stupid things, like develop outrageously agriculture. One must not let go. (interview 18, France)

Thus, a number of interviewees consider that there are some possibilities for rural areas, but they also feel that strong policies are needed urgently in order to prevent young people from leaving these regions. Tourism could lead to the economic development of many rural areas, creating new job opportunities for the young people themselves in the process:

> Well, I think the region's future mainly depends on tourism... It'll depend on people and whether the tourism industry and all the others are able to make use of local resources. Local authorities will have to think about how to keep people in Murau. There are several things which have to be rethought, otherwise young people will leave. (interview 31, Austria)

Nevertheless, several young people did mention that an over emphasis on tourism development carried risks, which ultimately might compromise the attractiveness of the area. In the Irish case study area, concern was also expressed at the poor working conditions associated with tourism employment.

In many countries, a number of young people expressed the feeling that their opinions were not sufficiently taken into account. Many consider that the presence of young people is important for rural areas, and that they should be consulted more on prospective plans for their local area:

> I think young people can get quite a lot done. I am in the development group at school, and that's one way, at least. And in any case, if you only have the courage to say something you can put things right, if only you speak up. (interview, Finland)

The lack of attention paid to young people's opinions can also explain, to some extent, the fact that quite a large number of young people are not aware of what is happening in their locality and detach themselves from local affairs.

However, in all the countries, several young people said they were involved in local activities. Some had previous experience of setting up youth related activities whilst others were currently developing new projects in order to make the villages come alive again:

> With a group of friends, we have set up again the local fete committee. We organise the June fair, pancake day... We are in charge of all that. We got together and went to see the mayor, and she said ok. There wasn't anything anymore... The young want their

village to come alive again, and the older people appreciate, it makes them go out. We would be happy if more young joined us. (interview 2, France)

In the different PaYPiRD case study areas, there are various activities undertaken by the local youth. These relate to cultural activities, as in Mayenne, traditional and religious feasts as in Portugal, as well as humanitarian or social actions. These activities constitute an important element helping to integrate young people into their local communities, as well as helping to revitalise the area generally. These elements seem to contribute to the attractiveness of the area.

I've been a member of a local association, the Courcite young people's club, for two years and a half. I'm there every weekend, all the time. Every year we organise a theatre spectacle. We have many ideas. ...The association is twenty-five years old. There are thirty-five people registered, and we are regularly fifteen to twenty members. It's embedded in the area. Theatre is the traditional April activity. So I spend my week ends there, I enjoy that. (interview 15, France)

A number of respondents suggested that the local politicians were more interested in the old people's issues that in the problems of the youth. Several complained about the difficulties they encountered when they tried to organise activities. A remark which was often made concerned the greater attention given to sport activities whereas other areas, especially cultural activities, did not receive the same levels of support:

I don't feel things move here. I think young people are not listened to, except if they play football. It's football first, and the rest after. In all the villages of the area, it's like that. We do our theatre activities in a room we converted six or seven years ago. We asked for a proper place, but there's no chance for it to happen, we're not acknowledged. We're considered as jokers. Several times we asked for some financial help and each time it was very complicated, we had to explain why, while the football, they have all the money they want. (interview 17, France)

Many young people said that they felt excluded and had the impression that community development was the preserve of a limited number of mostly elderly people:

Perhaps they are simply indifferent if young people suggest something. Perhaps the older people in the council office think they understand better. (interview, Finland)

This gap between young people's rejection of 'Politics' and a desire to be more involved in their local community seems to be a very important issue, particularly with regard to the strong valorisation of the concept of "citizenship" that can be observed in the policy discourse. Efforts are being made and new measures applied in most of the European countries in order to increase communication and citizens' participation, and improve the integration of the inhabitants into their neighbourhood. But what is applied today in urban areas does not seem to have spread to the rural areas to the same degree.

9.   The Wish to Stay, a Need to Leave?

In all the countries, we observed that the young people have a considerable fondness for their region, and many of those interviewed expressed a wish to stay. This strong attachment to their home region, was considered as something quite normal, but difficult to explain:

> The freedom of being able to go out for a walk in the clean air and the environment. It's where I was born and it's where the heart is. (interview 9 Ireland)

> I'd never leave the Wesermarsch... I just feel so at home here. (interview 19, Germany)

This phenomenon can be related to elements, very strongly valued nowadays, which are linked to the search for "roots" and to the promotion of a specific identity. After many decades during which being from rural areas could have a more or less negative meaning, there seems to be, today, a kind a pride in coming from the countryside:

> I like the opportunities we have here like, for example, we have experienced things that people in the city wouldn't have, like the open space and all that. Like this year, we had a corncrake in our field and I mentioned it to a few friends from the city, and they didn't have a clue; they had never heard of it before. It's nice to be able to know these things. (interview 3, Ireland)

However, we observed some variations according to the age, the gender, the level of qualification, or the cultural and social backgrounds of the interviewees. The men often present economic or professional arguments as their reasons to stay or to leave – for example to take over the farm or for other job opportunities. Many young women expressed arguments related to personal or family situations – they plan to leave to follow their husband or friend, or, on the contrary, they plan to stay if their husband or friend is working locally:

> I am now training as a secretary, and work at the Alençon hospital. I enjoy it very much, but I would rather work in a municipality or a little firm. But I am not really mobile, because my friend lives in Javron, he is a farmer. We will probably stay together, and maybe he will need me to help him with the accounting, but in any case I won't work with him all the time. I'll see... I envisage staying here, having a family, but I want to have a job, a stable situation. (interview 14, France)

This uncertainty is usually related to the situation of the labour market:

> It's calm, definitely and that's what I like. But there's just no opportunity to get a job. It's too small. There are a few firms but too many young people are looking for an apprenticeship and the companies can't take all of them. (interview 29, Germany)

Several respondents explained that employment is indeed the main concern and that with a job, many young people are happy to live in the countryside:

Some of my friends have got an apartment, they have found a job, all is going well, it's a kind of happiness. Though they don't have a job they enjoy, they are happy. Most people want to stay, they feel attached to the area. Many do not see any reason to leave. They have their friends, their family, a house, a job, they do not see the point of going to look somewhere else. (focus group 2, France)

Several interviewees seem prepared to accept certain manageable travel distances related to employment. They have a practical approach, based on a realistic vision of the situation:

I want to stay in the north of Germany. But I'm fine with up to one hour drive, because in this area, it's pretty hard finding a job. (interview 18, Germany)

This readiness of some interviewees to commute, if necessary, corresponds not only to their wish to stay in the area, but also to their previous experiences (during their studies for example):

For me it's no problem. I also commute to Bremen for my practical course, and you just have to be flexible, you can't just stay in the area... Too many people wait for a job calling and saying: 'Hi, here I am, would you like to work?' (interview 19, Germany)

The most qualified people usually explained that unfortunately they had few chances of finding a job that fitted with their qualifications and expectations, and that they would probably have to leave the region:

I would love to find some way to reconcile the two, but I can't see how I can do it. I can't see what I can do in the commerce, trade and marketing, and all that and go back to Connemara. I wouldn't know what to do. (focus group, Ireland)

Recent research conducted in Finland explored this important "staying or leaving" issue, and showed that many young people, in spite of their satisfaction with their home region, were ready to leave in order to find a job.[12] Also, the fear of the decline of the region is an important feeling expressed by many interviewees. Many would like to stay in their home area but have the feeling that they will be more or less 'obliged' to leave for economic reasons:

Sometimes I like living here and sometimes I don't, it varies. Just now, I would like to be living somewhere else. It seems that the whole place is dying. There's nothing here. Everything is gradually closing down. I often find it very depressing. When I think about my own future, I can't see anything to aim at living here. I guess I should go somewhere else. (interview, Finland)

---

[12] Paunikallio, Merja (1997), *Helsingin yliopisto, maaseudun tutkimus-ja koulutuskeskus*, series B: 17, Seinäjoki.

In France for example, a number of interviewees explained that many of their friends had left the region, mainly for professional reasons, and there were few young people still in the area:

> Many of my friends have left. Some have gone to Paris to look for a job. Those who leave, it's first because there is no work in the field they are interested in. We just have to go. (interview 16, France)

However, the attachment to the area is sometimes so strong, that young people prefer to stay in their region, even if the employment conditions are not very good:

> Well I'm prepared for that, and if I work somewhere else, I'll commute. That's the way it is. It doesn't matter, anyway. Most people are commuting, there is no one who works at home, apart from farmers, of course. As for me, it hardly matters to me. I know that I always will be living here. (interview 27, Austria)

Nevertheless, several interviewees expressed a clear desire to leave the area. There are mainly two reasons. On one hand, there is the wish to travel, related to a sort of desire to "discover the world", which is not so much a wish to leave the area, than a desire to see something else:[13]

> I don't want to stay in the region, because I want to travel, to go abroad, work in the humanitarian field. But I feel a strong attachment to this area. I am not very much an "urban". I love the countryside, there doesn't need to be much liveliness. (interview 1, France)

This often goes with a wish to return to the area sometime or other, once the confirmation is made that it really is the best place to live in:

> I would like to travel to see a bit more of the world. I'd just like to give it a shot, 'cause you never know. I will always come back here at some stage, if it is six months, a year, five years, ten years, I will always come back. 'Cause it's just the place. You would miss the place. People say 'I'm dying to get out of here', but if you go abroad you notice the difference. (interview 2, Ireland)

On the other hand, and this can be related to the geographical situation of some of the rural areas, there does exist a wish to live in town, or at least closer to a town, in order to benefit from more activities and services. Some interviewees did mention the fact that life in rural areas was too dull and boring, and did not have much to offer them:

> People are about to leave, and Murau will be dead one day. You can say so. The younger ones will leave too, like the others. Even my sister is about to leave for Gratz to attend the Borg (a general high school), although there is one in Murau. (interview 18, Austria)

---

[13] However, this is not typical of rural areas, and many young people express a desire to travel before settling down, getting a job, or starting a family.

I would move to Bremen, Oldenburg, Hanover, just anywhere. I have absolutely no problem with that. I wouldn't like spending my whole life in Brake. (interview 28, Germany)

For other respondents, the choices seemed more open. Several young people explained that they were ready to stay in their local area or move to a town depending on job opportunities and family situations:

To stay here? It's only a question of professional opportunity, for me. But an opportunity that can also be related to my sentimental life: if I meet the man of my life tomorrow, I can easily stay here. I am not trying to run away from the region where I was born, nor trying to stay. For the moment I have no ties, I have my family but it's not something that attaches me. (interview 18, France)

10. Conclusion and Policy Implications

The analysis of the concept of attractiveness, such as it is perceived by young people, highlights the many advantages that young people find in living in rural areas, but also the difficulties they face. One of the main outcomes of this study is the importance of the staying or leaving issue. However, in considering policy recommendations in relation to young people in rural areas, it first must be stressed that there are still many young people that live in rural areas and who want to stay there. This confirms recent work which tends to emphasise a certain revival of rural areas in many European countries.

The other important conclusion is related to the similar problems that young people face in all the seven countries of this research. In spite of some particularities linked to specific national or local contexts, the appreciations, opinions and perceptions of the interviewees are very similar.

The main difficulty mentioned by the interviewees is related to the lack of choice, a crucial problem that affects many sectors: such as the labour market, the offer of leisure activities and services and transport possibilities. This lack of choice is, of course, linked to the weak density of population that exists in most rural areas. This situation seems therefore embedded into the rural contexts: weak densities induce weak opportunities. But this can be seen as a geographical viewpoint, which focuses on geographical conditions, and the present research also showed that most of the opportunities lie in the eyes of the interviewees. In addition, these characteristics can also be, to some extent, part of the elements which contribute to the attractiveness of rural areas.

So, instead of trying to make life in rural areas similar to life in urban areas, we suggest, on the contrary, to valorise the specificity and the resources of the rural areas, on one hand, and to improve the relations with the urban centres situated nearby, on the other. The policies should concentrate on increasing city-countryside relations. Not only is it necessary to develop services and jobs which are appropriate for rural areas, but it is also important to develop the mobility of the population and to improve accessibility to the opportunities that exist elsewhere.

The local actors and many interviewees themselves, stress the need to broaden the horizon of rural populations. It appears essential to be able to travel, to see other regions and to use the possibilities that are offered out of the home area. The policies should therefore try to develop the intellectual capacities, and therefore the "intellectual mobility", of rural youth through education and training.

Measures and policies should be undertaken to develop both physical and intellectual mobility. Improving the roads and communications between the countryside and the nearby cities can help to create new territorial networks. But it is also important not only to develop individual mobility (cars), which can exclude groups of people and which does not appear sustainable in an environmental sense, but also to promote other systems (train junctions, buses, car sharing, communal taxis, etc). Both the cities and the rural areas would benefit from this interdependency. The main issue seems to be the necessity to open up these rural areas and give them real functions for both the region and the country.

Alongside this investment in the human and social capital of young people in rural areas, there is an urgent need for economic development. Unless better quality jobs are available, which will require a more skilled and educated workforce, only disequilibria will be created through more emphasis on education and training. A better skilled and educated workforce requires better skilled and better paid employment, and vice versa. These aspects of policy are complementary and interdependent.

Of course, many measures should be taken locally to improve the life conditions in rural areas.[14] Though many concern the development of the labour market, the transport systems or the leisure activities, some of the measures do not imply financial support, but request a better understanding of young people's needs. One main demand concerns the possibility for the rural youth to participate in the local activities and to give their opinions. Therefore it is imperative that they should be listened to. A number of interviewees expressed their interest for environmental, social or humanitarian issues, and showed their eagerness to be considered as real citizens. Many young people want to be active agents of this "revival" of rural areas. Thus, the policies addressing young people should, first of all, be based on a clear knowledge of their specific needs and expectations. These issues will be explored further in each of the remaining chapters.

---

[14] Several lists of measures and recommendations were presented and analysed in the seven national reports.

Chapter 6

The Impact of Programmes under the European Employment Guidelines on Young People in Rural Areas

Gerhard Dietz and Gerhard Christe

This thematic analysis is one out of seven prepared within the framework of the PaYPiRD project. It asks: "How far can policies addressing the integration of young people into employment tackle social exclusion?" The objective of the development of this theme is to assess the impact of programmes and policies under the national employment action plans (NAPs) of the seven countries participating in this research and their impact on young people. These NAPs have been designed and implemented in response to policy guidelines established within the framework of the European Employment Strategy (EES).

The task of the German team in pursuing this theme was aided by information received from the other partners in the PaYPiRD project. This allowed for a comparative analysis of the integration policies that exist in the various countries. As with the other themes taken up by the PaYPiRD partner teams, it was envisaged that much of the data could be elicited from the National Reports. Because these drew heavily on the interviews with the young people in the different case study areas, it was anticipated that information could be gleaned on young peoples' responses to the different policies and programmes adopted by government and other agencies to address youth unemployment in rural areas. It proved, though, in the further course of the project, that young people appeared to be rather unaware of existing policies as well as of the impacts these had or might have on them. In view of this, there was agreement that where no other data would be available, the "impact assessment" would have to be confined to an examination of the principles underlying policies (by way of documentary analysis) and to relate this, as far as possible, to young people's experiences with education, training and the labour market. In addition, key actors' judgements about programmes or concrete actions should be taken into account.

Initiatives, programmes and policies to prevent social exclusion and to advance the integration of young people, generally speaking, are of various kinds. Different actors and agencies are responsible for their implementation and the programmes may be operative at different geographical and administrative levels. In a document issued by the European Anti-Poverty Network, the "essential elements of social exclusion" are characterised as follows: "denial of access: to "the full range of rights", to services, training and employment, culture, leisure, social protection, income, security and influence; marginalisation from the mainstream; denial or prevention of participation in society" (EAPN 1999a 112).

Processes of social exclusion and inclusion are related to overlapping spheres of integration. Thus, viewed as a multi-dimensional, dynamic concept (with an emphasis also on the importance of the local context), social exclusion – as elaborated in Chapter 2 – can be defined in terms of the failure of one or more of the following four systems by which resources are allocated: markets; the state; civil society; and family and friends. Each of these systems and their respective spheres of integration, in some combination or other, is relevant to each of the themes of this book, although each chapter may differ in the origination or initiation of the programmes or policies at issue, the levels at which implementation occurs, the categories of actors involved and the sources of data available.

1. Employment Trends and Policy Developments

Before turning to the NAPs, a brief summary of some previous developments and activities related to the issue of youth unemployment within the EU is necessary. While the economic recovery of the mid 1990s put a stop to a further increase in unemployment, it did not have a measurable positive effect on the labour market until autumn 1998, when the EU-15 overall unemployment rate dropped below 10% for the first time since late 1992. The rate fell again in autumn 1999 (9.3%), but with strong differences between the rates in the Member States remaining, particularly at the regional level. The statistics for youth unemployment followed a similar pattern: the EU-15 youth unemployment rate dropped from 19.6% to 18.3% between 1998 and 1999, and thus, on average, continued to be twice as high as the overall rate, again with wide variations across countries and regions (Chisholm 2000).

Despite this recent decline, which continued in 2000, the EU rate of youth unemployment today is still high. Because youth unemployment within the EU has been a problem for the last twenty five years, Member States and the European Commission, in political as well as practical terms, have, in the course of time, increased and more strongly co-ordinated their efforts to combat this problem and the related risks of social exclusion for young people.

Measures to reduce unemployment among persons under the age of 25 were subsidised under ESF regulations for the first time in 1977 and in the 1980s a number of sectoral action programmes were also set up, aiming to better equip young people for successful labour market entry. The ESF, which offered a greater number of better-funded programmes that other sources, was itself subject to reform in 1988. This reflected a higher priority being given within the EU to combat youth unemployment, a priority which has gained even more importance during the last decade.

In the early and mid 1990s, steps towards a proactive and more integrated European policy in the area of education and employment were the following (Chisholm 2000):

- the Delors White Paper on "Growth, Competitiveness and Employment" (European Commission, 1993) which highlighted the necessity of more adequate general and vocational education for all so that the Member States and the common market be better prepared for the challenges of an increasingly knowledge-based and globalised economy;
- the debate on "employability" in 1994 at the Essen Summit, which emphasised the importance of lifelong-learning and identified as a key area of intervention the improvement of measures in favour of groups particularly hard-hit by unemployment, including young people, the long-term unemployed and women;
- the Council's and the Commission's agreement in their 1995 "Joint Employment Report" (JER) that efforts in favour of the aforementioned groups should be intensified and, more specifically, the following three structural goals should be established:

  - All young people should be provided with the level of education, training and work experience needed to make them employable.
  - In the context of a more active policy for the prevention of long-term unemployment: all unemployed people should have the opportunity of retraining or reintegration before reaching the point of long-term unemployment.
  - ...the promotion of equal opportunities in the context of all public policies affecting employment... (European Commission 1995a);

- the launch in 1995 of common action programmes, namely Leonardo and Youthstart, both of which are now operative for another multi-annual cycle (2000-2006).

The Leonardo programme supports Member States' efforts to improve the quality of their education and training systems, as well as combating exclusion and unequal distribution of opportunities. The programme supports, for example, transnational activities and projects like "second chance schools" which, following the White Paper on Education and Training (European Commission 1995b), were launched as a tool to fight social exclusion by providing disadvantaged young people with knowledge and skills necessary to follow vocational training or to obtain a regular job.

In the field of employment, Member States' action is supported through the Youthstart programme, initiated by the Delors White Paper of 1993. Youthstart comprises actions within the mainstream ESF programmes under Objectives 1 and 3 as well as the Employment-Youthstart Initiative, both being mainly funded from ESF sources. In the period of 1995-1999, 20% of the ESF budget was allocated to projects within the mainstream programmes, designed to promote the occupational integration of young people under 25 seeking employment. The Youthstart initiative as one of the four strands of the Community's Employment Initiative was devised to promote the integration into the labour market of young people under 20 lacking basic qualifications or training, with particular emphasis on the exploration of innovative ways of access to employment. From 1995-1999, well over 1000 projects have been implemented. From other forms of assistance provided by the ESF, Employment-Youthstart differs in the following respects: it supports innovation and experimentation, it promotes activities which are transnational and have a multiplier effect, and the projects promoted involve a wide range of experts and local players (European Commission 1999b).

Following the implementation of the Leonardo and Youthstart programmes in the mid 1990s, efforts in favour of youth integration, the fight against long-term unemployment and the promotion of equal opportunities – as already outlined in the 1995 JER – were further stepped up by the European Employment Strategy called for by the Amsterdam Treaty of June 1997 and launched at the Luxembourg Summit in November 1997. Although this employment strategy (also referred to as the "Luxembourg Process"), is not only addressing young people, the importance given to actions directed at this group is one of its significant features (see below).

With the agreement concluded in Luxembourg, the European Union took a major step forward by the establishment of guidelines for a co-ordinated and integrated policy to fight unemployment and to promote employment through a combination of reactive and proactive/preventive measures. To this end, the Commission now formulates a series of formal annual Employment Policy Guidelines and Member States are invited to present National Action Plans (NAPs) for combating unemployment in line with these guidelines. The current number of which is 21. These are compatible with the broad thrust of macro-economic policy which is aimed at stability, sound public finances and structural reforms of the labour market and the markets for goods, services and capital. Given the differences between countries and the principle of subsidiary, the Luxembourg decisions ensure that national responsibility is preserved. The decisions also take account of the existing financial constraints and hence the need for budgetary discipline. They emphasise that the social partners share responsibility for solving employment problems.

It was clear from the outset that the European Employment Strategy would not lead to satisfactory results immediately, but only in the medium term. It was agreed, therefore, that the policy objectives were to be reached within a five-year period, i.e. by 2002, with 1998 being the first year for the employment guidelines to be transposed into NAPs and for these to be implemented.

2. The National Action Plans and Joint Employment Reports

Member States report to the Commission on the implementation of their NAPS. The Commission annually reviews both the NAPs and the National Implementation Reports and, in consultation with the Council, prepares Joint Employment Reports (JERs). These reports present comparative assessments of how the Member States have implemented the guidelines of a particular year and how they have transposed the (revised) guidelines for the following year in their NAPs. In these reports, special attention is paid to the way in which Council's recommendations with respect to their employment policies have been addressed by the Member States. Another issue dealt with in the JERs, and identified in the NAPs, is the use Member States are intending to make of the ESF, which is the major source for funding of active labour market and employment policy measures.

The JERs, of course, also undertake an evaluation of policy efforts, i.e. concrete actions, and of their impacts on labour markets. It is clear, though, that this evaluation which is based on a benchmarking approach very much depends on the transparency, sufficiency, systematicity and, in particular, comparability of the information – both quantitatively and qualitatively – provided by the Member States about their policy efforts and the respective outcomes. Benchmarking serves to set common standards by assessing which countries have addressed problems with the greatest success and how they were able to do so. An important aim of this whole monitoring and assessment procedure, which is a continuous process of mutual multilateral surveillance, is the harmonisation of basic objectives. A noteworthy element of this procedure is the so called "peer review process", in which Member States jointly examine examples of "good practice", i.e. Member States themselves select examples they want to present to the others and these examples are reviewed by those who declared their interest.

The Employment Policy Guidelines are organised around four so called pillars, or four main priorities which address the main problems identified regarding the overall employment situation, namely lack of qualification, lack of jobs, lack of co-operation between the social partners, and discrimination. The four priorities or pillars addressing these problems, respectively, are:

- to improve employability (first pillar);
- developing entrepreneurship to forward creation of businesses and jobs (second pillar);
- promoting adaptability through modernisation of work organisation and work contracts (third pillar);
- reinforcement of equal opportunities for men and women (fourth pillar).

All four pillars are closely related. While the fourth pillar emphasises social cohesion, the first three pillars emphasise labour market efficiency, their rationale being predominantly economic. Of the latter, the first pillar (employability) mainly concerns measures regarding the supply of labour (skills etc.) or aims at matching supply of and demand for labour, whereas the two other pillars (entrepreneurship and adaptability) primarily deal with factors influencing the demand for labour (encouraging job creation and preventing the loss of jobs, respectively) (Pascual 2000a).

As regards actions specifically directed at young people, the most important of the four pillars is probably the first, "employability", although in some countries young people are also covered by programmes under the pillars of entrepreneurship and adaptability. It is clear, of course, that – in a more general fashion – reinforcing equal opportunities or reducing inequalities between men and women (pillar four) also concerns young people, and that their labour-market integration may also be positively influenced by developing entrepreneurship to push job creation (pillar two) and by promoting adaptability through modernisation (pillar three) (Rychener 2000).

The importance given to youth employment policy at the EU level, as institutionalised and consolidated in the (revised) guidelines, reflects the recognition of the difficulties experienced by young people in their transition from school to work, especially, but not necessarily so, when they are poorly qualified. Integration of young people into the labour market today is characterised by lack of training places, intermittent employment, high turnover rates and prolonged uncertainty. The youth transition may be even more complicated in rural areas, as compared to urban ones, due to specific features of their labour markets, such as:

- loss of jobs in agriculture perhaps not being compensated by job-growth in other sectors;
- disinclination of young people to work in agriculture, because this may be perceived as unattractive and/or poorly paid;
- greater barriers for women to enter into male dominated crafts or trades due to the persistence of traditional cultural values;
- lack of quality jobs for those with high qualifications;
- the existence of only a narrower range of poor jobs, which increases competition among those with poor levels of qualification;
- partly seasonal nature of jobs available;
- recruitment for jobs often tending to be through good connections, thus putting at risk of exclusion those not favoured by support from a social network.

Several European countries have addressed this situation with a multitude of programmes and policies all aimed at easing the transition from school to work but adopting different approaches, depending on the context in which they were conceived. The Luxembourg Process has accelerated the development of youth integration policies and in this process each country has prioritised various aspects of the European Employment Guidelines in its National Action Plan according to the scale of the problem, cultural traditions and institutions (Pascual 2000b). Member States also differ with respect to the extent to which programmes already being operative when the NAPs were devised and implemented for the first time were continued or more or less modified. This is to say that the 1998 NAPs built on efficient policies that were already in existence, with some alterations made to them in order to strengthen the programmes in response to one or the other guidelines. Alternatively, new, innovative programmes, designed to avoid the pitfalls or negative impacts of previous policies, were introduced under the NAPs.

Of the nine guidelines under the employability pillar there are three in particular which call for strategies and actions in favour of young people (Rychener 2000). According to the first of these guidelines, Member States are asked to offer all unemployed young people a "new start" in the form of training, re-training, work practice, a job or any measure improving their employability before they reach six months of unemployment (guideline 1). With respect to strategies developed under this guideline it is emphasised they should build on the early identification of individual needs. Furthermore, the objective of offering opportunities for a "new start" within a six-month period is to reduce the inflow of young unemployed people into long-term unemployment. A wider approach to prevent youth unemployment, as compared to this guideline, is defined in the two other guidelines. Under their common objective of improving, or easing, the transition from school to work, there are two aspects. The first one is to improve the quality of the education system to reduce the number of early school drop-outs (guideline 7). The second one is to improve young people's preparation for working life by increasing their adaptability to technological and economic changes and equipping them with skills relevant to the labour market, through the extension or improvement of (apprenticeship) training provisions (guideline 8).

Before taking a closer look at some of the major programmes implemented under these three guidelines in the Member States considered in this report, (especially guideline 1), it seems appropriate to provide in a summary fashion the Commission's assessment and conclusions with regard to the relevant policy measures that were in force or planned in the seven countries by 31 May 1999, as set out in the JER 1999 (European Commission 1999c). This report was based on the Commission's analysis of the Member States' implementation reports on their 1998 National Action Plans for Employment and on the examination of how the 1999 Employment Guidelines (European Commission 1999d) had been translated into revised NAPs for 1999.

The reason for drawing on the JER 1999, therefore, is that this report is a documentation of the comparative assessment of the relevant policies which were operative in the second half of the same year, at a time when, over a period of several months, also most of the interviews with young people in the framework of the PaYPiRD project were carried out. This, at least in principle, opens up the possibility of relating our respondents' experiences with policies and programmes under the NAPs – as may have been made in 1998 and/or 1999 and as reported to us in the interviews – to the official assessment of the programmes concerned. In order to give an accurate depiction of this official perspective, reference in the following will not only be made to the JER 1999, but also to the JER 2000 (European Commission 2000), which partly builds on the Member States' reports on the actual implementation of their 1999 NAPs.

3.   Comparative Assessment of Employment Policies

According to the JER 1999 (Part II), all of the countries which are being considered here have used, to varying degrees and with somewhat different priorities, ESF resources to underpin the implementation of the employment guidelines. France, Portugal, Austria and Germany are identified to have concentrated on financing measures under the employability pillar, including measures for the integration of young unemployed persons, such as vocational training schemes etc. (pp. 33, 69, 63 and 15, respectively). As regards the other three countries, in the view of the JER, the ESF has been used "as an innovative tool" (Finland), ESF input into the NAP 1999 has increased (UK) and "budgetary information of ESF support is very comprehensive, but there is little indication of priority areas" (Ireland) (pp. 75, 87 and 39, respectively).

The JER 1999 (Part I) states, with respect to national policies under guideline 1, that "there is now a clear move towards a more preventive approach in combating youth ... long-term unemployment, but some Member States are more advanced than others in setting up the necessary framework ... to offer to all young ... unemployed a new start before six months of unemployment" (p. 31). As regards the countries considered in this thematic report the stages of implementation of guideline 1 they have reached are described as follows:

> In Austria, ... very few [young] unemployed cross the 6 ... months threshold without being offered a new start. Measurable efforts have also been undertaken to increase attendance of ... programmes of vocational training for the young unemployed. (JER 1999, p. 31).

> For young people the safety net ["Auffangnetz"] was quite successful as it reduced the strain on the apprenticeship market on a short-term basis. (JER 2000, p. 156).

> The UK concentrates on job search assistance to help the [young] unemployed back to the labour market before they cross the 6 months threshold through the JSA [Jobseekers' Allowance] scheme. The New Deal programmes ... intervene ... at 6 months, consisting of a range of measures including intensive counselling, training and subsidised jobs. For young unemployed, the UK claims a non-compliance rate of zero..., which is linked to strict benefit sanctions ... 18% of the young unemployed ... crossed the 6 months threshold. (JER 1999, p.31).

> Evaluation evidence is suggesting that the New Deal for Young People is having an impact on the off-flows from unemployment (JER 2000, p. 183).

> Ireland is implementing the preventive strategy in a phased approach ...The individual process starts with a vocational guidance interview carried out just before the end of the 6 month unemployment period, and is followed by referral to training, job or personalised job search assistance. Therefore, the majority of intensive employability measures take place only after the 6 ... month period ... it is possible to infer an average non-compliance rate of 7.5%, that is the share of the cohort of young unemployed which crosses the 6 ... months threshold without having been offered any action. (JER 1999, p. 32).

> A modest improvement in effort for the younger age group can be seen. (JER 2000, p. 129).

> Last year [i.e. in 1998] Portugal implemented a thorough reform ... which has yielded promising results as only 5.8% of young people ... becoming unemployed were not offered actions before reaching 6 ... months unemployment (non-compliance rate) in the

regions covered by the new policies (representing about one third of all unemployed). However, the number of those who did not come to the interview triggering individualised prevention remains quite high and more substantial progress is still required to achieve lower inflows into long-term unemployment (17.3% for young unemployed). The NAP 1999 foresees the extension of the new policies to 75% of the total population in 1999. (JER 1999, p. 32).

The programme dealing with young ... unemployed [INSERJOVEM] ... continues to produce significant results. The territorial coverage ... has been widened and 18.7% of young [unemployed] ... had not been offered an active measure before ... 6 months of unemployment. Assessment of this relatively low rate of non-compliance (one of the best performances among Member States) shall take into account that many unemployed ... 52% of the young ... do not come to the interview offered by the PES. [Public Employment Service] (JER 2000, p. 163).

France seems set to meet its objectives in terms of number of beneficiaries of offers of a new start ... A much better balance between preventive and active measures is necessary in order to block inflows into long-term unemployment ... The share of beneficiaries of preventive measures is expected ... to increase gradually ... In 1999, the new start should cover half of the young target group. (JER 1999, p. 33).

The "new start" measures ... did not achieve the objectives established. The non-compliance rate was 77.8% for young people ... beneficiaries of the "new start" measures ... have also benefited from the Trace programme (43,000 young people) and from all the measures under the Combating of Exclusion Act. (JER 2000, p. 122).

Finland launched an activation policy centred around the offer of a job seeking plan to all unemployed before the 6 ... months threshold, which is planned to be fully implemented by the end of 1999. Based on interviews ..., an individual job-seeking plan is worked out. (JER 1999, p. 33).

... significant progress was made ... in 1999. Of all [young] unemployed job seekers around 95% received an action plan before reaching the threshold. However ... the output indicator is still high: around 10% of ... young job seekers passed ... into long-term unemployment. (JER 2000, p. 170).

In Germany: Priority has been given to the prevention of youth unemployment in its wider sense, mainly through the extension of apprenticeship ... The new [Immediate Action] programme to fight youth unemployment reflects an additional step towards a preventive approach more in line with the first guideline and early results are encouraging. (JER 1999, p. 34).

74% of those [young people] who became unemployed in the course of 1998 started a measure within a concrete action plan before six months of unemployment. About 16% of those remaining jobless beyond six months have not started an active policy measure (non-compliance rate). (JER 2000, p. 100).

As to guideline 7 (improving the education system and reducing early school leaving), the JER 1999 concludes that "most member States address the reduction of school failure at all ... levels. They are therefore developing comprehensive strategies in which a better preparation and adaptation to working life is seen as a means to achieve the overall improvement of educational achievements" [e.g. the UK] The report continued ".... a few Member States, like Portugal, Ireland but also the UK have yet to overcome a significant problem of dropping out before the end of compulsory schooling" (p. 44). The report cited a number of examples of initiatives taken by specific Member States, such as:

> targeted intervention ... in economically and socially disadvantaged areas. (Portugal, UK, France, Ireland);
> alternative curricula or special classes (Ireland, Portugal, France), with the provision of specific individual support to pupils and students encountering learning difficulties;
> strengthened orientation and guidance at different levels of the education system (Austria);
> actions targeted at the most disadvantaged groups, including ethnic minorities (UK) and young people with disabilities. (UK, Germany, Austria) (p. 44)

Other efforts under guideline 7 mentioned in the JER aim at increasing the flexibility of the education systems through the creation of new bridges allowing for re-routing, the extension of practical training in working situations and (in the case of Portugal and the UK) enabling "the return to education of those young people already at work, despite a low level of educational qualification, so as to prepare them better for their future careers and minimise the risk of unemployment" (p. 44).

The view expressed in the JER 1999 with respect to guideline 8 (equipping young people with better skills) is the following:

> It is difficult to assess how the accession to the labour market ... is influenced by ... the nature of skills provided during ... training ... it is possible, however, to measure the employment probabilities ... within a year after leaving education. Female school leavers have ... only a 59% chance to find a job, compared to 64% of their male counterparts. This figure hides further wider divergences among Member States: employment probabilities are as low as 36% ... in Finland ... and as high as ... 86% ... in Germany. (p. 45)

The JER continues:

> The strategies developed to improve the preparation and adaptation ... to working life give a key role to the improvement of the technical and vocational systems.... Austria and Germany are pursuing the modernisation and expansion of their apprenticeship systems.... Germany increased public support to the SMEs and the New Länder ... whilst Austria has both extended the offer of apprenticeship places in new trades and implemented its special aid programme to accommodate young people who fail to find an apprenticeship place.... The participation in apprenticeship has also progressed in several Member States where it is not the main component of vocational training, like in Portugal..., the UK, [and] Ireland .... Several initiatives are being taken to improve the provision of technical and vocational training, such as:

- Revision of curricula at upper-secondary levels in view to include the acquisition of "key social qualifications" (Austria);
- Introduction of practical training at post-secondary level (Austria, Finland, France)" (p.45);
- Reform of technical and vocational programmes either to facilitate and extend access or to up-date and adapt their content (Portugal) (p. 46).

It is further stated that:

> France ... [is] also acting to reinforce the links between education and the business world by setting up new structures ... Nearly all Member States are giving priority to preparing young people for the use of new information and communication technologies and have ... schemes to equip schools with these technologies, including in some cases (Germany) special provision for the appropriate training of teachers. (p. 46)

4. Young People's Experiences of these Programmes in the Study Areas

To complement this overview of the Commission's assessment of the aggregate-level implementation of the three youth-relevant employment policy guidelines by the Member States, in what follows, these policies and programmes are looked at from a different perspective. The following, apart from views expressed by local key persons, is mainly based on young people's experiences of these policy measures at regional or local levels, as reported to the researchers in the study areas and elaborated in detail in the National Reports. This must be qualified by saying that only a certain proportion of the respondents – varying in size across study areas – actually participated in measures under the NAPs (or comparable ones, operative prior to the first implementation of such plans), because the different samples of young people interviewed were partly made up of individuals who have experienced rather smooth transitions on their pathways from school/university-to-work, thus there being no need for them to seek support through any of the schemes designed to facilitate labour market integration etc. by way of special training or otherwise. Accordingly, it is only the former group of young people whose experiences are appropriate for consideration in further developing this chapter's theme.

The underlying approaches and other characteristics, such as operational and outcome aspects, of some employability related policies and programmes and/or young people's experiences with these are dealt with in chapters 7, 8 and 10 of this volume. Therefore, to avoid overlaps, the remainder of this chapter focuses on the relevant findings from the (context, national, thematic) reports of the different teams for each of the case study areas in turn, according to the alphabetical order of the Member States.

Austria

Of the various programmes operative in the Austrian context, and addressed in the respective National Report, there are two in particular which interviewees from Murau, the study area, participated in and were able to report about. The first of these is known under the name of "safety net" (Auffangnetz). Based on the Youth Training Consolidation Act (Jugendausbildungssicherungsgesetz) and in response to guideline 8 (training provision), it was created in 1998 to secure sufficient vocational training options for young people with a school-leaving certificate (Hofstätter 2000). Safety net courses have a duration of 10 months. Participants receive a monthly allowance. The courses provide (partly firm-based) training in basic practical and IT-related skills, which usually are acquired during the first year of regular three-year apprenticeships. The training focuses on skills needed in crafts or trades where demand for labour exists. Standard vocational education within the Austrian apprenticeship system is a combination of work and school-based learning, the latter usually being restricted to one day per week. Participation in the 10 months-cycle of a safety net course counts as equivalent to passing the first year of an apprenticeship, giving credit for both work and school-based learning. Therefore when someone finds an apprenticeship place, subsequent to a safety net course, he/she will have to undergo another two years of training at the workplace, combined with attendance of vocational school.

An important task of the training centres where the safety net courses take place is to support participants in their search for apprenticeships. Termination of training and entry into an apprenticeship is possible at any time. When somebody does not find an apprenticeship place, he/she may stay on in training under the safety net beyond month 10. In order to apply for apprenticeships, the young people can use the training centre's infrastructure.

The disproportionately high participation rate of young women in the courses offered in Murau reflects the fact that in this study area young men's chances to find an apprenticeship without institutional support are considerably better than those of their female counterparts. Participants in the courses appreciated the training and, especially, the support they received in searching for an apprenticeship. This support kept them motivated and sustained their hope to find a suitable place. It was expressed that without such support one's activities to find an apprenticeship would be much less intense and discouragement would be much more likely. Disillusionment, nonetheless, did occur, when after weeks of participation in the course and numerous applications it was finally realised, how much luck one would need to get an apprenticeship contract. This was especially so in the case of young women whose frustration increased even more, leading to a sense of powerlessness, because of the observation that males, in comparison, were more successful in accessing apprenticeships. Some women complained about what they perceived as conservative attitudes on the part of employers, discriminating against them, and requested that firms no longer keep up barriers for women to enter as apprentices into male dominated crafts and trades. Despite their overall appreciation of the safety network courses, female participants considered it crucial that the training centre intensifies its placement activities.

The other measure to be described here is a regional initiative ("Women for Women"), jointly financed by the national employment service, the province of Styria and the ESF. Women in rural areas who have either low vocational qualifications and/or have interrupted their labour market participation because of family reasons have many difficulties to re-integrate into the labour market. The main aim, therefore, of the "Women for Women" initiative is to give women, subsequent to child-care leave, for example, an opportunity to re-orient themselves and improve their qualifications. The initiative also offers individual career planning. It is not primarily addressing young women, but covers the range up to age 45. The organisers of the initiative emphasise the necessity of widening the range of crafts and trades accessible for women, but progress in this respect so far has been limited, as the readiness of employers to accept women in "men's jobs" is still rather underdeveloped.

The initiative's overall results, nevertheless, in terms of participants' entry into employment after termination of the training, are stated to be quite encouraging (Sperl 2000). Yet, as regards their appreciation of the initiative, participants appear to have different views: Women, for example, who were referred to it by the employment service and did not take up the training because they themselves considered it desirable, were more critical towards it than others. This applied particularly to older women apparently not particularly prepared or motivated to re-orient themselves and acquire new skills, but also to young mothers. For the latter group the problem was to arrange for child-care in order to participate in the training (something for which one can not blame the initiative for, in the first place). Those, on the other hand, who were able to solve the problem of child-care, had a rather positive attitude towards the initiative and the training in which they participated.

Finland

Perhaps the most interesting measure in relation to Suomussalmi, the Finnish case study region within the PaYPiRD project, was the further development of the Youth Workshops, in which 8,000 young people took part in Finland in 1999. According to the Finnish NAP for 2000, 73 of the total of about 350 Youth Workshops in the country receive funding from the ESF. From the NAP, it does not become quite clear, though, whether the operation of the Youth Workshops is in compliance with guideline 1 (new start) or guideline 8 (training provision). Anyway, the workshops offer training, work and related activities for unemployed young people for a six-months period, helping them to manage their lives and providing the knowledge and skills needed for study or work.

According to the Finnish National Report, the Youth Workshop in Suomussalmi is a good example of a project intended to promote local initiative and the development of employment opportunities, and one that has some definite results to show for it. The young people who had participated in it were mostly satisfied with the experience, as well as with the remuneration by comparison with the usual unemployment benefit, although there were some young men who regarded the pay as low. The leader of the project indicated in the key actors' focus group discussion that she regarded its achievements as promising, and she emphasised that it was only very recently that they had reached a situation where real employment paths were beginning to open up for young people from the workshop, i.e. the testimonial received from there was instrumental in securing them a job, although admittedly not very often in Suomussalmi (Muilu and Onkalo 2000, 41-42).

The Finnish National Report further states that it appeared to be "difficult for young people in the interviews to make suggestions for measures that would be likely to improve their chances of gaining employment" (p. 42) and that in the focus group discussion with unemployed young people the view prevailed that the local council was not active enough to reduce unemployment (ibid.). The report also states that the participants in the focus group of professionals (local and central government officials) "were scarcely any more inventive than the young people" when asked for policy proposals and that the professionals' view was almost exclusively that of the public sector and the employment measures provided through it (p. 43).

Against this background it is interesting to note how the report continues with respect to the "great interest", apparently shared by young people in Suomussalmi, in the apprenticeship scheme, i.e. the idea of providing practical training through local partnerships (mentioned also in the Finnish NAP as a variant of action supported by the government). In the focus group of professionals another interesting discussion on possible measures [besides the one on the Youth Workshop] centred on the apprenticeship system, which is included in many official programmes. The young people were particularly interested in this, but the professionals appeared to have their doubts. In their opinion there were not enough companies in the area that were ready to commit themselves to an apprenticeship scheme for several years at a time. In any case, [in the view of the professionals] the young people had formed far too favourable a picture of the whole system:

> ...it means that a firm has to commit itself for two or three years if the apprentice is going to get a basic qualification... Few companies are capable of doing that... But another thing... is that many people... think... [an apprenticeship] is a great joy and blessing for anyone who can't face sitting in a classroom, that it's an easy way out and a sure way of qualifying for a trade. But it's nothing of the sort. You have to do an eight-hour day at work and then read for exams, or spend two or three days in the week travelling to somewhere [distant]..., wherever the theoretical teaching can be found for the particular subjects. In the end, it calls for twice the effort. There's a great difference of opinion over how much commitment it calls for and how easy it is. (opinion expressed in the key actors' focus group.) (ibid.)

The report concludes at this point by expressing the view that the apprenticeship scheme should, nevertheless, be developed further as an alternative route for entering work, and the "Top Job" partnership project that was initiated in Suomussalmi in 1999 by a local working group (including the Kajaani entrepreneurs' association) could well prove to be a crucial step in increasing the number of apprenticeship agreements in the area (p. 44).

France

France has set up a network of local agencies to put into effect employment assistance programmes implemented by the state and training programmes run by the regions and other social services, aiming at the integration of young people, provided by authorities at the level of the "departments". Related to this was a strengthening of contractual relationships between local authorities and the State, as well as efforts to encourage the development of local partnerships. In co-operation with Public Employment Service Centres, local agencies such as the so-called "local missions" or the PAIO (Permanence d'Accueil, d'Information et d'Orientation) offices are in charge of administering the programmes at issue established under the NAP. Two of these programmes, the "New Start" initiative and TRACE (Pathway to Employment; including combined job/training contracts), were set up under guideline 1 (employability pillar), while another one, "New Services – Jobs for Young People", is based on guideline 12 (adaptability pillar). The latter programme aims at the creation of jobs in new business lines catering to public needs not yet met by the market (cultural, educational, health and environmental services etc.). The Government contributes 80% of the minimum wage for the first five years of each contract established through the programme.

Besides the combined job/training contract mentioned above, there is a variety of other (apprenticeship, qualification etc.) contracts under which vocational training in France is provided. One of these forms of contracts, explicitly mentioned in relation to guidelines 7 and 8 in the 1999 NAP, gives young people the opportunity to obtain a basic-level "professional fitness certificate", or CAP. Thus, another task of the "local missions" or the PAIO offices is to assist young people in obtaining a suitable training contract.

In the French study area, Mayenne, the relevant local organisations are the (largely state financed) PAIO – specifically in charge of people in the 16-25 age bracket – and the Centre de Resources, which was set up by a group of local communities and which has some ESF funding. The PAIO and the Centre appear to play an important part in giving young people orientation, guidance and support – this not being restricted to the fields of training and employment, but covering also matters or problems related to transport, housing, childcare, health etc. As documented in the National Report prepared by the French team, a number of interviewees who had been in contact with these institutions were rather appreciative of the personalised guidance services and support the two public agencies provided.

Both organisations seem to have worked together well. Importantly, the staff were described by the interviewees as patient and receptive, and the quantity as well as quality of information offered on different job opportunities and career structures was warmly welcomed. The Centre de Resources offered a range of integration courses, for example, focussing on basic skills in French, Maths or IT, as well as on vocational preparation courses. At the Centre itself, though, no courses were offered that would lead to an acknowledged qualification. The respondents commented that one of the advantages the integration and orientation courses could provide was the practice periods associated with them, which facilitated their definition of a career plan (individual action plan). Some interviewees were also happy about the free access they had to the Centre's infrastructure (computers, internet), which facilitated searching for jobs and writing letters of application. In addition, it was appreciated that the Centre de Resources constituted a meeting point where people in similar situations could come together for the exchange of experiences – something which seemed to be particularly important for young people from more distant villages who can easily feel a strong sense of isolation.

While interviewees were satisfied with the services of the two agencies, some of those who participated in forms of training involving employers reported some negative experiences. Several respondents spoke of the difficulty of finding firms who would take them as trainees for the practice periods which were part of their courses. Others complained that firms had not kept them as employees upon termination of a qualification contract and/or that the pay was too low with regard to the hours worked, and/or that the quality of the training was rather poor.

Germany

As regards guidelines 1, 7 and 8, Germany has undertaken action to secure a sufficient number of apprenticeship places and ease the transition to training and work. This has involved the expansion and improvement of the apprenticeship system, as well as increasing the flexibility and differentiation of vocational training (guideline 8). An important scheme among measures under guideline 7 (improvement of education; reduction of drop-out) offers young adults without a school leaving certificate a second chance to prepare for and take the respective examination. In the NAP this scheme features also as an element of the German flagship programme ("JUMP") under guideline 1 (new start).

This "Immediate Action Programme" was put into effect in January 1999 and has been more successful than critics expected. Although initially limited to one year, it has been continued. "JUMP" is in addition to instruments which already exist. It is administered by the job centres. These enjoy considerable freedom as to how they make use of the money earmarked for "JUMP" (Government and ESF funding). For those entering the programme, individual career plans are set up, and the variety of measures available allows placements to be suitable to individual needs. Options include preparatory training, apprenticeships, further education or (first) employment etc. Wage subsidies serve to encourage firms to hire young people. Persons who refuse suitable training/employment, or break off a measure without good cause, face (temporary) suspension of their benefits. Reportedly, though, such disqualification only occurs in relatively few cases, which for the Ministry of Labour is an indicator that young people are highly interested in education/training and work. A crucial element of "JUMP" is outreach social work to reach those not registered with the job centres.

Each of the two job centres in the District Wesermarsch, the German study area, employs one social worker. These professionals have their offices – which are intended to serve as drop-in centres – not within the job centres, but on the premises of two (out of several) institutions in the area which offer training. Besides their outreach activities, the social workers deal with youngsters referred to them by the job centres and are primarily in charge of all those who are disadvantaged in more than one respect (education, finances, health, housing, childcare, relations with parents etc.). Their services include career advice, training or job placement and, most importantly, the co-ordination of all kinds of social and emotional support someone may need to be able to embark on a new start and stay on track. As regards the latter point, continuing case management is often necessary, because many clients lack staying power. The social workers collaborate with all relevant agencies related to training, employment and youth.

To be gainfully employed was important for virtually all young people that were interviewed in the District Wesermarsch. Correspondingly, and this reflects the area's economic situation as well as the educational deficits of a considerable part of the sample, but also the experiences generally made in searching for apprenticeships or employment as (un)skilled labourers, most respondents felt that government and/or companies should be providing more opportunities for apprenticeship training or employment. At the same time, the majority of the interviewees did not expect efforts in the creation of apprenticeships or jobs to be stepped up and had not much hope for a positive development of the area's economy.

Several interviewees had taken or were taking part in training schemes of the kind offered under "JUMP" or had experiences with work placements. However, while keen on the idea that such measures could increase their employability, those youngsters sometimes found themselves in places which they felt were not suitable for them, as they neither fitted their interests and aspirations, nor their abilities. Although the job centres received some criticism for poor services (unfriendly and disinterested staff; bureaucratic procedures) it was also appreciated that they provided training and employment measures. This is particularly important for youth without any or with few educational qualifications. In a number of cases, though, the problem remains of not having a school leaving certificate which, in a "credential society" (Collins 1979) such as Germany, is a prerequisite – not by law, but in practice – to gain access to an apprenticeship as an important step towards gainful employment in the future.

Young people's attitudes towards the services provided to them by the social workers were generally very positive, particularly due to the feeling that in their dealings with these professionals they and their problems were taken seriously. Nonetheless, some were quite frustrated because of the postponement of a course leading to a school leaving certificate, which had resulted from strong demand for courses of all kinds, and, correspondingly, from premature spending of the funds earmarked for "JUMP" locally. The social workers themselves expressed the view that it is necessary to set-up local offices of guidance and co-ordination for disadvantaged youth, offering a variety of services in one place. Relevant regional players, in fact, are presently considering the establishment of such offices.

Hence, although there is a lack of apprenticeships and employment in the District Wesermarsch, it can be argued that there is a "safety net structure", which comprises training courses and which constitutes a "second labour market". While this structure has been criticised, it is clear that without such support, prospects for the most vulnerable youths would often look bleak.

Ireland

The Irish government's policy in relation to unemployed young people is to encourage them "into employment and away from a reliance on welfare support through appropriate guidance, counselling, job-search techniques and to encourage those who have particular personal development or skills inadequacies into appropriate development programmes" (as set out in the NAP for 2000, in compliance with guideline 1 (new start)). This policy implies a more active engagement by the State with unemployed young people. The measure could also be viewed as the introduction of compulsion into the labour market / welfare policy domain. Currently, young people who do not take up an offer of training or employment run the risk of losing their benefits. Unlike some EU states where this type of policy is more associated with situations of economic decline, it occurs in Ireland at a time of high jobs growth – which suggests more of an emphasis on increasing labour supply than on reducing welfare dependence. However, it was suggested to the Irish team in the local policy actor focus group and previous interviews with the FAS (National Training Authority) official that the state will not pursue a policy in rural areas that will result in young people being forced to leave.

In relation to Guideline 7 on early school leaving, the most significant intervention in the Irish case study area is Youthreach. Since 1989, a Youthreach centre has operated in Letterfrack, under the County Galway VEC (Vocational Education Committee). Since the programme's inception, of 140 participants who completed it, one third went directly into employment, one quarter into an apprenticeship and one quarter into further education and training. From September 1999, the centre has offered the Leaving Certificate Applied to six students.

Nationally, the programme operates through 70 Youthreach Centres, 45 Community Training Workshops and 27 Traveller Training Centres, targeting young people aged between 15 and 18 who have left mainstream education without qualifications. Participants receive a weekly training allowance. The programme has five overall objectives:

- personal and social development and increased self-esteem;
- second chance education and introductory level training;
- promoting independence, personal autonomy and a pattern of life-long learning;
- integration into further education, training opportunities and the labour market;
- social inclusion.

Normally, a trainee will participate on the programme for two years and an important aspect of the programme is a work placement with an employer. The establishment of a system of Certification through the National Council for Vocational Awards (NCVA) has been important in providing a progression route for trainees.

In the view of the Irish team, the Youthreach programme constitutes a positive policy intervention in the area, achieving many significant results. This assessment is based not on any systematic evaluation of the programme, but primarily on observations, discussions with local actors, as well as discussions and interviews with participants of the programme. As a progression route for early school leavers, it has demonstrated considerable success in developing marketable job skills and personal development features that are needed to participate more fully in society. Youthreach places emphasis on skills acquisition, work experience and a curriculum that serves a wide range of interest and ability. The programme adopts a person-centred, supportive, flexible and non-formal approach to the learning process and is far more suited to the needs of many young people than the rigid and academic environment of school.

Portugal

Among young people in the study area of Santa Marta de Penaguiao (SMP), there are quite large proportions that drop out prior to completion of compulsory schooling (grade 9) or that do not complete secondary education (10th to 12th grade cycle). An important reason why students do not enter into or do not complete this cycle is their families' limited income: Schooling beyond grade 9 is not available in SMP, but only in neighbouring communities. In addition, while pupils may benefit from state grants during compulsory education, such financial support is not available beyond that level. Therefore, to go on with school implies considerable expenses (for books/stationary; transport; food) – a challenge for families with economic difficulties. For some interviewees, changing to a school outside of SMP constituted pressure in terms of making new friends and adapting to a more competitive school environment. If this is associated with inadequate selection of one's educational stream ("scientific field"), frustration is likely to occur. Several persons made a wrong choice, be it due to peers' influence, lack of teachers' advice or non-availability of a field they preferred. Other problematic aspects addressed were: poorly skilled teachers; too many courses; courses being irrelevant to students' needs and/or too theory-laden. It appears no wonder that some people started to skip classes, hung out with friends and, ultimately, dropped out. More than half of the sample expressed dissatisfaction with their schooling.

The National Report states a certain unwillingness among youngsters in SMP to contemplate the continuation of or return to education. It identifies several barriers to resumption of education: dislike of school; fear of peers' comments; wish not to give up present life style; and perceived irrelevance of education for current job or prospective employability. Such reservations are to be found among the least educated as well as those who have completed their 12th year. Those, on the other hand, who appeared willing to go back to school mentioned one or the other of the following as pre-requisites: access to transport; provision of child care; continued/resumed family support; post-work school time table plus adequate travel time; likely positive effects on performance/pay in current or other job; and courses suited to personal interests.

In spite of what may be an improved situation today, with the turn-over of teaching staff being minimal now, and material/educational improvements having taken place lately (this probably due to a strengthening of efforts at the national level in response to guideline 7), the research in SMP suggests that, in many cases, school has been unable to detect interviewees' abilities/skills and ambitions, and that, locally, specific counselling and professional guidance has been practically non-existent.

As with the school system, it is true that most of the respondents do not speak very highly of the quality of the services of the employment centre and related institutions either. Youngsters who were trainees in official programmes had difficulties to identify them by their names (e.g. the AGIR and INFORJOVEM programmes, established under guideline 8). Training for young people in SMP is provided by private and entrepreneurial organisations and the Institute for Employment and Professional Training (IEFP), which is associated with the Portuguese Youth Institute (IPJ). The IEFP and the IPJ closely co-operate with the Employment Centre, which is responsible for placements. As these three institutions are located in a town (Vila Real) outwith the SMP area, and, moreover, the majority of courses tend to be offered in neighbouring communities, this may work to the disadvantage of youngsters from SMP.

According to the NAP Implementation Report for 1999, the IEFP is also in charge of carrying out the interviews with the registered unemployed in the framework of the INSERJOVEM initiative (under guideline 1) with the objective of offering a new start and developing an individual action plan. With respect to this insertion programme, a key informant expressed his concern about the small number of employers or non-profit organisations in SMP ready to take on youngsters for training or subsidised employment.

Interviewees' experiences with the Employment Centre and the IEFP, particularly with regard to their usefulness and performance, were rather negative. This applies to the adequacy/quality of work or training offered as well as to the attitudes of the respective staffs, which were perceived as inefficient, indifferent and/or de-motivating. There were complaints about the length of time which passed without any significant action being taken by the IEFP. Some respondents registered with the IEFP only in order to be eligible for training, and not in expectation of ever getting a job. In the National Report it is viewed as problematic that the remit of the Employment Centre is to act exclusively as a mediator between the private sector and those seeking employment, all the more so as it is the public sector which is the key employer in less favoured rural areas. But because all public sector posts have to be advertised, there appears to be no requirement that the Employment Centre be involved or be informed of public sector posts which may be of interest to its clients.

As long as SMP youngsters experience institutional efforts (to improve their employability and/or to create suitable jobs) as insufficient and in their job search largely remain dependent on support from kin and other networks and as far as they are unwilling (or unable, due to low qualifications) to take up work that the local market provides, they may be forced to leave SMP in even larger numbers.

Scotland

Within the Angus case study area, the Government schemes that correspond with the youth-relevant Employment Policy Guidelines are 'Skillseekers' and the 'New Deal for Young People' (NDYP). Both of these programmes are, to some degree, based on ideas and principles formed during the previous government's term of office (Tonge 1999, 217-232). But though there is continuity of thought in some areas, the New Labour administration differs from the Conservatives with its emphasis on "joined up thinking", evident in their "welfare-to-work" package which has emerged through reform of the employment, tax and social security systems (Millar 2000, 7-10). The creation of a Scottish parliament offers the possibility of a different approach to youth unemployment but, as yet, and despite general support for a less coercive system – i.e. not taking up an offer of training or employment would not lead to loss of benefits – government in Scotland follows the UK paradigm in this area (Killeen 1998, 8).

The shifts in welfare and training provision stem from initiatives of the Labour Government and the new Scottish Parliament (UK Government 1998; Scottish Office 1999; Scottish Office 1998). Implementation of these initiatives has involved the development of regional and territorial partnerships. Regional partners – Local Enterprise Companies (Training and Enterprise Councils in the rest of the UK), local authorities, voluntary bodies – ensure that Government policies are adapted to meet local needs and conditions. One of their aims is to increase workforce inclusion by ensuring that people have the necessary skills to attain employment. This includes assistance for the school-to-work transition (Skillseekers) and support for a move into training or employment (NDYP). Under the youth training guarantee, all those aged 16 and 17 are eligible for the Skillseekers scheme which comprises training leading to a recognised qualification, an individual training plan and employer involvement (Scottish Office, 1999).

Among the young people interviewed in the Scottish study area no one had been on the Skillseekers programme, but several respondents had experience with the NDYP which, therefore, is further addressed in the following. In compliance with guideline 1 (new start), the NDYP was designed for those aged 18-24 who have been claiming jobseekers' allowance for over six months (Millar 2000, 1-5). Anyone joining the programme receives counselling and guidance in a 'gateway' period which lasts up to four months. The ultimate aim is to find an unsubsidised job for the young person – an effort supported by a personal adviser. If such a job cannot be found within the four months, there are several options: subsidised employment, full-time education and training, work placement in the voluntary or environmental sector.

The merits of the NDYP are subject to debate, with some commentators – as well as most of the interviewees who had been or were on the programme – criticising the coercive and disciplinary nature of the scheme, the poor quality of training provided and, perhaps most importantly, the effectiveness of the programme in generating new and sustainable employment (Burnett, Jentsch, and Shucksmith Scottish National Report 2000). Difficulties that have emerged with regard to the last issue, and the 'multiple disadvantages' that some young people have in relation to finding employment, are now being addressed by further adjustments to the programme. These problems were referred to by 'local actors' in the Angus case study area and provisions are now being introduced throughout the UK to improve basic literacy and numeracy skills and to ensure that prospective employees are better equipped to enter into the work environment.

But perhaps the singularly most damaging complaint is that the New Deal programme is too rigid and inflexible to the varied and fluctuating needs of the young unemployed (Millar 2000, 46). This is particularly pertinent for those who live in rural areas such as Angus, a marginalised group who face additional barriers, compared to their urban counterparts, which restrict their opportunities of finding employment. These barriers stem from geographical isolation and the limited opportunities available locally, difficulties compounded by the paucity of public transport, the lack of affordable housing, the strength of personal networks and the poor quality of jobs. Thus, in an area already disadvantaged because of comparatively low uptake of benefits and under-reporting of unemployment, imaginative measures are needed to increase the employability of young people. Pilot schemes designed to overcome some of these barriers have been introduced, and, with adequate backing from the relevant agencies, they can amplify the opportunities for young people to enter into the labour market.

5. Conclusion

By way of concluding this chapter, it must be pointed out, that the experiences of young people from the various study areas with some or the other of the different measures under the respective Member States' NAPs, as described in an overview fashion in the preceding pages, do not allow for any real or in-depth comparison(s). Nonetheless, based on the experiences which have been presented here, a number of aspects definitely deserve attention and could now be addressed. These issues, however, are all being discussed and put into the larger context of the other levels and dimensions relevant to the PaYPiRD research as a whole in Chapter 10. It may suffice, therefore, at this point, to refer the reader on to that chapter and the overall discussion which it provides.

Chapter 7

Rural Youth in Local Community Development: Lessons through Partnership[1]

Brian McGrath

1. Introduction

Introduction

The context of increased globalisation in 'late-modern society' has served to reinforce many concerns about democratic decision-making processes and the shifting balance of power away from the local level. Consequently, a feature of contemporary life in advanced capitalist societies is the re-emergence of 'community' as both a concept and actor on the development scene (Curtin 1996). As Giddens (1999) has suggested in relation to the emergence of new institutional structures and organisations: "globalisation underlies the recovery of local community power, the return of local cultural identity ... across the world. The impulse towards decentralisation is part and parcel of globalising processes".[2] This increased interest in local community power forms the centrepiece of the analysis presented here. More specifically, it seeks to identify the processes and practices arising out of local rural communities' engagement with the state in new institutional arrangements and how the pursuit of a common development agenda has impacted upon young people. This complex interface between civil society and the state is becoming increasingly attractive to policy-makers throughout the Member States as a means to addressing the most pressing needs of its citizens, particularly in relation to unemployment, service provision and other welfare

[1] The author would like to thank the Scottish team (Mark Shucksmith, John Burnett and Birgit Jentsch) for providing some of the case study material. Thanks to Jeremy Akehurst and Marie Jacques of Moray YOUTHSTART Partnership; Johnny Coyne of FORUM and Thomás Burke of Bord Iascaigh Mhara; and Dod Forrest, Scotland. The author would also like to acknowledge the other PaYPiRD partners for undertaking research in their respective countries and for offering advice on a previous draft of this chapter, especially the comments of the Austrian team. The Irish team of the PaYPiRD project also included John Canavan and Chris Curtin.
[2] Cited in OECD (2000a) 'Delivering on Social Exclusion: Lessons from the Local Development Programme'.

concerns. This new institutional approach towards the development process, referred to as a 'partnership' approach, is the context within which the analysis is undertaken. While partnership arrangements exist throughout Europe and the US (see OECD 2000b), the nature and form of partnership co-operation differs according to the context of governance in the various countries. In Austria, for example, partnerships (such as the territorial employment pacts) help to co-ordinate efforts between regional government and other regional organisations, such as the tripartite labour market board (AMS), while in Finland, strong local government has meant that municipalities have taken a lead role in establishing partnership arrangements. This chapter focuses on two countries of the PaYPiRD project – Ireland and Scotland – because of the key role played by the community and voluntary sector in partnerships in these countries. The partnership model offers an interesting framework within which we can observe the role of local rural communities and the voluntary sector as actors or 'stakeholders' in the development process. Case studies from the two countries are presented with the purpose of highlighting the commonalities in their approach towards rural youth inclusion. It endeavours to distil from the evidence some examples of good practice out of which we can comment on the role of local communities and the voluntary sector as 'partners in development'.

The remainder of this section offers a contextual look at civil society and what the new drive towards partnership with the state and other 'stakeholders' has signified. The overall structure of the report is provided towards the end of the section.

Civil Society and the Road to Partnership

It is often asserted that the vitality and stability of any democracy can be found in the strength of its civil society (Crotty 1998). Democratic development is viewed as hinging on the degree to which political accessibility is provided to a pluralism of interests and the extent to which participation in decision-making is made more inclusive, particularly for the least powerful in society. Consequently, there is growing interest throughout advanced capitalist economies in how civil society is negotiating its way into formalised political arrangements and ultimately how this process can be made more effective and inclusive. In essence, a civil society refers to the extent to which people's social lives – from the domestic sphere to activities of economic exchange – are organised in arrangements beyond direct state control. It encompasses a broad spectrum of organisations and institutions, suggesting a diversity not only in kind and structure but sophistication and advocacy strength (Crotty 1998, 9). The following groups and structures are said to qualify: professional, economic, trade, labour and civic associations; organised religions, grassroots and community organisations (including area-based or interest-based), social clubs, agrarian collectives and so on.

One of the more interesting arrangements to emerge in recent years in civil society-state relations is the notion of 'partnership'. 'Partnership' typically refers to co-operative agreements between state agencies, private interests, the community and voluntary sectors (or non-governmental organisations) and other interests such as farming organisations, trade unions and so forth (referred to in Ireland as social partners). As a means towards developing and implementing policy, 'partnership' structures are becoming increasingly popular throughout most OECD countries, with the OECD itself commissioning a number of reports (1993a; 1996b; 2000b) analysing the core principles and modus operandi of the new institutional arrangements. The focus of 'partnership', albeit depending on its context, has tended to fall within the following thematic areas: economic development, labour markets, employment and living conditions of disadvantaged groups, poverty alleviation, and matters relating to urban and rural environments (OECD 2000b). Tied to the notion of 'partnership' are a number of other public policy principles, namely 'local intervention' and 'targeting' (Duggan 1999). By 'local intervention' is meant the focusing of policies on a defined spatial or geographic unit, such as town, village, region, county or neighbourhood, while 'targeting', particularly in the case of anti-poverty and social inclusion partnerships, refers to the identification of those most disadvantaged and marginalised in society who ought to be the main beneficiaries of policy interventions.

It has been suggested that the genesis of these new institutional arrangements stem from official perceptions of crisis at both EU and national government levels (Curtin and Varley 1997). For instance, the emergence of the LEADER[3] and the Poverty 3 programmes are viewed by authors such as Curtin and Varley (1997) as efforts to redress any crisis that might threaten the legitimacy of the European Union arising out of its grand plan for economic and political integration. Rapid rural economic restructuring and the increase in social exclusion among the citizenry of the EU added particular urgency in exploring new solutions to the types of problems emerging. According to the authors:

> ...as much as the basic solution to the new and old poverty was seen to reside in market-led economic growth, a crucially important role was assigned to institutional arrangements capable of harnessing the energies of the public, private and voluntary sectors in new, dynamic area-based partnerships. (1997, 147)

However, the context of governance within individual Member States of the EU is particularly important in assessing the nature and effectiveness of partnership institutions. Throughout Europe, the nature of governance is quite diverse, suggesting that the types of partnerships that are emerging vary in terms of the geographical scale at which they operate, their membership and the level of autonomy they can exercise. The extent to which community actors are afforded a role in this process will consequently depend on a host of issues concerning local, regional and national governance. It is this level of involvement of local

---

[3] Liaisons entre actions de développement de l'économie rurale. The first programme, LEADER 1, covered the period 1992-1994. Its successor, LEADER II, ran from 1994-1999, while a LEADER+ programme is currently in preparation stage. The programme emphasises innovative agricultural diversification and support for small and medium-sized enterprise developments.

communities in partnership arrangements that is of particular importance in considering how local community power is said to be recovering.

While partnerships vary in form and strength across Europe, a number of national studies have helped to identify the positive outcomes of 'partnership' as a policy instrument. Recently, an OECD report on Irish partnerships (Turok 2000) has documented several positive characteristics, summarised as follows:

- The approach is a practical problem-solving one, where the needs of poor and unemployed people have been met through new and enhanced services and facilities. Local knowledge and consultation has effectively identified deficits in local service provision while the independence of partnerships has added credibility among local populations.

- As a means of bringing together agencies and organisations that have never before worked together there is a sharing of knowledge and information as well as co-ordination of employment and social programmes. A new dynamism and commitment is subsequently engendered.

- Many local communities and interest groups have greater input to how policies are formulated and resources utilised. In addition to providing a platform where there is direct engagement with providers, local communities have gained strength in their own right, through their ability to organise services, seek funding and learn from other experiences. It is claimed that communities can be empowered in the process.

- A change in mind-set is also a potential positive outcome, particularly in relation to the public sector. Through engaging with different organisational cultures, attitudes and ways of 'doing business', these agencies may become more attuned to individual and local conditions and may take a more proactive approach to development.

- The agenda of local development can become more wide-ranging as local circumstances and conditions are carefully assessed. A more integrated approach, encompassing sectors and areas, can be adopted.

- The lessons learned through innovation have the capacity for transferability.

However, 'partnership' raises as many conceptual and pragmatic concerns as it proclaims to offer innovative and effective ways of tackling poverty and social exclusion. In the Irish context, Curtin and Varley (1995) have referred to some of the constraining features of partnership arrangements:

> they can provide almost endless scope for conflict and disagreement, may become cumbersome and bureaucratic in their styles of operation, and may come to be viewed with suspicion by established agencies that see their jurisdictions being infringed and by politicians who see their role as local representatives being undermined. (1995, p.379)

Concerns regarding partnership participation among sectors that tend to have a weak voice in the political process, namely the community and voluntary sector

(Craig 1994; Crowley 1998[4]), also challenges the legitimacy of partnership as a policy instrument. Those who take a more pessimistic view of the 'partnership' model of development have suggested that the state's interest in engaging with community groups derives primarily from its need to control the economy (see Tovey and Share 2000). In the new consensus-based partnership model, it is remarked that community groups must adhere to the rules of the game as dictated by the more powerful stakeholders in the process, namely, the state.

In the OECD analysis of Irish partnerships in 1996, a further criticism was levelled against partnership organisations, principally in terms of their weak structures. It was suggested that weaknesses manifested themselves in their lack of representativeness and accountability to a local constituency (what the author of the report, Sabel, refers to as 'fragile democratic legitimacy') as well as their inability to forge effective co-ordination, both horizontally (between partnership organisations) and vertically (between government and partnerships). Turok (2000) suggests that partnerships should be particularly concerned with influencing the established partners (the statutory sector) to operate more flexibly and 'mainstream' those partnership measures which have benefited local communities. A more strategic approach is also recommended in order to strike an effective balance between direct service provision/project delivery and the broader remit of advocacy/policy influence/strategy development. Of particular import in Turok's analysis, however, is the need to recognise the underlying causes rather than symptoms of poverty and social exclusion. Without effective action at national policy level, in relation to infrastructural development and welfare reform for instance, then the efforts of partnership arrangements may be deemed ineffective.

In summary, partnership continues to be an attractive policy instrument for policy-makers throughout Europe. Through the co-operation and participation of different agencies and sectors in formally organised structures, it is envisaged that lessons can be learned in the process of governance and service delivery. As a means of combating social exclusion or generating economic development, the strength of 'partnership' is seen to reside in the maximisation of resources (both human and financial), its capacity to deliver in flexible and locally specific terms and the incorporation of efficient 'targeting' as a guiding principle. In some countries, the involvement of the community/voluntary sector as an 'actor' or 'stakeholder' in the development process has been a particular feature. There is ongoing debate as to whether this involvement has led to greater 'empowerment' or 'disempowerment' for the community/voluntary sector. While the debate hinges on the local specificities of 'partnership' arrangements it is suggested that 'partnership' holds out the possibility for greater 'participative democracy' in policy formulation and implementation (see Varley 1999, for discussion of this debate). However, as Conroy (1996, 36) reminds us: "an over-preoccupation with the techniques as opposed to the goals of partnership will only lead to partnerism replacing localism as the new barrier to local development." Notwithstanding the diversity of opinion on the merits of partnership, particularly where the community/voluntary sector is concerned, there can be little doubt that the nature

---

[4] Cited in Varley (1999) and Duggan (1999).

of civil society-state relations throughout Europe is undergoing a considerable degree of examination and change.

Structure of the Chapter

The remainder of the chapter is structured as follows: section two is a case study of natural resource development in North West Connemara, Ireland. It outlines a local partnership strategy to combat social exclusion and how young people were targeted as part of this process. Section three outlines a more recent partnership initiative in Moray, Scotland which attempts to promote social inclusion through the provision of intensive and preventative support measures to young people. The final section draws together the commonalities and differences in both countries and discusses the main implications of partnership for tackling social exclusion among young people in rural communities.

2.   Young People and Natural Resource Development

Case Study 1: North West Connemara, Ireland

This case study is concerned with how a local development organisation on the western seaboard of Ireland has actively involved rural young people in natural resource development as part of its strategy for local economic regeneration. The organisation referred to is a partnership arrangement, known as FORUM, which operates in the North West Connemara region of Ireland.

Location, Context and Origins

The case study area referred to in this section – North West Connemara – is the smaller of the two regions analysed in this report. The region is noted for being selected as part of the EC Third Poverty Programme ('Poverty 3') between 1989 and 1994 (see below; Mernagh and Commins 1997). With a population of 8,722 persons the region occupies 780 square kilometres, although much of the land is mountainous and uninhabitable. The major settlements in the area include Clifden (pop. 920 persons) and Roundstone (pop. 241 persons). The area is bordered on the west by the Atlantic Ocean and includes the island of Inishbofin. A previous study (Byrne 1991) indicated that the area suffered multiple levels of disadvantage and marginalisation, particularly in terms of high poverty levels, poor service provision, high dependency ratios and poor employment opportunities.

Official local collaboration between the state, community and voluntary groups and other interests, such as private sector and trade unions, has existed in Ireland over the last decade or so. In fact, social partnership at the national level has been heralded as a key instrument in defining Ireland's macroeconomic success in recent years. Of particular significance to policy analysis however has been the initiation of partnerships at local level, stemming from a period when Ireland's economic situation was less fortunate than at present. Out of the unemployment crisis of the 1980s, when governments recognised they could not contain the growing social polarisation that was becoming increasingly obvious, emerged the PESP (Programme for Economic and Social Progress) Pilot Initiative on Long-term Unemployment (1992-1994) which targeted 12 areas of disadvantage in a rural and urban context.[5] However, a particularly significant partnership model was initiated under the auspices of the EU a number of years prior to the PESP programme. Established in 1989, a total of 41 local projects throughout the EU were selected as part of a strategy to combat social exclusion in the Member States, known as 'Poverty 3' or the 'Third EC Programme to Foster Economic and Social Integration of the Least Privileged Groups'. Two categories of project were selected: (i) model actions (29 in total) which were based on geographical areas and combined the efforts of public and non-statutory partners in agreed plans; and (ii) innovatory projects (12 in total) which would target particular groups experiencing disadvantage (Mernagh and Commins 1997, 18). Two model action projects were selected in the Irish case, one of which was located in an urban setting (PAUL)[6] and the other, at the centre of this case study, in a rural location – FORUM.

The other context within which this analysis is undertaken is that of natural resource development and how this strategy of development has taken shape in the North West Connemara region. As a means for stimulating local sustainable development the utilisation of natural resources poses a significant challenge to policy formulation, particularly in the context of contemporary rural restructuring, where employment patterns, demographic formations, and uses of rural space are shifting ground. As traditional sectors of employment, such as farming, are increasingly in decline it is tempting to suggest that natural resource exploitation provides a potentially rewarding alternative means of earning a living for many rural dwellers. However, such an assertion is not so straightforward once addressed in the context of how resources are owned and managed. In many respects, the development of natural resources in North West Connemara, particularly the aquaculture sector, represents a microcosm of the larger debate concerning 'endogenous' (locally controlled) and 'exogenous' (externally controlled) development and what constitutes the core of 'sustainable development'.

Interest in the development of the region's natural resources precedes the formation of the FORUM organisation by at least fifteen years. The 1970s saw a growing curiosity among local community groups in North West Connemara in the possibility of developing shellfish production as an economically viable sector of the local economy. Such interest in the potential economic benefits of intensive shellfish production, particularly mussel cultivation, can be traced to the research endeavours of a marine biologist working in the region during this period.

---

[5] In 1994, under the Operational Programme for Local Urban and Rural Development (OPLURD), the initial pilot project was extended to 38 partnership companies in Designated Areas of Disadvantage and 33 community groups in Non-Designated Areas of Disadvantage. Funding increased considerably from £0.5 million in the pilot phase to £112 million over the period 1994-1999 (Crooks 2000).

[6] People Against Unemployment in Limerick.

Although there was much interest among the local community councils in operation at this time, the level of state interest was minimal. It took another four to five years, however, before the expressed interest in shellfish production and the research that was subsequently undertaken was transformed into action. Under the first Poverty Programme, from 1976-1980, the Community Action Project in the area initiated a number of efforts which led to the formation of a loose group of individuals interested in shellfish production. This subsequently led to the formation of Killary Co-operative, which was registered in 1982. In this year, a submission was made to the (now defunct) Youth Employment Agency to provide funding, for two training programmes, one of which was concerned with mussel production. This application was successful and led to the development of a training programme targeted at young people aged 18-25 years living in the area. While the project had limited success in its early years it was not until the formation of FORUM in 1989 that the momentum needed to develop the shellfish sector took hold.

FORUM – Organisation and Structures

The structure of the 'Poverty 3' programme required the model action projects to adopt a 'partnership' approach to development as well as having a multidimensional and integrated focus in its work programme. The FORUM organisation was and continues to be managed by a partnership committee of statutory agencies (health, education, training and local government) and the community/voluntary sector. It established six sub-committee groups with representation from these actors and other interests. The original sub-committees included 'un- and underemployment', 'the elderly', 'youth', 'women', 'community development' and 'education'. Since 1994, when Poverty 3 ended, FORUM has continued to operate with similar structures but with funding from the Irish Government, through the Department of Social, Community and Family Affairs Community Development Project. It also receives management grant aid from FAS (National Training Authority) to provide management advice and administrative services to a number of shellfish co-operatives.

Since its inception in 1989, FORUM, principally through the 'un- and under-employment subcommittee, has been engaged in a number of initiatives that have attempted to maximise the number of local people benefiting from shellfish production in the bays of North West Connemara. It has focused particularly on those who are disadvantaged and unable, without intervention, to set up their own farms. It was recognised quite early on by FORUM that the marine environment offered considerable potential to many low income families to gain full-time, part-time and seasonal employment by farming marine animals, mainly mussels and oysters. It was expressed clearly by FORUM that the target group for their shellfish production strategy should be drawn primarily from the local youth population, particularly those in the 18-25 year age cohort. The main work of FORUM in relation to this group has been the provision of training and practical assistance in setting up their own independent farms. Through the development of the shellfish co-operatives and collaboration with the local schools and Youthreach centre it has sought to strengthen the base from which young people can earn a sustainable living from the area's natural resources. In essence, FORUM has supported the co-operatives to become stronger and more efficient (see below) and assisted individuals with licence grant aid and loan applications. A development officer from Bord Iascaigh Mhara (BIM) was also employed through FORUM to animate and support the local co-operative arrangements in the area, through technical assistance and scientific research.

While the work of FORUM has been an ongoing process with producers, it is perhaps easier to appreciate its work in the context of the PESCA programme which it implemented in three stages over the 1995-2000 period.

Recent Programme of Activity – PESCA

Between 1995 and 2000 FORUM was involved in the implementation of three PESCA programmes in the area, with a total budget of £140,000 (177,800 Euros). The programmes have benefited at least twenty-six individuals, many of whom are aged less than 25 years.

The PESCA programmes were operated in close collaboration with the main shellfish organisations in North West Connemara – Killary Mussel Co-operative, the North Connemara Marine Co-operative and the recently formed Connemara Shellfish Producers' Co-operative. The most developed organisation in the area is the Killary Co-op, which is concerned with mussel cultivation, while the North Connemara Marine Co-op – concerned with oyster production – has effectively ceased operation. The Shellfish Producers' Co-op is, however, a loose organisation of those who were formerly involved with the North Connemara Marine Co-op. The distinction between the organisations is based primarily on two different types of farming – mussel and oyster production. Unlike mussel producers, oyster farmers have only begun production quite recently, in the last four to five years. In this regard, oyster production is still quite low and has not yet reached its full potential in terms of output. The returns from mussel cultivation also outweigh oyster production, where start up costs, in terms of the cost of seed,[7] are particularly high.

Killary Co-operative and Mussel Production Membership of Killary Co-operative consists of ten to twelve active producers. The co-op, which currently produces approximately 400-500 tonnes of mussels per annum, provides boats, equipment and landing gear to its members. Through the co-operative structure producers sell to a number of distributors, one in Galway and the other in Mayo, who then sell to the main market for mussels, France. It is estimated that a 3-4 hectare farm, producing 30-50 tonnes of mussels per year, is the optimum level for creating a full-time viable job in this type of farming. The return from mussels is approximately £450 per tonne (572 Euros). However, the Killary harbour has

---

[7] With oyster cultivation, the seed must be supplied by hatcheries. Mussels, on the other hand, occur naturally in the wild and so there are not the same costs for seed.

reached its full capacity in terms of the number of producers farming the bay, with the result that it is likely licenses will no longer be issued to new producers.

As part of the PESCA programme, training and the upgrading of the co-operative's equipment and facilities were provided. Training activity involved the construction and deployment of 50 barrel long lines onto licensed areas owned by the co-op. Training also involved participants in the ordering and pricing of materials. Overall, fifteen trainees participated in all or some of the training activities. Having leased the long lines from the co-op, from which they produced mussels to market size, trainees were encouraged to apply for their own licenses so that they could begin their own farm units on completion of the training programme. FORUM assisted these individuals in acquiring licences and applying for grant aid. In addition to on-site training a series of lectures and workshops were provided by both Bord Iascaigh Mhara (BIM)[8] and the Department of Marine and Natural Resources on a range of subjects such as mussel biology, purification schemes and shellfish toxins. As well as the upgrading of equipment on the co-operative's harvesting boat, a mussel landing and training area was constructed as part of the programme. Trainees were also instructed on the use of all facilities and equipment.

In addition to these actions FORUM has also been involved and continues to have some involvement in the following key activities with Killary Co-operative:

- It helped compile a three-year development plan with the Board of Management.
- Research was undertaken on market outlets for produce.
- Processors were targeted to ensure sales continuity.
- It organised co-operation between buyers on special quality product status to obtain premium prices.
- A weekly sampling programme was co-ordinated.[9]
- It submitted to and met with the Department of the Marine on licensing issues and campaigned for a planned development approach for the bay.
- It piloted trials on new species of shellfish.

An analysis of the change in producers and production levels suggests that the FORUM partnership has had a good deal of success in quantitative terms. For instance, in 1982, at the start-up time of the co-operative, five or six individuals were producing an annual tonnage of 15 tonnes of mussels, with a primary value of £6,000 (in 1984 terms). This had increased to 18 producers in 1999, producing around 600 tonnes, with an estimated value of £270,000 (342,900 Euros). It is suggested that this could increase further to 1,000 tonnes, valued at £450,000 (571,500 Euros). What is less apparent from the quantitative account is the 'process' and 'qualitative' shift in developmental terms. In a community

---

[8] The statutory Fisheries Development Board.

[9] This is a particularly significant activity in the current environment where the build up of harmful toxins to humans (but not mussels) is a constant concern. Monitoring is required twice a week in some cases.

development sense, there has been a particularly significant development of skills and knowledge among people in the area and a marked increase in the community's confidence and ability to influence local economic development.

North Connemara Shellfish Producers Co-operative and Oyster Production
Although oyster production is currently quite low in the area it is steadily increasing and has the potential to offer farmers a significant return compared to mussel cultivation. With a return of £1,100 per tonne (1,397 Euros) this crop is particularly attractive. There are currently twelve oyster producers and two producers interested in the development of clams affiliated to the Shellfish Producers' Co-operative, which registered in 1999. Many producers in this group had participated in a Community Employment Scheme sponsored by the North Connemara Marine Co-operative a number of years earlier. Overall, production is approximately 25 tonnes per annum in the region, although this output would need to approximate 250 tonnes per annum for it to have a significant impact as a resource development. Members of the co-operative farm several bays of North West Connemara, namely Roundstone, Clifden, Streamstown and Ballinakill. A good deal of assistance was provided by FORUM is setting up the organisation through licence and grant applications while they were successful in obtaining a grant of £16,000 (20,320 Euros) for seeding from Galway Rural Development Company (a joint LEADER and OPLURD partnership company).

Through the PESCA programme and in collaboration with the North Connemara Marine Co-op, training was provided to producers, including the ordering of seed and the preparation of orders for the market place. Site visits to various relevant operations throughout the country also took place. In addition, a number of consignments of juvenile seed were purchased from a variety of suppliers which enabled the co-op to experiment with grades and densities on their farm site. With this group of producers, the programme was successful in highlighting the merits of oyster production techniques. The PESCA programme has continued to assist this group through training and the purchase of equipment. Training consisted of sessions of relevance to the running and managing of their group. Capital assistance has been provided through the purchase of a mobile shaker grader for use among its members. Oyster cylinders were also purchased and trials were carried out at various sites.

Other types of assistance provided to the Co-op by FORUM include:

- The drawing up of a charter for successful development of oyster farming in the region.
- Facilitation of discussions on site expansion for new and existing members.
- Meeting owners of Ballinakill fisheries with a view to leasing the fishery.
- Testing animals and sediments of Ballinakill harbour for toxins.

Oyster producers face significant barriers in terms of developing production to its full potential. The development of land-based facilities – for purification, grading and packing – has been recognised as a particular need by producers in the area.

Also of critical importance to producers, in terms of control and add-on value, is the development of a hatchery or early nursery system for seed development. As it currently operates, producers need to make significant investments in an environment that can be quite uncertain in terms of returns. For instance, the purchase of 500,000 finger-sized oysters requires an investment of £5,000 (6,350 Euros), which does not necessarily guarantee successful results.

North Connemara Marine Co-operative This co-operative was established in the early 1990s with a view to reseeding the oyster beds in Ballinakill Bay which was undertaken in partnership with Bord Iascaigh Mhara and a local private hatchery company. While the reseeding programme has had limited success, the farm belonging to the co-operative has moved from an economic role to one used for educational training and demonstration purposes. FORUM provided the following services to the co-op:

- management advice and back-up administration;
- assistance with work plan for Community Employment Scheme;
- purchase of seed;
- presentation to CE participants and other members on how quality production should be undertaken;
- spot sampling for toxins.

Youthreach Sshellfish Training Programme FORUM engaged with the Vocational Education Committee (VEC) and Bord Iascaigh Mhara (BIM) in devising an innovative teaching/training module to trainees of the Youthreach programme (see Irish National Report). Ten trainees took part in the 'oyster module' which began in November 1998. The module is directly delivered by a member of the North Connemara Marine Co-operative who is employed by the VEC.[10] FORUM and BIM both provide back up assistance to the training programme. The module involves developing young people's skills in constructing materials and equipment, setting up a small on-site farm, care and maintenance of the farm and other aspects of animal biology and husbandry techniques.

Conclusion

Fishing has a long history in the North West Connemara area as a means of supplementing the local population's income. The area is endowed with a natural resource base that has been increasingly targeted for economic purposes since the 1980s, particularly in relation to aquaculture, or 'fish-farming'.[11] The increased incorporation of capital within the aquaculture sector is most evident in the salmon

---

[10] A statutory body operating at local level with responsibility for providing vocational and technical education.

[11] In order of economic importance, the main sectors within aquaculture in Ireland are salmon, trout and shellfish production, with shellfish production still regarded as being in its infancy in terms of output.

industry, where foreign capital has taken control and resulted in intensive production processes.[12] However, the shellfish sector has provided considerable potential as a means of developing sustainable development, in social and economic terms. It was recognised early on by many community activists that it is not enough to simply generate economic development without considering the more fundamental questions as to who benefits from the economic growth and how the benefits are distributed in a way that reflects the needs of the local community. In this sense, the case study here can be described as a demonstration in effective 'bottom-up' partnership development. However, the nature of the partnership can not be detached from the strength of local community development that has existed in the region over a long period of time.

Describing the process of natural resource development in the region requires that we compare current production activity to that which existed in the past. In quantitative terms there has been a substantial increase in the numbers of producers and production levels in the area over a twenty-year period. What is less apparent from these indicators is the changing 'process' and 'qualitative' shifts in developmental terms. From a community development perspective, there now exists a greater degree of control and ownership among local dwellers over the resource being developed. This has meant that the types of interventions undertaken by FORUM in the past are no longer appropriate in the sense they once were. Much of the operational procedure of shellfish farming is now controlled by the co-operative structures while knowledge and husbandry skills are shared among producers themselves.[13] Having instigated the strategic aspects of development, the knowledge and skills-base has achieved a level where it can be reproduced more effectively among community members now and in the future. Many young people are now engaged in full-time and part-time work on independent farms as a result of FORUM's efforts to shape a viable sector of the local economy and its enhancement of the infrastructural and skills-base in the region. As an effort in community 'capacity-building', the most striking outcome can be found in the increased confidence and ability on the part of actors in the community to affect future developments.[14] The challenge in the future will be to maintain that momentum and adhere to the fundamental ethos that has inspired change in the region, namely collective and co-operative action for social, economic and environmental sustainability.

---

[12] In 1991, 60 per cent of one salmon farm in NWC was owned by a Norwegian tobacco manufacturing company, while the second was, by and large, under the ownership of a large Irish tobacco manufacturer, Carrolls (Ruddy and Varley 1991, cited in Tovey 1996).

[13] In an interview with the BIM Development Officer (2 November 2000) he described how he is re-evaluating his role in relation to aquacultural development in the area. He sees his future role as more research-oriented rather than 'transferring knowledge and skills' to producers. Similarly, in an interview with the FORUM manager (15 November 2000) it was suggested that FORUM's role in relation to shellfish production would change from its animation and strategic development position in the past.

[14] As described by the FORUM manager (15 November 2000).

3. Young People and Integrated Support Service Provision

Case Study 2: Moray, Scotland

The following case study outlines the efforts of a partnership arrangement in North East Scotland in its involvement with intensive and preventative support services for socially excluded young people in the region. The analysis is based on the work of a recent organisation working in the Moray region, not far from Angus, known as the YOUTHSTART Partnership.

Location, Context and Origins

The region of Moray, located in North East Scotland and south of the Moray Firth, constitutes the geographical boundary within which this case study is framed. With a population estimated at 86,510 in 1996, the region occupies an area of 2,200 square kilometres, comprising mainly farmland, fishing villages and mountainous countryside. While Moray is the eight largest unitary authority area in Scotland, its population is the fourth lowest of mainland authorities, which means that it has one of the lowest population densities in the country. Most of the population lives in the towns and environs of Elgin, Forres, Buckie, Keith and Lossiemouth. The region is also noted for having the lowest average weekly earnings of the 21 unitary authorities surveyed in the 1997 'New Earnings Survey'.

The Moray YOUTHSTART Partnership is an organisation comprising partners from the statutory, community/voluntary and private sectors who work within a broad range of services in the region, including health, housing and employment (see Appendix 4 for list of partners). The origins of the Partnership are framed within the context of a new policy environment emerging in Scotland in relation to tackling social exclusion. In 1997, a Social Exclusion Network was established by the Secretary of State for Scotland, which comprised senior officials responsible for developing a corporate approach to promoting social inclusion at Government level. Subsequently, a new group known as the Scottish Social Inclusion Network was put in place to develop a Social Inclusion Strategy. Membership of this network consists of representatives of organisations with direct responsibility for promoting social inclusion and individuals with direct, personal experience of combating social exclusion, drawn from the community and statutory sectors. Its role has been to advise Government on its social inclusion strategy and to improve co-ordination between agencies. As part of the Social Inclusion Strategy, 47 Social Inclusion Partnerships (SIPs) will be established throughout Scotland on both an area-based and thematic (youth, older people, etc.) approach.[15] Overall funding for the SIPs amounts to £48 million over a period of

---

[15] In addition to designating new Social Inclusion Partnerships, the Government have converted existing Priority Partnership Areas (PPAs) and Regeneration Programme areas to SIPs, with a renewed emphasis on social inclusion and regenerating communities (Scottish Office Press Release 19/03/1999; http://www.scotland.gov.uk/news/releas99_3/pr0700.htm).

three years,[16] although the various partners are expected to support the partnership work by providing resources from their mainstream budgets (Scottish Office 1999). While SIPs are directly concerned with particular areas of disadvantage, several SIPs target young people in urban and rural areas of Scotland that are most at risk of social exclusion. The remit of these SIPs is to promote interagency co-operation in the provision of support and advice to young people and to improve service delivery and development for vulnerable youth.[17] The main areas of activity include health promotion, tackling youth homelessness, improving life skills of young people and assisting their transitions from school to further education, training, employment and independent living.

Moray YOUTHSTART Partnership – Organisation and Structures

The Moray YOUTHSTART Partnership emerged out of this new process and was established in April 1999 as a result of a successful Social Inclusion Partnership bid made to the Scottish Executive by the Moray council. The programme is funded until March 2002, although there are provisions for it to continue another two years after this date. The principal aim of the YOUTHSTART Strategy is to foster preventative, community-based services as a means of providing more effective support to children and young people. The target group at the centre of the Partnership's work programme is the 16-24 year age group, of which there are approximately 10,200 young people living in the region. However, a more recent initiative known as the 'Childcare Strategy' targets a younger age profile, namely those in the 10-18 year age cohort.[18] It is primarily those activities with the 16-24 year age group that informs this case study analysis.

In promoting a preventative, community-based services approach the Partnership views its strategy as challenging the traditional approaches to provision which it views as 'reactive' and 'institutional' in form, and creating too many pressure points at the 'high' end of service provision, particularly in residential and ancillary support services. The Partnership believes it is necessary to 'squeeze' the pressure points through the different service providers into preventative community based actions. As pressure is lessened through the early involvement of agencies, it maintains that the spiral of social exclusion can be prevented. It recognises that encouraging and supporting voluntary action from within the community is a crucial part of this strategy. This is reflected in its mission statement which outlines its vision in the following terms: "to meet the needs of

---

[16] An additional programme, known as "Listening to Communities" is also being developed by the Scottish Executive, to facilitate communities in participating in decision-making processes. It will provide £3 million over three years.

[17] 'The Excluded Young People Action Team' was established as part of the Social Inclusion Strategy and was asked to report to the Scottish Social Inclusion Network on how social exclusion among young people could be effectively tackled. It reported in 1999.

[18] The Childcare Strategy was adopted in 1997 and is a partnership between the Moray Council and two national voluntary organisations. In combination, the Youthstart Partnership and Childcare Strategy are seen as integrating the service needs of young people between 10 and 24 years of age, providing a continuity in care and support.

children and young people in their own families and communities wherever possible". The aims are set out as follows: "to ensure all young people in Moray have genuine opportunities to become full and active citizens, to contribute toward and benefit from, living in a healthy community". It also acknowledges the danger that since 'prevention' is difficult to measure and that 'community' equates with 'non-statutory', the possibility of losing priority in policy terms is a very real issue.

The stated objectives and priorities of the Partnership are fourfold:

- To assist vulnerable, excluded young people to sustain ordinary living and break the cycle of exclusion.
- To support disaffected young people through difficult transitions, to prevent exclusion and avoid the need for reactive, intensive services.
- To encourage and enable young people to become positive, active citizens within their local communities.
- To strengthen co-operation and co-ordination between Partners and with relevant other networks and initiatives (Moray YOUTHSTART Partnership Annual Report 2000).

While the entire region of Moray falls within the work of the Partnership its actions have been prioritised to meet the needs of particular vulnerable groups and areas of acute disadvantage. The strategy it adopts comprises four key components, namely: (i) the use of intensive community-based support for vulnerable young people; (ii) building on established links and rural area networks, developed through the 'rural family project', to promote community development; (iii) increasing the accessibility to community facilities for vulnerable youth; and (iv) supporting accommodation within a "scattered" foyer approach, initially in the West Moray area of Forres, which has a youth unemployment rate 50% above the national average.

The Board of the Partnership comprises senior officers of the local council as well as representatives from voluntary, charity and private interests. According to the Annual Report (2000), the level of private and voluntary sector involvement with the Board and working groups has increased over the first year of its operation. Their function is to set targets, commission activities and monitor performance. They are supported in this process by the Partnership Co-ordinator who was employed in December 1999. The partners usually hold meetings every two months. In addition, two working parties have been set up as sub-structures of the Board and concern the 'Youth Fora' and 'Housing'. The aims of its organisational framework are set out in the following terms:

- to be inclusive of all partners;
- to support the involvement of young people;
- to enable effective decision-making;
- to ensure lead responsibilities and delegations are unambiguous;
- to avoid unnecessary bureaucracy and meetings.

Within the framework the Partnership has proposed to establish a Youth Congress for involving the various partners and young people throughout Moray, through which they can review progress and objectives and identify strategic priorities.[19] At the local level, it is also planned that a number of Youth Fora will develop with the purpose of meeting Partner providers and commissioners to consider local issues and potential developments. The Partnership is still in the process of ratifying its constitution which will outline the operational aspects of the organisation. The constitution still requires agreement from the Youth Congress. From this, it is expected that two Youth Representatives will become members of the Board.

Current Activities and Future Plans

Related to each individual objective identified above, the Partnership has outlined a range of actions within its overall strategy. For each of the Partnership's programmes a number of core partners take a lead responsibility for its overall development, in the context of the Partnership structure. These activities are now summarised under each objective.

Objective 1: To Assist Vulnerable, Excluded Young People to Sustain Ordinary Living and Break the Cycle of Exclusion

There are two principal actions associated with this objective: (i) Intensive Support Service in Employment and (ii) Intensive Support Services in relation to Homelessness.

Intensive Support Service in Employment The partners involved in this project are Moray Youth Action (part of Aberlour Child Care Trust; voluntary sector) and the Moray Council (education and social work departments; statutory sector). Lead responsibility is taken by the former organisation who were responsible for establishing a programme known as the "16-18 Employment Initiative" prior to the Social Inclusion Partnership. The "16-18 Employment Initiative" is the principal project related to this objective, although the Partnership's emphasis on preventative work has had implications for this activity. Many of the young people originally helped through this project had experienced breakdowns in previous educational involvement, through social, emotional and behavioural difficulties. Intensive programme were put in place over a period of 12 weeks and comprised life-skills training and vocational skills development through workshop activity. The programme has close links with approximately 30 firms in the region who provide young people with work experience. However, in the first year of the Partnership's activities, a number of factors have led the Partnership to refocus the project to include the "15+Moving On Project", another initiative with a preventative, earlier intervention approach. The factors which have led to the Partnership's re-evaluation of the initiative include:

---

[19] The first meeting of the Congress was planned for 28/11/2000.

- recognition that new providers had moved into this area of work in Moray;
- less referrals were being made to the initiative. The lower number of referrals to the Employment Initiative may be attributed in part to the development of a local training and mentoring project initiated by the Forres Challenge Project, with assistance from the Partnership and the Drug Action Team;
- the success of the project in the first year was less than that during the pilot phase for reasons that relate to some participants having multiple offences and being unable to participate fully.

According to a social justice evaluation of the "16-18 Employment Initiative" (Forrest n.d.):

> It is clear from this case study that programmes which seek to enhance the employability of vulnerable, disaffected young people require a complex mix of formal professional support from a range of agencies. It is also evident that an agency able to offer an informal befriending or mentoring has the potential to enhance the prospects of employability. (p. 4)

The Moray Youth Action is viewed as an exemplary organisation for self-learning and one where internal self-evaluation and on-going self-management provides a setting for education, work experience and research (p. 80).

Intensive Support Services in Relation to Homelessness The Moray Council is the lead organisation with regard to this support service, while the active partners include National Children's Homes (NCH) Action for Children (voluntary), Moray Youth Action (voluntary) and Langstane Housing Association (voluntary). This work has involved the development of a scheme known as the 'scattered foyer' project whereby Social Housing Providers in the West Moray region contribute towards a suitable accommodation pool for young people. It is recognised that many young people are unable to manage their own affairs fully without the risk of losing their tenancy or developing other difficulties. This action aims to provide 'tailored' support programmes to its participants through a 'Housing Initiative' that combines advice and supports in relation to budgeting, education and employment. Through the 'foyer' system a more integrated service for young people is envisaged whereby services are provided in one central location. The scheme plans to have a small central unit and some 'scattered' flats across different locations in Moray, as not everyone wishes to live in Elgin, the location of the central unit. The overall aim is to reduce homelessness by 50% at the end of Year 2 of the scheme. It is hoped that by the end of Year 2 there would be a revolving stock of eight units available to the scheme. In the first year of its operation, the Langstane Housing Association (voluntary) purchased three properties for use within the project. In terms of general supports, the NCH 16-24 Housing Support Team (voluntary) received 37 referrals within the year, 24 of whom were homeless or threatened with homelessness. The Annual Report (2000) indicates that 30 young people were directly 'supported' through its activities. The Moray Youth Action organisation also provided intensive support services to five young people with 'borderline' learning difficulties.

Objective 2: Support Disaffected Young People Through Difficult Transitions, to Prevent Exclusion and Avoid the Need for Reactive, Intensive Services

Within this objective there are a range of activities, including the "15+ Moving On" Project that allows young people to gain work experience and develop a range of skills. This project is targeted at young people still in school but who are at risk of leaving the mainstream education system. The programme has its own centre where young people engage in practical training skills. Meetings take place regularly between the participants and tutors with the purpose of identifying and encouraging young people's progress. Sixteen young people received a service from the project in the first year of YOUTHSTART. One indicator of success of the project is the non-referral of participants to the "16-18 Employment Initiative" (see above). There has also been growing interest among secondary schools throughout the region that the project be expanded to include their students, which is a task identified for the remainder of the project.

Other activities as part of the preventative work include 'mentoring', promoting Youth Fora (see above) and Local Action Plans. As part of the work, research still needs to be undertaken to map the level of existing community-based services to young people to gain a better understanding of the challenges facing youth and to assess the role of service providers. It is envisaged that following the Youth Congress the first four (of eight) areas will be identified from which work can proceed. Four part-time youth workers (described as 'detached' or outreach workers) will be undertaken by existing staff. The identified tasks regarding this programme of activity include: engaging with local agency and 'stakeholder' networks; organising local 'forum formation' events; creating and prioritising local action plans; obtaining 'seed-corn' funding for the agreed local priorities; providing training and support to the local for a and networks.

Two development workers – a "Young People's Health Development Worker" and a "Teenage Parents Project Worker" – were appointed to undertake preventative work with young people at risk of social exclusion in the region and their roles are viewed as complementary to the wider strategy of the Partnership. In the future it is hoped that there will be more effective integration of local developments with these 'thematic' preventative services.

In its first year the Partnership supported a number of community-based projects including a peer-support group for young care-leavers; the creation of a bursary fund to enable disadvantaged youth to experience the Atlantic Challenge Moray Gig; a planned Forres Youth Café and FareTravel, a scheme designed to overcome access problems in sport and leisure through the provision of subsidised fares at weekends and evenings. These projects directly involved youth in terms of identifying needs, planning or both. Over the remainder of the programme there are plans to improve access to information through the development of a Youth Information Service with the Community Safety Strategy Task Group (of the Grampian Police) and 'Dataplace' (a local charitable organisation).

Objective 3: Encourage and Enable Young People to Become Positive, Active Citizens Within their Local Communities

The active partners regarding this objective include the Moray Council (statutory), Grampian Health Promotions (statutory), Grampian Police and Children 1st (charity). Work activity at this level has primarily consisted of planning, alongside the Community Learning Strategy, the Community Safety Plan and the Community Planning exercises. The Partnership initiated an "Open Space"[20] youth consultation exercise, with representatives from a number of working groups and young people. From this it is expected that the first Moray Youth Congress would be held in November 2000 and that the selection of localities for inclusion in the Youth Fora, Local Networks and Local Action Plans would commence. An officer with responsibility for "Children and Young Person's Rights and Representations" was appointed in January 2000 and her initial work primarily involved familiarisation, becoming known in the communities and establishing operational ground rules. A "Youth Inclusion Development" worker was also employed at this time and his work consisted in setting up the "Open Space" exercise and facilitating young people's involvement with this, commencing work on a Youth Services Directory and information service, setting up a Scottish Youth Parliament and planning for Partnership newsletters.

Objective 4: To Strengthen Co-operation and Co-ordination Between Partners and with Relevant Other Networks and Initiatives

In order to foster closer collaboration between partners, a number of working groups and steering committees were established for the Partnership's various initiatives and projects. The future work plan for the remainder of the programme has been outlined as the following:

- To achieve an effective, transparent, representative and adaptable organisational structure. This will involve developing the 'constitutional' document for the Partnership for agreement by all partners and the Youth Congress. It also proposes to define more clearly the relationships for developmental working groups, project steering groups and officers.
- To provide good quality information to partners and agency stakeholders. As part of this future dissemination strategy, the Partnership has indicated it will produce a bi-monthly newsletter and an interactive 'home page' on the internet. It also plans to undertake research on youth and social exclusion in the area.

---

[20] This was a consultation exercise with young people from across Moray from which they identified, with the help of a facilitator, issues they believed could make Moray a "better place to live in for young people". Small discussion forums were formed subsequently to develop their agenda for change.

- To increase net resources contributed through the Partnership. To achieve this it aims to co-ordinate funding applications and circulate funding opportunities through its newsletter.
- Shifting the balance of resources. The need to review services so that resources can be mobilised away from 'intensive' and into 'preventative' work will form the basis of future co-ordination.
- Monitoring and Evaluation. Ensuring that the programmes develop in response to young people's evaluations is key concern of the organisation. The Partnership hopes to address any mismatch between agreements/expectations and outcomes through the most effective channels. Regular reporting and identifying useful performance indicators and monitoring procedures will also feed into this process.
- Links to other strategies and initiatives. As part of this process, it hopes to clarify with Moray-wide initiatives their mutual agendas, roles, responsibilities, resources and plans.

A partnership co-ordinator was also employed in December 1999 and was invited to join the Moray Badenoch and Strathspey New Deal Steering Group, the Moray New Futures Steering Group, the Milnes New Community School Support Team and a Youth Information Services Working Group, originating from its Community Safety Strategy.

The sharing of projects and objectives among the partners has effectively added significant resources towards the Partnership's work programme. It has also meant that the partnership was able to successfully bid for additional funding, from New Futures and the Scottish Arts Council.

Conclusion

The recently formed Moray YOUTHSTART Partnership reflects a new approach to social inclusion in Scotland. In the current climate, closer collaboration of service providers is a pragmatic and potentially enabling direction for rural young people. Many actors, across a range of sectors and policy areas, have a good deal to gain from this 'partnership' arrangement. The preventive direction of the partnership as a critical guiding principle to its work programme provides a useful example of 'subsidiarity' since it advocates the development of support systems at the most immediate point to the individual, namely at family and community level. The strategic and integrated approach it adopts in supporting vulnerable young people has the potential to make significant inroads in tackling social exclusion among the youth population of Moray. In the future, the programme must learn from its piloting phase and continue to build on the benefits derived from partnership. As with all partnership arrangements, the complex process of engaging all partners in an equitable and equally influential manner requires close monitoring and evaluation. While an evaluation of the entire YOUTHSTART programme would be required in order to comment on the effectiveness of the intervention, an evaluation of the "16-18 Employment Initiative" of Moray Youth

Action highlights the benefits of partnership: "there is substantial evidence to show a strong coalition of interests evolving amongst the referral agencies and MYA. There is mutual gain for all the agencies through a sharing of resources and benefits the young person in a host of ways" (Forrest n.d. 35). The evaluator, however, outlines the underlying pressures of partnership, whereby the clash of different objectives and organisational culture among agencies results in a mixed approach towards younger people. It was suggested that the membership and functions of the Inter-agency Planning Group be reviewed and attention paid to the non-representation of particular interests such as housing, employers, trade unions and health organisations.

4. Discussion and Conclusions

The evidence presented here provides a mere snapshot of how the 'partnership' concept has been adopted in two European countries in an effort to tackle social exclusion among young people. Since the data is essentially incomplete the conclusions drawn can only be regarded as tentative. A more thoroughgoing assessment of both arrangements would be required if we are to say anything about the effectiveness of partnership as a policy instrument. However, the report provides some flavour of the processes involved in targeting rural youth in local community development and the means through which this can be made inclusive of all actors with a responsibility for defining and meeting young people's needs.

A useful starting point from which to conclude the chapter is to view 'partnership' in the context of community development. A description of community development provided by the Combat Poverty Agency in Ireland sees it as a connecting mechanism between social rights and local intervention to tackle disadvantage. It suggests that "from a social rights perspective local people need to be empowered and resourced to become involved in the political process, in the development of their own localities and in influencing and contributing to public service provision" (1991, in Curtin 1996, 266). In recent times, the means through which the community/voluntary sector has negotiated involvement in this process has typically occurred through 'partnership', principally with the state sector. As a means of fostering 'citizenship', through the incorporation and advancement of social, political and civil rights, the mechanism of 'partnership' has a good deal to offer. The effectiveness of 'partnership' in this regard is contingent upon a host of factors, including the history and extent of community activity in service provision; the degree of trust and co-operation between the various stakeholders; the level of autonomy afforded to 'partnership' and its capacity to influence policy-making. At least in rhetorical terms, it offers the chance to effect change in what can be described as innovative and flexible ways.

The case studies presented here outline two partnership approaches to combating social exclusion among young people in ways that are not radically dissimilar. Their differences are based principally on the strategies employed in tackling rural youth exclusion and the nature of community/voluntary involvement. While the Irish case study can be described as a lesson in local economic regeneration it represents, however, only one aspect of FORUM's broader strategy of empowering local communities in a multidimensional approach. The Scottish case represents an issue-based, i.e. 'youth', approach towards development. It also takes an explicitly stated 'social' and 'political' position on inclusion, particularly in relation to housing, education, work and youth participation. While both 'partnerships' have specifically targeted young people in particular geographical areas, albeit of different catchment sizes, their differences reflect the nature of governance in both countries. Firstly, the involvement of the community sector differs in terms of representation. In Ireland, community representation in the partnership was born out of the activism of the community councils that were particularly strong in the 1970s.[21] As such, there is no community representation in relation to a policy sector, such as housing or child care, as there exists in Scotland. In the Scottish case, while there appears to be co-ordination among partners and responsibility between them to take lead roles in particular activities, the Irish case suggests that it is the partnership itself that has initiated and delivered many of the programmes, overseen by the partnership management (comprising statutory, community and private actors). The form of partnership adopted in the two countries is therefore context-specific. Interestingly, while the two partnerships were established at different times, one quite recently and the other over a decade ago, they both emerge out of an 'official' recognition of the need to involve a range of actors in policy formulation and implementation. While the EU was the main instigator of the FORUM project, the more recently formed Scottish Executive has clearly indicated its regard for social inclusion partnerships as an effective policy mechanism in combating youth exclusion.

Earlier, the benefits of partnership were stated as centring on its flexibility and needs-driven approach; the harnessing of financial and human resources; its targeting and local dimensions and the capacity to draw on a combined range of experiences. In both case studies there is evidence to suggest that this approach is a sensible pragmatic one. While it is still too early to evaluate the effectiveness of the Moray YOUTHSTART partnership it is possible to point to the merits of its development strategy. The partnership adopts a multidimensional view of youth exclusion and has sought to combine the expertise of many organisations in a more closely collaborative approach. By drawing on the experiences and specialist knowledge of agencies across a range of sectors and policy areas, it has fostered an integrated strategy of including young people in their own social, psychological and civic development. It has sought to involve young people in all aspects of the decision-making process, including representation at management level. This is one of its key strengths in the pursuit of effective partnership. Another key component of its strategy has been to recognise the need for a preventative approach and not simply to deliver in crisis situations. It considers it essential to meet the needs of young people as close to their natural support systems as

---

[21] Community councils emerged from the vocationalist Muintir na Tíre organisation, founded in 1931. The councils comprised elected representatives, nominated representatives of voluntary associations and co-opted individuals. They were engaged in locally-specific social, cultural, economic, educational and recreational projects (see Curtin 1996).

practicable, namely in family and community settings. It is therefore a close approximation to the notion of 'subsidiarity', an approach favoured particularly by the European Union.

The Irish case study of natural resources and the inclusion of young people in local economic development is an older experience. As such it has demonstrated many significant results in the inclusion of marginalised or disadvantaged young people in their local communities. The approach has been one which recognises the need to develop and maintain sustainable economic development; essentially one where the economic benefits derive from local control and ownership. This concern for locally determined development is an important one. In marginalised communities located along Europe's peripheral regions there is understandable concern as to how social and economic development decisions are taken and to what effect. In the case of FORUM it was recognised that engaging in a 'partnership' approach offered an effective means of combating the worse effects of rural economic restructuring. As part of its strategy it continued to build on the achievements of local community development that existed in the region over a longer period before the introduction of 'partnership' from the European Union. As highlighted in this particular case, young people have benefited from a development agenda that purports to countervail 'exogenous' influences or the vagaries of externally owned businesses that can, at the stroke of a pen, decide to relocate to other more profitable locations. The development model pursued by FORUM is one that promotes petty commodity production, similar to conventional farming, where labour and capital are controlled by individuals working in co-operative arrangements.

This chapter has outlined the processes of partnership in two distinct, yet similar, contexts. While it is difficult to make generalisations across a European front, there are many benefits to be accrued from a partnership model. Notwithstanding the complexities of the approach and the potential for conflict, the strategic integrated tackling of social exclusion through the combined efforts of those with knowledge of and expertise in young people's affairs, including youth themselves and their local communities, presents a potentially influential public policy instrument throughout Europe. While there is a need to view partnership firmly in the context of how governance is performed in individual countries it is not unreasonable to assume that it will attain greater prominence in future public policy initiatives of some Member States.

Chapter 8

Rural Development Programmes and their Impact on Youth Integration

Thomas Dax, Ingrid Machold and Christine Meisinger

1. Introduction

With structural adjustment and integration of agriculture into the rural economy the concern for the development of rural areas in general has risen considerably over the last decades. Rural policy is no more primarily about agriculture but has to address specifically all different economic sectors and actors in the area. With fundamental changes in the market structures and relations, programmes targeted at specific rural areas cannot neglect the emerging interrelations to other areas. Hence a rural policy has to address directly its insertion into the regional framework and its relation to regional policy.

In recent years concern about social exclusion processes has reached also rural areas. Rising unemployment and the limited opportunities for young people have turned the attention of policy analysis to this social group. This chapter focuses on the assessment of rural development policies in the EU as they affect young people. To this end, the chapter starts with a presentation of the policy background and its evaluation, particularly with regard to its rising priority over the last EU-reforms. It continues with the investigation of a series of exemplary cases of policy measures and initiatives specifically addressing young people in rural development. In some cases a direct reference to young people's attitudes as expressed in the interviews with regard to awareness and assessment of rural policies and local initiatives is given. The concluding third section draws on evaluation studies on rural development programmes with regard to youth participation and explores the scope for future strengthening of respective activities and inclusion of young people concerns in rural development programmes.

2. Rural Development Policy

Before assessing the impact of rural development policies on young people's integration into social and economic life in rural areas we have to outline the policy background. Rural policy has received over recent years increasing political attention although there remain quite divergent views on the different concepts to be used and policy processes to serve the target of integration of sector approaches. The rural approach, albeit often alluded to as being similar to agricultural development, is in its core a territorial approach, applying regional policy measures for specific regions, the rural areas. Hence the following short introductory presentation focuses on both (a) the various policies with distinctive territorial dimensions and impact on rural areas and (b) rural development policy as addressed by EU policy reform and targeted at through EU agricultural policy via establishing a "second pillar" to Common Agricultural Policy (CAP).

Regional Policy's History – Basic Foundations of Rural Policy

In many countries of Western Europe regional and rural policy are closely interrelated and a sharp distinction between the two policy concepts cannot be drawn easily. It is therefore interesting to present here some remarks on the background of broader territorial schemes as expressed under the term regional policy.

In countries of Western Europe regional policy was introduced during the 1920s as a reaction to the strengthening of spatial disparities and the emergence of the first depressed regions, induced by sectoral crises (Artobolevskiy 1997, 32). All over the period since then social objectives have been the most important ones for regional policy. Though it was not officially established in all west European countries, in most countries key words depicting the main problems and regions of a country had been created by the start of the 1960s (e.g. Mezzo-giorno in Italy, Northern peripheral areas in Scandinavia, mountain regions). Many of these regional problem areas implicitly had a strong rural bias since large regional support areas covered regions with deeply rural characteristics. With rising criticism of regional policy in the 1970s and 1980s focus shifted towards policy priorities for increasing economic efficiency of the country. In many developed countries this led to a partial curtailment of regional policy and a reorientation from social to economic objectives.

It was only in the 1980s that the European structural policy which had previously just complemented national policies developed into a substantial Community structural policy. With the start of the reform of the Structural Funds the investment and volume had to correspond to the following 3 regional priority objectives since 1 January 1989:

- Objective 1: promoting the development and structural adjustment of regions whose development is lagging behind;
- Objective 2: converting the regions or parts of regions seriously affected by industrial decline;
- Objective 5b: facilitating the development and structural adjustment of rural areas.

The second reform of Structural Funds in 1993 confirmed the approach taken and EU-commitment for regional policy has been deepened continuously over the

1990s. Moreover, the Cohesion Fund, established with the Maastricht Treaty, has provided an additional instrument to support the four lagging EU-countries Greece, Spain, Ireland and Portugal in the preparation for the Monetary Union since 1993, and simultaneously to the economic growth process. With the EU-accession of the Scandinavian countries Finland and Sweden the situation of sparsely populated areas was acknowledged as a distinct problem pattern and led to a further regional priority objective:

- Objective 6: development and structural adjustment of regions with an extremely low population density

In the last decade the EU-measures to strengthen the cohesion and structures in less-developed regions have gained a substantive portion of the EU-budget. Since the second half of the 1990s the four Structural Funds and the Cohesion Fund together account for one third of the EU-budget which means about 0.5% of the yearly GDP of the EU-countries (Europäische Kommission 1996, 89). The four Structural Funds are:

- The European Regional Development Fund (ERDF);
- The European Social Fund (ESF);
- The European Agricultural Guidance and Guarantee Fund (EAGGF);
- The Financial Instrument for Fisheries Guidance (FIFG).

Besides the European Union has two more major financial instruments to implement its structural policies, the Cohesion Fund and loans from the European Investment Bank (EIB) which are both based on a project-financing approach and are governed by their own specific rules.

The major part is covered by the first four instruments which operate within an *integrated programming* framework according to a set of principles defined in implementing regulations. The outline of the objectives of the first programming period (1989-1993) have been prolonged, in general, for the second period. The programmes of this second period (1994-1999) have addressed specific regional problems under the above mentioned objectives and focused their activities on objective 1 areas, accounting for almost 68% of total resources.

At that period the population covered by the regional objectives amounted to 51% of the EU total. Some 55% of the total resources went to 16% of the EU population in four countries – Greece, Spain, Ireland and Portugal – mostly delivered through objective 1 programmes. During the second programming period (1994-1999) the regional scope and intensity has been increased, particularly in objective 2 and objective 5b regions.

In addition to the mainstream programmes there were separate Community Initiative programmes to support transnational, cross-border and inter-regional actions organised under 13 different themes, including the LEADER (and INTERREG) programme which focus on innovative actions in rural areas and building a European network of rural actors. In addition, a small proportion of total resources, some 1%, is reserved for technical assistance, pilot projects and innovative measures.

As recent analyses by the European Commission (1999a) pointed out there is now evidence available for actual convergence of lagging regions: From 1986 to 1996 GDP per head of the 10 poorest regions increased from 41% of the EU average to 50%, and in the 25 poorest regions it rose from 52% to 59%. This trend can also be seen at the national level, as GDP per head in the four Cohesion countries went up from 65% of the EU average to 75%, and, according to forecasts, to 77% in 1999. These regional shifts have a direct impact on rural areas, although the actual performance of regions is quite diverse. Depending on the territorial level of analysis further in-depth studies and inter-regional comparisons are needed to provide an advanced assessment on the impact for (specific) rural areas.

In many respects the reform of the EU Structural Funds in 1988 was accompanied by the rise of the debate on the "The Future of Rural Society". Through the commission paper under this title (CEC 1988) rural policy gained momentum as a specific European issue. Its underlying concept contributed to trigger the ensuing discussion addressing a much wider scope of functions for rural areas than had been considered before. The concept of an integrated approach for rural development programmes were reflected especially under the objective 5b-programmes but also in the objective 1 areas. With the ongoing discussions of the subject both the funds of the regional programmes enlarged (compare 1st and 2nd period of Structural Funds programmes) and new initiatives developed.

The most interesting element of Structural Funds from the conceptual point of view is the Community Initiative LEADER (Liaison entre Actions de Développement de l'Economie Rurale). It aimed at establishing local action groups, raising their awareness for rural development action and initiating this long-termed learning process. As the focus is on innovative actions and methods an important element is seen in the networking function of this Community Initiative.

The link between agricultural structural policy and a broader territorial approach was deepened for the regions targeted during the former periods by Objective 1 and 5b (and later 6) of the Structural Funds. Incorporating all actions envisaged under the different Structural Funds into a single programming schedule, pointed to the rising role of rural areas for the aim of "economic and social cohesion". It is in particular some of the remote rural areas which suffer under the most weak economic performances.

Although the regional objectives of the structural funds directly addressed rural features particularly in the case of objective 5b ("The economic diversification of fragile rural areas") rural areas occur under all regional categories of structural funds. The greatest relevance for rural areas has therefore not been bound to objective 5b-areas but is attributed to the great share of rural areas in objective 1 regions.

The assessment of economic development of rural areas in the EU in general is therefore largely related to the lagging regions in objective 1 areas: As has been mentioned previously there is evidence for convergence, as shown by figures for the poorest regions. However, at the same time disparities at the regional and particularly local levels persist (in particular, comparing poorest and richest regions) and call for ongoing Structural Funds programmes.

With Agenda 2000 reform the Structural Funds programmes have been concentrated. The territorial and programme concentration intended to reach particularly regions and people most in need of support and to avoid overlapping activities. Moreover, the period for Structural Funds programmes has been extended to seven years (2000-2006) which should allow to achieve longer-term targeting of the programmes through the continued commitment for objective areas. Actually the share of EU population covered by the regional objectives has been decreased to about 41% (and for national support areas to 35%). The objectives of the Structural Funds have been reduced to the three following ones:

- Objective 1: Development and structural adjustment of regions whose development is lagging behind.
- Objective 2: Economic and social conversion of areas facing structural difficulties.
- Objective 3: Adaptation and modernisation of policies and systems of education, training and employment.

Also the Community Initiatives have been restructured and limited to the four prime Initiatives INTERREG, LEADER+, URBAN and EQUAL. For rural development policy it seems important to have an Initiative like LEADER+ with a large scope for innovative actions, networking activities and, what is essential for the future perspectives, relying on a structure which allows an experimental character in its measures.

The actual rural development policy of the EU can therefore not be assessed easily by analysing one type of programme, but has to include elements from the following different EU-programmes, inter-linkages between these programmes, and further territorial actions provided by other programmes:

- Objective 2 areas (new), particularly those parts focusing on problem of rural areas
- LEADER+ programmes, Rural Development Plans, according to Reg. (EC) 1257/1999.

What has been said above, seems to be even more relevant to this period. The host of measures for rural areas have to be seen within Objective 1-programmes, and horizontal programmes (like Objective 3); moreover, other Community Initiatives, like INTERREG and partly also EQUAL, as well as local action group work, e.g. local AGENDA 21 and environment actions is of utmost concern to rural development. Having outlined the wide field of actions impacting on rural development it becomes clear that such a wide concept is not captured by the actual policy but lends itself heavily to the discussion of territorial development policy. It seems, however, promising that over the last years the preparation of the European Spatial Development Perspective – ESDP (CEC 1999b) has shown the readiness for addressing such viewpoints at a European level and, particularly, the high relevance of rural issues and its territorial implications on the agenda.

Evolution of EU Policies for Rural Development

Most EU documents state that the main means of support for rural areas of the European Union was the Common Agricultural Policy (CAP) and this still remains the case to some extent. This reflects also public opinion where rural is still strongly equated with agriculture or, at least, is seen as primarily agriculture driven.

The distribution of CAP aid within the farming community, in general, does not address territorial aspects and is often described as being quite regressive: "the main beneficiaries have not been the smaller farmers and poorer regions but the larger farmers and more prosperous agricultural regions" (Lowe et al. 1999, 57). The original EC member states were not concerned with regional inequalities and only the British Government saw regional assistance as a counterweight to CAP spending, and in 1975 the European Regional Development Fund (ERDF) and the Less Favoured Areas (LFA) scheme were set up. The LFA programme authorised member states to pay financial compensation to farmers operating in mountains and other "less favoured areas" in order to ensure the continuation of farming, thereby maintaining a minimum population level, or conserving the countryside. The programme operated very early through direct income payments to farmers and directly indicated through its aims the tight inter-relationship of agriculture and environment, particularly in such areas. However, from the introduction of LFA support to the appreciation of its impact on environmental performance under Agenda 2000 decisions was a rather long way (Dax and Hellegers 2000). At first, possibilities of support were broadened through the introduction of "integrated development programmes" (in 1979), particularly shaped to the need of Southern European countries through the Integrated Mediterranean Programmes (in 1985). After the commission paper on "The Future of Rural Society" in 1988 rural development has been seen largely on the way to be stronger integrated into Structural Funds programmes (see above). The designated "rural areas" under objective 5b and the LEADER Initiative are strong indication of this. The LFA scheme was drawn into the new Objective 5a combining together the horizontal measures for the improvement of agricultural structures. With the starting of the discussion of Agenda 2000 proposal, particularly induced by the Cork Declaration in 1996, discussion on the future of agricultural support and rural development policy and its relationship broke out. The outcome can be seen as a compromise between two opposite viewpoints: It attaches rural development more closely to agricultural administration and regulations, but on the other hand allows for some continuation of the concept of rural development going beyond agriculture. Yet, one can raise doubts about the opportunities for rural policies under these circumstances. These doubts relate both to the scope of activities being eligible or implemented as well as to the contents, e.g. with relation to its integrative capacity (c.f. Dax 1999, Lowe and Brouwer 2000).

Taking account of the broader concept of rural development within e.g. Structural Funds programmes it can by no means anymore be equated with agriculture or agriculture related development. Still many core documents (CEC 1997a) and the Regulation 1257/1999 adhere to the "old" view including rural development within agricultural policy. The concept of the "second pillar" of EU agricultural policy being provided by rural development also takes the agrarian viewpoint as starting point.

Integration Approach of Rural Development

However, there is concern and discussion on the widening of the concept, including the difficulties of acceptability in society and implementation in administration structures (e.g. Buckwell et al. 1997). In many different fields the interest for rural specificity has evolved and led to intensified debate. This concerns both the territorial dimension, and in particular regional policy which has extended its field of interest to local development processes and the interactions between different parts of the territory, in particular rural and urban areas. Besides the insertion of the discussion in the conceptualisation and implementation of the new Structural funds programmes for the period 2000-2006 these issues have been outlined and agreed upon in the European Spatial Development Programme (ESDP, CEC 1999b). Other policies, like environment, tourism, traffic etc. have to deal with their territorial impacts, and hence an assessment of the rural dimension. This wide concept has been particularly discussed over the last decade within OECD which tried to develop a common framework to provide orientation for the diverse national approaches towards advancing in the direction of a comprehensive rural policy in the interest of the society as well as rural people. Analysing the challenge of rural policy with a territorial perspective which allowed for recognition of individual place specific needs and underlined the importance of exchange with other areas, this phase of OECD work on rural development provided momentum to the international debate and strongly influenced the understanding of EU development of rural areas as well. Both the conceptual framework (OECD 1993b) and the implications of the diversity of rural areas (OECD 1996a) could underline that rural areas are not doomed to failure but that policy actually matters.

Whereas previously actions for rural development had focused on its backwardness and were restricted mainly to the agricultural sector, empirical studies at the international level have confirmed that there is no uniform development trajectory. In particular, this means that rurality in itself does not automatically mean lagging economic development. In particular OECD (1996b) has revealed through the establishment of a territorially disaggregated data set that for a series of countries employment increase (in the 1980s, and some recent data suggest also for the 1990s) was higher in rural than in urban regions. The argument was taken up largely in the international discussion. In many documents issued by the EU the large diversity of conditions and trends in rural areas is pointed out now (e.g. CEC 1997a).

This heterogeneity of performance of rural areas cannot be explained sufficiently by standard economic theory. It appears that in many cases intangible aspects are the most important in "making the difference" (OECD 1998, 12f.). Thus the reason for (economic) success does not just lie with physical capital but often must be sought in human capital (the ability of people to participate in the economy) and social capital (the capacity of communities to organise themselves). Hence the aim of rural policies consists in far more than simply compensating disadvantaged areas/people. It is realised that it is central to *initiate development processes* and to focus on the institutional framework for relevant initiatives. In such a context the contribution of the LEADER initiative, albeit small from its financial resources, might be crucial for the kind of discussion and processes required to overcome regional inertia which was prevailing in many rural areas. Its innovative character and its intention to foster inter-regional co-operation seems to be at the core of the development process. From its outset it has combined these elements with the notion of "bottom-up" approach, including a wide variety of local stakeholders and interests.

With regard to our topic we have to focus again on the role of young people in this process. There is no doubt that overall aims are not directed, or even mentioning young people as a target group. However, as we will show later, recently there is quite a distinct acknowledgement of young people in that process. Nevertheless we will have to approach the question by analysing the contents of programmes and by widening the scope of analysis in order to include measures impacting on young people. The next section therefore will concentrate on an overview of programmes and measures, and point to the specific features concerning young people or the treatment of young people in the programmes, in general.

3.   Young People in Rural Development – Experiences From Case Studies

The following presentation of the role of young people in rural development attempts to take a closer view on existing measures in rural development programmes, particularly in the regions and countries of the seven study areas of this project. It is intended to provide through this overview some insight into the situation and potential for youth specific formulation of measures and processes. Whereas the context of the Austrian study area Murau is analysed in greater detail, with the aim to explore also potential scope in a wider range of measures, only a selection of specific measures and programmes which seem due to some of its features of particular interest have been addressed for the other study areas.

Rural Development and Other Policies in Study Area Murau, Austria

In the district of Murau and in its neighbouring districts Knittelfeld and Judenburg which form together the NUTS III region Upper Styria West there are a lot of measures addressing, explicitly or implicitly, the development of rural areas. During the Structural Funds period 1995-1999 (for Austria, due to EU-accession in

1995) the district of Murau belonged to the objective 5b area and, for the period 2000-2006, just *partly* belongs to objective 2 (new). The objective 5b programme aimed at stimulating economic development of and enabling structural adjustments in rural areas. Three spheres of action were chosen in the Single Programming Document (SPD) as priorities for measures in Styria (Dax and Oedl-Wieser 1995, 21ff.):

- Diversification, adjustment and adaptation of farming activities, co-funded by EAGGF – Guidance, aiming at intensifying links between farming and other local businesses and the orientation of agricultural production according to market needs considering economical, environmental and social aspects (ÖROK 1999, 11). Six measures have been carried out in this sub-programme with the most important emphasis on supporting the use of regional potential of raw material, achieving added-value for forestry, preservation and improvement of rural areas, training and educational qualification, etc. (ÖROK 1999, 58).
- Development and diversification in non-farming sectors, co-funded by ERDF: The emphasis has been laid on creating positive premises for investments in tourism, environmental issues, modernising and structural improvements as well as attracting firms to create and secure job opportunities outside farming (ÖROK 1999, 11). Eleven measures have been carried out in Styria emphasising on modernising industry and business, marketing of tourism, and research (ÖROK 1999, 58).
- Development of human resources, co-founded by ESF, aiming at the reintegration of unemployed people into the labour market, especially through employment projects and qualification measures aimed at the needs of (the local) labour market. Under the five measures of this sub-programme the training and educational measures for unemployed people have been the most important. Measures with "youth dimension" are mainly found under this category (ÖROK 1999, 59).

The new objective 2 programme has not yet started to approve projects due to the scattered location of programme areas (arising from delimitation at the municipal level) in some parts of Austria, and particularly in the district Murau, one has to envisage that the regional dimension will be weakened for the benefit of more sectoral enterprise support. To maintain the regional aspects, it will become more important to utilise the opportunity of LEADER+ programme to include areas outside EU-target areas and thus follow a more distinct regional approach. It has to be mentioned in this context that the LEADER II programme has not been located in the study area of Murau. As there are now a great number of Local Action Groups (LAGs) proposals for LEADER+ programme which exceeds the maximum of LAGs to be selected for Styria (and Austria as well) there are still significant obstacles for the LAG Murau to be approved for inclusion in the new programme (decision to be expected in early 2001).

The regional proposal worked out for the planning period 2000-2006 addresses the strength of wood production in the region as the core issue and asset for LEADER+ activities. Expressions like "wood world Murau" and "land of (specific high alpine) pine trees" intend to coin regional identity for action under the programme. A range of projects will be encouraged focusing on issues such as "increasing people's awareness" of local community action and "developing adventure tourism". It is also intended by the regional management authorities to involve young people by incorporating schools into implementing processes of projects.

With the LEADER+ programme, at least mentioning young people as one target group among others, a base for an active integration is provided. However, given the regional institutional framework and recalling the views expressed by the young people in the individual interviews and group discussions (Dax et al., 2000) there are tremendous barriers to actually increasing participation of young people in the region. Nevertheless, as will be shown later, there is rising concern about the issue and a core group of local actors is committed to work for youth integration at different levels.

Regional programme structure   Following the application of the objective 5b programme and other rural development measures in the region some experience in rural development work has been achieved. In the survey the main priority activities are presented under the summarising label "wood world Murau" (Figure 8.1). This presentation gives an overview of the priority measures carried out actually in the district of Murau and groups together projects and measures under specific thematic headings. The perspectives underlying have been elaborated along work on the so called regional development model, co-ordinated by the EU regional management Office (in the years 1998 and 1999) and have been approved by the planning advisory board in June 1999. Its main intention was the formulation of objectives with regard to the economic, social and cultural development of Murau and the preparation for (future) allocation of financial aid (Chance 1999, 3).

The framework structure which can be seen as a further step to underpin the position of the EU Regional Management Upper Styria West as the turntable of the regional development is supposed to comprise all projects prepared and carried out in the district of Murau. Although Figure 8.1 is not exhaustive on all the measures and the single projects (see further differentiation later in this report) it shows quite clearly where the priority has been laid and will be for future projects in the region.

One of the most important leading themes concerns the stimulation of the economic situation including the wood processing branch in Murau, which will be linked to the educational initiative: Local education and training offers will be oriented   according   to   the   needs   of   the   labour   market   (business development/qualification/education). A further project theme concerns the linkage of the region by a four-lane highway to the national road system. It is seen as one of the most important prerequisites for improving access and the economic competitiveness of the region (public transport/traffic).

The development of summer tourism all over the region (Murtal) and the aim to become the second most important skiing region of Styria is another priority. The choice of Murau/Kreischberg to be the venue of the Snowboard world championship in 2003 will not only help to realise this plan but also to address young people to take part (tourism development).

As Murau does have a high percentage of people still engaged in farming there are many projects emphasising diversification and multifunctional issues (agriculture and forestry).

Cultural and art projects seemed to be important, too, but primarily mainstream driven and tourism-oriented. However, even under cultural and art projects very few projects can be found showing a "youth dimension" (art and culture).

A further desegregation of EAGGF projects funded under objective 5b programme shows that these are mainly to be summarised under "Village development". Eleven out of 35 municipalities have taken up such initiatives. Especially the development of tourism facilities of the kind "holidays on farms" are of importance as this might provide farmers with an additional source of income. The second priority of this part of the programme is the implementation of the "forestry management communities" which provide farmers with a chance to secure additional income. Especially young farmers to be trained wood workers seem to appreciate these training courses as they provide an additional job opportunity outside farming. Young farmers interviewed confirmed the importance of having an income which makes them independent from parents (c.f. focus group 1). The third type of EAGGF measures concerns diversification of farmers towards tourism. About 800 out of 1600 farms and about two thirds of farms offering "holidays on farms" have been involved in objective 5b-projects. About 80 jobs have been created and secured especially in relation to diversification of farms, and a budget of about 300 Mio. ATS has been spent on the projects whereby half of the budget consisted of money from EU Funds.

Rural development programmes and young people Many of the relevant measures for rural development relate to employment policy (like NAP programme) which are taken into account specifically by the thematic report of the German partner of this project. Therefore we limited information on such issues and did not analyse in-depth those measures. To sort out the overlap was not as easy because most of the measures or projects carried out in the district of Murau with a potential youth dimension focused to some extent on young people's integration into labour market. Following the framework structure shown in Figure 8.1, we were specifically looking for measures addressing young people explicitly as target groups, or addressing young people through the contents of projects (attractiveness of courses, education, innovation etc.). We also looked at possible impacts of these measures to improve the situation of young people in the study area. Following the conclusions in the national report we took four notions, namely education, employment, participation and mobility which are seen to be decisive for young people's integration and tried to link them with selected measures. The selection of measures esteemed useful for our theme is presented in Figure 8.2.

The main priorities and measures of the past rural development programme hardly reflected the needs and aspirations of young people nor have these been taken into account substantially in the planning process. To the young people interviewed such policy programmes are not relevant which means that they have hardly been confronted with the policies and that youth relevant parts of the programme could not be communicated as options to young people of the area. On the contrary, young people do not feel understood or appropriately taken into account in local initiatives. As has been mentioned, they deplore the small number of young people (after school age) which hinders building greater commitment strength involving them as local actors. (Dax et al. 2000, 8)

The visible lack of youth projects might derive from the fact that no need for such projects is experienced and expressed by young people, local actors and communities. It has been repeatedly suggested by young people and local experts that the situation looks different in other neighbouring districts (focus groups 1 and 2). This probably might be derived from *the predominance of local traditional structures which are still working very well* and reduce aspirations for change. On the other hand, young people interviewed criticised the lack of willingness of adults and the local/regional representatives to listen and understand young people's desire for participation in a more 'youth adequate' way.

Recent youth specific initiatives   In addition to the above presented measures directly youth oriented programmes should be analysed in the following. The focus on young people is explicit here, but the rural dimension, in general, is weaker. However, analysing recent initiatives one finds that territorial issues are seen increasingly as an important element and some of the measures concentrate on the rural dimension.

The most impressive youth future programme, called *nex:it*, has been started by the Land of Styria since May 2000. It encourages young people aged 15-25 and non-profit-organisations addressing young people as beneficiaries or target group to submit innovative projects for financial aid. The total budget of the programme amounts to 50 Mio. ATS. The call for proposals is quite open and criteria for project eligibility are limited to address young people and to present proposals with "new" approaches/initiatives (*nex:it* 2000).

About 500 projects have been submitted (by the deadline, June 2000) and up to October 2000 a number of 152 (out of 300 intentional) have been approved. Most of the projects are submitted by youth representatives and youth groups. It is not very surprising that most of the projects approved are based in Graz, the capital of Styria, and its neighbouring district Graz-surroundings as shown in Figure 8.3. At least 20% of the projects comprise more than one region (NUTS III), including a group of 10 projects which will concern the whole of Styria. Only a small number of six projects are located in Upper Styria West of which four in our study area Murau (see Figure 8.5). Although the quantitative distribution of projects can not be taken as an indication for the participation the small number of activities proposed in the study area reveals the level of awareness for youth involvement.

Projects submitted under *nex:it* relate to five categories, namely Sense of Community, Art & Fun, TEC-Future, Action of Music, and Clean World. As

Figure 8.4 shows most of the projects can be attributed to the category Sense of Community (57 out of 152) emphasising young people's participation, communication and disadvantaged young people. Forty one projects belong to Art & Fun comprising actions like workshops, literature and story telling workshops which will be presented through internet, fashion shows, film productions and acting, photography workshops, events, and sport activities. These projects are mainly aimed at participation of young people and integration of young migrants. TEC projects address issues concerning new technology and account for almost 20%. They comprise creation of online magazines provided by and for young people, internet platforms with information and discussions forums, youth radio and TV programmes produced by young people, training courses in radio, TV, and video technologies, and e-commerce, etc. Projects under Action of Music account for 18%, and 4% of projects belong to Clean World. Action of Music projects are mainly focused on the development of youth culture by supporting music bands, music workshops and organisation of music events. Under Clean World projects young people are trained to become "attorneys of nature", or go into matters such as fair trade and solar energy use.

As the response to *nex:it* has been quite high it becomes obvious that an enormous dynamic development can be set off by providing the 'right' framework conditions for activities. Providing easily accessible structures with few bureaucratic restrictions is as important as providing financial aid to ease potential participants to join in, especially if no adequate structure exists. The programme reveals also that the scope for experimental activities is taken up by various groups of young people and could be further developed. The fact that many projects comprise more than one district or region can be seen as a positive indication with regard to the persisting difficulties for co-operation among municipalities, regions, etc. The orientation on larger areas reflects the need for linkages between territorial units. Actions of this kind might contribute to break up existing barriers and improve co-operation activities and encourage others to follow.

Selected youth projects in Styria In recent years national employment policy and the Job Service Agency in Austria increased the emphasis on measures aiming at preventing youth unemployment. As actual unemployment among young people is not yet very problematic in Austria the focus was laid on placement of school leavers and measures which support young people in their transition phase towards integration into the labour market (AMS 1999, 10). Measures focusing on the improvement of placement are in line with the guidelines of NAP (National Action Plan) which aims at halving the rate of long term unemployment of young people. Qualification measures had been the most important strategy in 1999 with about 66% of budget spent on it. This group of measures comprises vocational career planning, preparation courses and job finding activities such as job coaching which have been extended at the expense of standard educational and vocational training (AMS 1999, 17). Employment measures such as "labour market oriented projects" with a high degree of direct responsibility of participants account for 25% of the budget spent in 1999.

Some of the labour market projects in Styria are described here as they particularly address the needs for specific rural areas. They can be understood as part of an integrated programme for rural development.

In Styria the focus of measures offered to young people is to ease their way into the labour market. In contrast to measures with a simple structure there have been some more challenging programmes developed which cope with the complexity of problems young people are facing when looking for a job. Such projects take a comprehensive approach by offering a toolbox comprising not only educational and vocational training, but also psychological and social support which might include also measures helping young people coming to terms with daily routine.

In Figure 8.6 selected projects addressing this complexity are presented as examples, particularly as they relate to rural areas or to approaches and methods which might be useful in the rural development context. The first two examples concentrate exclusively on young women in rural areas. As we discovered in the national analysis, young women feel especially restricted in their choice of vocational education and professional career in the region. They are closely tied to the local/regional offer which is strongly shaped along traditional and narrow lines. The two described examples "Mafalda" and "now@" try to meet the needs of young women to enhance their choices and opportunities in vocational aspects on the one hand, and, on the other hand, strengthen their self-confidence and self-assertion as women.

The other two examples are chosen between a range of labour market oriented projects. The projects show great efforts to meet young people needs but reveals at the same time the importance of (great) sensitivity with regard to social and cultural environmental aspects.

Mafalda is an organisation originally located in Graz addressing girls and young women. It offers qualification courses, professional and psychological consulting and leisure time activities. The awareness that women are still facing discrimination especially in the countryside has led to the project "Mafalda goes countryside" which was started in 1998. The intention is to improve general conditions for girls and young women and to increase sensitivity of the local society. Up to 1999 about 150 events had been organised in co-operation with schools, youth centres and consultation offices in various places all over the rural area of Styria. It is intended to intensify these activities because response to the offer was beyond capacity provided (Mafalda 2000).

Now@, established in 1996, is an initiative acting as an intermediary between women seeking a job and local firms in Graz and the surrounding district. Five projects are carried out so far of which the "Mobile InternetCafe for women" has already been mentioned above. "The regional centre of vocational management" is a further project addressing women who want to get a foothold in technical jobs. It offers not only comprehensive training courses but also individual career planning, a technological workshop, etc. As a further eight districts have implemented similar projects and are establishing regional centres of vocational management it could probably be seen as the start of a successful strategy covering a greater part of rural areas in Styria (Now@, 1999).

"Young people" belongs to the group of labour market oriented projects with a high degree of direct responsibility of young people mentioned above. The project was started in 1995 and lasted until 1997 to cope with unemployment among young people in the district of Bruck/Mur. The first course organised was a two-week course and was attended by 77 young people aged 15-25, mainly school leavers and mainly young women. Organisers had to learn through the drop-out rate immediately after starting the seminars (about 22%) that the programme did not respond adequately to the needs of young people. In particular it has been referred to *"young people's physiological and psychological deficits"* (Young people 1997) which means that a number of factors in the preparation for participation in such schemes has to be taken into account. Some of them relate to the personal psychological and social situation, others even to health constitution of participants. Many participants used the project for securing an apprenticeship by being consulted in the right way or at least having the chance of a practical training. As young participants increasingly asked for personal consulting this led to an unexpected financial increase on the consulting budget whereas the budget for qualification training was not utilised fully (Young people 1997, 6). During the course many young people couldn't cope with the projects requirements of finding their own way and doing work on his/herself. 56% of participants had secured a permanent job after the measure of whom 70% already got the job while they had been attending the course. Many of the participants have been asked too much with respect to self-organisation under this project which was partly due to the low age of participants. The experience from the difficulties arising from the complex influences on labour market integration seen from this project have been used for conceptualising the following activity.

In January 1999 a project called *"Mürztal 2000"* has been implemented by two districts focusing on young unemployed people and providing qualification modules to ease their way into the labour market. At the same time awareness of unemployment among young people should be increased which should give rise to a network comprising local actors, firms, the job centre, regional development organisations, etc. The project offers different qualification modules where young people can join in at any time. The qualification modules are accompanied by the activities of the enterprise contact platform and the "socio-pedagogical consulting centre". The platform should enable participants to get contact to potential employers and vocational training placements. The social centre's objective is to accompany the participants and to particularly support young people who have psychological and social problems. It is also the aim of this centre to raise the awareness of young people for the need of an active personal involvement and the request to take up responsibility for personal future.

As the interim report (Mürztal 2000, 18) revealed, the drop-out rate was considerably high. More than half of participants left the measure before it finished. Half of these young people left because they had got a job, half of them had other reasons such as lack of ability to join the measure or personal reasons caused by their social environment. Moreover the evaluation showed that participants were more inclined to take up social professions than anticipated or intended, and, unfortunately, it turned out that there has been no improvement in relation to gender biased job selection. The aim to have more women in non-traditional jobs could not be achieved. The failure in achieving the objectives can be partly attributed to the short term of the project and points to additional efforts required relating to information and raising awareness.

Exemplary Cases from Other Study Areas

Experiences from case studies All over the seven study areas it became clear that young people have not been a significant priority group of rural development programmes, if regarded as relevant at all. The missing attention towards youth issues in the programmes has been reflected by the statements of young people interviewed in the project. Participation in general was interpreted as a critical and somewhat awkward issue by young people and information on both national and EU policies was rather low. The multitude of measures on rural development which has increased over the last years due to the Structural Funds programmes and a general increase in the importance of territorial approaches have been performed without any significant awareness of these among the young. Yet, such programmes have always included as one important aim the aspiration to counteract out-migration from rural areas via these programmes. Only a few activities in our study areas, (but including all the EU measures, e.g. LEADER Community Initiative, objective 5b programmes and other territorial programmes) have directly addressed young people. That is why we have included in our analysis also horizontal measures which did reflect this issue already somewhat earlier.

We have gone into greater detail for Austria, as information could be made available for the study area and the provincial situation with regard to youth specific programmes. Our focus was to show that it is not primarily an issue of the detailed objectives towards youth policy which brings about respective activities, but the commitment and participatory elements in the rural society as a whole. Whereas specific labour market youth measures have been developed during recent reorientation and harmonisation of EU labour market policy only recently a series of innovative actions going beyond labour market aspects are available to young people or got some public relevance. This would seem to be a starting point for future inclusion in rural development programmes.

The situation in the other study areas was not presented in such detail and, in general, has been exemplified by one youth measure per study area which might serve in our opinion as reference with regard to the issues tackled or the methods used. Measures described range from:

- the co-operative work linking training and employment actors in a French rural context;
- the training of a youth theatre in Kainuu in Finland;
- the international collaboration of customer service training, based in Finland (and Scotland);

- the New Deal programme for Young People in the UK with a specific programme for musicians, but no clear assessment on its specificity for rural areas;
- to a Youthstart funded programme in Ireland (Mol an Óige), concentrating on in-school and out-of-school activities for those "at risk" of leaving the system.

Similar activities could be mentioned from the study area in Portugal, where LEADER activities tend to revive old local traditions of handicraft and look for young people participating in such schemes or, in an other interesting project, raising children's awareness of local development by having them draw how they perceive their area and how they would like it to evolve (ADICES, AEIDL 1997). Likewise in the German study area, corresponding to its socio-economic characteristics, labour market measures with relation to young people prevail.

When looking beyond our study areas there are some few relevant additional examples available:

- It seems that in several countries some LAGs had a specific focus on youth development (e.g. in France, LAG Périgord Noir and LAG Bugey, LAG Bazois-corbigeois and LAG Dinan Sud; in Germany LAGs in the regions of Mecklenburg-Vorpommern and Niedersachsen; in Ireland in Cavan-Monaghan and in the UK in the Oswestry Hills – AEIDL 2000b), all these activities specifically targeting at young people and bringing together local agencies working with young people.
- Moreover the FAO work on increasing the involvement of young men and women in rural development as a strategy for rural development in the CEECs presented some interesting case studies. All of them relate to comprehensive territorial work applying a cross-sectoral approach. In particular, positive experiences from Portugal, Slovenia and Northern Ireland are presented there (FAO 1998).

Although the cases examined seek to address the great variety of fields of actions and aspects of youth development, all of them share the general objectives of either addressing aspects of integration of young people in the rural context or raising awareness of the community and young people about their importance to the community and encouraging them to participate actively in local development initiatives.

France: *Centre de Resources*   The organisation of the Centre de Resources is a vivid example of the importance of intermediary agencies which fulfil tasks of networking activities of people in the region, both vertically and horizontally. The emphasis is put here on matching education offer and demand at the local and regional level. The example shows also that quite different funding has supported activities and contributed to human resource development and employment creation in a deeply rural area.

In France the basic ideas were to create a "House of employment and training" with a structure related to local needs and also to create a "Centre de Resources", corresponding to the LEADER concept. Like there it was intended to offer innovative training and support actions to local firms.

The aim is to have a structure which is a link between different local economic and training actors. The decision for establishing such a structure came from the Communautés de Communes de Villaines la Juhel (the so called CCV), part of the study area Mayenne (the following case presentation is based on the context report of the French team, Auclair and Vanoni 1999). The CCV is an association of 11 municipalities in order to develop common actions and programmes. Therefore the Centre de Resources is considered a public service offered by the CCV to the inhabitants of the different municipalities concerned.

The Centre de Resources addresses the whole population and not only young people, although young people constitute an important part of the people who visit the Centre. The main actions of the Centre de resources relate to information provision/exchange: the Centre offers information mainly about training and employment by providing a documentation room, collaboration with the National Job Centre (notice board), collaboration with the "Missions locales" and the "Permanences d'accueil, d'information et d'orientation" (PAIO) which is located in the capital of Mayenne. An agent of PAIO comes several days a week in the premises of the Centre de Resources and provides assistance to young people from 16-25 years.

The agents of the Centre provide on one hand collaboration with local firms and employers through regular visits to local firms in order to identify their needs, in terms of training for the employees or in terms of qualification requirements for future employees. On the other hand, the Centre organises the training offer by contacting different training institutions and adapted training offers to the local needs. Thus the Centre de Resources can act as a link between training institutions, local firms, and trainees.

Additional support is given, e.g. through assistance to unemployed: A club of job searchers established in 1997 is linked to the National Job Centre. It is a new service which is part of a wider national program with the aim of offering individual or collective support to unemployed people, and to help them define a professional project, write letters and CVs.

There is also support available to help people to create their own business. They organise a virtual firm and then organise a training course on the basis of this firm, which is used as a pedagogical example. This club is part of a national network that counts 150 other similar clubs.

Very recently the director of the Centre was working together with the agents of the "Pays du Haut Maine et Pail" which is another local development structure representing the collaboration of four overlapping co-operative activities of municipalities in the area (CCV and three others). The common aim is to attract firms and employers into the area, the Pays being in charge of the economic development, and the Centre being in charge of the training aspects.

Organisation and budget of the Centre de Resources: The Centre's benefit is a public service which is mainly financed by the Communautés de Communes. At the beginning there was financial aid from Leader I to buy a building. Nowadays financial aid is available for some of the training courses from ADAPT programmes and ESF funds, and premises used in training courses will be rented as the need arises.

Evaluation: The structures of the Centre de Resources induces a strong dependency on the local governments, and therefore on the local politicians, especially the President of the Communautés de Communes; though up until recently the director (a woman) had quite a large autonomy to develop new projects. There has not been carried out any specific assessment concerning the Centre de Resources, but the interviews taken with different local actors and young people by the French team confirmed the very good opinion people have concerning this structure.

Finland: The youth theatre's training week in Kainuu One of the few examples of cultural activities is the youth theatre's training. This project is located in Kainuu the study area of Finland and addresses young people aged 12-25. It is conducted by the LAG Organisation "Kainuu Businesswomen LEADER II" and funded by Leader II. During the course young people study theatre production in a number of forms. Course participants come from all round the Kainuu region and also from other regions in Northern Finland (AEIDL 1999).

Finland welcome host – learning customer service The SHEP training programme is an international project of the study area which is run together with Scottish Ross & Cromarty Enterprise (Scotland-Highlands and Islands) and Savo Amazon LEADER, an other Finnish LEADER area. Pupils from the Reisjärivi and Haukivuori senior secondary schools attend a customer service course and will be trained on themes concerning customer service with an international aspect. The basic aim is to teach young people the importance of good customer service, the development of tourist environment, as well as marketing and teamwork in tourist industry. A course was held in January 2000 at the local hotel-restaurant and holiday centre. It consisted of three days of theory and two days of practice, and during the course students learned the basics of tourism and customer service in both Finnish and English (AEIDL 1999).

United Kingdom: the New Deal The New Deal is a key part of the Government's Welfare to Work strategy. The New Deal programmes have been set up since 1998 with the aim to improve job opportunities for people out of work. It gives job seekers aged 18-25, 25 plus and those with disabilities an opportunity to develop their potential, gain skills and experience, and find work. There are six main New Deal programmes, varying in a number of ways: size of target group, key aims and objectives, eligibility rules, conditions of involvement, type of support offered, etc. (Millar 2000). With regard to our theme the New Deal programme for Young People (NDYP) is presented as elements of the programme are affecting performance in rural areas.

The New Deal for Young people is targeted on 18-24 year-olds who have been claiming Jobseekers Allowance (JAS) for at least six months. The measure is compulsory, and includes a "gateway" period of advice and support followed by four options: subsidised employment, full-time education and training, voluntary work, environmental work (Millar 2000). Recently, a specific programme, the New Deal for Musicians under the NDYP was designed and developed with the help of the music industry. It is intended to help young musicians who are eligible for NDYP and who are seeking a career in the music industry (Jowell 2000).

By February 2000 just under 440,000 young people had been through the NDYP and in total about half of them had found jobs (Millar 2000). Of these, about 146,000 lasted 13 weeks or more and this is about 34% of all participants, lower for women (31%) and ethnic minorities (27%). Millar assumes that "about half of these people who had found work through NDYP would probably have done so anyway". It is projected that about 250,000 young men and women will find work over the four years planned for the programme which should make this programme almost self-financing over that time.

As Millar (2000) assumes in her research on the New Deal programmes, the response to participation in programmes were positive, because "participation boosted confidence, enhanced job-seeking and improved skills". In contrast, young people interviewed in the sample of this research project by the UK Team seemed to have more negative than positive impressions on the New Deal programme (Shucksmith et al., 2000, 50-56). It was perceived by those interviewed that the primary motives of the government behind the scheme was to get people into the programme so that the unemployment figure, in statistical terms, would fall (Shucksmith et al., 2000, 53) although this may have been a hangover from the previous government's Youth Training Scheme. Young people also criticised the compulsory element of the programmes linked to benefit loss in case of refusal (Shucksmith et al., 2000, 52). In general compulsion has been assessed to be more favourable for certain groups such as young people and long-term unemployed than for others (older workers, lone parents, disabled people, and partners) (Millar 2000). Experience has shown that participation in voluntary programmes was low, although it was not only due to the fact that people were choosing not to take part. The personal advisers approach has had a positive impact on both participants and providers and might probably be one component which could increase voluntary participation.

As an important output of the evaluation it can be mentioned that sometimes people felt a large gap between the individual assessment and the fixed requirements to be followed. As "Labour market programmes seemed to be more effective for those already closest to employment", Millar (2000) noticed that the New Deal programme will have to work harder in order to reach especially those groups of people with multiple disadvantages and special needs. Further refinements to achieve this have recently been introduced.

Similar critiques have been raised by young people interviewed in the Angus study area. In particular, they felt that employers voluntarily seized the opportunity to take advantage of the cheap labour force offered by the programme (voluntary work, environmental work). Some interviewees had the impression that participation in New Deal measures was received negatively by potential employers and that difficulties to break this vicious circle still persist (Shucksmith et al., 2000, 52).

Ireland: Mol an Óige In Ireland a high percentage of young people still cease education at the age of 15 years (or less). The early drop-out rate in the study area of Connemara is about 38 per cent, somewhat higher than the national level with 26%. Mol an Óige was a four year Youthstart funded project in Co. Tipperary, (January 1996 – March 2000), which addressed the 10-19 year-olds at risk of failing in school by developing and testing innovative approaches to the issues relating to educational disadvantage (Mol an Óige 2000, 1).

The concept of "Collaborative Action Planning" was adopted in Mol an Óige project as a strategy for tackling early school leaving. Analysing its performance at school level, teachers and school management have been allowed to critically evaluate school practices in relation to young people "at risk" of leaving the school and to respond in a flexible way to the needs of them (MacGrath et al., 2000, 40).

Evaluation results in relation to the project Mol an Óige reveal some additional key approaches, and operational features are considered significant in enhancing educational provision and participation (MacGrath et al., 2000, 40).

- Educational provision and development should incorporate schools, pupils, communities, parents, community development agencies, youth work organisation and statutory bodies. This will provide considerable potential for resource provision and commitment to success through shared project ownership.
- Developing support for young people in terms of their intellectual and emotional needs. New measures in-school and out-of-school are needed to develop the interests and commitment of young people especially of those "at risk" of leaving the system. Personal development of skills which enhance self-esteem and assertiveness, leadership strategies, learning support and career counselling are examples of in-school measures. Community action projects, where young people are actively involved in local community development initiatives is an example of out-of-school activity which might enhance participation of young people generally and, hence, their educational participation.
- Initiating mentoring support for pupils by non-teachers. Mentors act as positive role models, and provide advice and assistance to youth at a number of levels.

The Irish government will spend 28.4 million IrL over the next three years to provide schools throughout the country with resources to tackle early school leaving. Initiatives such as Mol an Óige could serve as "models of good practice in enabling schools and communities to deal effectively with education disadvantage" and provide an idea how measures could be implemented in practice (MacGrath et al., 2000, 39).

4.   Perspectives for Increasing Involvement of Young People in Rural Development

The low awareness of youth as a target group of rural development is reflected by the singularity expressed in case studies presented in the previous section. Few regions took the option to include youth workers in their territorial approaches nor to take the viewpoint that future orientation has to be based on youth development. Consequently, evaluation studies did not pay any attention to the issue either, wheter it was evaluation of regional programmes (objective 1, objective 5b) or of Community Initiatives (LEADER) the issue of raising participation was evaluated by referring only to the dimension of overall participation of local and regional actors, with no specific consideration of young people.

As insight of young people interviewed into the specific policy programmes is limited, statements with regard to rural development programmes and measures can be traced only with considerable difficulties. To a large extent they are included in views expressed on the general policy framework and their estimation of the relevant local actors. As the interviews arguments therefore are less focused on rural development programmes there is no section under this chapter dealing with the voices of young people. However, much of the analysis and interpretative work with regard to policy assessment in the seven "national reports" of this project and statements of young people quoted in chapter 6 are very relevant for rural development issues as well.

Experience from Programmes

Although a series of evaluation studies has focused on this very issue, of raising involvement of local people and increasing representation of relevant groups of local society, youth was hardly mentioned as such a group in these studies. For the scope of our analysis we only took into account those evaluation reports made available recently at EU-level, and those carried out for the Austrian programmes. In core, this refers to intermediate evaluations of Objective 5b programmes, carried out around the years 1997 and 1998. Moreover reference is made to the general assessment of the regional programmes of the first two Structural Funds periods (Europäischer Rechnungshof, 1998) and the EU evaluation of the LEADER I outcome (Dethier et al., 1999). The thrust of evaluation studies for rural development programmes had to fulfil requirements concerning the quantitative assessment of programmes' progress. The financial performance, aspects of coherence and effectiveness, quantitative impacts and issues of efficiency have been the focus of the evaluations prepared for objective 5b programmes for some countries, and most of these commissioned by the European Commission DG VI; UK (PACEC 1998), Finland (Malinen et al., 1997), Ireland (Brendan Kearney and Associates 2000, on LEADER II Community Initiative), Germany (Tissen and Schrader 1998), Spain (Isla and Soy 1998) and Italy.

In addition to its main quantitative outline these evaluations did stress a number of more qualitative issues which have an impact on the issue of how to handle young people's involvement in rural development. In particular the following aspects emerged:

- The great variety of projects and the request of complimentarity with other Community, sectoral, national and regional policies, in some regions created confusion and increased costly bureaucracy, pointing to a need to increase integration of the different initiatives (PACEC 1998). This uncertainty about orientation in the programmes available is particularly pertinent for those groups of local population less acquainted with institutional regulations and lower experience of participation. A substantial number of young people can be counted among these groups and, as our interviews confirmed, don't feel attracted by the confusing sets of regulations and "rules" for participation.

- Overall there was a high degree of synergy between the EC funds and national measures, particularly with regard to Objective 5b programmes and LEADER II. Problems cited relate primarily to "limited integration in administration procedures and limited information flows" (PACEC 1998, 50). "An improved co-operation and co-ordination of actions supported by the structural funds involved for the purpose of reaching synergy effects is particularly important on the local level" (Tissen and Schrader 1998, XV). It will be important for the implementation of future programmes to maintain the high level of synergy achieved and, where possible, to enhance programmes' functioning by increased distribution of information. With regard to young people it is extremely important to regularly address this aspect and to question the meaningfulness of information available. Young people interviewed had a tendency to feel informed only superficially and to be not directly addressed by information and public discourse.

- Although the programmes evaluated have induced a wave of assessment of regional strengths and weaknesses and local actors' involvement, evaluations suggest that local activity should be stimulated further and options to increase awareness and consequently improve co-operation with different sectors through programmes should be used (PACEC 1998, 57).

- Developing skills is a priority chosen in almost all rural development programmes. In countries with high levels of education achieved also in rural areas one has to adapt carefully new training programmes to local and regional needs. For example, Finland is indeed producing an especially good all-round educated population, but there are certain needs within the objective 5b regions at the intermediate and higher levels (Malinen et al., 1997, 23 f.). It is assessed there "that there is a requirement for experimental work and ESF financing is very well suited to that task". This statement is underlined by experience from many programmes and reflected in the presentation of selected projects in the previous chapter. Moreover, it is complained that linkages between training and other actions have been weak in the past and evaluations point out a move towards closer interaction in the future (Isla and Soy 1998, 73).

- It has not been feasible to approach each issue of problems for all the regions. The priorities on the aspects to analyse, the methodological estimates and the content differ from region to region and thus synthesis reports could not deal with some interesting issues (Isla and Soy 1998, 70). It therefore becomes important for future programmes to highlight youth participation as a potential field of activity for rural (and territorial) development programmes.

- The desegregation of the actions and measures at the local level is of major interest for the analysis of the programme's impacts. In fact, the consideration of, exclusively, the overall impacts could disguise important and significant territorial disparities (Isla and Soy 1998, 7f.) which seems particularly relevant for the situation of remote rural areas, e.g. in mountain regions as can be seen for the Austrian study area.

- Although it is well known, and has been extensively explained, one has to respect that there is a considerable trade-off between innovativeness of projects and programme implementation. In general, traditional measures are easier to apply and show greater rates of accomplishment (Isla and Soy 1998, 71). One is also inclined to see a preference for more harmonic regional strategies taken by responsible administrative institutions at all levels. This tendency has the implication to neglect the needs and ideas of local populations not included in core participant groups or primary stakeholders. Young people's aspirations tend to be seen as immature and provocative and hardly fit into a more traditional, harmonic approach.

- In many contexts the central role of intermediary agencies and the specific tasks of Local Action Groups (under the LEADER Initiative) have been addressed (e.g. ÖROK 1998 and 1999). It arises from the widespread European experience that local development is not a mere local task but has to be achieved in co-operation with regional and national authorities. The long-term commitment of "facilitators" can not be over estimated as a crucial element for enhancing participation and ensuring outcome of programmes (see also Shortall and Shucksmith 1998).

A more comparative work is available through the EU-wide ex-post evaluation of the LEADER I Community Initiative (1989-1993). This evaluation, conducted by the Commission, was realised by independent experts, including around 60 experts from 12 countries. The final report published in March 1999 (Dethier et al., 1999) allows a thorough insight into the achievements of the first generation of LEADER programmes and also can serve as starting reference for evaluation of rural development programmes with more complex methods. Although the work was based on a number of quantitative techniques the report has drawn in its conclusion the attention towards the importance of a more qualitative evaluation approach.

In many aspects LEADER I was a pilot scheme and can be "considered as provider of a precious stock of knowledge about rural Europe utilised for a better targeting of rural policy actions" (Dethier et al., 1999, 166). The demonstration effect that was an objective of LEADER did influence rural policy ideas and led to a "reconsideration of traditional delivery systems for rural development support" (Dethier et al., 1999, 179) also at national and regional levels.

However, the lessons learned for rural policy are not always clear-cut. Although the experience of LEADER initiatives was highly appreciated, particularly in Southern Member States and in Ireland where LAGs were significant in number, the innovative aspects of LEADER "did not really affect the implementation of mainstream rural policy" (Dethier et al., 1999, 179). Even when in LEADER II the number of LAGs has risen substantially and implementation affected a number of areas almost five times greater than in the first period the link to mainstream policies remained weak. There is scope to investigate the lack in the transfer of experiences to general rural policy.

Some of the obstacles might be seen in the fact that an experimental programme induces processes which need time. Positive returns become visible only in the long run and a minimum degree of continuity is needed. Moreover core aspects of the LEADER programme, such as the participatory approach, innovation or networking have been less relevant within the framework of LEADER I and contributed marginally to its value added. In the evaluation report it has been assessed "as a weakness that should be strengthened" (Dethier et al., 1999, 180). Indeed it appears that meanwhile much greater priority has been laid on networking and participation, to be explored in more detail in chapter 7 and 9.

The evaluation report, of course, does not refer directly to young people as actors or as a target group in rural development. However, the important impact which is seen in the better qualification of human resources through training activities and the emphasis put on questions and issues that different stakeholders may have in terms of information needs indicate fields particularly relevant to young people. Moreover, the LAGs are categorised as being a) dominated by the local public administration, b) by private interests and c) by a well-balanced situation between public and private interests.

Even in the last case, variables such as democratic participation of the population and the territorial diagnosis were largely missing. The report continues: "This finding should not be taken as an indication of irrelevance of these aspects but the contrary: when they were applied the results were indeed impressive". (Dethier et al., 1999, 173). In addition it is made clear that representation of local actors should be extended (to more than just one interest group) and LAGs should not remain the single specific focus of activity but insure also the inclusion of other innovative actors.

Youth Integration – An Emerging Requirement of Rural Programmes

It is particularly in the Irish context that rural policy has dealt extensively with the problem of social exclusion, even addressing the issue directly in its national rural development plan. The ex-post evaluation for LEADER II in Ireland also has elaborated quite straightforward proposals that situations of social disadvantage or exclusion have to be checked by LEADER groups and the "youth sector should also be given specific recognition" (Brendan Kearney and Associates 2000, 59f.).

This notion has already entered into the official requirements for LEADER+ programmes for the period 2000-2006. The guidelines for the Community Initiative set out in the requirements for the development strategy (Kommission der Europäischen Gemeinschaften 2000, para 14.2(a)) that young people (and women) provide useful inputs to the development of rural areas and therefore strategies have to look for better employment chances for these target groups. The criteria for selecting pilot programmes have to reflect this Community priority. Moreover under para 14.2(b) it is referred to the socio-economic situation of the area and an approach is required which does not reduce options for future generations. The inclusion of young people as a distinctive target group thus is a clear reference that from now on a closer examination of the role of young people in the rural development process will take place.

Obviously, this shift in priority of EU requirements has not been translated into the spirit of the bulk of the new programmes which had to be conceptualised before the guidelines have been published. Yet, young people have to be mentioned now explicitly as target groups and potential local actors.

The inclusion of this reference to young people in the guidelines has to be seen as a consequence of the discussion in the 1990s, and for example culminating in the set of principles laid out in the "Cork Declaration", including the desire to encourage participation in the formulation and delivery of rural policy. However, the time constraints inherent to formulation and strategy conceptualisation for (the former) objective 5b and LEADER programmes act as an important limitation on the scope for EU programmes to foster truly participatory forms of rural development.

The debate on participation in rural development has taken up elements from the policy and programmes on social exclusion. Recently, the often overlooked tendency of young people to out-migrate from rural areas has been addressed and the long-term historic trend has been assessed as detrimental to rural regeneration in general. The effect of marginalising young people in rural areas is best reflected by the very limited number of options facing young people there: to remain unemployed or to emigrate (Lowe et al., 1999, 40f.). Although the situation has to be differentiated according to the regional (and local) contexts, and unemployment is not the only problem for young people, one can find supporting information in the interviews of our research project that young people face considerable difficulties with regard to being accepted in the rural society and hence see primarily obstacles when trying to "participate" more intensively in their communities.

Enhancing Participation Activities

The combination of young people and rural development is, as has been shown, a rather new priority in EU rural policy, and has only been applied up to now in some exemplary cases concentrated in countries with a priority for action against social exclusion. However, when looking at global literature on the issue, it becomes evident that the issue is of much greater magnitude in developing countries. There the economic development and the future perspectives are more directly related to young people as these represent a much greater share of population. Case studies reported from Asia (Reddy 1990; Young India Project 1988; Reinhold 1993; Anwar 1994; Anwar et al., 1994; Anwar et al., 1995), Africa (Guijt et al. 1994) and Latin America (Dirven 1995) reveal the relevance for the territorial development in those areas. The approach has been of similar interest to the Eastern European countries (Pavelka and Stefanov 1985). Moreover case studies on experiences from North and South have developed a set of approaches, known as Deliberative Inclusionary Processes (DIPs) recognising that citizens should play a role in informing and shaping environmental policy (Holmes and Scoones 2000). Experiences from that work could be used for policy formulation targeting at an increasing involvement of young people in rural development.

Lowe et al. (1999) see a wide scope for effective local participation in the economic development and planning of rural areas and regions. There is, however, surprisingly little written about why participation is so important. It is argued that during the 1980s both the assumptions underpinning regional development policies and academic research began to shift. The new paradigm emerging did not any more see rural (and peripheral) areas as just externally-driven locations but paid increased attention to the potential of local actors for endogenous development. The development of rural pilot schemes in Austria, France and Spain at the start of the 1980s particularly centred on accentuating the internal forces of those areas. The development of EU rural policy, and in particular the LEADER initiative, took the same approach and thus has seen participation as a central element in the rural development process. However, later on in the 1990s with increasing experience of different regional cases the assessment made of these programmes underlined the need for widening the group of actors. The domination of traditional institutional structures had the effect that processes of participation evolved more slowly than anticipated, and action remained limited to core representatives of local (rural) society in most places (e.g. Dax and Hebertshuber 2000) leading to the discussion of how to achieve inclusion of larger parts of rural populations. As has been shown, recent EU guidelines give scope not just to allow for such considerations but even to require them as an integral part of programme formulation and evaluation.

The shift in discussion can also be seen in contents, as the focus is not any more on reaching consensus but increasingly on addressing conflicting positions of different stakeholders. The rising complexity for the regional work is addressed in many recent practical and theoretical studies (e.g. Bratl 1996, Scheer 1998). The requirements for the integration of young people in this process of enhancing participation activities are similar to those reflected in comprehensive approaches for environmental activities. A Handbook for Good Practice on local community involvement, prepared for the European Foundation for the Improvement of Living and Working Conditions (Chanan 1999) gives a number of proposals on extending horizontal and vertical participation. They relate directly to the Structural Funds and rural development programmes.

Lessons which could be drawn from this approach address the different benefits that different people will gain from participation according to their starting point. It is suggested that "for young people, taking part in sports, arts, social clubs or issue groups can be a way of developing a sense of responsibility and gaining recognition of talent" (Chanan 1999, 37). As the integration of diverse groups in this process is a long-term objective, a multi-level strategy is needed which would allow for increasingly widening involvement. Participation could therefore be conceived as a pyramid in which all residents of the area have at least one potential entry-point. From "lower" to "higher" levels one could see the following five steps (Chanan 1999, 38):

- Being a member or user of a community group or voluntary organisation.
- Taking a developmental role in a group or organisation.
- Helping a group/organisation to co-operate with others.
- Helping groups and organisations form a network.
- Representing a network or forum in an official scheme.

For our theme it appears important to emphasise those forms of participation which reflect the objectives of excluded young people, and young people in general, which include widening the networks of established organisations and giving opportunities to excluded individuals. This last notion allows us to address the issue of limited options, experienced as the core problem for young people in rural areas.

5.   Conclusion: Participation of Young People and Social Development

BIG-Bruck/Mur From the interviews with young people in the seven study areas it has appeared that actual involvement in local rural development is rather limited. It is more expressed by those young people who enjoy closer relationships to local key actors and who are better integrated in social networks. Most young people are hit by the changes in labour market features, rural changes in general (e.g. due to technological and societal changes), regional weak performances and uncertainty about usefulness of acquired skills. The interviews have, however, shown that there is a strong willingness to participate in community development. Conclusions from the analysis of the interviews and the respective literature (FAO 1998; Lowe et al., 1999; Johnson et al., 1998) point to the following main points:

- Young people in rural areas experience limited options for future life chances; the restrictions felt are relevant both for the economic and social spheres.
- Specific groups of young people in rural areas are affected by multiple barriers and special needs which might evolve into a vicious circle, leading to situations of social exclusion.
- Information available to young people on opportunities and life chances is lacking and there is a feeling among young people that their information need is only partly met by authorities. There is a search for a deeper understanding of the usefulness of education, training and transition options.

- Community development that engages with men and women of all ages requires a catalyst, i.e. a facilitator working with all people. One should look to increase the role of professional youth workers trained in interpersonal skills, advocacy and community development.
- Basic requirements for youth participation include capacity development of young people to articulate their needs, make plans and assert their rights, as well as technical assistance.
- The experience from youth future programmes reveals that an enormous dynamic for development can be sparked by providing the 'right' framework conditions for activities. Providing easily accessible structures with few bureaucratic restrictions is as important as providing financial aid to ease participation, especially if none exists.
- It is essential to develop parallel processes with adults and young people, as participation can only develop in a social context open for dialogue between these groups.
- Given the lack of local and regional strategic considerations, there is scope for using LEADER+ (and similar Community Initiatives and innovative programmes) as a pilot action for involving young people in rural development. Such action would address the experimental character as a means to allow creative enhancement of young people's involvement in local action and might serve as useful reference and motivation to participation and programme implementation in other rural regions.
- Economic integration is in general the leading issue when analysing young people's problems in rural areas. However, the social dimension and the inter-relationship between culture and young people's participation must not be overlooked. There is a need to extend emerging experiences of children's and young people's participation (Der Spiegel 2000), especially since such initiatives have strong implications for their subsequent participatory roles as adults.

Young people have the feeling that adult policies for young people concentrate on education and future employment issues. The views adults commonly hold of children and of the young represent them "as ignorant, irresponsible, immature, incapable, a nuisance and a resource". Such views focus on output driven notions and don't address personal development. "Seeing children as social actors opens up a new and wonderful world in which adults facilitate more than teach and children show that they can do much more than adults thought they could" (Johnson et al., 1998). Such an attitude is reflected in recent activities which seek to enhance participation through actions like "kids voting" in the USA which has been followed by German actors organising "political voting" which influences behaviour of children *and* their parents (Der Spiegel 2000). The recent innovative actions for youth participation has lead to a "youth future programme" in Styria, Austria, as outlined above. Using German experiences it is hoped to raise awareness skills of young people to deal with youth issues and to participate in projects and local actions (Der Standard 2000). Avoiding the dangers of over-simplification of such activities, one might see a wide scope for application of such initiatives, particularly in rural areas. Whereas previous research has focused on exclusion processes in urban areas this project has stressed the rural dimension and pointed to the multiple dimensions of problems in those regions.

Future rural development programmes therefore could become increasingly meaningful by including participatory approaches of young people in their development strategies. With adaptation to the relevant regional context, the recent discourse on social development and participation could be utilised for conceptualising development options for young people. As rural areas are addressed by the LEADER initiative, a programme of a highly experimental character is available which should be seen as an asset and used for more youth specific initiatives. When innovative projects in this field could be developed, this might have wider impacts on overall development of society.

Figure 8.1 Regional Measures Framework

Planning region "Wood world Murau"

Business development/qualification/education			Agriculture and forestry		Art and culture	Public transport/traffic	Tourism development			
Wood processing	**Business support**	**Education initiative**	**Adventures in rural areas**	**Additional sources of income**	**Art and culture**	**Public transport/traffic**	**Skiing region**	**Life world – water**	**Wood region Murau**	**Local specific measures**
Specialised wood processing techniques	Business park Scheifling	*Regional education platform*	Adventures in rural areas	Forestry close to nature	Art and culture of Murau	Increased mobility	Development of skiing resorts (Kreischberg/Frauenalpe)	Wildlife park Grebenzen	Concept of "Wood street Styria"	Health tourism (Krakautal)
Murau's workshop	Market in Niederwölz	Regional employment platform/JUPRO		Sustainable energy/heating	Regional festival Grebenzen/Styriarte (classical festival)/Jeunesse	Regional concept of transport and traffic	Apartments for tourism (St. Lorenzen)	Vivarium Stadlob	Wood museum Styria	Health centre (Stolzalpe/Murau)
Centre of wood world	Virtual centres Murau	*Women for women*		Provision of community services	*Cinema Scheifling*	Regional cycling program/paths	Local development (Turracher Höhe)	LIFE-Nature Hörfeld-Moos	Focus on Wood Products	
		Youth education		Agricultural education	"Water is alive"	Expanding the network of streets		Etc.	Walking and Trekking	
Murtal@at Connection						Coordination of public transport facilities	*Snowboard championship 2003*			

Note: Measures in italic are presented in Figure 8.2 (Projects of Youth Impact)

Figure 8.2 Selected Measures/Projects of Youth Impact in the Study Area Murau

Project Description (funding Sources)	Education	Employment	Participation	Mobility
Murau's Workshop: Distribution and Marketing of Products: Carpenter's workshop and Higher Commercial School Judenberg (school): Combination of new technology and conventional methods in cooperation with pupils; Development of distribution channels (ERDF, objective 5b)	X	X		
Connection: Mobile Internet@cafe for women. Providing computers for interested communities for one month: internet courses offered to women as private persons and employees in Murau (ESF)	X	X		X
Information Guide for Young People/Murau: Information about institutions such as official authorities, clubs, etc. and initiatives and cultural entertainment offered through internet and a brochure. Helps young people to establish a network (*nex:it*, Land Styria etc.)		X	X	
Regional Employment Platform: Discussion forum to create measures in the frame of the Territorial Employment Plan to increase job chances by educational and vocational training. Young people will be a specific target group (ESF, EQUAL)		X		
JUPRO 15-25: Application and vocational training of 6 months duration; funded by Land Styria (NAP: Job 2000)		X		
Women for Women: Innovative and local programs to improve women's job skills. Basic and advanced education and training opportunities, help to secure jobs in non-traditional branches, individual career planning, practical training, etc. (ESF)		X		
Cinema Scheifling: Cinema and entertainment centre (Clubbing, events); young people can rent a room for parties (private funding)			X	
Snow Boarding Championship 2003			X	

Figure 8.3 Youth Future Programme's Projects (*nex:it*, Styria), Regional Distribution NUTS III Level

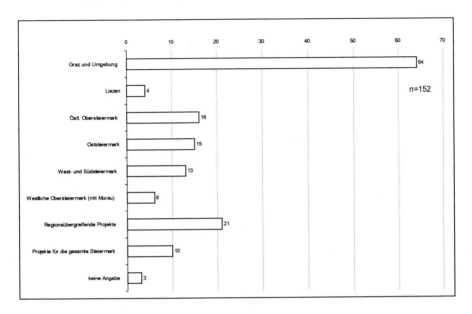

Figure 8.4 Youth Future Programme's Projects, Spheres of Action (*nex:it*, Styria)

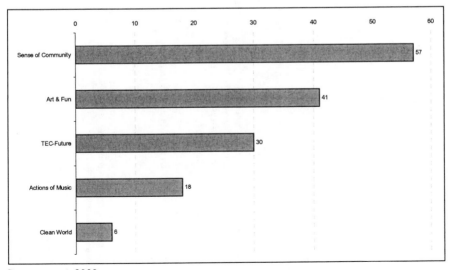

Source: *nex:it* 2000

Figure 8.5 Youth Future Projects in Murau

Title	Description	Duration	Category
Information Guide for Young People/Marau	Information Guide for Young People/Murau. Information about institutions such as official authorities, clubs, etc. and initiatives and cultural entertainment offered through internet and a brochure. Helps young people to establish a network	15.05.2000 – 31.05.2001	Participation
X-Treme	Recently a new Youth club has been established in Neumarkt in the district of Murau. The youth club arranges music events especially for young people who live there (easy to reach for the young people)	01.04.2000 – 16.09.2000	Participation, Mobility
Adventures for you too	Young addicted people should be helped through adventural projects to manage their day-to-day life (horse riding, painting, spending nights in self-catering flats)	01.07.2000 – 01.06.2001	Participation
Project N: nature in young people's hands	60 young people out of Styria will be trained to become a competent and committed "attorney of nature"	01.09.2000 – 31.05.2001	Participation

Source: nex:it 2000

Figure 8.6 Selected Youth Projects in Styria

Projects	Education	Employment	Participation	Mobility
"Mafalda goes countryside": offers courses about self-confidence, self-assertion and self-defence, workshops about "body and sexuality" as well as "new technology" to young women (only).	X	X	X	X
Training course for CNC specialists for women: In co-operation with a local firm a training plan has been created which offers women the opportunity to become a CNC specialist. The training activity has been funded by LMS, Land Styria and ESF. In 1999 15 women (12 aged 20-22) participated.	X	X		
"Young people": In 1995 a labour market oriented self-arranging project **"Young people" started with 77 young people aged 15-25.** The project lasted 14 days and was funded by ESF, Land Styria, and regional municipalities. In co-operation with the Labour Market Service (LMS).		X		
"Mürztal 2000": A network will be implemented which should secure employment for young people. The project comprises several modules such as clarifying needs, consulting, educational and vocational training, job finding and support to people in work. Funded by NAP, two municipalities are joining the project.		X		

Chapter 9

Social Networks, Labour Market and Policy Impact in Santa Marta de Penaguiao

Chris Gerry, Patrícia António, Carlos Marques,
Jose Portela and Vasco Rebelo

1. Introduction

This chapter summarises the results of the thematic research conducted by the Portuguese PaYPiRD team on *Social Networks, Labour Market and Policy Impact* in a small rural county (Santa Marta de Penaguião) in the Douro region of North Eastern Portugal into how social networks help rural school-leavers both to access information about job opportunities and, indeed, to secure employment. The chapter also describes the practical functioning of these mechanisms and, in doing so, tests the validity of a broad conceptual framework that was developed at the beginning of the research (Gerry 1999).

It was hoped that, by providing an assessment of the importance of rural social networks in the study area, relative to the functioning of both the labour market and the policy environment, and the extent to which they provide a means of securing more satisfactory employment for rural youth, further insights might be gained into the way in which market, policy and the local community articulate in other localities and contexts. If so, the analysis could provide a valuable input into attempts to improve the relevance, design and targeting of policies to promote employment and combat social exclusion in rural areas, by providing policy makers, prospective 'outside' employers and investors, with additional insights into the contexts in which such rural economic initiatives are made.

2. Why Study Social Networks?

Our interest in researching the functioning and involvement of rural social networks derived from the recognition – based on substantial prior sociological and economic research on rural Portugal – that the combination of the market mechanisms and government/EU policy *alone* determine neither rural employment and income outcomes, nor the broader social and cultural dimensions of rural livelihoods. It was strongly felt that rather than focusing narrowly on supply and demand, along with the policy measures ostensibly designed to improve the efficiency and equity of their interaction, it was the factors that lay behind the laws of supply and demand that demanded more detailed analysis. Intuitively, local (and local – extra-local) social networks also play a significant role in providing access – privileged or otherwise – to employment, and it is their form, functioning and relative importance that the Portuguese team sought to investigate and assess.

Rather than limiting the analysis by assuming that negative features of the structure and dynamic of rural youth employment could be largely explained by the failure of market and/or corrective policy to work properly, it was felt that greater emphasis should be placed on examining the nature of the interaction between (a) the market, (b) social network-based, and (c) policy mechanisms – along with their corresponding arrangements and institutions – so as to produce the employment and social inclusion/exclusion outcomes that currently characterise rural youth in Europe.

In tracing how rural social networks contribute to given outcomes for rural youth, and in identifying the "bridges" and "barriers" characterising the contours of market, policy and network, we have to be mindful of the fact that, directly or indirectly, in distinct circumstances of rural development, social networks, the labour market and policy measures all produce, alone or in combination, both wage-employment *and* self-employment opportunities. These are discrete forms of income generation, reflecting distinct social relations (in the broadest sense of the term), with correspondingly specific values, attitudes and social relations and, as such meet the aspirations of rural youth to a greater or lesser extent. Additionally, the fact that in many rural contexts economic pluri-activity (i.e. multiple employments and income-sources) is the rule rather than the exception increases the complexity of articulation between market, policy and network.

Traditionally, one of the key variables in influencing the outcome of social change and, in particular, the distribution of its benefits, has been the acts of solidarity that bound together members of the same socio-economic class. With the onset of the debate on post-modern society, the concept of class began to lose popularity and legitimacy among social scientists, and much of late 20th century sociology has placed greater emphasis on other criteria for inclusion and identity, such as common ethnicity, community, neighbourhood, family, gender or generation. Indeed, the sociological literature – in particular that relating to emigration, the persistence of smallholder agriculture, the informal economy, and ethnic minority entrepreneurship – is replete with references to the importance of networks (Portela 1988, Panayiotopoulos 1993) based on such non-class types of solidarity in determining who benefits and to what extent from the opportunities created by social change i.e. the very outcomes upon which recent concepts of social exclusion and inclusion have been constructed.

The literature on social networks that emerged in the 25 years following the Second World War is particularly rich,[1] though much of this tended to focus on the micro-phenomena of urban life, and/or on the persistence and adaptation of so-called 'traditional' forms of family- and ethnically-based solidarity as members of the rural populations in developing country increasingly established themselves in metropolitan settings. However, the literature on continued recourse to social networks in rural areas (i.e. the other side of the migration and adaptation 'coin') and, particularly, their functioning in the Southern European context, is less plentiful.

More specifically, the contemporary models of how the transition between school and work takes place, and how employment pathways are constructed, owe much to the seminal work of Beck (1992). However, these seemed inadequate – at least in the Portuguese case – to the task of making sense of not merely a residual persistence, but the continued vigour and indeed prevalence of social networks throughout rural society.[2]

The two main changes that Beck considers have marked the transition to a "risk society" are, on the one hand, the supplanting of traditional family solidarity by various types of institutional support and, on the other, the relentless penetration of the market and its attendant values. With regard to the school to work transition, Beck's conclusion is that youth, cast adrift from familiar support systems, and required to confront an ever more competitive, hostile and unpredictable labour market, are increasingly obliged to adopt a much more 'individualised' approach. It is in this context that youth are seen to be more and more constructing their own employment pathways and their own biographies.

Assuming, for the purposes of argument, that the Beckian hypothesis holds – i.e. that, in a risk society, youth do construct their own biographies, it is important to point out that the notion of choosing and constructing one's own 'biography' (as against accepting ascriptively attributed attitudes and behaviour) has two quite distinct but interrelated dimensions:

- *identity* – or the (mainly) subjective perception of self, constructed out of both subjective/internal and objective/external/structural elements, and its 'projection' onto or into concrete situations (e.g. identifying with particular groups, patterns of behaviour, norms, values, etc.); and
- *pathways* – based on the extent to which this process of 'projection', along with the context into which one's identity is 'projected', produce an outcome commensurate with expectations (i.e. job, lifestyle, prospects).

---

[1] See e.g. Mitchell 1969, Boissevain and Mitchell 1972; for more recent reviews and contributions, see Wolfe, A. 1978, Johnson 1994, Nardi, Whittaker and Schwarz 2000 and Fernandez, Castilla, and Moore 2000.

[2] For a recent account of the functioning of social networks, seen from the standpoint of the articulation between group and individual and between network and market, see Nardi, Whittaker and Schwarz 2000 and Molm, Takahashi and Peterson 2000.

For a number of reasons, the traditional family structure and its provision of solidarity and support still remains largely intact in some rural areas in Europe, notably the area under scrutiny here. Furthermore, while it is clear that, to a significant extent, demographic decline has retarded – or perhaps the term 'deflected' would be more appropriate – a fuller and deeper penetration of the market in rural areas. Finally, government policy has largely failed the rural areas and, where it has succeeded, this has often been due to the 'lubrication' it has received from the functioning of social networks in general, and clientelist relations, in particular. This should not be a complete surprise – as Giddens (1999) has recently argued that:

> in the industrial countries (...) traditional ways of doing things [have] tended to persist, or be re-established, in many (...) areas of (...) everyday life. One could even say there was a sort of symbiosis between modernity and tradition.

Paradoxically perhaps, Giddens' conclusion echoes one drawn by Lenin, almost a hundred years before, when he conceptualised the apparently contradictory co-existence of the modern and the traditional in Russian society in the following way:

> The development of (...) social relationships in general, cannot but proceed very gradually, among a mass of interlocking, transitional forms and seeming reversions to the past. (V. I. Lenin 1967, 536)

The Portuguese team's knowledge of and previous experience in rural and agrarian research suggested that, *a priori*, while a rural school-leaver may indeed initiate the search for employment on an increasingly "individualised" basis, with policy intervening – with more or less success – to mitigate the worst effects of labour market imperfections and/or supply-demand imbalances, a further component – namely the operation of mainly localised social networks of information, influence and solidarity – had to be incorporated into the analysis, if it were to provide a more complete assessment of market efficiency and policy effectiveness.

3. Methodology

The methodology adopted for the research as a whole did not generate the type of information that network analysts customarily dealt with. Both the data from the questionnaire survey, and the results of the open-ended interviews generated information, reflected the current situation and past experiences of a small sample of young people from a wide range of local communities, class backgrounds and educational levels. Due to this degree of geographical dispersion and socio-economic heterogeneity, it was not practicable to undertake detailed mapping of the social networks individuals used (or had deployed on their behalf) in pursuit of employment. Thus, regardless of the Portuguese team's preferences with regard to established conventional methods of network analysis, an approach had to be adopted that was relevant to the type of data collected. It was felt that, given the data that the project would be generating as a result of its wider, common concerns, and the current paucity of knowledge and analysis of how social networks operate in a rural Portuguese context, it was justifiable to limit our analysis to the following two main objectives:

- testing our initial typology and hypotheses concerning the nature and dynamics of rural social networks; and
- identifying the extent to which such mechanisms were currently used by and for youth, in substitution for, or as a complement to, market and policy mechanisms.

Nevertheless, the research into rural social networks in Santa Marta provides the basis for future, more detailed research with some or all of the following aims in mind:

- follow-up of the experiences of Santa Marta interviewees; and/or
- assessment of the performance (and recent improvements) in key policy measures; and/or
- a deepening of the analysis of preferment (*cunha*); and/or
- comparison of network forms and functioning in neighbouring counties/regions; and/or
- comparison of deployment of social networks by youth in more urban, yet non metropolitan contexts.

4.   Social Networks in Santa Marta: A Broad Conceptual Framework

Introduction: Networks, Markets and Policies

In Santa Marta and, by inference, in much of the rural interior of Portugal, not only do social networks play a crucial role in the search for employment in the private, public, NGO, and other sectors, but recourse to them is generalised. Indeed, their use would appear to be on the increase, mainly due to the pressures and difficulties young people experience in accessing stable and satisfactory employment.

While social networks clearly constitute one of the three key forces that determine employment outcomes – the others being the market and policy interventions – it would be inaccurate to see them as being a comparatively minor and residual factor, or merely a complementary component of the overall mechanism. All three factors interact and the relative weight and determinacy of each will vary according to the local circumstances and the prevailing economic and political conjuncture. Just as government policy is often seen as an (ostensibly temporary) imperfection that is imposed on the market with a view to achieving an improvement in overall equity and a targeted increase in welfare, so social networks can also be regarded as market imperfections brought about by local actors in pursuit of a distribution of benefits that is more favourable to them.

In the specific case reported on here, it would be more accurate to say that social networks are the predominant factor in explaining how young people find work for the first time, and how they take the first steps on a pathway leading either to stable (though not necessarily satisfactory) employment and relative socio-economic inclusion, or to precarious employment and possible socio-economic exclusion. In some circumstances they constitute the essential lubricant in the process; in others, they are the only significant force providing information, support, advice and assistance in helping youth to avoid long term unemployment. In extreme cases, the may operate to the complete exclusion, and prevail in spite of the dictates of the market and/or the targeting priorities of policy. Thus, in rural areas, it is the market and government policy that play secondary – and in some cases residual, neutral or even negative – roles in the process of matching *some* young people to the available employment.

It is therefore important to see the functioning of social networks not only in their own terms, but in their policy and market context. Access to appropriate social networks is a necessary but not sufficient condition for successfully making the transition from school to work: alone they provide no absolute guarantee of advancement. In order to be appointed to a particular position – however modest or senior, temporary or permanent, "dead-end" or promising it may be – normally a number of prerequisites will have to be met. This is all the more so when the post is filled through formal market mechanisms, i.e. open recruitment, advertised posts, interviews, ranking of formal and experiential qualifications, etc. Thus personal initiative, educational and/or technical qualifications, work experience, social networks and, frequently, luck may all combine to improve or diminish the likelihood that a given youngster will be successful in gaining a first and subsequent footholds on the employment ladder. Each of these prerequisites may be subject to limitations, and some criteria may need to be filled if others are to have influence: for example, family influence may only be invoked if the candidate for the post in question has the appropriate minimum educational qualifications.

Principal Features of Social Networks

Typically, rural social networks are not homogeneous, nor do they function in a simple or mechanical fashion. Indeed, the very term 'network' suggests complexity and flexibility. The operational form of the social network tends to be lighter, less structured and institutionalised, its functioning more flexible, and its interests and aims broader and less explicit than that of the social group. Networks are not typically constructed between people, enterprises and/or institutions on the basis of equality, but on the supposed identity, similarity and/or complementarity of their interests. Sometimes these interests are general (e.g. family solidarity); sometimes they are presented as being quite specific (e.g. business co-operation). Furthermore, networks consist of various types of asymmetrical interpersonal relations that can be deployed continuously and/or intermittently to achieve mainly economic outcomes by non-market means.

The generational, class and gender composition of a network's membership – be it homogeneous or heterogeneous – will have significant effects on the actions of those that participate in it, and the distribution of the benefits that accrue to them. Indeed, network membership of itself, guarantees little or nothing: benefiting from participation in a social network requires the continuous and/or intermittent management of its aggregate resources and its potential benefits, both by the individual and by key groups operating within given networks. Furthermore, network benefits are unlikely to be distributed on an equal basis, though implicit norms of both eligibility and relative equity of treatment will apply.

There are many types of networks and many of them interact. Network heterogeneity will influence the nature and outcome of a network's interaction with (a) social groups, (b) other networks, (b) policy-related institutions, and (c) markets. However, as an analytical starting point, the types of relations and transactions in question can be thought of as a continuum, ranging from acts of intra-family solidarity, through support provided within the extended family and between close friends (either inter- or intra-generationally), and networking within work-based and professional groups, to various forms of nepotism, and traditional and new forms of clientelism, including political and/or economic preferment, graft and corruption.

While the analogy of the transaction has traditionally been used to clarify certain aspects of how social networks function, this term tends to connote an essentially short-lived, act. However, the types of inter-personal and inter-group reciprocity referred to here – be they balanced or asymmetrical – may have considerable longevity, with myriad intermittent repetitions and cumulative interactions over time. Thus rural social networks tend to be lifelong phenomena: they are constructed, cultivated, extended, managed and maintained, restructured and revised, activated, suspended and reactivated throughout their members' life-cycle, from youthful dependence, to adulthood and relative family autonomy and back again to the relative dependency of the aged.

Thus multiple 'chains' of relationships stretch from inside the nuclear and extended family, across generations and between genders, extending to the local community, institutions, polity, economy, and beyond. The activation of these chains reinforces and/or restructures the pre-existing networks of asymmetrical relations – whether they be based on relations of solidarity or clientelism – altering both the context in which additions to and management of the network may take place, and the outcomes that may be expected by those involved.

Managing the Network

Neither young people, nor their older or elderly counterparts ever confront networks as ready-made structures and mechanisms. To a varying degree and, in particular, during the years of adolescence and early adulthood, networks are both subjectively construed, concretely constructed and increasingly deployed by youth as components in the exercise of some degree of control over their lives (in general), and over their employment pathway (in particular). For example, on the basis of their (albeit limited) knowledge of market and policy circumstances, and their assessment of probable outcomes, in seeking to achieve their own short term objectives or longer run ambitions, young people may perceive a clear distinction between the use of (a) ready-made and apparently secure and predictable connections provided and activated by their parents or close adult relatives, and (b) networks made oneself at school, in training and/or placement situations, in military service, and actively manifest a preference for one over the other.

There is a further and even more important distinction to be made between *membership* and *management* of social networks, which helps to explain the scope that exists for internal differentiation – both potential and real – inherent in them. Of themselves, networks do not guarantee an 'edge', a competitive advantage, or privileged access either to information and/or advancement. The ability to *manage* one's network(s), and to adapt network use to the prevailing circumstances – be they subjective (aims, aspirations, ambitions) or contextual (e.g. market conditions, shifts in politics or the balance of economic power) – is absolutely crucial to the improvement of employment, or any other sort of outcome.

Perhaps the best way of linking the subjective and objective dimensions highlighted above, would be to recognise that, over time, individuals activate and reactivate their networks, are more deeply or more marginally involved in them, and draw more heavily on or contribute more significantly to them as the circumstances dictate. Indeed, the skill with which one 'manages' one's network(s), i.e. maintains contact with fellow members, even when their contributions are not being called upon, may well be reflected in the overall long-run success with which networks can be used. This continuous 'management' may need to be undertaken not only when no network benefits are being sought, but also during periods of often extended absence, as in the case of emigrants.

For some, this network management may be a largely natural and instinctive process, while for others it can be conscious, planned and premeditated. Not only is the temporal extent of these rural social relations considerable, but so is their spatial scope, with network "tendrils" extending out to other areas, linking young married couples' own families, migrant relatives and friends, class mates who have moved to the city, fellow squad members from military service, fellow workers from building sites and fruit harvests in distant regions of the country or across national frontiers. The interpersonal proximity and shifting, and asymmetrical interdependency that any form of networking implies and, indeed, demands, not only has palpable benefits, but can also generate friction, and this may lead to individuals withdrawing from or even dismantling and restructuring the network, particularly in cases of (e)migration.

The notion of youth constructing, tending and occasionally 'pruning' their network of advisors, informants, patrons, mediators and 'fixers', contradicts to some extent the stereotype many adults have of youth – namely that they are typically immature and irresponsible.[3] Notwithstanding the prevailing image of youth culture as a 'live now, pay later' philosophy and practice, the reality is far more complex and contradictory. Youth not only have what we might call 'pre-

---

[3] Note, however, that this is only half of the 'Janus-face' that adults attribute to youth: the other half consists of the belief that youth are creative, intuitive and the repository of humankind's hopes for the future.

career concerns', i.e. about gaining access to employment, accumulating "credit" with potential employers that may serve them in the future, and finding the most advantageous trade-off between effort and reward. They also worry about which careers they will end up in, regardless of how closely these may correspond to childhood dreams, aspirations and ambitions. Conscious of the hardships past generations have suffered and how poorly many of the rural elderly still live, rather than simply 'living for today', they may contemplate some distant 'post-employment' future – what their pensions will be worth and who will look after them.

5.   The Use of Social Networks in Accessing Employment: A Summary of Results

The View from Below: Social Networks and the School to Work Transition

Before looking at the extent to which social networks are used to complement labour market and policy mechanisms in Santa Marta, it would be helpful to try to picture how the contours, trajectory and direction of the youth employment pathway, and thereby, young peoples' employment outcomes, are influenced by some of the key components of social networks alluded to above.

Typically social networks may link the parents of a recent school-leaver asymmetrically and intra-generationally with those who may be able to offer help, advice, information, influence, or even have the ultimate decision-making power in determining who is employed. Where such relations exist, young people themselves and/or by their parents may bring them to bear – successfully or not – on the problem of gaining a first foothold on the employment ladder.

Figure 9.1 below is an attempt to visually represent the first stages of such an employment pathway.[4] In this hypothetical case, not untypical of the situations encountered in the interviews and in the focus group meetings with youth from Santa Marta, an uncle acts as intermediary between his niece and a friend who works for the Local Council, with a view to securing an employment opportunity; later, the girl's mother's previous collaboration with a local development association paves the way for a temporary job in a hotel that is participating in a project to promote rural tourism, but also because the candidate, on her own

---

[4] For the sake of diagrammatic simplicity, it is assumed that the impact of factors influencing the direction and dynamic of the employment pathway is felt at the end of a distinct stage when, in reality, their impact may be felt throughout that stage and even beyond.

initiative, sought to improve her language abilities by spending time with relatives abroad. This experience, combined with volunteer work, along with her contacts, gave her the edge when applying formally for a more permanent post.

Figure 9.1 The Influence of Social Networks on the Employment Pathway

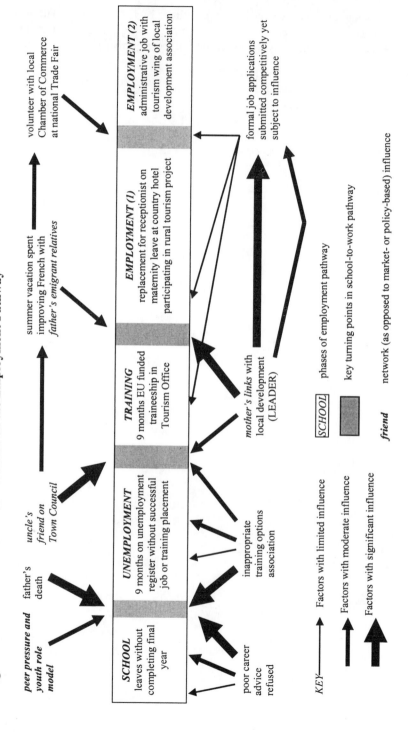

The View from 'Above': Social Networks, Markets and Policies

Networks do not exist and are not built, managed or modified in a vacuum, i.e. outside the context of market and policy, and that is why it is essential to examine the relationship between the three components of the network-market-policy "triangle", and how this articulation determines the eventual employment outcome, as Figure 9.2 below illustrates.

Figure 9.2 Employment Outcomes and the Network-market-policy 'Triangle'

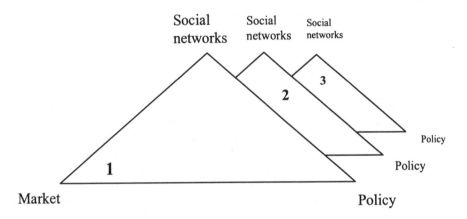

Market forces, policy measures and social networks combine differentially to bring about overall employment outcomes 1, 2 and 3, in which the influence of market, policy and social networks predominate, respectively. Put another way, these three positions reflect three types/degrees of 'market imperfections': relatively freely operating labour, capital, land and other markets, largely policy-induced and predominantly network-induced, respectively. These three outcomes could also characterise situations in distinct territories (metropolitan, intermediate, 'marginal'/rural) or, broadly speaking, distinct periods in which different economic and/or policy paradigms predominate (e.g. neo-liberal versus interventionist).

Analysts are accustomed to looking at the interface between policies and the market, but relatively little work seems to have been done on the articulation between non-market networks (either of the 'traditional' or 'modern' type) and either the market and/or policy interventions.[5] The three conditioning factors are not mutually exclusive; they may complement each other or conflict with each other. In reality, the 'spheres' of network, policy and market overlap and interact

---

[5] However, see, for example, Hadjimichalis and Papamichos 1991, and Hadjimichalis and Vaiou 1992.

substantially, since networks may be used (a) to secure employment/training that has arisen out of a particular policy initiative, and (b) posts that ostensibly are to be filled via the market mechanism; furthermore, policy shifts may constrain or widen the opportunities for networking, and shifts in the labour market may make networks less effective or attractive.

Thus the interaction between market, policy and networks may be of a more dialectical nature, with outcomes more complex than mere trade-offs.[6] Thus it may be more helpful to base our analysis less on the concept of the trade-off and more on the notion that rural social networks are created, maintained, managed and extended, mutually articulate and interact with markets and policies on the basis of *synergies*. Thus, in principle, the use of a social network, alone or in articulation with other networks, and/or market and/or policy factors, may produce a more satisfactory employment outcome than may be expected from reliance on market and/or policy measures alone. A more complex model is called for, given that the argument that relations of interdependence between different categories of rural resident are typically asymmetrical is more compelling – both on theoretical and empirical grounds – than the assumption that inter-network permeability is uniform, and network access is evenly distributed.

There is also the question of how networks change, adapt, and reconstitute themselves over time. Does this depend on how 'formally' they are internally structured and operate, or is it determined more by their articulation with other networks, institutions and markets? Is there an articulated set of "modes of advancement" along the employment pathway, linking not only market place, policy measures and social relations, but also bringing together various types of networks, each differentiated by function, generation, periodicity and extent of use?

If the future growth and adaptability of enterprises (and, by extension, other types of organisations) will depend more and more on network-based synergies, as suggested increasingly nowadays by management analysts, then it would be logical

---

[6] Some hypothetical, yet entirely plausible examples may serve to illustrate the problems of using the assumptions of narrowly-defined rational, optimising economic behaviour explicit in the concept of the trade-off and the zero-sum game approach: (a) *Young Farmers:* What are the costs of a young farmer withdrawing partially from family and/or community-based social networks in order to engage more actively/extensively in market-based initiatives via an EU subsidy and training programme (i.e. shifting from 3 towards 1 and 2 in Figure 9.2)? (b) *Youth Culture*: Is there a loss (or some kind of more complex qualitative shift) in the solidarity provided by a network of unemployed or unsatisfactorily-employed youth, when one member accepts a new job (i.e. does the shift from 3 to 1 permanently undermine the influence of 3)? (c) *Youth Training/Employment Initiatives Policy:* When rural youth participate in a given policy initiative, are there competing claims of family, friends and community (on the one hand) and of (new) policy-partners – some of whom may be peers (colleagues and collaborators), others who may be managers and/or decision-makers? (i.e. does a shift from 3 towards 2 undermine the effect of 3, or enlarge and redefine its influence?)

to conclude that networks offer opportunities that neither the market nor conventional corporate structures can provide.

6. Family, Friends, Classmates and Colleagues: Nurseries for Networking?

Introduction

Most of us assume, on an intuitive basis, that, to an appreciable extent, policies formulated to support youth employment achieve their stated objectives. As a result of our own day-to-day experience and observations and the effects of the prevailing policy discourse, we are conscious of the activities of whole sections of the state apparatus – the Ministry of Employment, Job Centres, the Institute for Employment and Professional Training, the Portuguese Youth Institute, etc., as well as myriad non-governmental and private agencies, intervening directly and indirectly in the labour market in a variety of ways, such as work experience programmes, training initiatives, self-employment micro-credits and advertising and information campaigns.

At the risk of caricaturing an undoubtedly complex situation, the interviews conducted in Santa Marta revealed that the intervention and intermediation of a series of people was of substantial importance in bridging the gap between school and work: parents, uncles and aunts, cousins, neighbours and even relatively casual acquaintances of the family, as well young people's own friends, former class mates and colleagues on training and work-experience programmes

The Primacy of the Family

One of the most important conclusions drawn from the research was that, among the local social networks to which youth had recourse, the immediate family was the foundation on which job-seekers depended for help and advice. The primacy of the family – both nuclear and extended – was reflected not only in the provision of general support (emotional, motivational, material, etc.) to youngsters, but also in attempts to maximise the employment opportunities open to them by activating any and all available networks, or by mobilising what some authors, in a somewhat differing context, have variously referred to as "social capital", "cultural capital", "relational assets", "powers of association", or "untraded dependencies" (Amin and Thrift, 1995; Storper 1995). In other words, rural families indulge in networking, deploying a complex web of relatives, close friends and even relatively casual acquaintances, with quite different socio-economic statuses, characteristics, assets and interests. Thus, typically, parents and other adult relatives were the first and crucial collaborators in the search for employment and, not infrequently, their efforts meet with considerable success.[7]

---

[7] This conclusion mirrored the situation found in some of the other European study areas, notably Austria (to a comparable degree, it seems), as well as Scotland and Ireland and, to a lesser extent, France.

Parents themselves make a number of direct inputs that assist their sons and daughters in finding employment or, at least, help them through the difficult period of waiting for an opportunity to emerge: principal among these inputs are:

- moral support and both "strategic" and "tactical" advice regarding both personal and employment related issues;
- continued free/subsidised food and lodging;
- child-care for offspring who have already started their own family;
- 'on the job' training and experience in agricultural and construction skills on the family plot and/or in the harvest, during repair/rebuilding of the family home and, in some cases in a family non-farm enterprise;
- land for own house construction;
- land, capital (including secured guarantees) and other inputs for a small business project (self-employment) to fully or partially occupy the son/daughter's time and provide a full or part income;
- access to privileged information and/or influence (*cunha*).

School as a Networking Opportunity

Its geographical position between Régua and Vila Real, and the closure of many village schools as a result of demographic decline and urban concentration, has meant that there is no secondary education beyond 9th grade in Santa Marta. Thus youngsters who wish to stay on and complete their 12 grade are forced to accommodate themselves both to new educational and social environments, with their associated benefits and distractions. There is not only a new institution to get used to, but also a new town and its extra-curricular attractions to explore, perhaps for the first time. Not only do youth have to construct a new set of peer relationships in their new environment (e.g. through new classmates and their siblings and parents), but they may perhaps also try to simultaneously maintain contact with existing friends. Despite the difficulties encountered (to which many interviewees alluded), this brief period of final schooling does provide young people with opportunities for broader-based socialisation, the building of new friendships and the widening of existing networks. To some extent, it may also enable youth to exercise greater autonomy over their use of networks.

To the outside observer, the strength of school-based friendships and classmate solidarity in Portugal may seem quite remarkable, and these values are particularly persistent in small towns and rural areas. It was quite apparent from our contact with the interviewees that attended Contact Group meetings (amounting to one quarter of the young people surveyed) that there existed strong ties between many of them: regardless of the differences in their ages, this bond was based on their attendance at the same secondary school, their same place past/present residence or employment (in the case of those from or working in Santa Marta town), complemented by common experiences, including the type of networking that has already been mentioned as one of the key sources of information in seeking and securing employment. As one interviewee explained:

There was this girl I knew from school who was there on an IPJ [work experience] scheme with two others. One left and the girl asked me if I was interested in working there instead. I said I was, went to talk to the people at the Local Council, and there we are. If it hadn't been for her, I would never have known about the job.

It is also worth noting that, with only one school providing secondary education in the county, it is at school that many young people begin to establish their first emotional relationships; as individuals develop stronger and more permanent relations with potential partners, there may be additional opportunities to expand networks that hitherto have been largely based on family/family friends. When a couple start to date regularly, their networks naturally expand, not only through mutual friends, but also through their respective families. The more permanent the relationship, the more integrated the networks become. Thus both of the young people involved gain access to specific sources of advice, information and influence, that would not have been otherwise available. Indeed, the interviews revealed a number of cases in which job opportunities were indicated and/or facilitated either by boyfriends or girlfriends.

Parental Influence Over Employment Outcomes

Continuing family support after sons and daughters have left school, clearly raises questions about the extent to which sons and daughters are involved in family decision-making, and the influence that parents and other adult relatives exert over youngsters' employment decisions. The extent to which young people themselves may participate in the deploying of connections and influence, in the discussion of options, and the taking of decisions is likely to be highly variable.

However, there was only a relatively small number of cases in which youth decisions had conflicted with parents' advice. Specific cases of disputes tended to involve leaving school against the parents' wishes. I such instances, parents may reluctantly accept their son's or daughter's decision, or try to reverse it by denying (or threatening to deny) access to family-based employment opportunities, contacts or influence, as Rosa's experience indicates:

My dad wanted me to carry on at school, and told me that if I wanted to start work, not to expect him to arrange it for me (...) [When I found a potential opening myself] my dad said, "Look, you can either wait and see if something comes up at the Town Council, or I can talk to someone". Anyway, not long afterwards, the Council offered me a job, but my dad had already starting talking about calling in some favours.

Parents may exert considerable influence over the occupational choices of their offspring (and the choice of school subjects each option would require) either openly or in subtler ways. Their inputs can provide useful guidance, but also may seriously misdirect the young people concerned, precipitating either quite radical and stubborn opposition, or an excessive degree of passivity and diffidence on their part, as the following case (among several others) illustrates:

I had thought of taking Arts and Design. I wanted to but my mother wouldn't let me. She said "Not Arts and Design – that's just for little fools". That's it, that's how she talked at the time (...) I wasn't going to attend school any further [i.e. above the 6th grade] if I was going to have to take a course I didn't like. What would be the point? But later *I got used to the idea of working here* in the family shop [our emphasis]. (Dulce, female)

However, despite stiff opposition from their parents, it was nearly always the son's or daughter's wishes that prevailed; various strategies to overcome parental opposition were used, including deliberately failing the year and/or persistently absenting themselves from classes. A small but not insignificant number of interviewees dropped out either well before compulsory schooling had been completed, or even when the option of further education was open, simply because they felt that the time had come to help the family economically, instead of being a financial burden.

There are also cases in which the family environment is far from conducive to positive educational and/or employment outcomes. For example, particularly after his mother left, Gonçalo received no support from his 'primary' family. He was forced to take care of his younger siblings and thereby forfeited any chances he had of completing even his primary education. But his 'secondary' family – namely that of his uncle – provided the basis for positive change, through the improvement in his immediate home and emotional environment, and his uncle's sound advice and network of contacts in the village.

My father was a labourer on the Council's road-mending gangs and, well, there wasn't much chance of me staying on at school, because I always had to take his lunch to wherever he was working. He drank a lot, too, so when my mother left, someone had to look after the house and the other 4 children. I didn't get on with his new wife either, so when I was 17, I went to live with my uncle. He got me started in the construction business — the builder I work for is from the same village. When things are quiet, I go abroad for the tomato or strawberry harvest. Some of my friends have ended up in prison, you know, but I've managed to avoid that. I've got my own wife and kids now.

Domestic Chores, Family Businesses and Employment Pathways

In principle, integration into family-based economic activity – either run by one's own parents, extended family, or family friend/acquaintance – may constitute a stepping stone in terms of experience, skills and confidence, as well as for the establishment of networks that may facilitate the search for more definitive and stable employment. Before they find work, or during periods of (temporary) unemployment, young people may simply help out at home or, in those cases in which the family has a small, vineyard, farm or family a small business, they make a contribution to the family's own productive activities. As Castro, now an agricultural labourer, told us:

I like what I'm doing. It may seem to some that vineyard work has nothing to offer but, for me, it has. But it's not easy: like everything else, you have to learn. You can't turn up one day and just do it. I worked with my father, so it's always been familiar work. Even when I was still at school, I was interested, so we'd work weekends, and I'd see what he was doing, when it had to be done and why. I learnt alongside my dad, seeing what people did in the vineyard. I didn't get paid for helping, but I still enjoyed it.

In some cases, the inputs provided by youth may be sporadic, largely symbolic and unpaid while, in others, they may constitute a real and valuable contribution to the enterprise that may warrant some remuneration over and above the board and lodging the family normally provides.

Clearly, involvement in domestic and home-based chores (ranging from housework, through childcare of siblings, to tending the vegetable plot) begins long before youngsters leave school and continues, to some extent or another, for some time afterwards. There were numerous cases of young women making significant inputs at home, particularly in the case of sick or disabled parents or grandparents. Indeed, in some case this quite clearly interfered with looking for work, i.e. interrupted the school to work transition.

Temporary involvement in a family business may become more permanent. Despite the limited capacity of the typical rural family to absorb in this way sons and daughters that have left school, it can nonetheless provide an important "cushion" while employment options are identified and explored. Almost one in five of the young people interviewed (9/46) had worked or were working in what we could describe as their own family's firm – using the term in its broadest sense. In three of these cases, the job has become permanent, while in the remaining 6, the employment was clearly temporary 'stop-gap' measure rather than a specific 'stepping stone' that improved future employment chances.

There was, however, anecdotal evidence that 'informal' job experience training is provided in micro-enterprises through the extended family and/or intra-family networks, in preparation for future employment in which not only will experience be necessary, but where it may be more difficult to bring influence to bear, i.e. where the market will play a more leading role. As one key informant, suggested

> Something I've learned from my experience in business is that cunha doesn't typically operate as a means of arranging what we might call 'real' employment (...) Where it does function is when parents talk to friends or acquaintances and say "I've got this son who's just finished his studies, but who knows absolutely nothing about the real world. Couldn't you take him on for 6 months, so he could get a bit of experience?" And that's the way it works – you use a *cunha* to get your son or daughter some experience (...) even if they don't always get a salary. (TS, Focus Group meeting of institutional actors, 30.05.2000)

It is not clear to what extent such network-provided 'stepping stones' are restricted to this work-experience and informal training function. However, if this stage in the school to work transition is relatively common among youngsters actively seeking employment, then its prevalence would constitute a profound condemnation of the formal training services, not to mention the inappropriateness of much of what is taught in secondary schools, universities and polytechnics.

Family Strategies and Employment Pathways

Often an explicit family strategy is developed in which the economic activities of parents and the future employment of sons and daughters (or at least the first steps along their employment pathway) is indissoluble. In at least three cases, parents of interviewees developed a strategy that relied upon the active (or at least passive) co-operation of their offspring in subsidised business investment initiatives, and from which the sons/daughters potentially could benefit. In one case, a father had sought a subsidised loan from a EU-supported small business promotion programme to open a shop which would diversify his car sales and repair business, and which his daughter was to manage. In another case, both parents had encouraged both their sons to apply for a Young Farmer training course and helped them to submit a vineyard project to the government's agricultural credit agency IFADAP for subsidised investment funding. It was clearly the parents, rather than their sons, who would take charge of the new vineyard; as one of the boys, Xavier, said:

> Yes, it was their idea – Dad and Mum's. (...) The paperwork's already been handed in. It's a vineyard project – the land's registered for Port grape production, near Régua. The project had to be in our names: it's a question of age – if it was in their name they'd get nothing. But it'll be them who'll handle the farming side. Nowadays Young Farmers can spend less than 50% of their time on the farm and they still get the money.

In a third, a father and son felled and sold wood; the son was to apply for the same type of subsidised investment described above, but the father was to take the major responsibility for the vineyard.

Training and Networking Opportunities

With regard to post-school determinants of the employment pathway, once young people have definitively left school, they may participate in training programmes or undertake work experience placements. There is a strongly-held belief among economists, policy-makers and training professionals, not to mention some – but by no means all – potential trainees, that training will have positive effects on young people's employment prospects. In this section, the question being addressed is not "does training enhance employability?", but rather "does the training experience also help to expand networks?". In principle, training brings young people into contact with others of the same age and background, but from other counties, as well as training staff and administrators from outside their field of experience.

Given the very real problems that confront the training system in rural areas (see Section 10.5.), there exists a very real threat that courses and programmes may have little or no tangible effect on youth "employability", let alone on building their confidence, or realising ambitions and potentialities. There is some evidence from Santa Marta that youth derived other types of benefits from training and work experience placements: (a) purely pecuniary ones since, in many cases, trainees receive allowances and payments; and (b) the opportunity to build networks – including clientelist ones – that might be deployed (not always successfully) in attempts to secure more permanent employment, either where the placement was undertaken, or elsewhere. While the information gathered on the extent to which training and similar experiences may help to create/extend networking between young people is somewhat patchy, it nonetheless corroborates what had frequently been mentioned in interviews: young people roundly criticised Job Centres, careers advice provision and the poor range and relevance of training schemes, yet they suggested – often indirectly – that, within strict limits, training does provide a basis for extending one's networks. The key question remains – do such additions to youth networks have positive effects on employability?

While many training programmes themselves encourage networking in the broadest sense, others actively encourage trainees to seek subsidies, sometimes together, so as to maximise the initial capital available and to spread the risk. Some trainers – particularly in programmes that have self-employment objectives – felt under pressure (and this is inevitably sensed by the trainees, too) to direct young people towards the subsidised business credit initiatives that central government provides and that are managed by various public institutions. As one young woman, aged 23, remarked:

> There were only a few of us from Santa Marta on this Parks and Gardens training course in Régua, and I was by far the youngest. There was a lot of pressure on us to make group applications for small business loans. As I didn't know anyone there, I just kept quiet.

Also, it can be extremely difficult for a young person to put together the capital necessary to launch a small business. Family may help (Gerry et al., 1999), but so may the constitution of a more or less formalised partnership. However, the extent to which youth (or, indeed, the parents that may be required to act as partial guarantors for subsidised loans) may extend their trust to young people from outside their own community and/or network, remains to be seen. In conclusion, while there is some evidence that training *can* be an experience that enlarges young people's networks, the particularities of the training systems would suggest that training perhaps provides rather better employment opportunities for trainers than for trainees,[8] and that the networking it may encourage is not as conducive to the creation of sustainable youth employment as it could be.

---

[8] Recently, the take-up of trained professionals has been higher in institutions active in the welfare/charitable (NGO), training, and agricultural/sectoral and local development spheres than in the traditional providers of local employment (namely the Local Council and the Wine Co-operative). It is important to stress that such activities constitute a relatively new type of network, that may intersect with those habitually used by rural youth in their search for employment, and that may constitute a new source of networking benefits. However, it remains to be seen whether (a) recruitment and advancement in these has more immunity from the influences of *cunha* than the more traditional institutions, and/or (b) if, through their employees, these organisations also provide preferment to members and clients and their families, over and above the services they are constitutionally committed to providing.

7.   The Evidence from the Santa Marta Interviews

Patterns of Recourse to Different Types of Networks

Our analysis of recourse to social networks (i.e. intra-family or friendship-based solidarity and co-operation) is based on what interviewees said about their *own* employment pathways; however, many of the references made more specifically to *cunha*, favours and preferment were contextual i.e. they appeared to relate more to what respondents had heard from friends than to their own employment experience. Clearly, it is extremely difficult to distinguish accurately between (a) comments that are rationalisations and/or self-justifications of an unsatisfactory employment situation, (b) experiences that are attributed to others, when in fact they apply to the respondent, and (c) comments that fairly and explicitly refer to objective circumstances, practices and outcomes. We can exclude neither the possibility that some youngsters' reflections on their own failure to get the employment they wanted, or to advance along the pathway desired, were simply "sour grapes" – a not inappropriate metaphor to use in a wine-producing county such as Santa Marta.

Furthermore, given the limited size and representivity, and *purposive* nature of the sample, the figures mentioned below and the percentages presented in Table 9.1 reflect the tendencies that emerged from the interviews conducted with young people in Santa Marta, and should not be interpreted as being anything more than suggestive of circumstances existing among youth in Santa Marta in general.

Notwithstanding these reservations, the interviews showed that, in general terms, a strong sense existed among virtually all the 46 young people surveyed that social networks were of invaluable support in finding employment and, in many instances, had been used for this purpose in their own particular cases.[9]

It should be stressed that only 8 of the 46 young people interviewed provided no information with regard to the use of social networks. Five of these were still at school, and therefore would have had little direct experience of the social relations on which they were invited to comment. Thus, of the remaining 41 respondents, only 3 failed to provide substantive information on this theme, either because it had played no role, or due to embarrassment on the issue, or their more general reticence or shyness. Two-thirds (27) made multiple references (averaging two significant comments each) relating to the use of social networks of various types at various times. The multiple responses either related to employment outcomes in which (a) two types of network had been simultaneously used (e.g. family member giving information, family friend/acquaintance as provider of or intermediary in the provision of a favour or, indeed, a favourable decision regarding employment), or (b) in which different types of networks were used in finding successive jobs.

Ten young people had obtained their current, or some past employment through the use of *cunha* (i.e. via preferment that transcended the more 'horizontal'

---

[9] The three interviewees that attributed little or no importance to this factor had no personal experience of unemployment.

practices of intra-family or friendship-based solidarity, a phenomenon dealt with in more detail in Section 5 below), which constituted somewhere between a quarter and one-third of those interviewed. There were cases of both personal and 'institutional' *cunha*, as well as those in which the client's 'reward' was not necessarily as permanent an employment as they had perhaps expected. Though it was not possible to quantify the proportion of *all* jobs that had been the result of *cunha*, the indications were that it would be somewhat higher than one-third of all cases.

With more specific regard to the use of social networks in accessing employment, the interviews yielded a total of 86 experiences of work (or various types and durations), a figure that excluded the incipient employment histories of the 5 individuals still in full-time schooling and the three non-respondents. Qualitatively speaking, family- and friendship-based networks were found to provide not only information and intermediation/influence that facilitated job search, but they sometimes also directly provided employment. The distribution of the use of different types of networks was as follows:

- Family- and friendship-based information networks: In 30/86 (or a little over one third of the cases) family, close kin and friends provided information which facilitated job-search and, in many cases, the securing of employment.
- Family- and/or friendship-based employment intermediation: 19/86 or approximately one in five of the employment opportunities taken up by our interviewees were created through the substantive intermediation of kin, other intergenerational or friendship-based intragenerational networking.
- Family- and/or friendship-based employment provision: 13/86 or one in seven of the employment opportunities taken up by our interviewees were created directly by a family member or by a friend providing work.
- Employment via own initiative: 8/86 or one in eleven of the employment opportunities taken up by interviewees since they left school being primarily as a result of their own initiative, providing evidence, albeit limited, of the extent to which social networks are either are not available to or are eschewed by youth when seeking work.
- Employment found via institutional preference for kinship-based recruitment: 4/86, or one in twenty of the past or present employment opportunities taken up by interviewees were due to an institutional preference for recruiting kin of present employees; however, this apparently insignificant number should be considered an underestimate, since there were further interviewees whose application for entry into one or other the uniformed services was at some point "in the pipeline", and these are precisely the organisations that still – formally or otherwise – have this preference for kin-based recruitment.

The details of the analysis of the transcripts of individual interviews and focus group meetings are summarised in Table 9.1 on page 209.

Relations of significant interdependency exist between parents/adult relatives and friends and acquaintances on the frontier between the nuclear family and what we could more accurately describe as key social networks. Such networked relations of solidarity support constituted almost 14% of the references youth made to sources of help in accessing/securing employment. Here we should stress that activation and management of these wider networks may often be initiated by parents and adult relatives, thereby complementing their own intra-family assets and efforts.

It is not surprising that networks that include family friends and acquaintances, being more extensive and with greater potential interconnectivity, exert a greater influence over employment outcomes than is the case with family-only networks. While family friends and acquaintances tended not to be substantial direct providers of employment (only three of the jobs surveyed), they nevertheless were an appreciable source of information and/or influence (9 responses).

Compared with their parents, parents' relatives and friends, young people's own friends constitute a more significant source of information (13 responses). While the total volume of information (ultimately useful or otherwise) that flows between members of the same generation remains unknown, there are strong indications that the above figure underestimates the overall scale of peer-provided data.

Surprisingly, given that we might assume that influence is correlated with age and experience, friends of the same generation are the most significant source of influence. Over one in ten responses referred to friends, former classmates and 'cousins' (often a euphemism for distant relatives of similar age), compared to the 6 and 3 cases respectively that mentioned the influence exerted by close kin and family friends, in accessing and/or securing jobs.

Gender Dimensions of Social Networks

With regard to the use of specific types of social networks in seeking and securing employment, there were relatively few differences that could be discerned between the 19 young males and 21 young women interviewed. Discounting non-respondents, over a quarter of all interviewees' responses mentioned their ability – if necessary – to call upon the networks and influence of their parents in securing employment. More than half of the 22 interviewees that referred to family-based 'fall back' support were female. Furthermore, women constituted six of the eight interviewees who had found their present or previous employment primarily through their own initiative, i.e. without appreciable recourse to any form of social network. This finding indicates that, predictably, in a society that is still extremely male-dominated, despite the growing feminisation of employment, and ostensibly greater priority and more effective targeting of women's employment, the principal job-related social networks still tend to function disproportionately in the interests of men.

Table 9.1 Types of Social Networks used in Seeking and Securing Employment

NETWORK CATEGORY	TYPE OF SUPPORT	N°	NETWORK %	SUPPORT %
1. Intra-familiar and inter-generational i.e. support from parents/close kin [10]	(a) information only	2		2
	(b) influence ('go-between')	3	14	4
	(c) employment provided	7		8
2. Family influence as a fall-back [11]		22	26	26
3. Extra-familiar, inter-generational i.e. contacts between parents, friends and/or acquaintances [12]	(a) information only	5		5
	(b) influence ('go-between')	6	16	7
	(c) employment provided	3		4
4. Intra-generational friendship friends, class-mates, cousins [13]	(a) information only	13		15
	(b) influence ('go-between')	10	30	11
	(c) employment provided	3		4
5. Traditional kin recruitment [14]		4	5	5
6. Own initiative/ own business [15]		8	9	9
TOTAL		86	100.0	100.0

Source: Transcripts of interviews conducted in Santa Marta, November 1999 - January 2000.

---

[10] Intra-family support (advice, information, influence, and direct provision of employment in family undertakings) is assumed to be inter-generational, i.e. limited to solidarity from parents and close kin.

[11] Information was taken mainly from a specific set of prompts in the open-ended interviews, in which young people were asked whether they could rely on their family's privileged contacts, if they were unsuccessful in securing employment through the labour market. Even those who had little to say about social networks in general often replied in the affirmative. Overall, 20 of the 46 young people interviewed, reported that they felt confident that they could count on this type of family back-up.

[12] Employment found through parents' friends far outweighed the cases in which success was due to parents' influence with 'mere' acquaintances. While, in a sense, 'everyone' knows the Mayor, relations with the President of the local Parish Council may not only be closer, more familiar and easier to activate, but highly localist territorial solidarity will almost certainly be a further factor in determining whether a 'favour' can be expected.

[13] It may be thought that cousins should be included in the category of *intra*-family solidarity, support and contacts. However, due to the small (demographic and geographical) scale of the communities in question, as one interviewee put it, "more or less everyone's your cousin here". There is of course a hierarchy of (near) peers who are lateral blood/marriage relatives: first (or 'direct') cousins being offspring of one's parents' siblings. Yet people commonly refer to their ties with second cousins, and even more distant 'cousins' by marriage, as conferring special consideration and solidarity.

[14] Partly due to the security of salary and tenure that the employment offers, there are still a number of occupations in which recruitment from the same family predominates: for example, the various uniformed branches of the police service, the post office, the local voluntary (paid) fire brigades, among others.

[15] There were a few cases in which the interviews pointed to employment being secured largely as a result of the interviewee's own initiative, not in the market-place, or in employment related institutions, but via either direct contact with potential employers, or seeking out those they knew to be well-informed and/or in possession of 'inside' information.

Finally, male interviewees were the exclusive beneficiaries of what we called 'traditional kin recruitment', whereby institutions such as the post office, some branches of the police force, etc., demonstrate a strong preference for the recruitment of relatives of currently serving staff.

Of course, these results may be biased by broad factors such as the degree of detail and/or candour to be found in interviewees' responses regardless of gender, or more specific factors such as a more characteristic unwillingness on the part of males to admit to family support even as a 'fall-back' option. However, the researchers' own observations, contextual evidence, and the results of other studies (Estanque and Mendes 1997) would suggest that our modest conclusions are not too far wide of the mark.

Class Dimensions of Social Networks

Extra-familiar social networks (e.g. those between parents and their friends/acquaintances, and between youngsters and their former classmates) often cut across class lines and, as such, tend to reflect the dominant position of clientelist structures and ideologies in rural society. Just a very few families completely dominate Santa Marta's economy and society, and these constitute an extremely powerful interconnected elite that together controls most of the key institutions and decision-making processes in the county. The fact that there has long been a close correlation between land-ownership (either private/family-based, or corporate), and economic and political power, is reflected in the still high proportion of landless agricultural wage workers in the county, compared with much of the rest of rural Portugal. Though this situation may be changing now as a result of migration, mechanisation and the (albeit limited) diversification of the rural economy, it nevertheless raises the interesting question whether those more 'proletarian' backgrounds tend to use social networks any less than those from other socio-economic categories. Indeed, the poorest rural families may suffer significant and chronic network exclusion (See section "Too poor for *cunha*?" page 221).

What the data seems to show with regard to the class dimensions of social networks[16] is the following: among the small number of youth with 'white collar' parents, corresponding to the 'new' rural petty bourgeoisie of public functionaries, managers and professionals, there were very few cases of extra-familiar, inter-generational social networks being used, though there was a high level of confidence that the family could provide the safety net in the form of access to social networks that could be useful in accessing employment. In contrast, among

---

[16] Parents' occupation constituted the nearest proxy indicator for socio-economic class on which data was collected via the questionnaire survey. There is a longstanding and highly polarised debate on whether meaningful conclusions regarding class positions, attitudes and actions can be drawn from standard occupational categories; notwithstanding the quite legitimate reservations that critics of this approach have advanced, it is clear that, on the basis of such a small sample, no very firm conclusions could be drawn.

youth with 'blue collar' parents (farm labourers, construction workers etc.), i.e. those with what might be termed agrarian working class characteristics, intra-generational friendship networks were of particular importance in supporting job-search and contributing to success in finding employment. Youth whose parents are self-employed, and whose socio-economic class position is that of the traditional rural petty bourgeoisie (shopkeepers, small farmers and small entrepreneurs), appeared to use all possible networks and social relations in their search for employment.

Network-Accessed Employment: Stop-Gap or Stepping Stone?

Almost one in five of the young people interviewed (9/46) had worked or were working in what we could describe as their own family's firm – using the term in its broadest sense. In three of these cases, the job has become permanent, while in the remaining six, the employment was clearly a temporary 'stop-gap' measure rather than a specific 'stepping stone' that improved future employment chances. However, there was, however, anecdotal evidence that 'informal' job experience training is provided in micro-enterprises through the extended family and/or intra-family networks, in preparation for future employment in which not only will experience be necessary, but where it may be more difficult to bring influence to bear, i.e. where the market will play a more leading role.

If there remains some doubt about precisely what function the 'stepping stone' performs, then it is essential to determine how many young people whose first job is of this variety (i.e. acquired through family/social networks), and what proportion find their subsequent jobs using less clientelistic means. Obviously, to detect this 'stepping stone' effect, we have to look at those who have had more than one job experience. Obviously, with such small numbers of cases, the results of this analysis have little or no statistical significance, and are purely suggestive of phenomena and explanations that will require further investigation.

- Youth with experience of two jobs: If we compare the way in which youth with experience of two jobs at the time of interview obtained their first and current jobs respectively, then we find that in the overwhelming majority of cases, both family and/or friendship networks continued to be involved in securing the second employment opportunity. This was the experience of at least eight out of the 12 cases analysed.
- Youth with experience of more than two jobs: For those with more than two work experiences, i.e. cases in which any 'stepping stone effect' would be more clearly visible, the situation was extremely variable. However, very few used the 'family/friend' circuit in finding either (a) their first and subsequent job, or (b) in finding their current job. In the first case, this was the experience of, at most, only three of the 11 cases identified; in the latter case, the figure was only 4/11.
- Youth with experience of two or more jobs: If we compare current and previous employment of the 34 cases in 1) and 2) above, 28/34 (i.e. well over

three quarters) found their current employment through family and friendship-based networks and, taking into account that 13 youngsters were in their first job at the time of interview, 16 of the remaining 20 (again, the vast majority) also found their previous jobs through similar network-based channels. In other words, the market and policy-related mechanisms functioned directly and/or exclusively in no more than one in five of the cases examined.

By way of comparison, it is worth referring to the findings of the Scottish PaYPiRD team, who applied Beck's (1992) conceptual framework of the 'risk society' and the associated 'individualisation' of employment pathways to their data from the Angus area, and concluded that social networks tend to channel youth primarily into *temporary/seasonal*, low-skill and poorly paid jobs. Moreover, there was some evidence from other study areas to support the wider validity of these findings. However, the situation in Santa Marta was marked by some subtle, yet important, distinctions. In order to access employment and as a means of constructing a first phase of their employment pathway, young people tended to deploy social networks rather more, resorting less (and less directly) to the market and to policy measures. Also, there was a strong indication that social networks were used far more extensively, i.e. not simply to find casual, temporary and/or unskilled work. The data further suggested that, in many cases, such jobs constituted neither a mere 'stop-gap' measure, nor a stepping stone to more satisfactory or longer term employment.

While the number of cases in the Portuguese study was insufficient to draw any firm conclusions, the evidence suggests that, when social networks are deployed, they do typically lead to low-skilled, poorly paid and potentially 'dead-end' jobs, as in the Scottish case. However, rather than taking advantage of temporary and/or seasonal jobs as a sort of 'stop-gap' until more stable employment is found, the structure of employment opportunities faced by young people in Santa Marta is typically much less varied, and, in many respects, far less promising. Many of those interviewed had taken a succession of *potentially permanent* but usually low-skill and low-paid jobs that they only abandoned if and when a better alternative presented itself – either via network-generated information and/or influence, or through unmediated market and/or policy mechanisms.

If we compare how interviewees found their *first* and *subsequent* employment, in almost half of the cases (5/11) youngsters moved from one (potentially permanent) low-skill job to another, equally low-skill job, usually on their own initiative or with family/friends' assistance. Furthermore, if we compare how interviewees found their *previous* and *current* employment, just as many youth seemed to move from one low-skill job to another equally unpromising job as a result of the market and/or policy-measures, as change jobs exclusively with the help of family and/or friends.

In part this is predictable, since geographical factors may limit both the functioning of local networks; furthermore, access to the type of favours (jobs, small business contracts, training and investment subsidies) that the local elite may bestow on local youth may be restricted not only by ethical considerations and/or the more rigorous application of transparent selection procedures, but also by supply factors. For example, influence may be more readily exercised in certain sectors (in which employment growth is limited and/or where subsidies are being tapered off), than in others.

However, as can be seen from the data above, there is also evidence that social networks, particularly those based on family (rather than friends/acquaintances) are a plentiful and essential source of employment. Some of the jobs are in small family firms, which is predictable in profoundly rural areas. Others are provided by uncles and aunts, cousins and godfathers, both in the locality and elsewhere (due to extensive out-migration).

The fact that casual and/or unskilled employment tends to be the norm rather than the exception in Santa Marta, could explain the predominance of networks and the determinant role they play in accessing employment there. However, this suggests a rather simplistic and deterministic correlation i.e. that the more pervasively rural is the local economy, the more network-based will be the society. Or, put another way, at one end of the rural continuum (e.g. Angus, in Scotland), social networks simply complement the market, while at the other extreme, (e.g. Santa Marta), the market and policy merely support the operation of networks.

The fact is that, in Santa Marta, the family retains a very strong (though adaptive) influence, despite the influences that have fed back into local society from the emigration experience. Furthermore, pre-modern rural social relations – which were very much based on the *quinta* (the large estates) and on economic and political clientelism, have also persisted and still play a fundamental and pervasive role in influencing both the local opportunity structure and the prevailing norms of social, economic and political behaviour.

8. Influence, Preferment and the Job Market in Santa Marta

> We're talking about a county [that's] (...) profoundly rural in character, where, essentially, access to the labour market is achieved through personal influence. This means that most of the very few posts that become available in the local council, wine co-operative, schools and (...) the police are filled via someone's intervention. (institutional actors focus group meeting, 30.05.2000)

Introduction

The range of non-market relations that form the subject matter of this study constitute a continuum stretching from (on the one hand) various forms of intra-family solidarity, through neighbourhood- and community-based mutual aid, labour-exchange and information-swapping, to (on the other hand) clientelist favouritism, discrimination based on friendship and/or political connections, acts of quite brazen nepotism, and even financial corruption, all exerting an influence over the employment pathways rural youth may be able to follow. These latter practices are broadly referred to in Portuguese as *cunha*. However, in its colloquial use, the term tends not only to cover a multitude of sins, but myriad acts of what could even be described as kindness and unselfishness, aimed consciously or otherwise at defending the sustainability of the local community.

Literally, *cunha* means a wedge, and is used to describe the advantages enjoyed by those who have influence, "clout", "pull", "friends in high places", the ability to "pull strings", provide preferment or "jobs for the boys", either on a narrowly nepotistic, broader friendship-based, partisan political or more generalised clientelistic basis. It thus refers to a whole range of discriminatory and unethical practices of preferentially allocating people to posts and/or contracts to companies. Furthermore, the term is used both to signify the relationship, as well as the 'price' of the favour.

Cunha involves privileged access to influential people, through whom information, further contacts, or even direct preferment e.g. in the form of a job, a contract to supply goods or services, may be arranged. Such advancement may be achieved either via a direct and immediate exchange of favours, including payment in money or in kind for 'intermediation services' (i.e. 'rent-seeking', or outright bribery) and/or deferred return of the favour, either 'in the same coin' (between those whose socio-economic status is similar), or in some different form i.e. political reliability in voting or decision-making, or 'transactional' preferment (as in business relations). Furthermore, in the case of those with lower socio-economic status and the least to offer, the patron may be able to rely on (or exact under pressure) a series of minor (even symbolic) acts in repayment of the favour.

The high degree of concentration of decision-making power – as exemplified in 'elite pluri-activity', or the widespread interlocking and overlapping of political, institutional and economic activities of the individuals and families that constitute the local elite – is due, in part, to the small scale and limited resources of rural communities, but it also has its origins in the pervasive and deep-rooted inequalities that have long dominated Portuguese rural society that have been reproduced over the years and, more importantly, *adapted* to fit present day conditions.

Asymmetrical Interdependence and the Dangers of Moralising

In analysing *cunha*, we should avoid moralising about the market. The hegemony of neo-liberal theory and practice has transformed the hypothesis that "the market is the most transparent and fair mechanism available" into an uncritically accepted certainty. It is worth reminding ourselves that not only is the real extent of market liberalisation frequently exaggerated, but also the remaining 'imperfections' still far from perfectly understood. Those who see the market as guarantor of both efficiency and equity conveniently forget that social and economic anthropologists, along with applied development economists, have long identified "networking", and the deployment of "social", "ethnic" and/or "community capital" as key processes in how the real economy functions – particularly in the attempts of both disadvantaged workers and out-competed small businesses to subsist and survive, often in contexts in which forms of economic intermediation such as rent-seeking by more privileged members of society, along with widespread clientelism, tend to be the norm.[17]

Furthermore, networking is now considered a *sine qua non* of success in corporate business, non-governmental organisations, and academic research. Indeed, in recent years, the growing flexibilisation of labour and employment, coupled with the revolution in information- and telecommunications-based technology, the expansion of outsourcing, and the unprecedented integration of media, entertainment, telephony, computer and internet businesses, has further emphasised the strategic importance of networking, both in the old and the new sense of the term (Nardi, Whittaker and Schwarz 2000).

Cunha, both as a practice and as an attitude, remains strong and persistent, and links individuals and/or whole families in asymmetrical clientelistic relations over the generations and in this respect is similar to social networks based on more egalitarian solidarity. However, "keeping it in the family" is a two-edged sword, and it is extremely easy in highly competitive circumstances to blur the dividing line between (a) solidarity in pursuit of greater local social justice and (b) corruption as a means of concentrating the spoils in a few privileged local hands. If the 'horizontal', more symmetrical functioning of social networks represents a strategy of the poor and less-privileged trying to increase degree their inclusion in the few available opportunities over which they have no direct control, then it may seem that the more 'vertical' and asymmetrical interdependencies explicit in *cunha* represent a strategy of excluding all but a chosen few from a share in the few available opportunities over which the patron exercises direct control.

The passage from traditional values to modern ones, or from regulated to more freely-operating markets has often been portrayed as a transition from arbitrary/ascribed distributional principles and practices to more legitimate/equitable ones. However, many analysts would still claim that the triumph of the market has merely replaced one set of asymmetrical interdependencies with another. The perhaps unpalatable reality is that in an unequal society, solidarity-oriented social networks and discriminatory *cunha*, localist cross-class solidarity and self-serving clientelism are indissoluble, each contributing to an environment that is conducive to the development of the other and neither, ultimately, facilitating the reduction of inequity and injustice, let alone the eradication of social exclusion.

Supply and demand aspects of cunha Paradoxically, or so it would seem, *cunha* continues to flourish even now that the dominant ideology and discourse is that of the free market – ostensibly the more anonymous, rational and just mechanism of allocating resources to their most appropriate, efficient and productive uses.

---

[17] Social networks are fundamental to the overall structuring and regulation of migrant labour flows, as well as in providing on an inter-ethnic (or intra-community) basis for the solidarity that allows migrants to plan in advance (or, at least, approach with some degree of confidence) their upcoming resettlement, permits new arrivals to settle, find work and shelter, negotiate bureaucratic hurdles, or have others do so on their behalf.

On the 'supply side', i.e. from the perspective of the patron, no type of organisation seems exempt, be it private sector, public sector, government service, or NGO. In general, it's through friends that the parents approach what you might call Santa Marta's employers – the Council, the Wine Co-operative. Well, there's not many other places to look for jobs, is there? They plead, they promise, they even try to enlist the support of well-known people, or members of the same political party (Father M., initial contextual interview).

Indeed, we should not assume that favours and favouritism do not apply where the recruitment process is more regulated and greater formal transparency exists, i.e. in the public sector, and/or in the recruitment of higher level, professional and related staff. Furthermore, there is concern among youth about the appointments to more permanent jobs being made on the basis of candidates' political affiliation and not their fitness for the job.

As far as the private sector is concerned, it has long been commonplace for building contractors, vineyard owners and wine co-operatives to use local social networks for the recruitment of both permanent and temporary (seasonal) labour. However, local government throughout rural Portugal has a tendency to weight key decision-making criteria in a way that is often questionable, and to use procedures that are less than completely explicit or transparent bot only when allocating short-term work-experience and similar posts funded by central government, but also the adjudication of local construction, maintenance, service or supply contracts. Furthermore, there is growing concern that in appointments to more permanent posts candidates' political affiliation and not their fitness for the job is often decisive. Also, as a general rule, conflicts of interest that would otherwise exclude individuals from key public decision-making processes tend to be ignored.

Where favours are provided through political networks, asymmetrical interdependence also exists. From the perspective of the job seeker (or his/her family), political connections may improve the chances of success. From the standpoint of the political elite, the clientelist management of employment outcomes facilitates the building of alliances and the consolidation of privileged position and power.

From the 'demand-side', i.e. that of the 'client', social networks in general, and 'pulling strings' in particular, also constitute a very palpable and influential part of the rural mind-set. Recourse to family and extra-family networks remains an almost instinctive response among rural residents, particularly the relatively powerless. Firstly, the specific historical features of Portuguese rural life, the miserable living conditions that the vast majority of the inhabitants of the countryside experienced in the past, along with the particular forms of institutionalised clientelism and vote buying that developed during the Republic and under the Salazar dictatorship, have tended to reproduce this psychological conditioning and predispose much of the rural population to excessive deference to and dependence on local political and economic elites. As a key informant explained:

The importance of the *cunha* – at least in psychological terms – is that people (...) have got it into their heads that they won't get anywhere in life without 'knowing someone'

(...). So they make a point of talking to Mr. X, or Dr. Y. or Mrs. Z. about some employment opportunity or other that they think may exist for their son or daughter. And these people reply, 'Don't worry, I'll talk to so-and-so, everything will turn out OK'. And even if the intermediary doesn't do anything or hasn't really got any influence, maybe the young person concerned gets the job. So the whole thing becomes an accepted and normal procedure. (FR, initial contextual interview)

Additionally, demographic and economic decline in many regions of the Portuguese interior, and more intense competition for ever fewer job opportunities that these processes have generated, have caused those seeking employment – in particular, for the first time – to call on any and all resources that might ensure them of success. Indeed, even in the absence of concrete evidence that deploying clientelistic relations may have some positive effect on job prospects, youth and adults alike will automatically assume that their interests will be served by the activation of whatever network of family, friends and acquaintances they may dispose of, and by soliciting favours from ostensibly better placed individuals to provide them with "inside information", to "put in a good word" for them, or in some other way to promote their cause.

Clearly, however, supply and demand aspects cannot be seen in isolation. By definition *cunha* is a 'two-way street' – benefiting employer and employee, patron and client, along with any intermediaries involved – albeit unequally. The use of networks and the exchange of favours facilitate recruitment in a context characterised by labour/skill shortage. Furthermore, it structures and concretises employer-employee relations by subjecting the performance of the 'client' not only to conventional employer pressure, but also to the pressure of his/her network, his/her 'helper' or intermediary. In short, the intermediary in the provision of *cunha* stands as guarantor for the performance and reliability of the person whose case has been advanced. Finally, the top-down, clientelist management of employment outcomes by a local elite provides a means of building alliances and consolidating its position, power and privilege.

Limits to Cunha

Notwithstanding the pervasiveness of *cunha*, there are limits to its use and effectiveness. As we have seen, where the market is less well developed, where factor markets neither function nor articulate fully, and where information is both imperfect and circulates less than freely, access to employment via privileged information and/or influence is crucial, and clientelist relations will play tend to play a more significant role in determining employment outcomes.

Firstly, while social networks may be useful, influence normally need not be deployed in order to access labouring jobs. When discussing the use of influence, interviewees often made an interesting distinction between 'work' and 'employment', the former term being used to describe labouring jobs in agriculture or construction, the latter exclusively reserved for office-type jobs in the private or public sector. Typically, *cunha* is not required for hard physical labour, as the following young woman confirmed:

> When it's just a question of hard work, all you have to do is talk to the farmer or whoever. They'll say straight away – "You can start tomorrow" (...) So you don't need to know anyone to get that type of job. But for decent jobs, you need influence. (Rita, female, 2nd focus group meeting, 27.05.2000)

However, where influence can improve an applicant's chances – or even guarantee a job – a *hierarchy* of influence exists; in other words, the 'market' for *cunha* is itself imperfect, its supply is limited, family and individual network endowments are unequal and differentiated, and therefore competition for access to the benefits of *cunha* is fierce. As one interviewee admitted, somewhat ruefully:

> Any influence I've got doesn't count for much. If it did, I'd already have a permanent job with the Town Council (...) I suppose I've got *some* clout – the problem is that others have got much more.

Firstly, from the client's standpoint, the success of *cunha* may first depend on choosing whom to approach in which particular circumstances. Naturally, this is determined by the clientelist networks to which one has access. The more extensive and complex the network or networks, the greater will be the number of points of access. For those with multiple, differentiated and intersecting networks, there is also the problem of deciding at which point or level in the formal (workplace, decision-making) or network (influence-deploying) hierarchy the approach would be most effective, remembering that you "don't ask a general to do a major's work". Clearly, where a 'chain' of influence has to be activated, it is important to have as much confidence as possible in those playing an intermediary role between the potential beneficiary and the person from whom preferment is being requested.

Secondly, the success of *cunha* may also be contingent on deploying other assets, or fulfilling other criteria, such as educational prerequisites. Thirdly, and in spite of having the right formal qualifications, and regardless of having 'pulled strings', the approach may be misdirected (i.e. lead to nothing), be rejected (the 'brick wall effect'), rebound on the client concerned (the 'boomerang effect'), or be successful, yet prove too costly in terms of future favours, in comparison to the value of the preferment being sought. Both the 'operational' complexity and indeterminacy of outcome that characterise the use of social networks in general, and *cunha* in particular, are exemplified in the following examples.

Educational prerequisites for cunha   Our data showed that those who have completed 12th grade experienced most problems in gaining stable employment, and often suffered longer periods of unemployment, and/or a succession of more unstable and unsatisfactory short-term jobs. Nevertheless, those who had still not completed the compulsory 9th grade, or who were studying privately, or after work, to complete their 12th grade, were conscious that these qualifications would allow *cunha* to be deployed:

> I've got a guaranteed job as a secretary next year, with a friend of my mother's, at the telephone company in Vila Real, as long as I pass my 9th grade. (Luísa, first Contact Group meeting, 20.05.2000)

Some interviewees implied that, naturally, they needed to have the educational qualifications required by a particular post, but as long as they fulfilled that specific criterion, networks, clientelism and favours could help to "move them up the list":

> Just recently, there was an administrative assistant's job going (...) [where I work], and of the three girls who applied, two of them hadn't even finished secondary school, and another applicant had a degree. But she didn't get the job, because one of the others had an 'inside line'. (Rosa)

The 'brick wall' effect One of the main reasons why young job-seekers may find their pathway blocked is that there exists a hierarchy of *cunhas*, i.e. even if one can bring some small influence to bear on the situation, someone else may be able to deploy more or better *cunha*. Thus those with no or little influence through their social networks may find that their legitimate claim to a job, or at least a chance to be interviewed, is undermined by less well qualified applicants with better connections and/or better information. Drawing on their own and others' experiences, many youngsters draw the general conclusion that the skills, qualifications and commitment they have to offer is not taken into consideration when employment decisions are made:

> I put in an application, but I didn't have any luck. Things worked out differently from what I'd imagined. I thought your qualifications and skills would count for more than just *whom* you know. (male interviewee)

Another conclusion that they may draw is that their own influence failed to work, people did not keep their promises, or that someone with a better *cunha* got the job:

> I've tried four years in succession to get a job that way [using *cunha*], so that I could study and work at the same time, but it's never resulted in anything (...) The people I talked to at the place where I was trying to get a job were just ordinary folk, a teacher, for example. Friends of my parents. But it didn't come to anything. (Luísa, first Contact Group meeting, 20.05.2000)

Further, they may also perceive that, as far as access to information is concerned, no 'level playing field' exists, and that some people are always at the head of the queue:

> I heard from my girlfriends that there were work experience placements that you can apply for, that pay the national minimum wage. You work in the Town Hall, or in a play-school, or something like that. But [before you can apply] (...) you find out that so-and-so already has a placement, and she got to know about it at the Job Centre. And you ask yourself, how did she get the job? "Oh, you had to apply, and then get selected", she'll say. But how are you supposed to know about these competitions? And even when they have to be advertised, it's always the same people who are 'in the know', and who seem to move from one of these types of jobs to another every 6 months. Selection should either be competitive, or not – one way or the other. As it stands, it's just not fair – it's always the same people who get the jobs." (Zulmira, female interviewee)

The 'boomerang effect' In rural communities characterised by asymmetrical interdependencies, the use of social relations to gain preferential access to employment tends to reinforce both inequality and solidarity at the same time. This means that every favour has consequences, not just in terms of the need to return or repay it in some way, but also because it often places parents and/or friends in a position where they stand as guarantor for the behaviour, performance and reliability of the person on whose behalf the favour has been asked.

Judging from the open-ended interviews, there were at least seven cases of what might be termed a 'boomerang effect' in the use of clientelistic relations and networking. By 'boomerang' effect, we are referring to attempts to use *cunha* to get a job that, for any one of a number of possible reasons, in fact may work *against* the potential client. Preferment that was solicited and expected fails to be delivered, bribes lead to nothing, or the sometimes exaggerated expectations of both youth and their parents regarding the efficacy of "having friends in high places", or putting "a word in the right ear", are not met. There may be cases in which the effect may be immediate, as the quote from Ana (interview 18) below indicates; a relative tried to intervene on her behalf, only to find that their own social and/or economic status in the community precludes help. Sometimes, as Rosa's comments below suggest, seeking a favour means taking a risk: though the effect may be deferred, under specific circumstances and after some time has elapsed, the boomerang can return to injure its thrower:

> My father-in-law said to the Mayor "Look, Chico, couldn't you find a job for my daughter-in law?" And he says, "It's you that's in the best position to find her a job, not me, what with all your money and your houses and so on!" (Ana)

Or, as one interviewee explained, advantages that a client may gain on the basis of a patron's transient decision-making power, may be eroded in the future, if circumstances change:

> Both my dad and I have done a lot of work for the party, so I had that edge over the others when a job came up in the Town Hall. The Mayor's in the same party – but if he lost to the opposition at the next elections, and power changes hands, then I'm done for. I wouldn't lose my job, but I'd never get promoted, that's for sure. (Rosa, first Focus Group meeting, 20.05.2000)

From the perspective of some of those with decision-making power, rather than being an exclusive form of nepotism, *cunha* provides a means of inclusion, reflecting the responsibility of the rural elite towards their less-favoured neighbours. Unlikely as it may seem, some members of the rural elite would judge whether or not to favour a particular petitioner on grounds that they would consider to be ethical, namely that the use of *cunha* should be limited to those really in need of support. This is so, even if the act earns the patron some small – sometimes merely symbolic – favour in return, either immediately, or at some time (or several times) in the future. Thus we can almost talk of an "ethical *cunha*", distinct from real corruption, that concretises the responsibility the rich and powerful feel towards their less-favoured neighbours – an attitude that is firmly rooted in conservative ideology. Nevertheless, they may find their use of "petty *cunha*" constrained to some degree: patrons may be subject to denunciation, public ridicule and even social ostracism, if they are seen to exceed the bounds of acceptable behaviour.   Also, the patron's willingness to provide preferential treatment is linked to their position relative to the 'petitioner', and the extent of the former's 'social exposure'. The corollary of these limits to the exercise of *cunha* is that it is generally held that it should only be used to help those really in need of support.

Too poor for cunha?[18] Pre-existing social and economic exclusion may also make it difficult for certain sections of the rural population to access even the small favours that are often associated with traditional clientelist relations. In some more marginal parts of Santa Marta county, economic and social deprivation is still marked, levels of educational attainment are still much further behind average European levels than elsewhere in rural Portugal, and demographic decline constitutes a major threat to local socio-economic viability. In such contexts, the combination of poverty and physical isolation. Thus some families may be too poor, and parents and their children too poorly-socialised, to be able to establish either the type of varied and extensive social networks or be able to deploy the type of *cunha* that, as a rule, those living closer to the county seat take for granted. A former Santa Marta teacher explained this problem of 'network exclusion' in terms of:

- the autonomous (rather than predominately wage-working) 'mode of production' that characterises the more isolated highland villages of the county, where the local economy is based on cattle rearing rather than vineyards, and where the latter's characteristic clientelism is largely absent;
- the fact that their communities are smaller, more isolated, and in sparsely populated areas where physical access is more difficult; and
- the fact that, paradoxically, children's overall socialisation is impeded rather than assisted, from a very early age, by the way that education is organised.

Most children have to travel to school from the age of 6 or 7, leaving very early in the morning and returning only late at night. Since many are forced to rely on public transport, interaction with their parents, most of whom may be relatively poorly endowed in educational terms, is reduced to a minimum. Indeed, the children may not even have the dubious advantage of being bombarded by TV in what remains of their evenings, since the signal will be too poor or non-existent in the areas where they live. While, according to conventional evaluations, the school performance of such children may not be noticeably lower than their more urban lowland counterparts, their socialisation is poor, and their interpersonal skills less

---

[18] This section draws heavily on an early contextual interview with Francisco Rocha, 30/11/2000.

well developed. This in turn implies more limited networks and less effective networking skills.

Regardless of where people live, however, the present generation of young people in general has a much greater likelihood of gaining the educational qualifications that would take them out of the socio-economic category to which their parents typically belong. Yet young people still marry rather early, and therefore their parents may be as young as 35-40 when their children begin to contemplate married life, and this may limit the scope and maturity of networks and *cunhas* that parents can deploy on their behalf. Even those with reasonably extensive networks may find that they are inappropriate to meet their children's aspirations and/or potentialities.

Cunha and the 'accumulation of credit'   When the labour market is tight, young job seekers frequently accept permanent posts that neither match their qualifications, nor meet their salary expectations. The decision is often seen as a worthwhile investment in the longer term, inasmuch as it "builds up credit" with a new employer, and may provide the basis for future advancement and promotion. Seen this way, i.e. as a stepping stone rather than a stop-gap measure, there is clearly a deferred exchange of favours involved, with the new recruit making a commitment that may be rewarded in future, and thereby laying the foundation for easier and more rapid promotion later.

However, this deferred exchange of favours does not only apply to the well qualified (i.e. those with 12th grade or a degree). There is a certain acceptance that working on work experience programmes, despite the very low wages, offers a way of accumulating 'Brownie points'. Several interviewees with only low qualifications took up such opportunities, partly in the hope/expectation of building up their 'credit' either with the employer involved (e.g. crèche manager) and/or with decision-makers in the allocating agency (e.g. Town Hall and/or Job Centre). Youngsters calculate that, by taking such posts, regardless of the skills they may require and/or acquire, it may be possible to transform a short-term temporary job into more promising programme-based employment, and/or access state-promoted training, or even convert temporary employment into a permanent 'staff' position.

The following conversation, taken from one of the Focus Group meetings, exemplifies the theory and practice of 'accumulating credit':

> "No-one likes working all day, all month, on the Unemployment Fund and earning only 18,000 escudos [€90], but a lot of kids accept the low wages because you're sort of earning your place". (...) "You know, a job in the future. Often, when they advertise a post, the first thing they ask is how long you've been on the Fund". (Luzia). "You were already working in the School Office, weren't you? You'd done your time, and you still didn't get the next job that came up, did you?" (Sebastião). "No I didn't, but that was because there were two women ahead of me who'd been on the Fund longer, so that was fair enough, even though one had only 5th grade and the other only 6th, while I've finished the 12th (...) Still, if there's a chance of a real job, it's worth the investment." (Luzia, female, and Sebastião, male, 2nd focus group meeting, 27.05.2000)

In order to put a foot on the first rung of the employment ladder, a youngster may have to accept what may be a poorly-paid waste of time, providing little or nothing in the way of training, and that may in fact confer greater benefits on the 'patron', via the filling of quotas, and meeting programme targets. Later, the fact that he/she has 'collaborated' may improve his/her chances of a better and more permanent job, and may permit existing networks to be extended, thereby creating a better platform for subsequently accessing *cunha*.

Politics and Preferment

As we have seen, in the particular circumstances of Portuguese rural society, there are practical advantages of deploying social networks and a strong psychological predisposition to use them. Furthermore, local politics in rural Portugal is perceived as a personally- and territorial-related exercise: it meshes with family life and prospects, as well as with the functioning of social networks. It can therefore be legitimately argued that local politics often act as a driving force for both social "inclusion" and social "exclusion". Throughout the Portuguese countryside, those who have close ties with the mayor, with members of the ruling party, with local leaders, or with those who are integrated in their social networks, succeed in entering specific social spheres; the rest are simply "left out". However, this does not prevent the majority of people, with the exception of those who are wholly marginalised from the centres of political decision-making, from perceiving the Town Hall as a potential source of preferment. As one key institutional informant maintained:

> Here, lots of things operate on the basis of *cunhas*. People expect this. They seek out those who have influence and, I don't know whether this is because it's a small community, but it's all very politicised, too. They go to the Town Hall a lot precisely for this reason. I suppose they feel that it's the Council's duty, somehow, to find work for those who have none. And they really do go looking for favours! Just like beggars asking for alms.

Local political power tends to be built upon social networks. Some informants openly recognised that both the family and peers strongly influence one's links to the life of the political parties. One girl stated explicitly that she joins the party's marches as much to have fun with her friends as to express her political commitment; other informants spoke of their political involvement as an integral part of family life. Eça, a young man whose family is involved in Santa Marta politics, and who has been politically active himself, could not have been clearer:

> My father is a [local] politician. (...) Personally I do not like much politics: I think it's rather a dirty business (...) Politicians do a lot of deals under the table and behind people's backs (...) As for me, you see, it was more... [a case of being involved] since I was a child (...). I later joined my father in this 'business', in political campaigns and so on (...) I started to get more and more involved, and I was eventually pressured into a post with the local youth branch [of the political party], and that's all there was to it.

Some young people, having gained a degree of political experience, become socialised into the prevailing opinion of their party leadership regarding the role youth should play in politics and the value of their ideas. It would be legitimate to ask why the some youth persist in giving their time and energy to political activity, when there exists such a mismatch between the high costs (in terms of commitment and work) and the low returns (little attention to and limited acceptance of young people's ideas and proposals). Furthermore, given the disrespectful and rebellious reputation young people have, would it not be reasonable to expect some sort of reaction, other than fatalism and apathy.

Why do young people apparently allow politicians to 'use' them? Some of the data collected in Santa Marta may support the idea that, after all, the unbalanced nature of the transaction between politicians and young people is not a long-term phenomenon. Youth 'play' with politics for the fun it involves, and 'drop out' of politics because of its frustrations. On the other hand, they may keep a low political profile by missing the regular party meetings, tolerating the above mismatch mentioned for a while in the hope that it may turn out well.

The politician and public servant's capacity to intervene on one's behalf is, however, frequently overestimated, even though their activities are frequently under close scrutiny. Indeed, three informants revealed that their current jobs were obtained (two became civil servants and one has had several temporary jobs through the Local Council), due to their political membership and activity. The researchers also became aware of their sombre expectations if local political change were to occur: both career promotion and the availability of temporary work could come to an abrupt halt.

9.   Social Relations in Other Case Study Areas

It seems unlikely that Portugal is the only case study area among the seven analysed in the PaYPiRD project, in which the degree of rurality (however defined) is sufficiently high, the absence of a "proletarian milieu" and frame of reference so great, and the transition to a "risk society" – with its attendant individualist perceptions and patterns of employment – so incipient, that social networks (of solidarity, clientelism, etc.) continue to play a preponderant and/or determinant role? Do other study areas – such as the French case (despite the nearby large factories) or the Irish or Scottish cases (despite the proximity of relatively large urban centres compared to Santa Marta) or the Finnish case (with its extreme physical isolation, though at a higher level of income and material development), provide any evidence in this regard?

Again, the researchers' own observations, along with data from contextual interviews and other studies, would suggest that the discussion of this hypothesis cannot be restricted to data relating to first experiences of relatively low level employment. Regarding the applicability of the 'Scottish hypothesis' to Portuguese rural reality, it would appear that, due to the absence of fully functioning market mechanisms, the limited relevance and impact of past rural- and youth-oriented policy, and the heritage of clientelist practices and mind-sets, social relations (in general) and *cunha* (in particular), both help to channel individuals into a very wide range of jobs – from the most temporary, unstable and low skilled employment, through more permanent and stable jobs with potential for advancement, to the most responsible posts in which the incumbent exercises substantial power over others.

An initial evaluation would suggest that these same networks do operate (albeit to a lesser extent) in other rural areas studied in the PaYPiRD project, in market/structural contexts that are by no means ideal, but nonetheless relatively 'rich' compared to that of rural Portugal. Questionnaire data on social networks in all seven of the study areas indicated that they were of great help in accessing employment in five of the seven cases, their use being least marked and/or appreciated in the German and Scottish study areas.[19] In a group of cases – France, Finland, Austria and, particularly, Ireland – there was more evidence that social networks played a role in helping youth to find work. In the latter case, it should be noted that as many as one out of six of respondents felt that social networks were irrelevant.

Table 9.2 Importance of Social Networks in Finding Employment: The Seven PaYPiRD Study Areas Compared

	Great Help	*Some Help*	*Irrelevant*	*Total*
Portugal	36	6	3	45
Ireland	24	15	2	41
Austria, Finland, France	49	26	15	90
Germany, Scotland	13	38	8	59

In the Finnish and French cases, Job Centres were the key provider of information, motivation and opportunities, almost to the exclusion of social networks; in Ireland the importance of Job Centres was less marked, though still important, whereas in Austria, they were infrequently cited as being of value. However, it was in rural Portugal that social networks were shown to be most valued by respondents, with policy and market-related mechanisms (except for newspaper advertisements) proving to be of little significance in accessing employment.

More specifically, in Ireland, the extended interviews showed that social networks particularly helped youngsters to make better-informed decisions based on the current/past work and training experience of friends. From the potential recruit's standpoint, this provided an opportunity to gather information about working conditions, prospects, etc., in specific workplaces or training programmes, and thereby verify whether a given opportunity would provide a 'better match'

---

[19] However, these data must be interpreted with great caution, due to the specific "anchor effects" detected in answers from several countries. Comparatively, with regard to *all* factors affecting the ease of getting a job, the response category "some help" was much more favoured in Scotland and Germany; in Austria, the view that social networks were "irrelevant" appeared to be disproportionately high; Portuguese interviewees opted more often for the response "great help".

than other options, prior to making a decision. Networks also provided a potential employer both with a 'richer pool' of recruits, whose commitment and behaviour could be vouched for by those friends and relatives already working there, as well as a 'better match', since new recruits had been recommended by those more knowledgeable about the demands of the job. There was also a sense in which youth felt that a small local clique of well-networked economic and political leaders exercised too tight and exclusive a control over local affairs, and that this had potentially detrimental effects both on individual prospects and the community's future. This criticism was coupled with the familiar equivocation concerning the advantages and drawbacks of small community life – namely that it provides a sense of belonging, delivers solidarity, and yet encroaches on the need for privacy and anonymity that young people understandably value.

The Mayenne study in France also reflected somewhat the Scottish findings, with networks being mainly deployed for access to unskilled local factory work, but they provided little or no advantage in finding employment in more traditional artisanal small businesses. Nevertheless, there were exceptions that corresponded more closely to the Portuguese case, and it was quite clear that the family played an important role in generally supporting the search for work and subsequent early stages of the employment pathway, mainly via advice, and financial help to enable transport and/or housing problems to be overcome. Some French interviewees referred to the same advantages and disadvantages of rural life that Portuguese and Scottish youth had emphasised – the lack of facilities for youth, the generally difficult conditions of life, and the familiar contradiction between intra-community solidarity and intrusiveness.

In the Scottish case, social networks appear to provide youth with temporary, low-skill and low-quality, fall-back employment, and sometimes, perhaps, "stepping stones" to better employment prospects. Thus the operation of networks complements both the labour market and employment-related policy measures, rather than markets and policies complementing a complex of social networks – as seems to be the case in the Portuguese study area.

The social networks (and, in more extreme cases, the so-called *cunha*, or clientelist and discriminatory preferment) that function extensively in the rural areas of Portugal, clearly play and extremely important role in providing some youngsters with a way of remaining in the area where most of them were born and brought up, and yet avoiding a life in agricultural employment in a community where local employment alternatives are extremely scarce and largely unsatisfactory, even for those with minimal education and skills.

10. Reflections on Networks, the Market and Anti-Exclusion Policies

Despite the key role played by social networks in the study area in particular, and in Portugal in general, the importance of policy and the market cannot, of course, be underestimated. Clearly, the specific features of the articulation between social networks, the labour market and the policy context needs further research, if the market is to function more efficiently and equitably, policy is to be relevant to the specific problems rural areas face, and abuses of power and position are to be contained.

If employment outcomes are determined by the respective strengths of the three forces in the market-policy-networks 'triangle', then in Santa Marta it is networks that are disproportionately influential. While the specificities of the Portuguese situation have theoretical implications for how the three forces articulate, more practically, they raise questions regarding the extent to which policy could and should be "re-engineered" to take these complexities (and inter-local differences) into account.

The research on social networks suggests that, from a policy standpoint, the following priorities should be following emphasised.

Policy Recognition of the Role of Social Networks: Towards More Network-Sensitive Policies and Improved Youth Targeting

Due to the danger of undermining what is undoubtedly a key mechanism in the construction of employment pathways, policies devoid of local relevance have to be avoided. Due to the multiple temptations of top-down, often supply-led rather than demand inspired blueprint policy solutions, along with persistent institutional discrimination, target groups (women, youth, and the disabled) often tend to be little more than caricatures. Rather than targeting broad characteristics assumed to be associated with exclusion, it is the key relationships that need to be the focus of policy attention. The policy-maker's view of who the client is needs to be broadened to take key youth-youth, youth-adult and youth-elderly relations into account.

Policy means need to be found to enable youth to position themselves more centrally both in the networks on which they clearly depend to a significant degree, and in the implementation of policies aimed at improving their local employability. In short, this means

- more network management by youth, as opposed to adults;
- more policy inputs by youth, as opposed to adults; and
- more accurate and effective policy targeting (by public decision-makers and public, private and NGO local development actors) on those young people who are particularly excluded from the networks on which the building of successful employment pathways so crucially depends.

For example, in situations such as that of Santa Marta, rather than imposing policies that undermine the legitimate use of what we might call benign (informational) networks, more care should be exercised in designing policies that not only support youngsters' capacities to use existing social networks to improve their employment opportunities, but also foster greater youth autonomy and inputs into the use and, above all, the construction of new networks.

If the important function played by social networks is not recognised by and integrated into policy design, future measures may result in perverse effects. For example, attempts by policy makers to reverse rural demographic decline by 'fixing' young population in the countryside (i.e. by strengthening the market and related institutions), may 'backfire' unless the positive and negative dimensions of network use are recognised. Young people may find their local social networks undermined by policy initiatives that are both more neo-liberal in inspiration, and less amenable to clientelist influences. Paradoxically, as the design, objectives and targeting of inclusion-promoting measures become more influenced by the logic of the market, policy makers may find it increasingly difficult to successfully promote and/or deliver sufficiently attractive and stable employment. Unwilling (or unable, due to low qualifications) to accept the type of work that the market is able to provide, youth may be forced to leave such localities as Santa Marta de Penaguião in even larger numbers.

The Need for More Autonomous Space for Youth

Young people in Santa Marta are very conscious of the extent to which their lives are run, and their futures determined, by adults. Specifically, many of the young people we interviewed complained about the lack of 'dedicated facilities' available to them. On the other hand, the political elite, parents and decision-makers tend to say that young people today have everything laid on for them – everything, that is, that adults want them to have, or feel is appropriate.

After they definitively leave school, where do youngsters go to maintain their contacts, improve their sources of information, work out new strategies? Even though school, in addition to its primary function, also provides informal opportunities for youth to hone their social skills, build their own networks and exchange ideas and information, it only provides very limited formal opportunities to develop the confidence to become more active and autonomous in local affairs, more informed about the institutional structures and the policies that ostensibly support their successful social inclusion, and more wary and critical of local clientelist practice.

From this standpoint, it is interesting that our research produced references to the importance of other local facilities as centres for networking, socialising and the brokering of influence. Foremost among such entities is the local café, which is of particular importance to adults, in general, and to males in particular. Whomsoever it serves, the café or club, or similar facility, is not simply as a meeting place, but somewhere that information, influence and favours are all exchanged. To run a café successfully, one needs lots of friends with money and influence, who can constitute both a regular clientele, and a networking 'node' that will attract other customers. While they can evolve their own relationship with the existing networks in such cafés, young people are at the disadvantage of not having even something as basic as a specifically youth-oriented bar that could act as an autonomous meeting place. Given that such establishments as cafés often do operate in this way in adult networks, there is every reason to believe that something as simple as a bar, club or other establishment could assist in the creation of more effectively functioning information networks, not to mention providing a physical and organisational focus for other activities (such as training, health education and the like) with stronger youth involvement and management. Indeed, the employment-related difficulties that some youth face spring simultaneously from the (a) physical inaccessibility, bureaucratic attitudes, poor performance and relevance of official institutions (b) youngsters' lack of dedicated facilities, combined with (c) their own ignorance of what institutions are responsible for which initiatives.

Given the paucity of truly youth-oriented collective spaces (clubs, cafés, etc.) and the consequently limited opportunities for individual or group learning experiences, the development of greater organisational autonomy and meaningful institutional involvement, and with Job Centres located where they are and conceived and operated as poorly as they tend to be, youth tend to fall back primarily on the networks that family and friends can provide. Nevertheless, the provision of more youth-oriented space provides no guarantee that youth will be able to develop greater confidence and, thereby, be able to participate more fully in local decision-making. For that to happen, more intractable problems have to be confronted, requiring more fundamental change in the attitudes that colour the relations that adults in general, and policy-makers in particular, establish with young people.

Operationalising the Discourse of Youth Citizenship and Participation

It is one thing to bewail the cynical use of young people as 'troops' in electoral campaigns and quite another to propose practical ways to build a local political culture that is more participatory, and less dominated by a relatively elderly and conservative power elite. Nor is it sufficient to exhort youth to participate more, and to demand more from the adults that run local political parties in return for their political support. In a sense, this would replicate the classical *caciquism* of the past, by which the elite received the votes of their social subordinates in exchange for employment or income-related favours.

The lack of any real "grass roots counter-culture" constitutes one of the key obstacles to the emergence of a stronger and more confident youth 'voice' at local level, and their greater participation in local political decision-making. In order (a) to overcome the fatalism, passivity and social deference that characterises the attitudes and practices of the majority of rural youth (not to mention their elders), and (b) for youth to acquire the confidence and social skills on which their wider and more profound participation depends, there must be an intensification of the dynamic, activities and autonomy of (in)formal groups and networks in which they are already involved.

Here we have a chicken and egg problem: the emergence of a more confident and assertive youth culture runs counter to the interests of the local political and economic elite, and would undermine the very clientelist relations that contribute significantly to the reproduction of their power. This elite has had considerable success in 'managing' youth energies and initiatives, i.e. confining them to issues and areas that support rather than challenge the *status quo*. In 'managing' the space in which cultural organisations (and, indirectly, some of the networks based on – or intersecting with – such organisations) operate, the local elite has tended to politicise them in its own interests. Furthermore, "elite pluriactivity" (namely the overlapping of local business, political and institutional interests), ensures that local groups and their members remain dependent on favours, often distributed through clientelist networks, in which policy-makers (or at least local policy interpreters and implementers) are to some degree complicit. This inevitably constrains and/or compromises such groups' ability to achieve their interests and objectives, and further reduces their extremely limited their autonomy.

Local economic interests as well as politicians at local, regional and national level need to be educated and motivated to take the young more seriously in both political and economic terms. Entrepreneurs, institutional leaders and the political elite are not the only stakeholders in local development, and yet to date policy has tended to favour the construction of a local 'enabling environment' that tends to serve their' needs above those of youth themselves. A local enabling environment needs to be created in which inclusion objectives are defined with youth as *subject* and not merely *object* of policies and their ostensible benefits.

Changes in the power relations between the local elite and such groups, organisations and networks will require that the latter be integrated into local development in a completely different way. This means that, from the policy standpoint, local cultural, community and other groups in which youth are involved can no longer ignored, or simply perceived as a relatively unimportant afterthought, or patronised in a clientelist fashion, either by the local elite, or by policy-makers.

Improving Provision and Dissemination of Information

There is an urgent need to improve the quantity of information and its relevance to the particularities of the rural areas, as well as to improve substantially the quality of information, and the skills and insight of those who disseminate it. The vicious circle referred to above can, in part, be broken, if the diffusion of information were to be radically improved at the local level. This would help to short circuit the clientelist intermediaries, both public and private, who tend to monopolise and channel strategic information in support of their own interests, and provide the basis for more informed and more autonomous decision-making on the part of youth.

Improving Training Performance

The supply of training inputs will not be qualitatively improved, unless courses are made more relevant to the demands both of potential employers, local economic potentialities, and the needs of local youth themselves. This is particularly so if future opportunities are more likely to emerge in the sphere of self- rather than wage-employment. Attaining this objective will be no easy task, given some of the particularities of the market for training in rural Portugal (and elsewhere):

- *Difficult access:* evidence from Santa Marta (as in Angus, Scotland and other case-study areas), suggests that training is generally regarded as rather difficult to access, and that the opportunities for 'real' training (i.e. in line with young people's aspirations) are few and far between.
- *Inappropriate motivation:* in Portugal (as elsewhere), greater emphasis has been placed on the provision of *paid* training schemes than on the relevance of their content; this means that programmes are mounted (often with little if any prior assessment or subsequent evaluation of the trainees) and youth will frequently sign up opportunistically for almost any course, often a succession of courses, having made no real assessment of what it may or may not deliver in terms of improved employability.
- *Management priorities:* Also, there seemed to be a disproportionate institutional emphasis on encouraging young people to sign up for courses, regardless of the willingness/aptitude of the person, or the relevance of the course; in part such attitudes are the result of supply-led approaches to training, and the pressure on government departments to spend budget allocations and meet targets – the latter still predominantly defined in terms of *inputs* (e.g. number of trainees attending), rather than *outputs* or *outcomes* (i.e. number of well-trained, more employable, more self-confident youth).
- *Competition among training agencies:* similar pressure to prioritise quantity rather than quality is felt by the burgeoning private and NGO training sector, whose own organisational dynamic and financial sustainability depend on meeting similar targets, if future government and/or EU funding is to be secured.
- *Eligibility for training:* due to the extent to which young people in Santa Marta have abandoned their studies in the last 10 years or so – not untypically before compulsory schooling has been completed – many remain ineligible for training, and are therefore excluded from some of the more promising employment opportunities.
- *Inequitable distribution of training:* some of the youth interviewed in Santa Marta felt that the placements were distributed inequitably, on the basis of favouritism and corruption, often predominantly to those "in the know", and repeatedly to the same people.

Against this background, it was not surprising to hear youngsters in Santa Marta expressing their profound frustration at the way in which the employment and training services operate.

As suggested above, it can be the case that filling the quota of trainees, and encouraging the take up of loans, comes to take precedence over the relevance and viability of the small business initiative proposed, and the degree of preparedness of the trainee concerned. Worse still, given that for the elite of university- or polytechnic-trained young people based in the towns and cities surrounding the rural areas, the organisation of training courses (either as a self-employed 'trainer' to whom agencies and organisations 'outsource' their own contracts, or as a salaried trainer and/or training manager), constitute a significant growth sector, training and work placements may offer greater opportunities to the trained than to the trainee. In other words, working in this burgeoning sector, may enable public/private sector training professionals as well as private economic/business consultants (locally, often referred to as *projectistas*), to extend their own networks (not to mention clientelist relations) into the youth cohort, thereby benefiting their own employment pathways, rather than those of local youth.

Finally, there is a danger that the siting of training courses will discriminate against youth in the remoter or less favoured rural areas, with the result that those who are able to attend may be attracted away from their locality once they have qualified. As a key informant explained:

> The vast majority of vocational training courses have taken place in just about every county around here *except* for Santa Marta. Perhaps the sponsoring organisations feel Santa Marta is too small. Paradoxically, while they'll put courses on in Régua or Vila Real, the bulk of the trainees will be from here (...) As for the Employment Insertion Programmes (...) there simply aren't enough sponsoring agencies (...) In the first year, there were two private non-profit organisations, but last year there was nobody from Santa Marta, and this year, it'll probably only be the Council that will take up youngsters (...). (Contextual Interview, 30.11.99)

Certifying Training

Furthermore, rather than seeing youth training as something that only qualitatively improves the supply of labour, its role in building more active citizenship should be recognised. From this perspective, a further policy initiative that would help to build experience, confidence, organisational skills and leadership among young people, would be to ensure that appropriate training inputs are made to the type of local organisations mentioned above. This will inevitably mean weeding out those training institutions – be they private companies, NGOs or (semi-)public organisations – that have been motivated more by accessing EU funding than effectively providing relevant training to young people. It is no coincidence that while training has become a boom sector, providing significant employment opportunities for better-qualified labour market entrants, dissatisfaction among young people with the quantity, quality and spatial distribution of training provided seems to have escalated.

A rigorous process of certification of training institutions needs to be implemented without delay, along with greater control of the quality and relevance of the skills they provide, so that the benefits of the "training business" can be more equitably distributed between the training institutions that have proliferated in rural areas in recent years, and rural youth who have yet to feel significant impacts of institutionalised training on their employability.

11. Conclusions

The evidence from the Santa Marta de Penaguião study strongly suggests that social networks offer opportunities that neither the market, nor policies nor conventional corporate structures can provide. Perhaps the prevalence and apparent growth of the type of networks analysed in this chapter could be interpreted as a partial rolling back of the market, in response to and in compensation for the excessive withdrawal of state interventionism in the 1980s. By analogy, the rise in the importance of social networks in underpinning rural livelihoods could suggest that a continuation (or restructuring) of productive market-network synergies has been taking place – more in recognition of the limited penetration of market than its excessive penetration. It may even be that, in localities like Santa Marta, the market mechanism and pro-market policies are progressively being restricted to the types of resource allocation to which they are "best suited", with social networks in general, and clientelist preferment in particular, continuing to play a key, and sometimes dominant, role.

However, as a result of demographic decline, the continued concentration of population in the urban centres of rural regions, and the extended and intensified commoditisation of life that globalisation is bringing about, it is more likely that there will be an ongoing penetration of social networks by market norms and values, not to mention a further penetration of social policy by precisely the same imperatives. Paradoxically, this may simultaneously strengthen some existing social networks and promote the establishment of others, in an attempt to preserve the benefits they are known to generate, as well as giving rise to new network-based imperfections in markets.

Whether overall welfare gains or losses will result from this type of network-market articulation and who will enjoy the benefits and who will bear the costs is unclear. Nevertheless, rather than witnessing the rapid erosion and terminal decline of social networks as a valid and viable means of achieving economic outcomes in rural areas, networks – through the people that construct, constitute and operate them – are showing themselves capable of adapting to and benefiting from their articulation with the market.

The same sort of scenario could be applied to the interaction and mutual articulation of rural livelihood networks and policy. Given that current policy discourse emphasises the need (and the efficiency) of building local institutions that are conducive to the growth and development of such networks, we are also likely to see complex synergies, characterised by an uneven mix of more heavily politicised networks and more locally-networked policies emerging in this context too.[20]

Whether aggregate welfare gains or losses will result from this type of network-market articulation, and who will enjoy the benefits and who will bear the costs is unclear. Nevertheless, rather than witnessing the rapid erosion and terminal decline of social networks as a valid and viable means of achieving economic outcomes in rural areas, rural social networks – in Portugal at least – are showing themselves capable of adapting to and benefiting from their articulation with the market.

The results of our analysis of social networks and *cunha*, and the way in which they mediate between individual job-seekers (on the one hand) and market mechanisms and policy measures (on the other), may provide policy-makers with some food for thought. Given the importance of rural social networks, policy makers have to be more sensitive to the impact that policies may have on their effective functioning. If young people find that a major factor in constructing minimally acceptable employment pathways in their rural localities are undermined by policy initiatives that are both more neo-liberal in inspiration, and less amenable to clientelist influences, they may simply vote with their feet. Unwilling (or unable, due to low qualifications) to accept the type of work that the market is able to provide, youth may be forced to leave such localities as Santa Marta de Penaguião in even larger numbers.

Notwithstanding the difficulties of motivating the local elite to give youth a greater say in local decision-making, there is an urgent need to negotiate new spaces – both physical and organisational – as well as new structures for young people, not least of all so that they can develop the confidence and skills to participate more actively in local politics and policy initiatives. In spite of the high priority given to formal education and training in the general and policy discourse of adults formal and informal, the school system, employment service and training framework appear largely unprepared and unable to identify and respond to the dreams and the legitimate, concrete aspirations of their "clients", namely young people in the school to work transition. It is no wonder that many of them look elsewhere for better "niches" in life, and have recourse to other sources of support, influence, advice and consolation as they attempt to construct their employment pathways.

One step that policy makers could take along the road to responding more to the needs of young people, instead of simply evoking the now prevalent and familiar discourse of market fatalism, would be to radically improve the diffusion of information at the local level, not only in terms of the quantity and quality of information, and its relevance to the particularities of the rural areas, but also the skills and insight of those who disseminate it.

---

[20] For example, the fact that the central government contracts regional business associations to promote, process and adjudicate the allocation of subsidies to local micro-enterprises under their 'jurisdiction', does not bode particularly well, either for the autonomy of such associations, or their continued local legitimacy or, indeed, for the effectiveness of government enterprise promotion policies.

Finally, rather than seeing youth training as something that only qualitatively improves the supply of labour, its role in building more active citizenship should be recognised. From this perspective, a further policy initiative that would help to build experience, confidence, organisational skills and leadership among young people, would be to channel appropriate training inputs to the types of local organisations in which youth have both a stake and a real interest, through which they could more rapidly gain experience, and create opportunities to exercise influence in how the future of rural areas is envisioned, and the corresponding employment opportunities there may be generated.

Chapter 10

Experience of Rural Youth in the 'Risk Society': Transitions from Education to the Labour Market

Birgit Jentsch

1. Introduction

The aim of this chapter is to examine young people's transitions from education to the labour market, including their plans and strategies for accessing the labour market. Here, the premise is that 'transitions' involve multiple processes, which differ according to the socio-economic background of the young person. They have no definite point of arrival. The context of the transitions may be educational failure, institutionalised discrimination and high levels of unemployment (Wyn and White 1997, 95), which may result in "delayed, broken, highly fragmented and blocked transitions" (Chisholm 1993, in Wyn and White 1997, 95). In other words, transitions will rarely comprise 'linear' processes, but have become less predictable than in the past, for which the changed and changing labour market can certainly be made responsible to a significant extent. Experiences of steps in the transition process were examined bearing in mind Beck's (1992) individualisation hypothesis, which makes particular reference to the lives of young people. While Beck's theories have been criticised on a number of grounds (see, for example, Adams 1995; Dingwall 1999) nevertheless, this chapter uses this perspective heuristically as another potentially useful ankle to analysis.

2. Young People in the 'Risk Society'

It was Beck's (1992) contention that in late modernity, lifestyles and 'risks' have become increasingly individualised. Particularly interestingly for our purpose, Beck (1992) addresses the issue of how individualisation can be understood as a change of life situations and biographical patterns. One central claim is that people are cut loose from traditional social commitments and assurances, but encounter new forms of control and new dependencies. Beck points to the removal from status-based classes, which have moved on from changes in the sphere of production (e.g. general increase in educational levels, juridification of labour relations while fundamental social relations of inequality have remained) to changes in the area of reproduction. The 'proletarian milieu' has been dissolved in the view of, for example, tendencies towards differentiation and pluralisation with regard to family structures, housing conditions, neighbourhood relations, and leisure time behaviour (Beck 1992, 129). Hence, there is a range of different lifestyles, subcultures, social relationships and identities to choose from for people with the same income range or 'social class'. While class differences and family connections are not entirely disappearing during the individualisation process, they assume a lesser role when compared to the 'new centre' of the biographical life plan which has come into existence. Interesting in this context is also the situation of women who have been 'liberated' from marital support and thus their traditional housewife role with the effect that the whole structure of familial ties experiences pressure for individualisation (Beck 1992, 129). The special feature of 'individualisation' then lies in its consequences: it is claimed that "it is no longer social classes that take the place of status groups, or the family as a stable frame of reference that takes the place of social class commitments. The individual himself or herself becomes the reproduction unit for the social in the life world" (ibid 130). In other words, individualisation involves Freisetzung ['liberation'] from status-based classes. Freisetzung implies that the individual is removed from status-based classes and thereby freed from the collective conscience (Adams 1995, 182).

At the same time, new dependencies emerge, highlighting the inherent contradictions in the individualisation process: the newly emerged individual situations are thoroughly dependent on the labour market.

> They are, so to speak, the extension of market dependency into every corner of (earning a) living, they are its late result in the welfare state phase. They arise in the fully established labour market society, which barely remembers traditional possibilities of support any longer, if at all. (Beck 1992, 130)

The dependence on the labour market and money has a knock on effect on other areas on which the individual is now dependent, including education, consumption, and welfare state regulations and support. Hence, biographical patterns become institutionalised, overlapping with or replacing status-influenced, class cultural or familial biographical patterns (Beck 1992, 132). Parallel to the increased institutionalisation of biographical patterns, there is a growing mistrust of expert opinion, supported not least by the increasing influence of rational theory over policy making. According to rational choice theory,

> behaviour is governed primarily by an individual calculus of advantage. [The approach] claims that politicians propose policies to gain votes rather than meet needs, and that the officials and professionals who deliver services are more concerned with their own position as determined by the size of their budgets or their control over their work-load than the public interest. (Taylor-Gooby, Hartley, Munro and Parker 1998)

One of the consequences of 'individualisation' and the mistrust of experts is that individuals become aware that they cannot avoid a greater share of responsibility for managing their own needs. It is clear that events and conditions do not just happen to individuals, but are also consequences of decisions they have made, and which have to be treated as such. Social inequalities are not disappearing, but they do not necessarily operate at the level of social class any more, but increasingly at the level of the individual (Evans et al., 1999, 136). In relation to social class, Beck emphasises that despite the weakening of class ties, the vulnerability to 'risks' is unequal:

> Like wealth, risks adhere to the class pattern, only inversely: wealth accumulates at the top, risk at the bottom. To that extent, risks seem to *strengthen*, not abolish, the class society. Poverty attracts an unfortunate abundance of risks. By contrast, the wealthy (in income, power or education) can *purchase* safety and freedom from risk. (Beck 1992, 35)

More and more, 'failures' are considered to be of a personal kind, whether this concerns exams, unemployment or divorce, so that risks are individualised. Hence, "in the individualised society, risks do not just increase quantitatively; qualitatively new types of personal risks arise, the risk of the chosen and changed personal identity" (Beck 1992, 136).

Risk Society and Young People

What are the implications of the risk society for young people, who find themselves at the stage of emancipation, i.e. in the process of developing and asserting an independent identity? In modern age, the identity of young people, which has been ascribed or derived from families of origin, is gradually being replaced by an identity which is negotiated between self and the other. Emancipation then involves a break with communities as well as with other traditional networks. It has been pointed out that during this process, many young people, especially in rural areas, leave their homes and communities (Jones 1999, 2).

At the same time, according to the individualisation hypothesis, crises which young people are likely to experience are less regarded as outcomes of processes which are beyond an individual's control, but are related back to personal characteristics of the individual as the 'centre of action' (Furlong and Cartmel 1997, 4). In the area of employment, this could mean that those people who fail to secure a job (of a certain status) explain this with their own perceived shortcomings, rather than with structural causes. Such common perceptions may result in fewer calls for political action. Instead, problems are attempted to be solved at an individual level.

This includes decisions young people have to take in the context of an increasing demand for credentials when traditional ties and support are lacking.

> The traditional links between the family, school and work seem to have weakened as young people embark on journeys into adulthood which involve a wide variety of routes, many of which appear to have uncertain outcomes. ... Because there are a much greater range of pathways to choose from, young people may develop the impression that their

own route is unique and that the risks they face are to be overcome as individuals rather than as members of collectivity. (Furlong and Cartmel 1997, 7).

Notwithstanding the greater individualisation of experiences among young people, for this group, too, experiences are still shaped to a significant extent by the categories of class, gender (as explained by Beck), and also 'race'.

What all youth will tend to have in common though is the fact that the school to work transition has become protracted, with young people remaining dependent on their families for longer periods of time than used to be the case (Furlong and Cartmel 1997). At the same time, there are also new opportunities, which have arisen through individualisation, and the liberation from the traditional ties: young people have more control over the choice of their own particular life-course as their biographies become and continue to be self-produced. Under certain conditions, the individual may be able to take advantage of exceptional opportunities. Recent research in England and Germany has shown that young people manifest 'active' and 'passive' transition behaviours, the former being associated with high achievers and strong social networks, and the latter with low achievers with weak social networks. The career patterns related to those behaviours were rooted in structures of social class, gender and region (Evans et al., 1999, 136-137).

It seems of particular interest to consider Beck's hypotheses in the rural context, in which some of these assumptions related to the 'risk society' can certainly be challenged. Research in the area of community life in Scotland has yielded mixed results. Most people would probably agree that there are still relatively close communities and familial ties in rural areas. Young people regarded this fact either as a bonus (the 'community spirit' and closer links to people), or as a disadvantage (rumours and gossip) (Chapter 5 of this book; Jones 1997; Shucksmith, Chapman, Clark et al., 1996). The findings of our research will grant some insight into the forces of support, pressure and disappointment which young people have experienced, and the resulting strategies, which they developed. Before the presentation of the data, however, a brief account should be given of the research methods adopted.

Researching Rural Youth in the 'Risk Society'

The study is based on a total of 254 individual interviews carried out in the study areas of seven European countries as well as a total of 16 focus groups with young people. In addition, in all study areas bar the German, one focus group interview was carried out with key personnel working with and for youth. In Germany, 8 members of local key personnel were interviewed individually.[1] As far as it was

---

[1] The interview with the latter group gave us the opportunity to feed back some preliminary findings to those with some power in decision-making processes, as well as informing us about their insights into the barriers and enabling factors young people may experience during transitions leading towards adulthood.

possible, the sample of young people in each study area comprised similar proportions of pupils, students and trainees, employed, and unemployed youths. In most cases, similar numbers of men and women were included. Accessing the young people turned out to require a range of techniques, from a very informal process in Portugal, which mainly relied on approaching youngsters in public spaces and snowballing, to a rather formalised approach taken in France, where youth organisations assisted in identifying potential sample members. Other study areas used a combination of those two approaches. As to the characteristics of the different study areas, Table 4.1 (see Chapter 4, 66) gives a broad overview of the areas in terms of strength of the local labour market, remoteness, and other social and cultural variables.

Amongst other items, the interviews explored young people's perceived risks and uncertainties, as well as possibilities, during the transition from school education into training, further/higher education and employment. What are the factors which young people consider when taking decisions regarding their educational qualifications, training or employment? What are their personal responses to the perceived difficulties and opportunities? What is the relative importance of different support systems, namely traditional ties and social forms (family, social class) and secondary institutions and support relationships (labour market, social policies, such as education policies and social security)?

3. The Route to Educational Qualifications and Higher Education

Let us begin with the interviewees' experiences of school education. The importance of education – including school qualifications – for accessing employment should be uncontentious. An OECD report shows that "[t]he level of education is a factor influencing participation rates in the labour force and the quality of economic activity. ... The higher the level of education, the higher labour force participation is" (OECD 1995, 32). It is clear that 'good' formal educational qualifications can confer advantages in training, apprenticeship and the labour market, and that premature school leaving can be associated with disadvantages in all these areas. It is therefore not surprising that the National Action Plans[2] also show concern with the area of education. The general focus is on the upper secondary level of education. It is worthwhile noting though that from the countries included in our study, Ireland, Germany and Portugal are also paying special attention to the problem of young people dropping out before completing their compulsory schooling. Looking at the drop-out/failure rates in our sample, it can be seen that quite a large proportion of our study participants have experienced difficulties also at lower secondary education level.

---

[2] As explained in the first PaYPiRD report for the European Commission, the decision to develop NAPs was taken as one of the results of the Luxembourg Job Summit in November 1997. The aim of the NAPs is to implement the EU guidelines, fight against unemployment, and the harmonisation of basic objectives.

Figure 10.1 Highest Level of Formal Education Attended

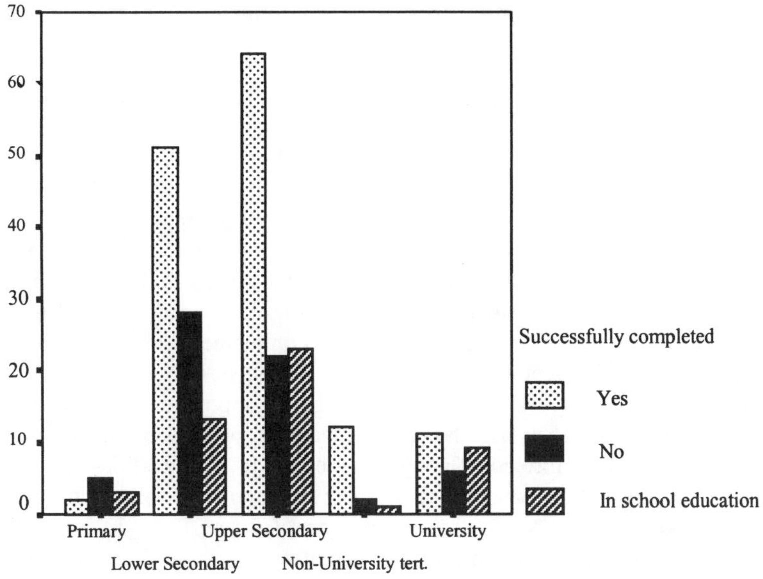

The qualitative data shed light on possible explanations for early leaving and/or failure to complete, as well as on the reasons behind experiences of success. Regarding lower and upper secondary education, the Scottish study area seemed particularly remarkable in that the vast majority of the young interviewees gave a positive account of their experiences. While Finnish interviewees also described their time at school in mainly positive terms, the opposite seemed to have dominated the experiences of many or most interviewees in the other study areas.

However, it is interesting to note that the factors, which were mentioned by participants from all countries as contributing towards a more or less enjoyable and worthwhile school experience, were surprisingly similar. Let us look at the reasons why some young people's accounts of their secondary education were so positive.

Teachers and Peers

Aspects of their school time which the Angus study participants appreciated in particular and mentioned repeatedly included the positive atmosphere at school, created by teachers who awarded pupils respect and a significant measure of responsibility. The good relations amongst pupils were also emphasised as helping to turn the school into a "happy, fun place (...)". Moreover, good educational qualifications were equated with better opportunities in the labour market, and therefore seen as worthwhile achieving. These comments were very much in accord with the views of the Finnish interviewees as they described the educational opportunities in Suomussalmi. Moreover, some accounts were given of how the influence of teachers could promote better performance. For example, a female postgraduate student from Angus described how she had encountered

> a teacher who believed in me and gave me so many opportunities and felt that I could progress to university to study English. I mean, without her support, I probably wouldn't have considered doing it (female, 23 years old, Angus, Scotland).

However, a minority of the Finnish and Scottish participants were more critical. They either pointed to aspects of their schooling they had enjoyed less in the context of an overall positive account, or talked about the bad time they had suffered as the predominant memory of their school time. With regard to interviewees of the other study areas, reports on the negative aspects of their school lives prevailed. Interestingly, many of the features of education the interviewees in all study areas disapproved of were directly in opposition to the positive aspects listed above. The reasons why a significant proportion of the Irish sample left school early (i.e. before completing their second level education) included negative teacher/pupil relations, and a loss of interest through lack of support and attention, as well as bullying (McGrath, Canavan and Curtin 2000). In other study areas, there were complaints about a lack of a motivating atmosphere at school, where it remained unclear what advantages good educational qualifications could confer. In addition, poor attitudes by teachers towards pupils were commented upon, which then could hinder good performance, as was described in the following examples.

> They just weren't nice teachers ... A lot of the teachers aren't from around here, so they thought they were above us ... they thought they were doing us a favour by coming out in the morning and sitting there. A lot of them I just didn't get on with and I wasn't the only one. A lot of us didn't get on with all the teachers really, and even the local ones weren't the greatest. (female, age 20, Galway, Ireland, commenting on school education)

> I didn't like school. I had thought of trying to finish the 4th year, but I started to have problems getting on with the teachers, and from then on, I never wanted to continue. (female, age 16, SMP, Portugal, commenting on school education)

> Most of the teachers were old and rather bad as teachers. Because, once, we had an alcoholic and another time, it was somebody ... who only yelled and screamed. Well, that wasn't the right thing. (female, age 16, Murau, Austria, commenting on school education)

> There were teachers that one could get on with, but others just went about looking for difficulties. They would come around grumbling when we were working even when there was nothing wrong. It wasn't nice. The teaching there wasn't as good as it could have been. (male, age 19, Suomussalmi, Finland)

> I didn't get along with the teachers. One of them was really bad, if your level of performance wasn't as he wanted it to be, he was through with you. Then you realised

you had drawn the short end of the straw. ... I had arguments with him all the time. (female, age 21, Wesermarsch, Germany)

Hence, when accounting for their school experiences, and educational decisions taken on that basis, young people often recognised that there were external factors, which defined that experience. Such factors could sometimes operate on a sub-conscious level. For example, where a 'culture of low ambitions' prevails in a community, and the pursuit of the 'lowest' educational stream is the norm, this seems a difficult context for young people to fulfil their potential – an observations from the Austrian study area. Related to these less tangible, 'cultural pressures' an interesting gender issue was referred to in the Scottish context, where it was argued that males were disadvantaged (especially in terms of educational achievements) due to a culture of 'laddism'. The dominant values of young men who are part of this culture seem to be incompatible with trying hard at school and achieving good qualifications.

Returning to the quality of the educational provisions, it is worthwhile noting that pupils experienced the same provisions and teachers quite differently – highlighting the fact that their perceived and actual needs, wishes and expectations are different. For example, by contrast to those who had enjoyed friendships with their peers at school, others had become victims of bullying (for example, in the Irish and Finnish sample), which could have led these youngsters to leave school early in order to escape a threatening environment. While some youths reported how their performance and confidence took off with the support of their teachers, others found themselves disadvantaged by teachers who tended to channel their energy into those pupils who were doing well, and neglected the poorer achievers. Similarly, a number of Irish interviewees observed that streaming according to ability tended to increase inequalities between students at the ends of the ability and social class continuum. Those factors seemed to be very important in encouraging or discouraging youth to stay on or to leave school at the earliest possible moment, sometimes even without having completed compulsory education and having acquired the minimum qualifications. Such cases existed especially in the Irish, Portuguese and German sample, in the latter of which the issue of racism emerged. A person of minority ethnic origin made the following statement:

> If it hadn't been for him [the headmaster], I would have gone on to grade 9, which would have been my tenth year altogether, and obtained my certificate. I had applied for permission to continue with school. But our head-master turned me down, he is kind of a racist. And he turned down the applications of almost all students who were not native students, and who like myself had fallen behind in class. (male, age 18)

Hence, when explaining their experiences at school and rationales behind staying on or leaving, the foci of many interviewees across the seven study areas were on individual teachers' approaches to the pupils, as well as on peer relations. Although it may be argued that it could just be 'unlucky' if a pupil experiences poor rapport with peers and teachers, this seems an easy excuse for not tackling a problem, which is likely to have deeper roots. Especially the Irish study emphasised the disruption which continuous staff turnover can cause for pupils. Here, one focus group discussed the nature and effect of a high turnover rate of teachers at their school. A participant of the discussion made the following observation:

> There is a good few teachers trying but there is a lot of them in there that it is just a stop gap; filling in time until they can escape somewhere else. There is not a huge commitment from any of them in extra-curricular activities. It's fairly poor. There are a few that try, but in general they don't seem to get the right teachers in the school.

There is evidence on the quality of rural school staff from other research which can lead to different conclusions. A study of four types of rural areas in Scotland concluded that "[r]ural primary school posts were 'prime' appointments and respondents felt that the high numbers of primary school teachers living in rural areas ensured a competitive labour market for teaching posts, and the appointment of high calibre staff" (Shucksmith et al., 1996, 321). The same situation was reported to exist for the teaching staff at secondary education level, who also "were perceived to be of a very high calibre" (Shucksmith et al., 1996, 326), and the schools in general were described as being "of a very high standard" (Shucksmith et al., 1996, 326). However, there clearly are rural areas, which are affected by the problem of a high turnover of professional staff in different services, as described in the Irish case study area in relation to secondary schooling. In fact, it has been recognised that many professionals encounter significant problems, for example, when having trained in metropolitan area institutions and then relocating to small isolated communities. In the Canadian context, it has been suggested that strategies have to be developed to help prepare professionals for the social differences which will confront them (Gougeon 2000). Such support could make a significant difference in the retention of professional staff, thereby ensuring higher quality services. As concerns the specific subject of young people at school, this is likely to have some impact on their decisions whether the school experience is worthwhile and merits pursuing, or whether they drop out early. In addition, there are other issues which also require attention.

Focus on 'Self'

In a few cases, interviewees seemed to make themselves responsible for failed exams, and subsequent dropping out, as was described in the following two examples.

> I failed only one examination, just for one course, I was on the borderline. I reacted badly to that failure. (female, age 20, SMP, Portugal)

> For me, it was strange. I had never failed, and I lost my motivation. (male, 20 years old, SMP, Portugal)

Perhaps more significantly, regrets were expressed retrospectively about having left school early – a step which was regarded as a personal mistake by a number of pupils from the Austrian, French, German, Irish and Portuguese case study areas.[3] This recognition seemed mainly to be related to the realisation that job choices and opportunities were reduced. In the Irish case study area, some of those who had left school without their Leaving Certificate[4] commented as follows.

> I would like to have furthered my education. I only have a junior cert and that is not worth anything to you at the moment ... It would have opened up more jobs for me now. (male, age 17, NW Connemara, Ireland)

> I am regretting it now ... that's probably one of the reasons why it's so hard for me to get a job. (female, age 18, NW Connemara, Ireland)

A German interviewee also mentioned that if he could start all over again, he would do everything different, and would now try harder to obtain his leaving certificate as well as completing his apprenticeship. As concerns Austrian interviewees, the 'regrets' they expressed were of a less fundamental nature. Here, interviewees with a higher educational level reflected that if they had the choice again, they would prefer a different type of high school. Those who had opted for an apprenticeship sometimes found that a different vocation would have been preferable, although the choice for dual education was still considered good.

The Curriculum and Structure of School Education

Some criticism of school education voiced by the youngsters can be interpreted as being related to structural issues, although this was not necessarily the way the interviewees explicitly presented issues themselves. Certainly, where school is seen as 'boring' and even irrelevant for the lives of the young people, we may be inclined to look for causes, which go beyond the characteristics of the teaching staff and the relationship amongst pupils. The school curriculum, and the rigid way, in which it is being delivered, could be of prime importance here. It has been claimed before that "[t]he longest distance in the world is between an official state curriculum policy and what goes on in the mind of a child" (Peter Schrag 1998, in Innes 2000, 9). Such an observation does not seem to be out of place in the context of our research findings. In exceptional cases, young people said they enjoyed the contents of the classes – and their good achievements. However, especially 'early leavers' from all study areas mentioned that there was a discrepancy between the perceived academic and dry lessons taught at school, and some pupils' desire to engage in some 'hands on' practical courses which they assessed to be more interesting, as well as more relevant and useful for their employment opportunities.

---

[3] In the case of the Portuguese interviewees, nearly three quarters of the young people mentioned that if they wanted to change some event in their past, it would be their choices related to school education.

[4] The 'Leaving Certificate' is the final and highest examination at second level education (McGrath et al. 2000).

While this situation led some of the youths to leave school at the earliest possible moment and find manual unskilled or semi-skilled employment, others looked to colleges to provide them with more rewarding learning experiences.

Other problems with the curriculum can be identified. Especially in the Portuguese sample, several young people felt that there was a mismatch between their perceived own capabilities and the demands placed on them at school. Sometimes, particular life events a young person had encountered could be made responsible for difficulties. Reports of how 'unexpected events' can interrupt the 'normal' educational pathway can highlight the inappropriateness of a rigid learning system. It is clear that children and young people cannot be expected to be ready to learn at any time or place. In each case study area, there were several examples of young people who had experienced unexpected personal problems, which resulted in difficulties at school. Some had suffered from health problems, or had to deal with death or illness of close family and friends, parents' divorce, or unplanned pregnancies. In these situations, they were faced with a school situation, which made few concessions to their complicated lives. While the young interviewees in such situations rarely blamed an educational institution for its failure to accommodate difficult life situations, they neither regarded themselves responsible for a lack of achievements. Perhaps they acknowledged that with the occurrence of particular life experiences, control over the pursuit of one's life-plan will inevitably be lost for some time. It should be added here though that whilst sometimes the life events which the interviewees' parents and other family members had encountered could interrupt the progress in education, it was often the same family relations who tried to ensure their children would continue, even if the motivation was low.

> I completed 12th grade, but since the 9th I was only at school because my parents made me stay on. I was too young and I could not stay at home doing nothing. I was really fed up with studying. I had no great desire to go on, so I had no interest in the classes. Then I stopped. (female, age 21, SMP, Portugal)

> Each time I was at home I'd say I'm not going back and each time my mother would convince me to go back and it just came to the stage that no conversation was going to turn me around. (male, age 21, NW Connemara, Ireland)

Hence, although parental influence may have encouraged the young person to stay on for a bit longer, there ultimately came a point when the rewards of the educational experience appeared too small.

One specific problem with rigid school structures has been identified in the German sample for a group of young people who had moved into the study area from different countries. There were three youngsters whose families had migrated or fled from non-German speaking countries, while another interviewee tried to come to terms with the cultural differences she experienced after moving from Eastern Germany to the Western part. Two of the foreigners mentioned how language difficulties had resulted in problems at school, while the interviewee of Eastern German origin found the different set-up of the school was not easy to get used to. None of them had managed to obtain the leaving certificate, and had clearly been in need of special support the school had not provided.

Finally, there were those structural factors, related to the rural environment, which led young people to leave school early. Long distances to travel and the related issues of transport and finances could impact on school education, as was particularly emphasised by some Portuguese interviewees. They described the daunting prospect which pupils face when the attendance of upper secondary school involves moving from one school and place to another. The Portuguese youth explained how such a step implies new daily routines, new people and separation from 'old friends', as well as a more competitive school environment. From such accounts, it appears that for pupils deciding to choose this path, comprehensive support structures need to be in place to help with this transition. This would, of course, include advice on the educational courses, which may be most suitable for them. It is also worthwhile mentioning the issue of childcare here. Although not emerging as a major issue for the interviewees in the quantitative data, this can be attributed to the fact that young parents were hardly represented in our sample. However, where the respondents lived with children, they were likely to acknowledge the impact of children on their educational opportunities. Moving on from school education to further/higher education and employment, it is of interest to look at processes of decision-making and the support received.

4. Career Choices and Guidance

Lack of Information and Encouragement

A striking feature regarding pupils' or students' decisions over what to do after school or a course in further/higher education was their uncertainty. This could be experienced especially by those who were doing well at school, had relatively ambitious aspirations, and perceived opportunities to be available, although they had found little information as to what precise form those may take. The confusion, which resulted for the youngsters, seems inevitable. The combination of perceived available opportunities (in nearby cities) and relatively high educational levels applied especially to the Scottish interviewees. In some cases, when faced with the question of 'what to do next', the dilemma was solved with the decision to stay on at school for longer, thereby being able to follow 'just the same routine'. A similar rationale could also have applied to the young Scottish people who went on University courses, trying 'to buy time', although the lack of a career plan sometimes outlasted even graduation. French interviewees reported that feelings of uncertainty were particularly strong when a career plan had not worked out, which according to the interviewees, could have been due to a lack of information, a mismatch between their expectations and the labour market, or a lack of realism.

The situation was different for young people in all study areas who tended to have modest educational qualifications and who were looking for pathways into jobs through apprenticeships. Here, the sense of direction seemed to be clearer, although even once the young people had made up their minds that they wanted to participate in training, they complained about a lack of information on what was available, and how to access it (France). In the Finnish case, interviewees reported that only few places were available, and argued that local employers had not been prepared to take responsibility for wider provision. Moreover, interviewees from all study areas had experiences where after having embarked on a training scheme or apprenticeship, the experience turned out to be disappointing and not what the young person had expected, so that plans sometimes had to change on this basis. According to those concerned, the choice of unsuitable options could have been prevented had advice been available on what particular jobs and the training for them involved. In the German study area, a special situation arose where three study participants had to break up an apprenticeship or training scheme as it emerged that they were allergic to the particular materials which they had to handle on a regular basis. There, the question arose whether anything could have done before the actual start of the apprenticeship to identify potential difficulties.

Lack of information or discouragement in their plans was presented as reasons for young people to end up in posts which had not been a positive choice. The frequent resort to alternative, less desired options has been summarised in the Portuguese report as a 'downward revision' of the 'wish ladder': where young people did not succeed, or were discouraged from even trying to achieve their own goals, they were open to settle for other options. Following this, the young person could either get used to the situation, and settle with this option, or try for a gradualist, step-by-step approach to reach their goals.

With the large degree of uncertainty which young people experienced, the question arises what support structures – especially career guidance – there were available to help them. In the case of many interviewees, career guidance was either perceived to have been lacking from the early stages already, or to have taken unhelpful approaches. Young people from the Scottish sample mainly criticised the quality of the advice provided. They found it was counterproductive when as pupils, they were put under pressure to articulate a career wish only to satisfy the questioning of the teachers and career service. Such 'guidance' was described to be at best a meaningless exercise, and at worst channelling young people in directions, which turned out to be unsuitable. The Scottish interviewees had also observed a process where teachers tried to encourage pupils to pursue the academic pathway rather than the vocational. The teachers' main reference point for such 'advice' seemed to be school performance, but the interests of the young person were barely taken into account, sometimes leading people onto the wrong track. Such an approach also neglected the poorer achievers. Similar findings emerged from the Irish study, where in addition, some interviewees explained how teachers could be discouraging once the young person had formulated a career wish which teachers deemed to be too difficult to achieve.

> I remember somebody saying to me "what do you want to do?" and I said social science. "Oh that's very hard" she said and that was about it. We didn't get absolutely no guidance and I mean we asked for it but, no. (female, age 21, NW Connemara, Ireland)

I remember in fifth year we were having a career guidance class and the teacher started saying "do you have any idea about what you wanted to do?" At the time I had this idea in my head about doing veterinary so I said this to the teacher and the teacher said "don't be ridiculous; there is only one college in the country that does it and what makes you think you are going to get in there?" I was shot down. I was devastated. (University Focus Group; female)

Portuguese interviewees referred to a lack of vocational guidance at school, where they found that teachers failed to assist their pupils properly in the choice of suitable educational branches, which would have matched the educational and vocational interests of the person concerned. Similarly, interviewees from France judged their school orientation services to be lacking in precise information on training offers and job opportunities, and neglecting the importance of individual guidance.

As to the quality of vocational and employment guidance outwith the school, the verdict was not more positive. Several Scottish and Irish interviewees felt they were failed when career advice had comprised little else but the provision of information on the basis of career proposals which the young people had to make themselves. In other words, the re-active nature of the career advice received was deplored. Interviewees from the other study areas commented on the poor advice given (sometimes even misinformation), and a lack of information especially on *local* training and job opportunities. A conclusion drawn by interviewees in all study areas was that more individual guidance which would take account of personal circumstances and interests, together with detailed information on training courses was required.

With the picture of career advice being generally gloomy, there were some isolated positive experiences of young people in most countries, who reported that they had found the career advice received "helpful", with appropriate information and advice having been provided. This was particularly the case where individuals had already firm ideas about the career they wanted to pursue. Perhaps more significantly, in the French case study area, the two organisations of PAIO and the Centre de Resources – providing a variety of services, including career guidance-received wide support. Why was this the case, and what was provided?

It appears that a user-oriented and effective career advice is of particular importance in rural areas. By definition, young people in rural areas are less closely exposed to the wide range of opportunities which are available to them, which contrasts with the situation which many of their urban counterparts experience. The issue of information thus seems to be particularly pertinent to them. Two local organisations in the Mayenne study area (the Permanence d'Accueil, d'Information et d'Orientation (PAIO) and the Centre de Resource) played an important part in giving young people orientation, guidance and general 'moral support'. The former organisation is specifically in charge of the 16-25 year old people, and both centres seem to have worked together well. Importantly, the staff was described by the interviewees as patient and receptive, and the quantity as well as quality of information offered on different job opportunities and career structures was very much appreciated by the young people (Auclair and Vanoni

1999, 37). Turning to the Centre de Resources, it offered a range of integration courses, for example, focusing on basic skills in French, Maths or IT, as well as on vocational preparation courses. The young people commented that one of the advantages those integration and orientation courses could provide was the practice periods associated with them, which facilitated their definition of a career plan. In addition, it was appreciated that the Centre de Resources constituted a place where people in similar situations could come to exchange their experiences – a feature, which seemed to be particularly important for rural young people who can easily feel a strong sense of isolation, as described by the following interviewee.

> I knew the centre de resources, so I thought that instead of staying alone, at home, trying to find something without knowing exactly where to look, there were people who could help me. And I also wanted to meet people in the same kind of situation like myself, because the problem of the countryside is isolation. So when you are somebody very sociable, and used to live surrounded by people, it is difficult to find oneself in a situation of unemployment and isolation. (female, age 25, student)

Young People's Career Decisions

Where the formal career advice was perceived to be weak, how did young people respond? When asked directly, interviewees often indicated they had never discussed with anyone their options for the post-school future, and little reference to any key influences was given. However, in the course of the interviews, it emerged that certainly traditional influential forces had contributed towards filling the gap of formal advice, although the extent to which that was the case varied from study area to study area. The following interview excerpt shows that sometimes, the young person could be expected to uphold some 'family tradition'.

> Yes, it seems to be family tradition, because my mother has already visited the commercial school and my uncle too, and now I have to visit the commercial school too, seemingly. (female, age 21, Murau, Austria)

There are examples in all study areas of family members exerting pressure to ensure the young person would continue in the same line of work as their parents and relatives. Sometimes, strong attempts were made by family members to persuade the young person to pursue a job or educational pathway which was perceived to be more worthwhile than the employment option the youth was interested in. Several Scottish interviewees mentioned the possible pressure farmers' children could find themselves under when parents hoped their offspring would take over the farm. By contrast, in France, the farmers' families seemed to be the ones particularly supporting higher education. This must perhaps be seen in a context where the agricultural sector is facing grave difficulties from which parents tried to protect their children (Auclair, Faure and Vanoni 2000, 7).

As opposed to the situation where parents influenced their children perhaps quite unduly in their decision-making process, strong views were articulated to the effect that parents were very supportive during different phases of transition processes. It is worthwhile pointing to the general support many young people had gratefully received from their parents during transition periods. This applied to financial help, the lending of a car, general moral support, and the fact that the young people felt that they could return to their parents' home when their plans did not work out. In fact, the strongest links here certainly existed in the Portuguese study area, where not only did children seem to be able to completely rely on their parents' support, but parents also acknowledged the help children gave them, so that an inter-dependent situation was recognised. Examples for the consistently strong support Portuguese interviewees expected from their parents were revealed in their thoughts about future plans, and when reflecting on the question of how to address the problem of unemployment. In many cases, interviewees would begin their replies by saying "I am counting on the support of my parents".

Interviewees from other study areas also gave accounts of the support received from parents, but there were sometimes strong sentiments that this support should be accepted only in measures. An unemployed young person from Angus was playing with the idea of returning to University to complete a degree he had started before:

> Yeah, if I went back, I'd have to get some sort of job at Macdonald's or something and fund myself. Because I've had my bite at the cherry, my parents' help, and I couldn't use their money again. (male, 21 years old, Angus, Scotland)

In some cases, the unobtrusive nature of parental support many young people experienced was appreciated:

> They (parents) want me to do well but they don't pressure me whatsoever. (female, age 17, NW Connemara)

> They are totally behind me whatever I want to do. (Interview 18; Male, NW Connemara)

There were also occasions where interviewees seemed to take their parents' pathways as a reference point for themselves:

> But I always kind of thought, my dad went to University, and I've always kind of assumed that as a goal. (male, age 17, school pupil, Angus)

Apart from parental influence, friends' and relatives' weight in shaping career choices was also referred to:

> ... My auntie is in accounting and I've been spending a lot more time with her ... I could see myself in an office. Basically it's how I see myself in my mind. (female, 17 years, NW Connemara)

> You see my friends that went to different schools they didn't do transition year so they are in college this year. I have three friends in Galway so I was talking to them about their courses. (female, age 16, NW Connemara)

> No one really suggested that I should become a car mechanic; it was my own decision. Of course the fact that many of my mates were going to do the same had some effect. (male, age 22, Suomussalmi, Finland)

In other cases, subjects taken at school or placement experiences gathered helped to inform a career decision.

> Yes, I've always been interested in that field. My school has focused on education for several branches. There have been three different branches of which you could choose one. I got to know all three of them. I decided on the field which suited me best. (male, age 19, Murau, Austria)

To summarise the situation of young people with regard to their career choices, it seems that notwithstanding the frequent impact of parental advice and employment history on young people's decision-making processes, young people recognised the fact that many career possibilities existed which could be worthwhile pursuing. The range of opportunities may indeed give the appearance of a new freedom of choice and unprecedented numerous options of creating one's pathway. However, often, the details of particular job aspects were not clear, and the process of 'how to get there' appeared obscure. This situation contrasts with the traditional cultural practice, which allowed for only low or medium degrees of mobility on the part of the child (Büchner et al. 1995, 54). At that time, children would often have followed the footsteps of their parents as a matter of course – limiting them in their abilities to find 'their' vocation, and being accompanied with low degrees of satisfaction. At the same time, the achievement pressure and stress to which they were exposed would have been much reduced (Büchner et al., 1995, 54). Let us now turn from the process of career decision-making to young people's experiences with and thoughts about the labour market.

5. Accessing the Labour Market

The local labour market was mainly commented upon in negative terms. An important concern by interviewees in all study areas was the accessibility to training and employment, and related to that, the lack of public transport. In such situations, it is clear that access to private transport is essential. However, over one third of the young people in our sample did not have access to a vehicle. We can assume that especially in the less accessible and remote areas – the Austrian, Finnish, French, Irish and Portuguese study areas – the lack of personal transport will be particularly limiting. It also needs to be borne in mind that accessing jobs which require commuting does not only presuppose the willingness to travel, but also the resources to meet travelling costs, whether this involves private or public transport. Difficulties accumulate, of course, where the lack of transport is accompanied by a lack of opportunities in training and employment.

Access to and Quality of Training

In all study areas, interviewees complained about the lack of places for training, and the limited range of options available with regard to types of training. Additional difficulties with public transport were vigorously articulated in a Scottish focus group discussion. Participants reported how trying to reach possible training places would often involve leaving home early in the morning, and returning late due to few and awkward travel connections. For others, it seemed less the problem of transport that mattered to them, but the availability of training, especially training of a certain type. In Mayenne, where a number of interviewees pursued vocational training after completing their compulsory education, difficulties were expressed in relation to finding an employer for the practice part of the training.

> I tried to find a training place that I would like, but you don't really know where to go, and when you like something, you know it's completely full. (female, 24 years, Mayenne)

Austrian and German interviewees sometimes attributed the cause for too few training places to employers – an analysis which seemed to be accompanied by feelings of a lack of control.

> The firms should perhaps try to take more apprentices. But this is something we cannot change. (female, age 16, Murau, Austria)

In the Portuguese study area, it became clear that training courses were public and private supply-led rather than demand-led. In all study areas, some of the training opportunities which interviewees managed to secure were found to be of poor quality, with little of the training element the trainees had hoped to benefit from, and aspects of work which did not seem to promote skills and experience. Hence, it was difficult for them to obtain marketable skills. In Wesermarsch, especially those with no formal school qualifications experienced difficulties. Since all vocational qualifications in Germany require College attendance ('Berufsfachschule') or the completion of an apprenticeship in the dual system, for which the access prerequisite is a school qualification, some young people have severe difficulties. They may not even be able to secure unskilled jobs, as employers prefer to employ young people with some educational merit, which appears to be regarded as a proxy for a good standard of work and commitment.

Notwithstanding problematic training situations in most study areas, an example from the Irish context was rated to have been successful. Young people at an educational disadvantage could benefit from the 'Youthreach' scheme.[5]

---

[5] Youthreach is a training scheme which was developed in 1989. It targets young people aged between 15 and 18 years who have left mainstream education without qualifications. It is funded by the EU, through the Department of Education and Science (McGrath, Canavan and Curtis 2000, 2).

Participants mentioned how the programme provided the opportunity to acquire specific qualifications suited to their career choices, a curriculum which was geared towards their interests and the chance to undertake mainstream courses such as the Leaving Certificate in a less authoritarian environment than school. (McGrath, Canavan and Curtin 2000, 44)

Moreover, the opportunity to take part in a formally recognised apprenticeship training was regarded as very attractive. The fact that all Youthreach participants receive a weekly allowance, which granted the young people a certain degree of independence, was commented upon favourably. While the scheme was thus well liked by those who could now compensate for their poor school performances in the past, those who were interested in general training suffered from similar difficulties as their counterparts in the other study areas. This situation has clear parallels in the area of employment.

Lack of Certain Types of Jobs

The problem of availability of employment featured in all study areas. A *general* lack of jobs in the local area was deplored in particular by interviewees in the Austrian, Portuguese, and Finnish study areas. In addition, a more complex picture emerged. Scottish, Finnish and Irish interviewees judged the local labour market situation to be fair for casual jobs, but commented on few opportunities for jobs requiring 'better' educational qualifications, and with good promotional prospects. This seemed to be also true for the French and German study area, where a lack of employment was reported to exist particularly for those whose educational achievements were at either end of the spectrum: the highly qualified, but also those with little if any qualifications. In Mayenne, the reason for the poorly qualified struggling to find employment did not seem to be related so much to a lack of jobs requiring few skills. Rather, it was pointed out that the labour market situation was such that it allowed employers to hire people who were overqualified.

Other complaints were made by Irish and Finnish interviewees about a shortage of jobs in those specific areas of employment in which the young interviewees had gained qualifications. In other words, a perceived mismatch existed between the education and training the young people had obtained and the type of jobs, which was available. This situation seemed to be particularly acute in the Finnish case, where the local authority – the main employer – was cutting positions in which many young people had been trained. It was also in the Finnish, as well as in the German study area, where young people commented on the observation that there had been a reduction in active measures to promote employment and in job creation schemes. Interestingly, in the Austrian and Scottish situation, where interviewees mentioned the problem of private employers closing down, no mention was made about the possible role the government could take here to compensate.

Poor Working Conditions

Related to the kind of employment which was described as being available, the interviewees voiced dissatisfaction with employment conditions. Young people in all study areas had complaints which concerned the poor wages to be gained in the local economy, which were sometimes reported to be close to benefit levels, resulting in a 'poverty trap'. Scottish interviewees who were college or university students described difficulties in gaining temporary jobs, and had observed that school pupils were preferred due to the lower wages they could be paid. There was also mention in Scotland of inadequate employment rights hindering the retention of jobs. Similarly, low earnings, poor working conditions and status were mentioned by Portuguese and Irish young people. This applied to family employment in the vineyards in Portugal and in Ireland, especially to the service industry, which is dominated by females. In Finland, too, it was mainly women who found their working conditions hard, as in this example.

> I was working at a home for the mentally handicapped. It was quite nice, but the work was really hard, especially because I was almost always working nights.... It was easier in summer, because the nights were light, but it was terrible as autumn came. Eventually I was just waiting for it to end so that I could get a good night's sleep. It feels funny now, though, to think that the work has finished. (female, age 23, on her last day of holiday pay after six months on a job creation scheme, Suomussalmi, Finland)

Gender and Employment

In fact, gender issues, such as the rigid division of employment between the sexes, were prominent in most case study areas. In Murau, evidence was shown that not only are women's vocational qualifications regarded as less valuable than men's. Moreover, the local labour market was argued to be mainly restricted to male workers, with women not being accepted in 'men's jobs'. However, the women themselves did not perceive employment as secondary. Rather, they would postpone their plans of starting a family to a later stage in life to take advantage of employment opportunities when in the rural community, the view prevailed that women should at least in part fulfil their traditional roles. In the French case study area, it was found that the reason for women's under-representation in certain employment areas was related to the fact that women did not avail themselves to jobs or training considered 'male'. However, this was coupled with perceptions of discrimination against women to whom certain jobs would not be made available. The situation has become more severe in recent years due to the contraction of private and public services in the study area, affecting in particular the female workforce. Furthermore, where working conditions are defined by long hours, so that childcare problems inevitably arise, it is obvious that this affects more women than men. This is also true for communities with poor provision of childcare. In the Austrian case, it was observed that the lack of public childcare for under two and a half year olds is leading to female unemployment, and the lack of childcare was also a matter of concern for Irish participants. One German interviewee referred to a situation which could pertain in particular to contexts where health and safety in public life are highly regulated, and where businesses are small. She talked about her repeated attempts to access employment in a typically male job (decorator), where she was continuously turned down, as the small employers never fulfilled the requirement of having two, separate toilets for male and female employees.

In other words, it appears that a mixture of individual and structural factors has caused the traditional employment patterns, which have been reported upon in the study areas. The former includes women's 'choice' to opt for particular jobs, and their decisions to put their private obligations before possible aspirations in the public domain. The latter includes lack of public childcare, but also (indirect) discrimination, which has manifested itself, for example, with strong gender-stereotyping, namely when 'typically male' jobs are to be occupied and women are ruled out as potential post holders. It is difficult to establish any causality here between the individual and structural factors. Yet, it is certainly possible that female behaviour is at least to some extent shaped by employers' discrimination coupled with structures, which infringe on the obligations that mainly women feel.

The Role of Social Networks

Notwithstanding the fact that there was a wide range of negative observations and experiences with the local labour markets, some young people –albeit a minority– had also commented positively. Here, reference was often made to employment secured through social networks. For example, occasional, part-time jobs and employment in the vineyards in the Portuguese study area, while rated as not worthwhile by some interviewees, was recognised by others as having the benefits of strengthening transferable skills, and helping to put the foot on the first rung of the occupational ladder. For other youngsters in SMP, social networks could help them to avoid employment in the widely undesired area of agriculture, or could cushion difficult times, which young people may experience after leaving school without any employment lined up. Where parents had a small business, farm or vineyard, children could be taken on either temporarily or long-term. This situation similarly applied to the Irish case, where the other side of the coin of the perceived exploitative family business was argued to be an opportunity to gain work skills and experience.

In all case study areas, the role of the family and social networks was mentioned in relation to employment matters. On the positive side, family business was rated to provide an important context in which work skills and experience could be gained. More generally, in all study areas, interviewees reported on the common situation of indirect help received from relatives and friends who had connections with employers, and who negotiated a place for the young person; or who informed him or her about the availability of employment. However, there was also a downside to the reliance on family and social networks. In the Scottish case employment, which could be gained from social networks, was mainly confined to temporary, seasonal and generally low paid jobs. Moreover, an interviewee revealed how her access to employment through, and then her work for a friend, restricted her in negotiating appropriate working conditions, as she did not want to be perceived as criticising her friend. A German interviewee mentioned his reluctance to work in the same organisation as his relative, since he had experienced that this situation could lead to comparisons being made between the related employees. It can then be easily assumed that "what he can do, you have to be able to do as well" (male, 21 years old, Wesermarsch, Germany).

A perhaps even greater cause for concern is the fact that an inevitable consequence of the importance of social networks is that those who are lacking 'good connections' or community approval, for whatever reasons, will find it difficult to access labour. Incidences of the former kind were observed in all study areas, and particularly emphasised in the Portuguese case.

> And even when they [the jobs] have to be advertised, it's always the same people who are "in the know", and who seem to move from one of these jobs to another every 6 months. Selection for these programmes should either be competitive, or not – one way or the other. As it stands, it's just not fair – it's always the same people who get the jobs. (female, 22 years old, SMP, Portugal)

> If you want to know about somebody in the agricultural business, you ask somebody else and they will probably know them, you know, and word gets round about, you know. 'You don't want to look at such and such, he's a bit of a crook', you know... 'oh, and I'd be wary of him'. And word gets back, you know, so yeah, ... I suppose you would call it the old boy network. Word gets out, you know. (male, 21 years, Angus, Scotland)

> When you want a job here, you need to have connections. But if they hear anything bad about you, they'll say straight away: 'We don't want you'. (female, 21 years old, Wesermarsch, Germany)

> The town is small, and the employers know each other. When somebody has screwed up in one company and wants to start with a new employer, then there is a chain of phone calls. Everyone is well in the picture then, and the person has no chance any more, and must see where to go next. (male, 18 years old, Wesermarsch, Germany)

To summarise young people's perceptions of employment in the local labour markets, most of their accounts emphasised difficulties either in terms of availability or quality of jobs, or both. There tended to be a good degree of acceptance of the situation, and although employers and the government were often held to be responsible, few suggestions were made about how the conditions could be remedied. While several young people relied on informal networks in their attempts to secure jobs, young people in all study areas showed awareness of the possible drawbacks arising from this situation, and sometimes had themselves been affected detrimentally. Those issues will be further discussed in the context of unemployment.

6. Unemployment

What experiences and views did the young people have of unemployment? A range of patterns seems to exist, and the context in which they occur needs to be considered. Let us look at the unemployment figures for our study areas, or the nearest administrative level for which comparable figures were available.

Table 10.1 Youth Unemployment Rates of EU and Seven Sub-regions in Percentage

EU/ Sub-region	Young people's (under 24 years) unemployment
EU	*19.6*
Angus (Scotland)	2000 males: 24.5% females: 31.5% [6]
Westliche Obersteiermark (Austria)	1999 males: 4.7% females: 10.9% total: 7.4%[7]
Suomussalmi (Finland)	1998 41.8%[8]
Mayenne (France)	12.4%
Wesermarsch (Germany)	Sept. 2000 9.9%[9]
West Ireland (Ireland)	Clifden RD:[10] 15.0% West Region: 9.0%
Douro (Portugal)	1997 7%[11]

It is interesting to note that the unemployment figures for youth go alongside very different total unemployment rates, the former being often significantly higher than the latter, with the exception of the two similar figures in Germany. Hence, it could be that interviewees' perceptions of the labour market situation is influenced by an

---

[6] Information supplied by Office of National Statistics. The percentage figures provided represent the proportion of unemployed young people from the total of all unemployed.
[7] From labour market service.
[8] This rate was not officially published, but compiled by Toivo Muilu from the data, which was provided by the provincial office of the Ministry of Labour. In 1998 the total labour force in that age group was 383 persons, of whom 160 were unemployed.
[9] From public employment service. The basis of this percentage is the dependent civilian labour force. It comprises those in employment covered by social security (statutory employment insurance, health insurance and pension schemes), those in 'marginal' part-time employment below a minimum level of hours/wage (without liability for social security contributions), civil servants, and the unemployed.
[10] From Census of Population, 1996.
[11] From National Statistics Institute.

awareness of the general situation, that of the peers or both. It can be seen that youth unemployment is around the 10% mark in most of the study areas (or the nearest administrative level), with Finland having a significantly higher percentage. Most study areas are therefore markedly below the EU average. However, we need to take into account that the situation in the specific localities where the young people were recruited from may divert from this wider picture. In the French context, it has been pointed out that in the North East of Mayenne, "several relatively important factories offer many low skilled or semi-skilled jobs. Therefore, the general impression, confirmed by statistics, is that there are no real unemployment problems in the area" (Auclair, Faure and Vanoni 2000, 7). In addition to the existence of large factories, low unemployment has also been attributed to out-migration movements of a large part of the population, especially the highly qualified. As concerns the Austrian study area, the rate of unemployment would be higher if people were not prepared to commute long distances to their jobs, sometimes only returning home on weekends. In Suomussalmi – the Finnish study area – unemployment was around 30% at the time of the fieldwork (Muilu and Onkalo 2000, 5). It is thus perhaps not surprising that 'a lack of job opportunities' was quoted by the interviewees as the chief cause for unemployment in Finland. However, this analysis happened in conjunction with references to negative personal traits, such as laziness, which were seen as causes for unemployment especially by school pupils and those with the highest educational qualifications (32/33).

In the French case study area with very low levels of unemployment, the focus seemed to have been on the circumstances and personal traits of the unemployed person in the context of structural difficulties. Particular mention was made of the early school leavers, young mothers, and youth with difficult social backgrounds who experienced difficulties at school. A correlation was seen to exist between those young people who had left school early with no qualification and difficulties in formulating a career plan, and their reduced possibilities in obtaining appropriate training or jobs. Another correlation was argued to exist between young, partnered women with children who have little job experience and difficulties in job search. The French study participants also argued that young people who have experienced social or family problems, as well as having encountered problems with their school performance require a long period of orientation and training in order to be able to access employment. Consequently, although the French interviewees found that anybody could get a job if they really wanted one, which seems to be supported by the low unemployment figures, the focus was on the 'deserving' unemployed who fitted in any of the three categories mentioned above, and they were not blamed for their fate.

Despite the relatively small number of interviewees with children in the sample, the issue of limited employment opportunities for mothers, as mentioned by French interviewees, featured consistently where parents were included in the sample. Women with children in the Austrian case study area reported on the difficulties they had experienced in gaining employment. This was in part due to the fact that the reconciliation of family and employment limited the working hours and the distance they could travel. In fact, even gaining access to vocational schools or training can be difficult unless good childcare is available. Other reasons for unemployment which were presented by the Austrian interviewees included illnesses or accidents, and subsequent needs for retraining. An issue, which particularly the Austrian study participants seemed to demand from the unemployed was flexibility in terms of the commuting distance, but also in relation to job choice and retraining. The context here is a remote geographical area where long distance commuting to work is seen as a 'normal' strategy to gain employment. This was coupled with expectations that people are flexible in their job aspirations, and prepared to settle for something available, rather than waiting for a preferred option. The expectation that 'commuting' should be accepted as a normal part of employment contrasts with the French case study area. Here, local actors observed that young people's perceptions of space and distance were very narrow to an extent that 'transport' to get to education or employment was not mentioned as a problem, since a large number of people neither travel nor easily consider it (Auclair, Faure and Vanoni 2000, 18). Moreover, examples exist in Finland and Ireland, where young people did not accept the premise dominant in Austria that any job was better than no job. Rather, the expectation was that jobs should be profitable, and considerably better paid than the benefits available through the welfare system. While there were thus different views on the 'problem' of a lack of flexibility leading to unemployment, there was more agreement on other personal traits, which the young people claimed they had commonly observed as causing unemployment. Such traits included the personal characteristics of laziness and lack of motivation to break the routine of unemployment for individuals. However, in only very few cases did interviewees relate those negative traits to themselves while unemployed, rather than suspecting others of such characteristics.

In addition, young people in all study areas found that the lack of working experience and vocational skills could pose a barrier to employment, this time not blaming the people concerned, but rather seeing those characteristics in the context of wider structures of poor opportunities. A vicious circle was described where it was only possible to access employment with certain levels of experience, but where the possibility of gaining experience depended to a large extent on having employment. There also seemed to be general concern about the fact that young people felt they were suffering from a lack of awareness of the local labour market situation. This made it difficult for them to take the choices in training and further education, which would enable them to find employment in their local community. Moreover, there was the issue of confidence. A lack of confidence was either referred to in a general sense, or was seen to be particularly pertinent to rural places. Where young people are used to being 'a big fish in a small pond' a move to the city for the purposes of education, training or employment may appear a daunting task.

Once young people found themselves unemployed, a range of strategies could be adopted and the various means of support offered by government agencies was an option the young people were often keen to try out, even if only modest expectations were held. In many cases, those agencies did not manage to contribute a great deal towards the interviewees' integration in the labour market. In the

Austrian case study area, the main provisions the young people took advantage of were labour market measures and courses for reorientation to facilitate easier access to employment or allow for improved qualifications. However, the value of the courses was difficult for young people to assess, with emphasis being placed on the writing of speculative applications and the contacting of employers. Such exercises were often done in vain, as the example illustrates of one young men, who had called 140 firms in the tourism sector to finally gain a job as a waiter.

In fact, those Portuguese participants who were first time job seekers at the time of the interview in part attributed their on-going difficulties in their job search partly to the ineffectiveness of those agencies, which are responsible for dealing with unemployed youth. While they registered at the relevant institutions to be eligible for training and/or placements, they criticised the indifferent, pessimistic and even de-motivating attitude of the staff, and the lengthy periods, which passed without any noticeable action having been taken.

> I had to register three times, and the last time they managed to lose the papers for a training course. It was last September, I went back there, and they said there was something wrong with my application, they'd lost something, and I'd have to start all over again. (female, 18 years old, SMP, Portugal)

When young people were offered training opportunities through governmental agencies, the focus was on what was available, rather than on which the young person was interested in.

In Suomussalmi, young people commented that they had little hope that the Labour Office could help them, as notification of vacancies would rarely reach that office, so that similar to their counterparts in other study areas, informal channels became all important.

> It's more or less a matter of who you know when it comes to getting a job here. They're never announced; you just get to hear about them somehow. You have to go and ask about work yourself... They say that if someone is interested enough in work they will come and ask... The notices of vacancies never get to the Labour Office in time, or else they are never sent, as an employer will prefer to take on someone he knows and can be sure about... Knowing the right people counts for a lot... All the Labour Office can do is hand out quarantine notices. (Focus group with unemployed, Suomussalmi, Finland)

In Angus, several young unemployed took part in the governmental training scheme designed to reduce unemployment, the New Deal. However, while keen on the idea of obtaining training which could increase their employability, those youngsters often found themselves in places which they felt were not suitable for them, as they neither fitted with their interests and aspirations, nor with their abilities. The prospects of finding employment as a result of participation in the New Deal were considered slight and exaggerated by the government. Furthermore, the fact that participation in the scheme was compulsory met with resentment from the youngsters.

However, there were also positive experiences, which were highlighted in the German context. Although the governmental Job Centres received some criticism for poor services (long waiting times; unfriendly and disinterested staff), it was also appreciated for its role in providing young people with fixed term, subsidised employment or training measures. This is of particular importance for youth without any or with few educational qualifications, who have dropped out of apprenticeships and who are unemployed. In this context, it is also important to refer to the measures taken in the wake of the NAP programme, which allowed for two outreach social workers to be employed through the *Beratung-Entwicklung-Arbeit* (Advice-Development-Employment) programme, which was founded by the local authority. The social workers' task is to help young people in their career choices and search for employment, whereby their work involves collaboration with all relevant agencies related to employment and youth. Hence, although there is a lack of employment and training places in Wesermarsch, it can be argued that there is a 'safety net structure', which comprises training courses, and which constitutes a 'second labour market'. Although the structure has been criticised, it is clear that without such support, prospects for the most vulnerable youths would often look very bleak.

Only very few young people seemed to pursued strategies independent of formal and established provisions. An unemployed female in Murau took the initiative by deciding to attend a computing course which was not paid for by the job centre. She managed to obtain a job on this basis:

> What I did and paid for myself were computer courses in F. That's what I did by myself. Excel, Windows, Power Point, the common things. And I passed an exam to get a certificate for these courses. That's what I did by myself. [...] And that's what's needed on your CV. Some of the first things demanded when a job is advertised are, first, work experience and computer knowledge. (female, age 22, Murau, Austria)

A particular feature of the Portuguese study area was young people's deliberations about leaving their country to pursue employment elsewhere, as they had often observed their parents and relatives doing. A social worker and a school teacher of SMP secondary school, two of the key informants of the Portuguese research team, both stressed the great magnitude of the local, traditional emigration as follows:

> They [the youngsters] do think a lot about emigrating. As it happened with their uncles as well as with their cousins, as it happened with their parents they think over it.

> School leavers have little ... they do not have a great will of working [in farming and building], so to speak. What actually they say and argue is that, as soon as they are old enough and get the necessary conditions, they will go elsewhere, in or out of the country.

Moreover, there were preventative strategies, which could perhaps apply to most study areas. Some young people in Murau tried to match their studies and training towards the jobs, which they knew were available in the region. Alternatively, they adopted a frame of mind, which was characterised by various degrees of flexibility in relation to geography and type of job, up to a point where the young people were willing to take 'anything'.

It is probably in unemployment when the general support from parents and friends will be particularly appreciated by the person concerned. While in most cases, parents were very supportive of their jobless offspring, there were also situations where parents showed less than an understanding attitude, as the following contrasting examples show:

Question: "And what about family's pressure for being unemployed?"
"No. On the contrary, my mother-in-law and my father-in-law themselves tell me not to despair concerning work. They tell me that I need to take care of my little daughter. But it is also annoying because I also want to have money for my things and I have not got it, have I?" (female, age 24, SMP, Portugal)

Without my parents I'd never survive on [the unemployment benefit]. They help me; I get food off them so I wouldn't have as many bills as other people. If it wasn't for them I'd be in serious trouble; I'd probably have to leave. (male, age 20, NW Connemara, Ireland)

At first there were threats [from the parents], so I have written a lot of applications and then you always receive negative replies, they turn you down. Then I thought to myself, 'I am not doing anything more, I am not interested in it'. So they put pressure on me with so many things and made me feel guilty. [...] My parents only complained about me, that I don't have a job. And they did not even believe that I have written all those applications. (female, age 16, Murau, Austria)

To summarise, for those who were unemployed, different forces were at play which could either put them under pressure to take any available job, or could take them to a mental and material state where it was acceptable to still search for a preferred employment option. The former situation seemed to apply where welfare regulations and/or the general approach to unemployment taken by the family or the community at large were such that unemployment was regarded as 'unacceptable'. From the cultural perspective, this situation was perhaps particularly true for the Austrian study participants. The opposite appeared to apply to the Portuguese situation, where parents were ready to give general support when children were trying to define their pathways. As to welfare provisions, it was the Finnish study area, where young people were by and large satisfied with the unemployment benefit they could gain, and where not just any, but an adequate job was widely regarded as important. It seems that only in exceptional cases, young people took the initiative and 'took risks', for example by financially investing in a course instead of pursuing governmental options, in the hope that such a step would pay off.

7. Discussion

What can be said about young people's transition from education to employment on the basis of some comparative data, and to what extent can analysis related to the 'risk society' hypotheses help us to better understand our findings? One issue, which seemed to underlie many aspects of young people's transition was the role of parents. Parents were found to be influential when youngsters considered leaving school early; they could shape to a significant extent young people's choices related to further or higher education; they gave direct advice with regard to career options, or had experienced careers which their children chose to follow. Their general support in all steps and phases during the transition was often referred to, not least when the young person experienced unemployment, and knew there was always a place to return to. Of course, the nature of parental input could differ, and although most young people tended to regard parents 'advice' as generally being well meant, they occasionally felt it could take an overly leading form. For example, farmers in the Scottish case often seemed to struggle hard to persuade their children to take over the farm. Other examples could be found in all study areas, where some parents were concerned about upholding a 'family tradition' in a certain branch of employment. In other words, a small minority of parents seemed still to adhere to traditional cultural practice, which the 'risk society' was supposed to have left behind. The majority of youngsters though suggested that their parents had provided unconditional support independent of their employment or educational choices. While this kind of support appeared to have been particularly welcome by the interviewees, we may also place this into the context of the 'risk society'. It can be envisaged that with the changed and changing labour market conditions over recent years, parents recognise not only that there is a wider range of opportunities than what had been offered to them, but also that those opportunities are difficult to understand and realise. Certainly, they will often be outside the parents' experiences, so that the parents themselves feel most comfortable with the thought that the ultimate responsibility for decisions will lie with their children. To some extent, similar observations could apply to the professionals, who should act as key supporters for youth.

For example, teachers who strongly advocated further/higher education independent of their pupils' interests – as was prominent in Angus – may well have thought that in the current situation, this seemed the 'safest' and most promising option with regard to employment possibilities. Where career guidance has widely been experienced as re-active, responding to some ideas of the young person, rather than exploring with them the range of possibilities, this also appears a risk-adverse approach, which can contribute towards keeping youth in traditional and well established fields. If a young person wanted to entirely rely on such guidance, he or she would effectively be denied a choice. By contrast, where career advice takes an approach which is focused on the individual in general, helps the individual to explore and articulate their interests and talents, and takes this as a departing point to examine possibilities, there may be more uncertainty involved, but also more suitable options discovered. Such an approach gives a young person the 'possibility to choose'. It appears that this latter approach mainly existed in the French study area, whilst interviewees from other study areas usually complained about the deficient former model of 'advice'. It was also noticeable that in situations where the formal career advice received was regarded as disappointing, the main influence on possible pathways seemed to have come from traditional networks.

In this context, it is interesting to look more generally at how young people rated other institutional provisions, which they experienced during their transition. While even the same provision had often been perceived differently, which depended on young peoples' personal experiences and needs, some patterns emerged. School education had been enjoyed by a large number of interviewees in Scotland and Finland, and positive features of education were highlighted in those contexts. This situation could be related to the composition of the samples, which in both cases included a disproportionate number of relatively well educated interviewees compared to the other study areas. At the same time, the factors which were mentioned as constituting 'good' or 'bad' educational systems were similar in most places, including those where young people had tended to leave school early. The fact that in many cases, interviewees from all study areas placed priority on the relevance of the knowledge and skills imparted at school for the labour market can lead us to refer again to the 'risk society'. Notions of 'dependency on the labour market' can make access to employment the dominant concern, and education can be a means to this end. However, the data points to a situation, which is more complex than that. In Austria, values such as doing well in the labour market through good educational qualifications had to compete with cultural notions that mediocre qualifications are all which is required. Similarly, it was argued in Scotland that 'laddism' can prevent young males from doing well at school, so that performance in the labour market is unlikely to be at the forefront of their minds. However, modest educational qualifications were, of course, rarely a 'chosen' option. Rather several young people in all study areas seemed to have accommodated themselves with the recognition that sometimes, due to unexpected events, the time and place for learning cannot be right. Poor school performances during serious illness and times of emotional distress were almost accepted as an unchangeable, if unfortunate, fact of life. There was no mention of any school in the seven case study area, which was trying or had managed to accommodate such not unusual cases. From a policy point of view, it seems unreasonable to expect young people in these circumstances to attempt to 'fit in' a system, and it will be more helpful to design flexible systems which can fit around the changing needs of individuals. In the case of our interviewees, it is clear that such flexibility would have provided them with far better opportunities and prospects than the difficult dead-end situations they could often find themselves in.

Another pattern, which emerged across most study areas, is worthwhile considering. In most cases, young people's experiences regarding labour market related institutions included strong elements of unreliability, where the main stability came from relatives and friends. The youngsters were reflexively aware that many of the provisions and services, which are designed to support certain steps in the transition processes, were weak and inadequate for their ideas of a future adult life. The list of voiced complaints about public institutions and services is of considerable length. School education was often regarded as uninteresting, taught by disinterested staff, and not leading to the skills perceived to be required for successfully accessing the labour market. Career guidance was rarely seen as having had a significant impact in helping a young person to define his or her pathway. Local training and employment opportunities were perceived as being poor, which sometimes was thought to have been caused by calculating employers, or the lack of governmental intervention. Where governments had intervened to 'support' the unemployed, the nature of the programmes was often criticised. However, similar to the findings of the research which examined people's attitudes towards welfare provisions in Britain, the perceived weakness of provisions did not lead the interviewees to simply mistrust or reject (welfare) state institutions (Taylor-Gooby et al., 1998). Perhaps more interestingly in our context, in very few occasions did our interviewees try to move outside the criticised formal, well established structures as a consequence of the perceived shortcomings. Rather, they attempted to manipulate the variables within them. For example, during unemployment, governmental training schemes were attended even if not liked, but under the premise that minimum effort would be invested in them, and priority be given to locating other possibilities. When preferred employment options were not available, expectations were lowered, and alternatives accepted, although the 'dream occupation' was not discarded, but its achievement postponed. Even where unemployment was high, hardly any young people played with the thought of, for example, becoming self-employed, or had undertaken steps to seriously consider such a career move. Similarly, only one example was provided of an Austrian young woman, who had gone outside the publicly funded educational sector, and had pursued a course which she herself saw as guaranteeing her employment – a strategy which paid off. The vast majority of interviewees, however, were considering the existing framework of youth and employment support, and suggestions were made how in the face of social and economic changes, institutions could usefully adapt to become more effective. It needs to be borne in mind here that most interviewees in our research constituted those youngsters who had chosen to stay in their rural community. Had 'leavers' been included in the research target group, we may have found significantly different strategies – an area meriting further research. On the basis of our findings though, it seems clear that better provisions are needed for those youths whose strategies focus on established structures. For them, Beck's notion of institutional 'dependency' has certainly become a reality. However, the important point is that such 'dependency' can in practice mean very different things for life opportunities. Our research has illustrated that conditional on what those institutions offer, 'dependency' on them can either severely limit people's agency, or give young people time and support for the planning of their biographies. A case in point is the career advice many French interviewees had enjoyed through the *PAIO* and the *centre de resources*, which helped in the definition of career plans by taking a youth centred approach that allowed young people to explore suitable possibilities. By contrast, in other case study areas, 'career advice' sometimes did little else but limiting young people's perspective. In the area of employment, the Irish 'Youthreach' programme, as well as some governmental schemes in Germany, provided for those vulnerable youngsters who, without such support seemed to have had little other prospects but unemployment. Other provisions such as the New Deal in Scotland were sometimes severely criticised for their perceived strong disciplinary component, and the lack of feasible options, notwithstanding the favourable formal evaluation of this scheme (e.g. Millar 2000a, b).

If we want to support young people in their attempts to act as the 'centre of their biography', then there seem to be three main issues for the design of 'good services' for young people. First, we need to introduce flexibility in rigid structures, which lead to the exclusion of many youths who have often already been disadvantaged by personal misfortune. Second, we need to ensure that our provisions are youth centred by taking into account young people's needs, strengths and aspirations when professionals explore with youth possible opportunities – the focus of this chapter. Youth centred development should, of course, also be relevant for areas of life other than employment, such as arts, sports and leisure in general. Third, while 'dependency' on institutions related to the labour market can well be regarded as a part of today's reality, examples of 'successful practice' from the young person's perspective proves that there is room for creativity, which can provide young people with options despite certain constraints. This is true for career advice, training and employment programmes, as well as for provisions for the unemployed. The challenge seems to be to move from those structures of provisions, which promote feelings of 'dependency' to creating dependable provisions, which young people know they can rely on when the uncertainties of the 'risk society', which can be associated especially with the transition period, demand this.

actively with markets, the state and civil society, as well as drawing on a wider range of role models from their more varied social networks. Interestingly, Olk (1988) has suggested that segmentation of labour markets has allowed the middle-classes to maintain stable, predictable transitions from good schools through higher education to core jobs, such that those occupying advantaged social positions retain the ability to transmit privileges to their offspring. Indeed, Zinneker (1990), follows Bourdieu in arguing that 'cultural capital' has become increasingly central to the reproduction of social advantage in individualisation.

The uneven process of individualisation may thus be enabling to some while constraining to others, and Beck himself acknowledges that in the 'risk society' risk is distributed inversely to social class. Working class children will be most at risk of poverty and unemployment, for example, as they undergo the transition to adulthood, and our evidence supports this. Yet, it is hard for the observer to judge how far such forces 'hinder' or 'promote' young people's ability to manage risk and welfare. After all, our decisions about what is desirable are influenced by our environment, and our preferences may be unconsciously adjusted to 'prescribed' goals. Examples from the Scottish and Austrian study areas show how cultural factors influenced young people's (short-term?) ambitions in the formal education system, leading, at best, to modest qualifications. While this may illustrate the strength of traditional influences (peers and the wider community) in a way which appears to us to be detrimental, young people themselves may not see it this way. The example from the Portuguese study area of young people committing themselves to the care of an ill parent could be a case in point. Such circumstances may be constructed as having interfered with the possibility of a good career, and can be said to have limited a person's ability to construct their biography. However, life plans can have other objectives than those related to the labour market, and can also change over time as personal circumstances change. Subjective assessments are as valid as experts', and these are known to diverge in relation to rural disadvantage (Shucksmith et al. 1996). There are also more basic questions about the existence of such life-goals beyond the short-term, and how easily these may be revised.

As a corollary, we may want to conclude that the process of 'individualisation' has different relevance in different contexts, influenced not least by cultural factors. It impacts on people's lives in complex ways, the quality of which is difficult to assess other than subjectively. Another conclusion is that people's pathways are rarely linear and planned from beginning to end, and this may be particularly true of the least advantaged young people. Changes of plans, ideas and aspirations are especially likely to occur during the 'transition', and it is for this reason that social provisions must be able to adjust to individuals' changing needs. This was emphasised in Chapter 10, where the requirement for increased flexibility in provisions was established in the context of the transition from education to employment.

The phenomenon of uneven individualisation, and the non-linear complexity of individualised youth transitions, has several implications for policy. In relation to rural economic development it suggests that a long time horizon and continuing animation and work with marginalised young people will be necessary in 'bottom-finding is that young people's social inclusion was found to be multi-dimensional, extending much more broadly than simply integration into the labour market.

In seeking to research this topic we have found it useful to consider the processes of change in terms of four systems which are analytically distinguished from one another according to the means by which resources and esteem are gained in society: these are markets, state, civil society, and friends and family networks (Philip and Shucksmith 1999). In practice, these systems interact in many ways, for example as social networks mediate young people's labour market opportunities and information. In drawing conclusions and policy recommendations we are therefore concerned not only with the state itself but also with the state's interactions with the other systems relevant to young people (especially labour markets). It is from this perspective that we begin by asking how policies affect young people in rural areas.

1. Policies and Their Impact on Young People

It was one of the objectives of this research to analyse the effects of policies on young people across rural areas in Europe, using a bottom-up approach (i.e. from their own perspective). The first thing to note is that young people were largely unaware of existing policies, and especially of those of the EU. Of course, this lack of awareness may not be specific to young people and may well be shared by adults. It is sometimes in the interest of member states, local agencies and gatekeepers to obscure the EU's role so that they can themselves take credit and maintain their clientalist relationships. Young people's unawareness of policies appears to derive both from poor access to information (often in faraway urban centres) and from the inaccessible form and content of the information, which could be made more user-friendly and be delivered in more appropriate ways. It would help if there was better co-operation between advisers and a single point of access.

In the process of the research, it also became clear that at European as well as national levels, while there is a range of policies for young people concerned with employment issues, such policies tend to neglect the rural dimension (see Chapter 6). At the same time, where policies and programmes focus on rural development, young people are often ignored. Chapter 8 reports our attempt to locate and evaluate local rural development programmes with some youth dimension in our study areas. It proved difficult to identify any such rural development programmes, and even where a youth component could be found, there was a tendency to work *for* young people rather than *with* them. There is an opportunity for the LEADER+ initiative to help local actors to pilot and then mainstream innovative ways of engaging with young people in rural development.

While promoting social inclusion amongst young people can arguably be an objective of rural development, it is also clear that the aims of rural development ('retaining local youth' in the rural area) can conflict with those of youth work ('promoting increased opportunities for young people'). MacDonald (1988) argued that 'getting on' (through education) is often undertaken as a means of 'getting out' (of the restricted options available in local labour markets in rural areas). This potential conflict was alluded to in Chapter 5 in the context of the perceived attractiveness of rural areas for young people. Many young people wished to remain in their rural communities, but achieving higher educational qualifications tended to lead to their being 'educated out' of the rural areas, where suitable jobs for the highly qualified are rare. Again, this confirms earlier findings by Jones (1992) and Shucksmith et al (1996) among others.

A number of difficult questions seem to arise here. First, to what extent should training and further education opportunities be adapted to local labour market needs, and local youth be encouraged to pursue such routes *in order to increase the likelihood that they will stay*? After all, rural communities tend to regard youth migration as a cause of grave concern. On the other hand, shouldn't we accept, or even encourage, young people's desire to *leave* their community? Leaving their homes may mark an important point in the transition from youth to adulthood, and can aid the process of emancipation from parental authority. Not to take advantage of such a possibility may mean a missed opportunity – itself a form of exclusion. Perhaps this dilemma can only be resolved through providing both 'support to leave' alongside 'support to stay'. Support 'to escape' might include comprehensive provision of information, and help when the change to a new, competitive environment away from social networks seems a daunting task. Materially, young people would need transport to relevant educational institutions, and perhaps also help with their housing costs. Support 'to stay' might emphasise the creation of 'quality jobs' in rural areas, accommodating the needs of those with high formal qualifications. The lack of such jobs was recognised by those interviewees with better qualifications, and frequent mention was made of the prevalence of poor working conditions, including experiences of pay below the statutory minimum wage. Either way, such 'support' will not be easy to provide.

Alternative approaches to this issue were reported in Chapter 7, each involving the interaction of civil society with the state in innovative partnerships. One approach, pursued by FORUM in Ireland, emphasised economic development and specifically the promotion of young people's engagement in petty commodity production; while another approach, pursued in Scotland by Moray Youthstart, emphasised the provision of services to young people as the means of inclusion. Such differences in approach reflect the differing institutional contexts in these cases, but often may also reflect compartmentalised policy and funding structures. Earlier research on partnerships (Bryden 1994) has suggested that few embrace both economic and social actions, and this is supported also by the recent findings of Westholm, Moseley and Stenlas (1999). Too often policies and programmes appear designed for the convenience of the providers rather than to suit the changing and varied needs of individual young people (see below).

Bearing all this in mind when trying to create more opportunities for young people, it seems essential to recognise that 'rural youth' are a diverse group, and interventions are likely to have winners and losers as a consequence (see Williamson 1993). For example, focusing on the creation of 'quality jobs' will mainly benefit those who have gained good qualifications in urban places, and who would like to return to their home communities. However, such an approach is unlikely to help those with few or no educational qualifications, lacking access to adequate housing, and trapped in insecure jobs (Dey and Jentsch 2000, 23), unless linked to training and further education opportunities. In Chapter 3, it was shown that it is particularly young people in *rural* areas (at least in the two countries for which data was available – France and the UK) who suffer low pay. Labour market segmentation theory was mentioned too, in Chapter 2, as one attempt to explain why, for example, certain locations and social groups have fared better in the labour market than others. In particular, Jones (1992) and Rugg and Jones (1999) have shown how social class and educational attainment underlie some young people's orientation to national as against local labour markets, and the different trajectories which follow. In addition, we may want to take into account cultural values and prejudice when explaining the position of many young people in rural areas in the lower segments of the labour market. It is perhaps those excluded young people who deserve our main attention.

In order to formulate concrete policy proposals on many of those matters, there is a need for better data and statistics. Such data must be able to take account of the diversity of rural areas, as well as helping us to understand the differences in experiences between urban and rural youth. Specific problems identified on the basis of this analysis are as follows:

- *Problems of international statistics.* Despite the best efforts of Eurostat to harmonise the statistics, the different statistical systems in different countries can still cause problems related to, for example, different dates and methods of data collection. This may cause problems like missing data. It will take a long time to resolve these problems and in the foreseeable future there are new problems to be faced, like the enlargement of EU and its effects on the international comparability of statistics.

- *Problems of regional units.* There are still no Eurostat statistics available at a more accurate level than NUTS3, and even this level is fairly rare in regional statistics. NUTS4 or even NUTS5 level data would be very useful for the international analysis of labour markets, and many other phenomena. It would also enable the comparison of NAPs of different countries at a regional level if more localised regional units were used in them.

- *Problems of classifications.* For some indicators, like sectors of employees, it would be useful to have more accurate categories. Classification into only three main sectors is insufficient to permit analysis of which parts of the regional economy are growing.

- *Problems of age analysis.* The main indicators like unemployment and activity rates are classified both by sex and age, but, for example, young people's employment by sector cannot be analysed at all since no age grouping is used.

- *The different national definitions of rurality.* Frustrate attempts at international analysis even where the datasets have been carefully harmonised, as in the Luxembourg Employment Study. It would be very useful if the OECD's rurality variable were applied consistently to each country's data.

Notwithstanding all these problems, an overall picture of labour market strength did emerge from the use of a range of indicators shown in Figure 3.3, providing a broad context for this study and offering a useful tool for mapping local labour market strength across rural Europe.

2. Young People and Their Impact on Policies

Turning from the impact of policies on young people, the question arises of what effect young people in rural areas feel they have on policies and decisions affecting them. How 'included' are they in the democratic and political processes in their areas? Do they feel 'citizenship' in this respect? This is another element of the multi-dimensional inclusion of young people in their communities, going far beyond access to 'good jobs', and is implicit in 'bottom-up' approaches to rural development. This study found very little involvement of young people in decision-making. The widespread wish of Austrian interviewees to have a voice and to participate contrasts sharply with the opportunities available there for youth involvement. Interestingly, such views also contrast with young people's attitudes in the Scottish study area. Despite local authorities setting up 'youth forums', specifically to involve young people in local decision making, most interviewees in Angus were unaware of this. Moreover, several perceived the Youth Congress to be boring (as were all local political organisations and institutions), and irrelevant, with little impact on local policies (see Scottish National Report). Problems were also perceived with the inclusiveness of the forum, with the suspicion being voiced that the congress had a middle-class bias.[1] Such forums tend to assume certain skills, competencies and material possibilities (access to time, transport, childcare possibilities, etc.) which are unevenly distributed across the population. Young people across all study areas felt unhappy with the institutional frameworks provided for youth "participation". In general, youth organisations (including the youth forums which have been recently established *for* young people primarily by adult people) are seen in a rather ambiguous way and are rejected as not pertinent to their aspirations and youth cultures.

Political commentators have frequently drawn attention to young people's lack of political awareness, to political apathy, to a disinterest in politics and to their lack of participation in the political process (Furlong and Cartmel 1997, 96). To some extent, the views found in our study may also reflect a cynicism and weariness with politics, found too amongst the older generation. Indeed, as Wyn and White (1997) point out, it is important to avoid seeing young people in

---

[1] There may be a danger that thoughtless pursuit of youth participation will lead to the 'normalising' of certain (middle-class) behaviours and the labelling of other behaviours lying outside these norms as deviant, so actually contributing to social exclusion in unintended ways (Shucksmith J 2000).

isolation from adults, society, their culture and history. For example, in Scotland, youth congresses were set up at a time when the government placed increasing importance on consultation with civil society in policy making. Of course, while many (middle-class) adults are used to reflecting on policies and socio-economic conditions, as well as consulting and advising, this is much less the case for young people. Hence, participation provisions for youth need to be properly supported. Problems may arise, for example, when a youth forum is set up but not run in a way where participants feel they have an opportunity to gradually learn, and eventually benefit – as some Scottish interviewees had suggested. 'Leaving young people to get on with it' is unlikely to lead to success, nor to encourage those young people who need extra motivation and competencies to come forward. A fine balance needs to be struck if adults' help is to be neither patronising nor inadequate when young people are presented with challenging opportunities to make a contribution as well as for self-development.

Amongst the ways in which young people can be supported are the following:

- Better guidance from schools and schoolteachers, from careers services, from training and further education institutions and from local employment services (see Chapter 10).
- A greater emphasis in schools on developing active citizenship skills (Fogelman 1996) and nurturing an awareness and understanding of, and an interest in, local politics (perhaps also through 'kids voting' as used in the US and in certain German *Länder* (Schumann 2000)).
- Building an explicit youth element into community development, with facilitators or animateurs employed to work specifically with young people, especially the least privileged.
- Promoting a local culture which accepts children and young people as social actors and as citizens to be included and valued.

A key issue appears to be the lack of feedback mechanisms to show young people who do participate that their ideas have been taken into account. Of course, continual rejections of suggestions will be demoralising and may signal that such a forum is merely a token gesture. Hence, the importance of raising awareness amongst local politicians of the value of young people's voices, and the need to recognise the potential of their contributions. In that way, both young people and politicians can benefit. For youth, the rewards can be in terms of their own personal development as well as through improving the policies and programmes themselves. Policy-makers can benefit by creating more effective policies and programmes, thereby increasing the public's confidence in them at a time when cynicism is widespread.

Fundamentally there is an issue of accountability to young people, with both the state and civil society generally failing to seek young people's voices or to consider their rights as citizens in our study areas (although it is notable that markets, in contrast, pay great attention to young people and their existing and potential purchasing power). According to many of our respondents, this failing is exhibited by local employment services, careers guidance services, training institutions and schools and teachers. One possible course of action would be accreditation of such service providers in which young people played a part. A glaring example of this is in the evaluation and monitoring of NAPs themselves, which relies entirely on analysis of aggregate statistics neglecting both the voices of young people themselves and variations in quality of the services from area to area. High priority should be given in all services to addressing this lack of accountability of professionals and institutions to young people.

3.   The Unevenness of Individualisation

A recurrent theme in this book has been that of the 'risk society' and 'individualisation', as we develop from traditional societies, in which support is provided by family, friends and church, to late modern societies in which people depend instead on markets and the state. Chisholm et al. (1990, 7) reviewed evidence that:

> the youth phase no longer consists of a standard sequencing of life events which mark transition stages to adulthood. Young people can no longer count on a secure labour market slot, they do not necessarily want to establish a 'conventional' family, and the ages at which the various transitions are accomplished vary widely.

Coles (1995) notes the emergence of *extended transitions* from school to work for some young people, and of *fractured transitions*, which may lead to unemployment, dislocation and homelessness, for others. Moreover, "change in the economic order, the dismantling of Fordist social structures, the extension of education and the associated demands for credentials mean that in late modernity individuals are increasingly held accountable for their own fates" (Furlong and Cartmel 1997, 8), however much these continue to be structured according to social class, race and gender.

  Chapter 10 highlighted the uncertainties young people face when trying to define their own individual pathways to adulthood and through life. The range of possibilities open to individuals means young people are constantly forced to engage with the likely consequences of their actions on a subjective level. Much of this report has been concerned with attempts by young people, and by institutions and others, to manage and cope with these uncertainties, drawing on social networks, civil society, the state and markets. Indeed it should be emphasised that this management of risk and welfare is a task not only for young people themselves (as agents) but also for those people and institutions which constitute the structures of opportunities (Coles 1995) within which young people must act. Our research has revealed a discrepancy between young people's wish to be able to count on the assistance and support of institutions during their period of transition and the inability of those institutions to meet young people's needs. Young people may seek independence but they also want dependability around them.

Beck's theory of individualisation, like Giddens' related theories of late modernity, is total, in the sense that it is applied to everywhere and to everyone. However, an important finding of this research is that individualisation amongst young people is highly *uneven*. The individualisation process operates in different ways, and to differing extents, for young people according to their location, class, gender and occupation, and can also change over time for one individual. Thus, it was found that traditional social commitments and assurances persist in many societies, to varying degrees. For example, young people often rely on their own or their parents' social networks in locating and accessing employment, and this was particularly emphasised in the Portuguese study area. The implications of this for the young person reflexively involved in 'life politics' (Giddens 1991) varied. Those with strong positive connections might indeed be able to pursue their life-plans with the enabling support of social networks. On the other hand, the prominent role of social networks could lead young people, as in the past, to follow in the footsteps of their friends or relatives as the safest option, albeit not the most satisfactory. A gender-stereotypical pattern of 'choices' is likely to be reinforced either way, whether following established pathways, or relying on other people's judgement of 'appropriate jobs'. In contrast, for those young people lacking significant contacts, the dependence on social networks could effectively exclude them from accessing their preferred jobs, leading them instead to develop alternative plans. In the Portuguese study area this was referred to as "exclusion of dreams". Finally, where there remained a context of strong mutual obligations and commitments young people often felt obliged to offer their parents support. Hence, in circumstances where parents required help or care, there existed a stronger sense in the Portuguese study area than in other study areas that parents' needs ought to be put before one's own labour market aspirations. This example illustrates clearly the uneven extent of individualisation (i.e. the degree to which young people could rely on or felt constrained by traditional support mechanisms), as well as the resulting impact on the young person's ability to pursue their life goals.

Individualisation may also differ according to the gender and social class of the young person. The research found that traditional cultures and social norms forced many young women in the study areas into 'women's work'. In Austria and Portugal this was lamented by several female respondents, and even in rural Finland most young women who stayed looked for employment in the public services, the traditional provider of female employment opportunities. In the Scottish area there was less evidence of this, however, demonstrating the unevenness of individualisation. Young men thus appear often to have more freedom to shape their own biographies than young women, despite women's better educational qualifications. This is not always the case, though. Young men were sometimes expected to follow traditional male pathways into farming or vineyard labour, especially in more agricultural areas, raising the possibility that the degree of individualisation may also vary by occupation.

Social class, though, is probably the most significant dimension of uneven individualisation. Although the data are poor in this respect, it appears that young people from middle class families were more likely to be encouraged, and educated, to formulate and follow safely their own preferred paths, engaging more

Chapter 11

Conclusion

Birgit Jentsch and Mark Shucksmith

The world into which children and young people grow is changing in many ways, as a result of globalisation and other processes of restructuring. In rural areas of Europe there is a structural decline in employment in agriculture and other traditional land-based industries, while new jobs are arising in the service sector. Many of the old certainties are ebbing away and some writers (Beck 1992; Giddens 1991) have argued that we are now entering into a much more uncertain phase of 'late modernity', during which we live increasingly in a 'risk society', dependent less on traditional institutions such as the family and church but instead on labour markets and the welfare state, which "compel the self-organisation" of individual biographies (Beck 2000, 166). Our ability to survive and prosper in this world will be more precarious because of the pace of change and the dependency on such impersonal systems and institutions, and these risks will not be evenly distributed through society but will be inversely associated with social class (Beck 1992, 35). However, Furlong and Cartmel (1997) have alerted us to the apparent paradox that while social structures such as class continue to shape young people's life-chances, these structures tend to become increasingly obscure as collectivist traditions weaken and individualist values intensify. "Blind to the existence of powerful chains of interdependency, young people frequently attempt to resolve collective problems through individual action and hold themselves responsible for their inevitable failure" (Furlong and Cartmel 1997, 114). Thus, social exclusion is "collectively individualised" (Beck 2000, 167). This is an important part of the context for our study of young people in rural areas of Europe.

In the early chapters of this book we sought to begin to understand the current circumstances of young people in rural areas through reviewing the literature and analysing statistical data. At the outset we discovered that there has been very little research on this issue, and that the formal data available are very poor. We make some recommendations below to Eurostat in this regard. In so far as the data allow, however, it appears that the circumstances of young people in rural areas of Europe are not very different from those in urban areas, although in rural areas, on average, low pay is more prevalent, education levels are poorer, and there is perhaps a narrower range of poorer jobs. However, there is no data on many important elements in young people's lives, and this study will therefore be of particular value in its use of qualitative methods to fill this gap. One notable up' initiatives if they are to build the capacity to act of all young people in an inclusive way. In relation to social policy, or equality policy, there is a clear message for policies and delivery mechanisms to reflect and address social differentiation: simplistic, off-the-peg approaches tailored only to standard biographies will address very few young people, and instead policies are required which can address their increasingly diverse circumstances and pathways. Flexibility to suit each person's circumstances will be essential. Policies of all types must also be adaptable to varying institutional contexts. Finally, there is an important role for not only schools and education policy but also for local political structures to foster active citizenship amongst young people so that they are better able to express their needs and shape policy, even if this is through a politicisation of personal moral issues (e.g. the environment, animal rights, nuclear power) rather than through the political pursuit of collective goals (Inglehart 1990; Bennie and Rudig 1993; Scarborough 1995).

A useful output of this project has been the identification of a number of models which appear successful in addressing some of these issues. In Austria, *nex:it* offers a model for just such a flexible youth-oriented programme which provided scope for young people to come forward with their own ideas and generated an enormous dynamic for development. In Ireland, *Mol an Oige* shows how innovative approaches can be developed to address educational disadvantage and early school leaving in particular, again by showing flexibility to individual circumstances. Also in Ireland, the *FORUM* project offers a useful model for involving young people in rural economic development, through a 'bottom-up' partnership seeking to promote opportunities in petty commodity production, and the *Youthreach* training scheme was valued highly by those young people who had failed to gain specific qualifications while at school. Some of the most useful models for labour market integration were found in France, however, notably the *Mission Locale* or *PAO*, and the *Centre de Resource*, which provided information and space for young people as part of a multi-sectoral, holistic approach. These had some similarity to the *Citizens' Shops* found in Portugal. These are described more fully in the national reports, and may offer some transferable ideas to practitioners in other rural areas of Europe.

4. The Transition from Education to Employment

All too often, rigid formal education structures seem to have disadvantaged young people in all the study areas. There was no mention by interviewees of any school which had managed to accommodate the quite frequent cases where personal, unexpected events prevented young people from successfully completing their school qualifications. Young people were expected to "fit in" to a system, rather than a flexible system fitting around these individuals' changing needs. Such a flexible approach, providing greater freedom for service providers to respond to individual needs in creative ways, would have provided our interviewees with far better opportunities and prospects than the difficult dead-end situations in which they often found themselves as a result of unexpected events or just a non-standard, non-linear transition. "The challenge is to develop policies which are based on the different realities of young people's lives, rather than on a fictional mainstream." (Wyn and White 1997, 110).

More flexibility in educational systems, to meet diverse individual needs, will also be beneficial for those who want to come back to education to acquire more qualifications at a later stage in their lives. Especially in the cases of the French and Portuguese interviewees, where early school leavers were well represented, several interviewees talked about their regrets at having left school early: many spoke of their intention to go back, if only the 'right circumstances' permitted. Prerequisites regarded as essential here included access to transport, provision of childcare, continued or resumed family support, post-job timetable plus acceptable commuting time, and a course design suited to their personal interests. It was also seen as essential that further education should have positive effects on job performance and pay in current or future employment.

Perhaps particularly relevant for rural areas is the issue of the 'distance' to educational institutions. Services are often centralised, for reasons of cost as well as of quality, such that even at quite an early age, some children and young people will have to travel considerable distances to complete their compulsory education and beyond, especially for more specialised subjects. There clearly is the question of how far it is reasonable to expect school pupils to travel without the distance having a detrimental impact on their school performance and on the general quality of life of youngsters who spend a significant time of each weekday commuting. Moreover, the distance to educational facilities may act as a disincentive for young people to continue their education. More research needs to be done to provide conclusive answers to these questions, and innovative policy and practice approaches are required to address those issues.[2] Our own study has demonstrated that, at least from the financial point of view, the families of some pupils will not be able to meet the costs involved in commuting, or will regard this as a poor investment. Depriving such pupils of public support will inevitably mean that even secondary education can become a privilege, rather than a right, and social inequalities will become perpetuated.

Of course, the issue of subsidising (at least some) pupils' travel costs to attend secondary school has a more general application. Once young people reach a certain age (probably related to the age at which employment becomes legal), the postponed higher rewards of further and higher education may seem unattractive. More importantly, the financial situation in the family, or pressure from family members, may encourage a young person to take up employment relatively early, and with few qualifications.

There are at least two policy implications here. First, there is the issue of whether public support should be provided for young people's maintenance if they continue their education at a time when they could legally seek employment. While in Portugal, the government provides grants to children with economic difficulties during compulsory education, this could be extended further as a means of

---

[2] See, for example, recent work on pre-school education in rural areas of Scotland by Copus, Petrie, Shucksmith J, Shucksmith M, Still and Watt (2001).

addressing inequalities of opportunities. Secondly, easily accessible 'second pathways in' are required for those to whom the idea of further/higher education appeals later on in life. It is clear that such pathways are more attractive when properly funded, organised, and flexible, allowing 'mature' students to combine their responsibilities and commitments with their education. Again in Portugal, provisions exist in the form of a state-sponsored taxi service to overcome the extra difficulties facing those in remoter areas attending evening classes.

The issue of guidance has been highlighted many times in this report, and should be underlined in this conclusion. This is especially important in the context of increasing individualisation. As Coles (1995, 55-56) observes:

> There is clearly a continued need for impartial guidance and advice on a myriad of complex career choices now facing young people. If a young person leaves school in the *mistaken* belief that a training programme will lead to work, or conversely, if they stay on and take a course of education in some *mistaken* belief that this will lead to a secure job, then, where they act on *mistaken* beliefs, they suffer welfare harm as a result... The rights to *impartial* knowledge, education, guidance and advice about the implications of different and competing career choices is, therefore, one element which is essential to the welfare of young people.

The experiences of the young people interviewed in this study suggest that current provision of guidance is deficient in many respects and that this is a crucial issue for policy.

Our interviewees' experiences of 'success' and 'failure' during the transition period seems to call for the following criteria against which institutions and services should be tested, if they want to promote young people's agency and social inclusion.

- Access must be enabled to good quality school/vocational/higher education, which is flexible enough to meet the changing needs of diverse individual young people, each of whom has an unpredictable life course. It should allow young people to achieve what they themselves want from education, while allowing them to take teachers', peers' or relatives' suggestions into account. It should also make information and individual guidance available at various stages to allow young people to prepare themselves for their chosen career when they wish, supporting them in breaking with traditional patterns of reliance on the knowledge and experience of their social network members.
- Access to desirable training places and jobs must be provided, together with information about the range of local and other opportunities, and about strategies for accessing these. This is a necessary precondition for young people's success, on their own terms.
- Different types of state support are required – allowing for 'breaks' in employment when there is a lack of jobs, and providing retraining when there is a mismatch between skills and labour market requirements. Support is needed for those who later on in life realise they would like to change career pathways, which may necessitate further education. It is also important for

the labour market to be regulated to ensure a minimum standard of employment rights for young people, including provisions for equal opportunities in training and employment.

* Young people especially require special protection from exploitation in the labour market. Policies must regulate working conditions and minimum pay for all age groups. Where different provisions apply for different age groups (as with the minimum wage and the absence of income support for 16-18 year olds in the UK), the implications of this need to be examined.

Although this research has not involved a formal evaluation of the implementation of NAPs in rural areas, it is clear that these policy innovations have made a considerable difference to young people in the last two years, even though they themselves may be unaware of these policies. However, the implementation of EU guidelines still suffers sometimes from difficulties and delays, as is recognised by the Commission. After all, it is for this reason that programmes like EQUAL were introduced to break up stale structures through regional development partnerships. In Germany, one problem appears to be the weak collaboration between the federal state and the *Länder*, but even France faces problems despite its more centralised structures, as the regions seek greater autonomy. If these issues could be addressed, and rural circumstances recognised in implementation, the effectiveness of the NAPs could be even greater.

In summary, labour market measures are recommended which:

* Are sensitive to the local context, which may be quite different in rural and urban areas;
* Combine top-down and bottom-up elements effectively;
* Pursue a holistic approach to young people, as whole individuals and as social actors;
* Promote connections and co-operation between local agencies (state, employers, civil society);
* Exhibit creativity and flexibility, reflecting the lengthening and individualisation of the youth transition, and its greater complexity and variety, as well as variations between areas;
* Pays most attention to those young people at greatest risk in rural societies.

5. Further Policy Recommendations

The report concludes with a number of additional policy recommendations to the Commission.

It is recommended that *Eurostat* works to improve the data available to support policies for young people in rural areas in the following respects:

* Greater harmonisation of statistics at regional NUTS4 and even NUTS5 levels.

- Statistics disaggregated by age are essential to inform policy regarding young people.
- More fine-grained statistics, for example on sector of employment.
- Disaggregation of statistics according to the common OECD rurality variable.

Many of the findings of this report are relevant to *DG Agriculture* responsibilities for rural development and agriculture, and there are several policy implications here:

- Young people will be less likely to follow their parents as a matter of course into farming, being also subject to individualisation. They will have more freedom of choice (and also a greater awareness of the risks involved), first of all in considering whether to succeed to the family farm, but it appears that there is little formal guidance and support offered to young people in making this crucial choice. Those who do become farmers are unlikely to be simply farmers following traditional practices, but will also experience individualisation in forming their own strategies for diversification, off-farm employment, or intensification, and again these choices would usefully be informed by individual guidance and support. They will also require training, education and retraining throughout their lives, and appropriate institutional support. There is an opportunity for these issues to be addressed through the implementation of the Rural Development Regulation by member states together with the Commission.
- Partnerships have become a central element in the Commission's approach to rural development, and much more could be done to involve young people in these, as suggested above, and to make them work much more effectively with young people. We recommend that the Commission uses the opportunity of LEADER+ to pilot innovative ways of involving and benefiting young people in local action, for subsequent mainstreaming.

Young people may often be seen as a concern of social and employment policy and accordingly there are a number of policy implications arising for *DG Employment and Social Affairs*:

- Although there are signs that the National Action Plans (NAPs) are effective in fighting youth unemployment, there are sometimes delays caused by the failure to commit national funds. Our main concern however is the method (and especially the aggregated level) of evaluation, which could not reveal the impact on youth unemployment in rural areas. We recommend the strengthening of these evaluations by disaggregating the quantitative indicators regionally, by including qualitative assessments of institutional co-operation within member states and regions, and by incorporating the views of service users and potential users (notably young people). These refinements would enable more effective implementation in rural areas.

- The other principal message for DG5 from this research concerns their responsibility in preparing young people for a precarious, non-linear transition to adulthood and work. Many detailed suggestions have been made in this chapter towards this end, touching especially on the need to connect (supply-side) labour market policies with (demand-side) job development policies, and to integrate these in turn with welfare systems (avoiding poverty traps and enabling labour market integration through transport and childcare services, for example) and with education and lifelong learning, and careers and guidance services. A recurring theme has been the call to design flexible, creative support structures which can address each young person's individual and diverse needs, rather than suiting the service providers' convenience.

There are also implications for *DG Regional Policy* arising out of these findings, including the points already made above in relation to young people's (lack of) involvement in partnerships which apply not only to rural development measures but also to the partnerships established to deliver Objectives 1 and 2, Interreg and other programmes. There are further implications in respect of the European Spatial Development Perspective (ESDP):

- Remoteness, accessibility and migration have been central issues in this research. A key question for young people is how 'growth centres or nodes' can be accessed: the ESDP places some importance on service provision through such centres but young people frequently lack the necessary transport to reach these, and this may force them to migrate to these centres. There is a danger that this emphasis in spatial planning will lead growth centres to 'suck' in young rural populations and hasten the functional differentiation between urban as the zone of production and rural as the zone of consumption.
- Generally more work is needed on urban-rural interactions from the perspective of young people in rural areas, and other social actors, to inform the ESDP more adequately.

Finally, the various *Youth Exchange Programmes*, funded by the EU, attracted many favourable comments from respondents. These were perceived as assisting the development of further useful skills, promoting self-development, and promoting knowledge-sharing and transfer.

Bibliography

ACRE (1994), *Rural life:Facts and Figures*, Cirencester, May.

Adams, John (1995), *Risk*, London: UCL Press.

AEIDL (1997), 'Raising children's awareness of local development: the initiative of the Dão-Mondego group (Centre, Portugal)':
http://www.rural-europe.aeidl.be/rural-en/action/dao.htm.

AEIDL (1999), 'Rural Europe, LEADER Observatory', *www.rural-europe.aeidl.be/*.

AEIDL (2000a), *Der Kampf gegen die soziale Ausgrenzung im ländlichen Raum*, 'Innovation im ländlichen Raum', Heft Nr. 8, Europäische Beobachtungsstelle LEADER, Brüssel.

AEIDL (2000b), *Information technologies and rural development*, Observatory Dossier no. 4, LEADER European Observatory, Brussels.

AEIDL (2000c), search on 'young people' http://www.rural-europe.aeidl.be.

Almas, R (1998), *Rural Development*, Centre for Rural Research, University of Trondheim.

Amin, A. and Thrift, N. (eds) (1994), *Globalization, institutions & regional development in Europe*, Oxford (Inglaterra), Oxford University Press.

Amin, A. and Thrift, N. (1994) 'Institutional issues for the EU: from Markets and Plans to Powers of Association'. Paper presented to 4th General Conference of the ESF's RURE programme, Rome.

Amin, A. and Thrift, N. (1995), 'Institutional issues for the European regions: from markets and plans to socio-economics and "powers of association"', *Economy and Society*, 24 (1), p. 41-66.

AMS (1999), *Österreichischer Jahresbericht 1999 des Arbeitsmarktservices*, Wien.

Anderson, V. (1991) *Alternative Economic Indicators*, Routledge, London.

Anwar, A.B.M.N. (1994), 'Involving rural youth in community service and culture and recreational activities', in: *Bangladesh journal of agricultural sciences*, Bangladesh Agricultural University, 21, no. 2, pp. 323-333.

Anwar, A.B.M.N.; Kashem, M. A. and Mahboob, S.G. (1994), 'Participation of rural youth in selected agriculture and income earning activities: an empirical study', in: *Journal of Rural Development*, Bangladesh Academy for Rural Development, 24, no. 2, pp. 49-62.

Anwar, A.B.M.N. and Kashem, M.A. (1995), 'Participation of rural youth in selected income - generating activities', in: *Bangladesh journal of agricultural sciences*, Bangladesh Agricultural University, 22, no. 1, pp.185-192.

Artobolevskiy, S.S. (1997), *Regional Policy in Europe*, Regional Policy and Development Series 11, Jessica Kingsley Publishers, London.

Auclair, E; Durand, F. and Vanoni, D. (1998), 'Le logement et l'insertion en milieu rural des exclus de la ville', in *Recherche Sociale* n°145, Janvier/mars 1998.

Auclair, E. and Vanoni, D. (1999), Policies and Young People in Rural Development, Interim-Report for the European Commission Research, DG B.I.2, chapter 3, 'Young people in Lassay les Chateaux, Couptrain and Pre-en-Pail in Mayenne, France', edited by the Arkleton Centre for Rural Development Research, Aberdeen, pp.106-130.

Bagnasco, A. (1977), *Tre Italie: La problematica territoriale dello sviluppo italiano*, Bologna: Il Mulino.

Beatty, C. and Fothergill, S. (1997) Unemployment and the Labour Market in RDAs, Rural Research Report 30, Rural Development Commission (Salisbury).

Beatty, C. and Fothergill, S. (1999) Labour Market Detachment in Rural England, Rural Research Report 40, Rural Development Commission (Salisbury).

Becattini, G. (ed.) (1987), Mercatoe Force Locali, Bologna: Il Mulino.

Beck, U. (1992), *Risk society: towards a new modernity*, London, Sage.

Beck, U. (2000), 'Living your own life in a runaway world: individualisation, globalisation and politics', in Hutton, W. and Giddens, A. (eds) *On The Edge: Living with Global Capitalism*, London, Jonathan Cape.

Bennie, L. and Rudig, W. (1993), 'Youth and the environment: attitudes and actions in the 1990s', *Youth and Policy*, 42, 1-5.

Berghman J, (1995), 'Social exclusion in Europe: policy context and analytical framework', in Room, G. (ed) *Beyond the threshold: the measurement and analysis of social exclusion*, the Policy Press, Bristol.

Besset, J. P. (1999), 'Les exclus convergent vers les zones rurales démunies', in *Le Monde* du 9 janvier 1999.

Böhnisch, L. and Funk, H. (1989), *Jugend im Abseits? Zur Lebenslage Jugendlicher im ländlichen Raum*, Deutsches Jugendinstitut, München, 285pp.

Böhnisch, L.; Funk, H.; Huber, J. and Stein, G. (1991), *Ländliche Lebenswelten, Fallstudien zur Landjugend*, Weinheim und München.

Boissevain, Jeremy and Mitchell, J. C. (eds) (1972), *Network Analysis: studies in human interaction*, the Hague, Mouton.

Bourdieu, P. (1993), La Misere du Monde, recently translated and published in UK as *The Weight of the World*, 2000, Polity Press.

Bradley, A. (1987), 'Poverty and Dependency in Village England', in Lowe, P. (et al) *ibid*, pp. 151-174.

Bradley, A; Lowe, P. and Wright, S. (1987), 'Introduction: Rural disadvantage and the welfare tradition', in Lowe, P.; Bradley, A. and Wright, S. (eds) *Disadvantage and Welfare in Rural Areas*, Geo Books, pp. 1-39.

Bramley, G., Lancaster, S. and Gordon, D. (2000) Benefit Take-up and the geography of Poverty in Scotland, Regional Studies, 34, 6, 507-520.

Bratl, H. (1996), *Regionen als wirtschaftliche Entwicklungssysteme*, Band 1, invent - Institut für regionale Innovationen, Wien.

Breeze, J., Fothergill, S. and Macmillan, R. (2000) The New Deal in a Rural Context, Report to the Countryside Agency (Wetherby).

Brendan Kearney and Associates (2000), *Ex post evaluation, Operational programme for LEADER II Community Initiative*, (Ireland), Interim Report.

Brown, L.M., Debold, E., Tappan, M. and Gilligan, C. (1991), 'Reading Narratives of Conflict and Choice for Self and Moral Voices: A Relational Method', in Kurtines, W.M. and Gewirtz, J.L. (eds), *Handbook of Moral Behavior and Development, Volume 2: Research*, New Jersey: Lawrence Erlbaum.

Bruce, A.; Gordon, D. and Kessel, J. (1995), 'Analysing Rural Poverty' in *Local Government Policy-Making*, Vol. 22, No. 1, July 1995.

Bryden, J. (1998), 'Less mobile resources in rural development', Report to OECD.

Bryden, J. (1999), 'Policymaking for predominantly rural regions', OECD Territorial Development Service, Working Party on Territorial Policy in Rural Areas, Paris, (working document).

Bryden, J.; Burnett, K.; Roberts, D.; Salant, P. and Shucksmith, M. (1996), *Broken Traditions: Agriculture and Rural Society in England*, A report for MAFF, March 1996.

Bryden, J., Hawkins, E., Gilliatt, J., MacKinnon, N. and Bell, C. (1992), *Farm household adjustment in Western Europe 1987-1991*, Final Report on structural change, pluriactivity and the use made of structures policies by farm households in the European Community, Arkleton Trust (Research) Ltd, Nethy Bridge, Invernesshire.

Büchner P.; du Bois-Reymond, M.; Krüger, K.-H. (1995), 'Growing Up in Three European Regions', in: Chisholm L., Büchner P., du Bois Reymond M., Krüger K.-H., *Growing Up in Europe. Contemporary Horizons in Childhood and Youth Studies*, Berlin, New York: Walter de Gruyter.

Buckwell, A.; Blom, J.; Commins, P.; Hervieu, B.; Hofreither, M.; von Meyer, H.; Rabinowicz, E.; Sotte, F. and Sumpsi Viñas, J.M. (1997), *Towards a Common Agricultural and Rural Policy for Europe, Report of an Expert Group*, European Commission, Brussels.

Burnett, J.; Jentsch, B. and Shucksmith, M. (2000), Young People in Angus County, Scottish National Report, Policies and Young People in Rural Development (PaYPiRD), Aberdeen.

Burnett, K. (1995), 'Rat Race Escapees or Rural Resource? Representations of Hebridean Incomers, Scotland', paper to XVI Congress of the European Society for Rural Sociology, Prague.

Byrne, A. (1991), *North-West Connemara: A Baseline Study of Poverty*, FORUM, Letterfrack.

Cabinet Office (2000) Sharing in the Nation's Prosperity, Stationery Office, London.

Carstairs, V. (1991), 'Suicide among men in the highlands of Scotland', *British Medical Journal*, 302, p. 1019.

Cartmel, F. and Furlong, A. (2000), *Youth Unemployment in Rural Areas*, York Publishing Services, York.

Castanheira, José Luís (1990), 'Atitudes práticas sociais de adolescentes', in *Desenvolvimento*, Ano III, N°. 5-6, Dezembro, pp. 23-36.

CEC (1998) *The future of rural society*, Brussels.

Chanan, G. (1999), *Local Community Involvement, A Handbook for Good Practice*, European Foundation for the Improvement of Living and Working Conditions, Dublin.

Chance. (1999), 'Regionales Entwicklungsleitbild Bezirk Murau', *Berichte und Standpunkte des EU-Regionalmanagement Obersteiermark West*, series 10, Juli 1999, Zeltweg.

Chapman, A. (1987), 'Class and social mobility: patterns of employment in rural and urban Scotland', in Lowe, P. (et al) *op. cit.*, pp. 175-194.

Chapman, P.; Phimister, E.; Shucksmith, M.; Upward, R. and Vera-Toscano, E. (1998), *Poverty and Exclusion in Rural Britain: The Dynamics of Low Income and Employment*, York Publishing Services, York.

Chasse, (1996), *Lanliche Armut im Umbruch. Lebenslagen und Lebensbewaltigung*. Leske und Budrich, Opladen.

Chisholm, L. (1993) 'Youth transitions in Britain on the threshold of a "new Europe"', *Journal of Education Policy*, Jan-Feb 2003, Vol. 8. No. 1, pp. 29-41.

Chisholm, L. (2000), Europäische Union, in Richter, I. and Sardei-Biermann, S. (eds) Jugendarbeitslosigkeit. Ausbildungs- und Beschäftigungsprogramme in Europa, Leske & Budrich, Opladen, 197-219.

Chisholm, L. & Bergeret, J.-M. (1991), *Young people in the European Community. Towards an Agenda for Research and Policy*, Report to the Commission of the European Communities Task Force Education, Training and Youth: Brussels: European Commission.

Chisholm, L.; Brown, P.; Buchner, P. and Kruger, H. (1990), 'Childhood and Youth Studies in the UK and West Germany: an introduction', in Chisholm, L.; Buchner, P.; Kruger, H. and Brown, P. (eds) *Childhood, Youth and Social Change: A Comparative Perspective*, London, Falmer.

Chisholm, L. and du Bois-Reymond, M. (1993), Youth transitions and social change. *Sociology*, 27, 259-279.

Clegg, Ian and Gerry, Chris (1990), 'On the analysis of the institutional dimension in structural reform', paper presented to the *Postgraduate Seminar on Economic Development and International Relations*, London School of Economics, England, 8th October.

Cloke, P.; Goodwin, M.; Milbourne, P. and Thomas, C. (1995), 'Deprivation, Poverty and Marginalisation in Rural Lifestyles in England and Wales', *Journal of Rural Studies*, 11 (4), pp. 351-365.

Cloke, P. and Milbourne, P. (1992), 'Deprivation and rural lifestyles in rural Wales II', *Journal of Rural Studies*, 8, pp. 360-374.

Cloke, P.; Milbourne, P. and Thomas, C. (1994), *Lifestyles in rural England*, Rural Development Commission rural research report 18.

Cohen, A. (1985), *The Symbolic Construction of Community*, London, Routledge.

Coleman, J. (1990), *The Foundations of Social Theory*, Harvard University Press.

Coles, B. (1995), *Youth and Social Policy: youth citizenship and young careers*, London, UCL Press.

Collier, E. (1996), 'Le revenu minimum de soleil', in *Le Monde* du 26 Mars 1996.

Collins, R. (1979), The Credential Society. A Historical Sociology of Education and Stratification, N.Y.

Commins, P. (ed.) (1993), *Combating Exclusion in Ireland, 1990-94: A midway report*, Brussels: European Commission.

Commission of European Communities (CEC) (1997), *CAP 2000 Working document, Situation and Outlook: Rural Developments*, Brussels.

Commission of European Communities (CEC), (1997), *Rural Developments*, Working document, Brussels.

Commission of European Communities (CEC), (1988), *The Future of Rural Society*, COM(88)601 final/2, Brussels.

Commission of European Communities (CEC) (1999), *European Spatial Development Perspective* (ESDP), Potsdam, Brussels/Luxembourg.

Commission of European Communities (CEC), (1999), *Sixth Periodic Report on the social and economic situation and development of the regions*, Brussels/Luxembourg.

Committee for Urban Policy (1999), *A Portrait of Finnish Cities, Towns and Functional Urban Region*, The Finnish Urban Indicators System, Helsinki.

Conroy, P. (1996), 'The Role of Partnerships in Europe: A European Framework', in Community Workers' Co-operative (ed.), *Partnership in Action: The Role of Community Development and Partnership in Ireland*, Galway: Community Workers' Co-operative.

Conway, E. and Shucksmith, M. (1996), 'Social Indicators for the Highlands and Islands', Report to Highlands and Islands Enterprise, Inverness.

Copus, A.; Petrie, S.; Shucksmith, J.; Shucksmith, M.; Still, M. and Watt, J. (2001), *Pre-School Educational Provision in Rural Areas*, summary "Interchange" published by the Scottish Executive Education Department, Edinburgh; full report will be available from the authors at the University of Aberdeen (see Interchange for details).

Crooks, T. (2000), 'An Overview of Local Development in Ireland', Paper Delivered at Conference: Delivering on Social Inclusion: Lessons from the Local Development Programme, Dublin, November 2000.

Crotty, W. (1998), 'Democratisation and Political Development in Ireland', in W. Crotty and D.E. Schmitt (eds) *Ireland and the Politics of Change*, London: Longman.

Curtin, C. (1996), 'Back to the Future? Communities and Rural Poverty', in C. Curtin, T. Haase and H. Tovey (eds) *Poverty in Rural Ireland*, Dublin: Oak Tree Press.

Curtin, C. and Varley, T. (1991), 'Populism and petit capitalism in rural Ireland', in Whatmore et al. (eds) *Rural Enterprise - Shifting Perspectives on Small Scale Production*, London: David Fulton.

Curtin, C. and Varley, T. (1995), 'Community Action and the State', in P. Clancy et al. (eds) *Irish Society: Sociological Perspectives*, IPA: Dublin.

Curtin, C. and Varley, T. (1997), 'Take your partners and face the music: The State, Community Groups and Area-based Partnerships in Rural Ireland', in P. Brennan, *L'Irlande: Identites et Modernite*, Cedex: Centre de Gestion des Revues.

Curtin, C.; Haase, T. and Tovey, H. (1996), *Rural Poverty in Ireland*, Oak Tree Press, Dublin.

Daly, H.E. and Cobb, Jr., J.B. (1989), *For The Common Good: Redirecting the Economy towards Community, the Environment and a Sustainable Future*, Green Print / Merlin Press, London.

Dawes, L. (1993), *Long-term unemployment and labour market flexibility*, Leicester: University Centre for Labour Market Studies.

Dax, T. (1999), 'Entwicklung des ländlichen Raumes - Kompromiß oder 'Zweiter Pfeiler der Gemeinsamen Agrarpolitik?' In: Agrarbündnis E.V. (ed.): *Landwirtschaft 99, Der kritische Agrarbericht*, Kassel, pp. 44-50.

Dax, T. and Hebertshuber, M. (2000), 'Rural and Regional Development in Austria: Leadership and Local Power', in: Woodward, R., Kovacs, I. and Halfacree, K. (eds), *Leadership and Local Power in European Rural Development*, Ashgate, London.

Dax, T. and Hellegers, P. (2000), 'Policies for Less Favoured Areas', in: Brouwer, F. and Lowe, P (eds), *CAP Regimes and the European Countryside, Prospects for Integration between Agricultural, Regional and Environmental Policies*, CABI Publishing, Wallingford, pp. 179-197.

Dax, T.; Machold, I. and Meisinger, C. (2000), 'Effective policies for social inclusion of youth?, First impressions and preliminary findings from interviews in the research project: Policies and Young People in Rural Development (PaYPiRD)', paper for the 3rd co-ordination meeting, 10-13 February, Vila Real, Portugal.

Dax, T.; Machold, I. and Meisinger, C. (2000), 'Policies and Young People in Rural Development, National Report, Study Area Murau, Styria', Bundesanstalt für Bergbauernfragen, Wien.

Dax, T. and Oedl-Wieser, T. (1995), *Ex-ante Evaluierung des Einheitlichen Dokumentes der Programmplanung (1995-1999)*, für die Ziel 5b-Gebiete Steiermark, Studie der Bundesanstalt für Bergbauernfragen erstellt für die Generaldirektion Landwirtschaft (GD VI) der Kommission der Europäischen Gemeinschaften, Wien.

Dax, T.; Oedl-Wieser, T. and Wiesinger, G. (1999), 'Policies and Young People in Rural Development', Interim-Report for the European Commission Research, DG B.I.2, chapter 4, 'Young people in Murau, Austria', edited by the Arkleton Centre for Rural Development Research, Aberdeen 1999, pp.131-154.

Department of the Environment, (1988), *Housing in Rural Areas: Village Housing and new Villages*, a discussion paper, July DoE, London.

Der Spiegel, (2000), Frühe Übung, Nr. 45, http://www.spiegel.de.

Der Standard, (2000), Jugend arbeitet in Gemeinde mit, Graz übernimmt deutsches Partizipations- und Ausbildungsmodell, 14 November, Wien.

Dethier, J.L.; Saraceno, E.; Bontron, J.C. and von Meyer, H. (1999), *Ex-Post Evaluation of the LEADER I Community Initiative 1989 – 1993*, General Report, Brussels.

'Développement local. accueil des urbains au village, un cadeau empoisonné' (1997) in *Vie Publique* d'octobre 1997.

Dey, I. and Jentsch, B. (2000), '"Quality Jobs" and "Real Choice" for Rural Youth: A reassessment', Arkleton Research Paper No. 6, University of Aberdeen.

Dey, I. and Jentsch, B. 'Rural Youth in Scotland: the Policy Agenda', in: *Youth and Policy*, winter 2000-2001 issue, January 2001.

Dingwall, R. (1999), '"Risk Society": The Cult of Theory and the Millennium? in: *Social Policy and Administration*, Vol. 33, No. 4, December 1999, pp. 474-491.

Dirven, M. (1995), Youth expectations and rural development, in: *CEPAL review*, Economic Commission for Latin America and the Caribbean, no. 55, pp. 127-141.

Douglas, JMD (1991) "Suicide among men in the highlands of Scotland", *British Medical Journal*, 302, p. 1019-1020.

Doyle, Y. and Conroy, R. (1989), "The spectrum of farming accidents seen in Irish general practice: a one year survey", *Family Practitioner*, 6, pp. 38-41.

du Bois-Reymond, M. & van der Zande, I. (1993), Young people in a changing society: the Netherlands, *Journal of Education Policy*, 8, no 1, pp. 61-72.

Duffy, K. (1995), *Social Exclusion and Human Dignity in Europe*, The Council of Europe.

Duggan, C. (1999), 'Locally Based Interventions to Combat Poverty and Exclusion: How effective can they be?' in *Administration*, Vol. 47, No. 2, pp. 56-77.

Durand, F. & Auclair, E. (1994), *Les conditions d'accès au premier emploi des jeunes en milieu rural*, FORS Recherche Sociale no. 130.

Edwards, W., Goodwin, M., Pemberton, S. & Woods, M. (2000) Community Action, Partnerships and Emergent Forms of Governance in Rural Wales.

Elias, P. and Steiner, V. (1993), *The causes and consequences of recurrent spells of unemployment in Britain and Germany*, London: Anglo-German Foundation and European Commission.

Epstein, E. (1961), 'The network and urban social organisation', *Rhodes Livingston Journal*, Volume 29, pp. 29-62.

Esping-Anderson, G. (1990), *Three Worlds of Welfare Capitalism*, Polity Press, London.

Estanque, Elísio and Mendes, José Manuel (1997) *Classes e desigualdades sociais em Portugal: um estudo comparativo*, Porto, Afrontamento.

Europäische Kommission (1996), *Erster Bericht über den wirtschaftlichen und sozialen Zusammenhalt 1996*, Amt für amtliche Veröffentlichungen der Eurpäischen Gemeinschaften, Brüssel/Luxemburg.

Europäischer Rechnungshof (1998), Sonderbericht Nr. 15/98 über die Bewertung der Strukturfonds-Interventionen in den Zeiträumen 1989 – 1993 und 1994 – 1999, zusammen mit den Antworten der Kommission, *Amtsblatt der Europäischen Gemeinschaften* C 347/1-47, vom 16.11.1998, Brüssel.

European Anti-Poverty Network (EAPN) (1999), *New strategies to combat poverty and social exclusion*. The situation in nine European Countries, Brussels.

European Commission (1988), *The Future of Rural Society*, COM(88)501 final of 28.07.1988. Brussels.

European Commission (1993), *Growth, Competitiveness and Employment*, White Paper, Brussels.

European Commission (1994), *Competitiveness and cohesion: trends in the regions*. Fifth periodic report on the social and economic situation and development of the regions of the Community, EC Regional Policies, United Kingdom.

European Commission (1995a), *Joint Employment Report 1995*, Brussels.

European Commission (1995b), *Education and Training*, White Paper, Brussels.

European Commission (1997), *Rural Development*, Brussels.

European Commission (1999a), *Sixth Periodic Report on the social and economic situation and development of the regions of the European Union*. European Union Regional Policy and Cohesion, Belgium.

European Commission (1999b), *Implementing the European Employment Strategy. The challenges of integrating young people into the labour market, long-term unemployment and equal opportunities*, Brussels.

European Commission (1999c), *Joint Employment Report 1999*, Parts I and II, SOC 438 ECOFIN 268, Brussels.

European Commission (1999d), 'The 1999 Employment Guidelines'. Council resolution of 22 February 1999, Brussels.

European Commission (2000), *Joint Employment Report 2000*, Part II, Brussels.

Eurostat (1997), *REGIONS: Statistical Yearbook 1997*, Luxembourg.

Eurostat (1999), *REGIONS: Nomenclature of territorial units for statistics - NUTS - May 1999*, Luxembourg.

Eurostat (2000), *NewCronos REGIO database*, CD-rom, version 30.05.2000, Luxembourg.

Evans, Karen; Behrens, Martina and Kaluza, Jens (1999), 'Risky Voyages: navigating changes in the organisation of work and education in Eastern Germany', in: *Comparative Education*, Volume 35, No 2, pp. 131-150.

Fabes, R.; Worsley, L. and Howard, M. (1983); *The Myth of the Rural Idyll*, Child Poverty Action Group, Leicester.

FAO (Food and Agriculture Organisation of the United Nations), (1998), *Increasing the involvement of young men and women in rural development in Europe*, FAO Regional Office for Europe, Technical Series 55, Rome.

Farrington, J.; Gray, D.; Martin, S. and Roberts, D. (1998), *Car Dependence in Rural Scotland*, The Scottish Office Central Research Unit.

Fernandez, R.M.; Castilla, E.J.; and Moore, P. (2000), 'Social capital at work: networks and employment at a phone center', *American Journal of Sociology*, 105 (5), 1288-1356.

Findlay, A.; Stockdale, A.; Philip L et al. (1999), *The Impact of Migration in Rural Scotland*, The Scottish Office Central Research Unit, Edinburgh.

Fogelman, K. (1996), *Citizenship Education*, conference paper, University of Glasgow, British Youth Research: the New Agenda, 26-28 January (cited in Furlong and Cartmel).

Forrest, D. (n.d.), *Moray Youth Action's 16-18 Employment Initiative: A Social Justice Evaluation*, Aberlour Child Care Trust.

Forster, M., Helliesen, A. and Kolberg, J.E. (1996), "LES: The New Challenge, An Introduction to Concepts, Documentation and Background Statistics", LES Working Paper No. 1, CEPS/INSTEAD, Luxembourg.

Francis, D. and Henderson, P. (1992), *Working with Rural Communities*, MacMillan, London.

Fuchs, Werner (1983) Jugendliche Statuspassage oder individualisierte Jugendbiographie? *Soziale Welt*, 34 (3), 341-371.

Funk, H. (1993), *Mädchen in ländlichen Regionen, Theoretische und empirische Ergebnisse zur Modernisierung weiblicher Lebenslagen*, Deutsches Jugendinstitut, München, 205pp.

Furlong, A. (1992), *Growing Up in a Classless Society? School to Work Transitions*, Edinburgh, Edinburgh University Press.

Furlong, A. and Cartmel, F. (1997), *Young People and Social Change: Individualisation and Risk in Late Modernity*, Buckingham, Open University Press.

Garner, C. (1989), *Does disadvantage damage?* Centre for Educational Sociology, Edinburgh University.

General Household Survey (1991), *People aged 65 and over*, OPCS, London, HMSO.

Gerry, C. (1999), 'Portugal: rural youth, networks & social inclusion', paper presented to the 2nd Meeting of PaYPiRD Project Co-ordinators, Vienna, Austria, 8th-9th of September.

Gerry, C., Caldas, J.V. and Koehnen, T. (1999), "O boom no investimento em estufas na região de Trás-os-Montes e Alto Douro, 1990-95: O perfil do 'novo' empresário agrícola", *Gestão e Desenvolvimento*, N° 8, Universidade Católica Portuguesa, Viseu, Portugal, pp. 69-94.

Gerry, C.; Portela, J.F.G.; Marques, C.P.; António, C.P. and Rebelo, V. (2000), *Social Networks, Labour Market and Policy Impact in Santa Marta de Peneguião*, draft Thematic Report prepared as part of the research project *Policies and Young People in Rural Development*, (FAIR contract N° 6-CT98-4171), Department of Economics and Sociology, University of Trás-os-Montes and Alto Douro, Vila Real, Portugal, December.

Gibb, K. (1997), *Housing Investment to Tackle Social and Economic Exclusion : A Report to Scottish Homes*, Centre for Housing Research and Urban Studies, University of Glasgow.

Giddens, A. (1991), *Modernity and Self-identity : Self and Society in the Late Modern Age*, Polity Press, Cambridge.

Giddens, A. (1999), 'Globalisation and Tradition', BBC Reith Lecture N° 3, April 1999, (later published as *Runaway World: how globalisation is changing our lives*, London, Profile Books, 1999).

Gilbert, A. and Phimister, E. (2000), *PaYPiRD: analysis of existing European level micro datasets*, Mimeo, Department of Economics and Arkleton Centre for Rural Development Research, University of Aberdeen.

Glatzer, W. and Noll, H. (1995), *Getrennt vereint – Lebensverhaltnisse in Deutschland seit der Wiedervereinigung*, Campus Verlag, Frankfurt/New York.

Gougeon, T. (2000), 'Orienting New Professionals to Small Isolated Communities', paper presented at the 'Rural Communities and Identities in the Global Millennium' Conference, Nanaimo, British Columbia, Canada, May 1-5, 2000.

Grabher, G. (1991), 'Rebuilding cathedrals in the desert: new patterns of co-operation between large and small firms in the coal, iron and steel complex of the German Ruhr area', in Bergman, E., Maier, M., and Tödtling, F. (eds) *Regions Reconsidered: Economic Networks, Innovation and Local Development in Industrialised Countries*, London, Mansell Publishing, pp. 59-78.

Granovetter, M. (1973), 'The strength of weak ties', *American Journal of Sociology*, Volume 78, N° 6, pp. 1360-1380.

Granovetter, M. (1985), 'Economic action and social structure: the problem of embeddedness', *American Journal of Sociology*, Volume 91, N° 3, pp. 481-510.

Granovetter, M. (1992), Economic Institutions as Social Constructions: A Framework for Analysis, *Acta Sociologica*, 35, 3-11.

Gregg, P and Wadsworth, J. (1994), *Opportunity knocks? Job separations, engagements and claimant status*, London: National Institute of Economic and Social Research.

Guijt, I.; Guglesang, A. and Kisadha, T. (eds) (1984), 'It is the young trees that make a thick forest: a report on Redd Barna's learning experiences with participatory rural appraisal in Kyakatabe, Masaka District, Uganda', International Institute for Environment and Development.

Hadjimichalis, C. and Papamichos, N. (1991), '"Local" Development in Southern Europe: Myths and Realities' in Bergman, E., Maier, G. and Tödtling, F. (eds) *Regions Reconsidered: Economic Networks, Innovation and Local Development in Industrialised Countries*, London, Mansell Publishing, pp.141-164.

Hadjimichalis, C. and Vaiou, C. (1992), 'Intermediate Regions and Forms of Social Reproduction: Three Greek Cases', in Garofoli, G. (ed.) *Endogenous Development & Southern Europe*, Aldershot (UK), Avebury, pp. 131-148.

Halfacree, K. (1993), 'Locality and Social Representation: space, discourse and alternative definitions of the rural', *Journal of Rural Studies*, 9, 1, 23-37.

Hanesch, W. (1995), Armut im vereinten Deutschland: konturen einer Armut im Umbruch, in Glatzer and Noll, *op cit.*

Hantrais, L. and Mangen, S. (1996), *Cross National Research Methods in the Social Sciences*, Pinter: London and New York.

Harvey, D. (1994), Social construction of space and time, *Geographical Review of Japan*, 67, 2, 126-135.

Hasluck, C. (2000), *The New Deal for Young People: Two Years On*, Sheffield: Employment Service.

Helsingin seudun nopeat indikaattorit (1996), Unpublished paper of project of Fast Indicators. YTV.

Henderson, P. and Francis, D. (1993), *Rural Action*, A collection of Community Work Case Studies.

Hingel, A. J. & Fridberg, T. (1994), 'Social Exclusion and the Fourth Franework Programme (Seminar on the Measurement and Analysis of Social Exclusion, University of Bath, 17-18 June 1994)', Brüssels: Commission of the European Communities, Directorate General XII: Science, Research and Development Joint Research Centre.

Hoggart, K. (1990), Let's do away with rural, *Journal of Rural Studies*, 6, 245-257.

Holdcroft, L. E. and Jones, G. E. (1982), 'The rise and fall of community development in Developing countries 1950-1965', in Jones, G. and Rolls, M (eds) *Progress in Rural Extension and Community Development*, Vol. 1, New York, John Wiley.

Holmes, T. and Scoones, I. (2000), *Participatory Environmental Policy Processes: Experiences from North and South*, IDS Working Paper 113, Institute of Development Studies, London.

http:// www.socreonline.org.uk/socresonline/1/1/2.html.

http://europa.eu.int/comm/employment_social/empl&esf/naps/commen.pdf.

http://www.oecd.fr/std/nahome.htm.

Hupasch-Labohm, (2000), 'Berufsausbildungsvorbereitung und Berufsausbildung in anerkannten Ausbildungsberufen im Landkreis Wesermarsch. Dokumentation der wissenschaftlichen Begleitung', Brake, April 2000.

Hutton, W. (1996), *The State We're In*, Vintage, London.

'Ils ont choisi la campagne' (1996), in *Le Point* du 18 mai 1996.

'Ils quittent la ville' (1996), in *Village*, n°21 juillet/aout 1996.

Inglehart, R. (1990), *Culture Shift in Advanced Industrial Society*, Princeton, Princeton University Press.

Innes, S. (2000), (ed.), *Children, families and learning. A new agenda for education*. Edinburgh: Scottish Council Foundation and Children in Scotland.

Ioan, G. (1993), *Land of my Fathers?*, Urdd Gobiath Cymru and YMCA Wales.

Isla, M. and Soy, A. (1998), Synthesis of the Interim Evaluations of the Objective 5B regions in Spain (1994 – 1996), Barcelona.

Jedrej, M.C. and Nuttall, M. (1995), 'Incomers and Locals: Metaphors and Reality in the Repopulation of Rural Scotland', *Scottish Affairs*, 10, 112-126.

Jedrej, M.C. and Nuttall, M. (1996), *White Settlers: The Impact of Rural Repopulation in Scotland*, Harwood Academic Publishers, Luxembourg.

Johnson, J. (1994), 'Anthropological contributions to the study of social networks', in S. Wasserman and J. Galaskiewicz (eds), *Advances in social network analysis*, Thousand Oaks, California, USA, Sage Publications.

Johnson, V.; Ivan-Smith, E.; Gordon, G.; Pridmore, P. and Scott, P. (eds) (1998), *Stepping Forward: Children and young peoples participation in the development process*, Intermediate Technology Publications.

Joly, C. (1998), 'La pauvreté moins dure à la campagne', in *Le Pelerin magazine* du 10 juillet 1998.

Jones, G. (1992), 'Leaving home in rural Scotland: choice, constraint and strategy', *Youth and Policy*, 39, 34-43.

Jones, G. (1997), 'The Policy Context' In: Henderson M. & Jones G. (1997), *'Rural Scotland Today. Policy Briefing. Young People in Rural Communities'*, Rural Forum Scotland, Part 2.

Jones, G. (1999), 'The same people in the same places? Socio-spatial identities and migration in youth', *Sociology* Vol. 33, No. 1, 1-22.

Jones, G. and Jamieson, J. (1997), *Migrating or staying on: decision-making and behaviour among young people in rural Scotland*, end of award report to ESRC, R000 23 5394.

Jones, G. and Wallace, C. (1992), *Youth, Family and Citizenship*, Buckingham, Open University Press.

Jowell, T. (2000), *New Deal – Young People Fulfilling Their Ambitions helps UK economy*, London, Department for Education and Employment, 415/00, http://www.dfee.gov.uk/news/00/415.htm.

Kaupunkipolitiikan yhteistyöryhmä (1998), *Suomalaisia kaupunkeja ja kaupunkiseutuja. Kaupunki-indikaattorit 1998,* Kaupunkipolitiikan yhteistyöryhmän julkaisu, Sisäasiainministeriö (Ministry of Interior), 123 p. Helsinki.

Kearney B, Boyle GE and Walsh J (1994) EU LEADER1 Initiative in Ireland : Evaluation and Recommendations, Dublin, Department of Agriculture, Food and Forestry.

Kearney, Brendan and Associates (2000), 'Ex Post Evaluation for LEADER II Community Initiative', Interim report.

Kempson, E.; Bryson, A. and Rowlingson, K. (1994), *Hard Times? How poor families make ends meet*, London: Policy Studies Institute.

Kesteloot, K. (1998), 'The Geography of Deprivation in Brussels and Local Development Strategies', pp. 126-147 in Musterd S and Ostendorf W (eds) *Urban Segregation and the Welfare State: Inequality and Exclusion in Western Cities*, Routledge, London.

Killeen, D. (1998), 'Poverty and Devolution', in *Poverty* (Journal of the Child Action Poverty Group), Spring 1998, pp. 8-9.

Kommission der Europäischen Gemeinschaften (2000), Mitteilung der Kommission an die Mitgliedsstaaten vom 14. April 2000 über die Leitlinien für die Gemeinschaftsinitiative für die Entwicklung des ländlichen Raumes (LEADER+), *Amtsblatt der Europäischen Gemeinschaften*, C139/5-13 vom 185.2000, Brüssel.

Kulkarni, G.S. and Rajan, R.S. (1991), 'Perceptions of development as empowerment', in O'Cinneide, M. and Grimes, S. (eds.). *Planning and Development of Marginal Areas*, Centre for Development Studies, UCG, Galway.

Lash, S. and Urry, J. (1994), *Economies of signs and space*, Sage, London.

'Le monde rural en mouvement', (1999) in *Territoires*, Hors série n°398 bis, mai 1999.

'Le rural en mouvement' (1998) in *Sciences de la Société* , n°45, 1998.

Lee, P. and Murie, A. (1999), *Literature Review of Social Exclusion*, The Scottish Office Central Research Unit, Edinburgh.

Leisering, L. and Walker, R. (eds) (1998), *The Dynamics of Modern Society: Poverty, Policy and Welfare*, The Policy Press, Bristol.

Lenin, V. I. (1967), *The development of capitalism in Russia*, vol. I of *Collected Works*, Moscow, Foreign Languages Publishing House.

'Les RMIstes aux champs' (1998), in *L'Express* 25 juin 1998.

Levitas, R. (1998) *The Inclusive Society? Social Exclusion and New Labour*, Macmillan.

Li, J. and Taylor, B (1991), 'Comparison of immunisation rates in general practice and child health clinics', *British Medical Journal*, 303, pp. 1035-1038.

Lievesley and Maynard (1992), *1991 Survey of rural services*, a report for the RDC.

Little, J. (1991), 'Women in the rural labour market: a policy evaluation', in Champion and Watkins (eds) *People in the Countryside*, Paul Chapman Publishing.

Little, J. and Austin, P. (1996), 'Women and the rural idyll', *Journal of Rural Studies* 12(2) 101-111

Little, J.; Collins, I. and Ross, K. (1990), *Women and Employment in Rural Areas*, National Rural Enterprise Centre.

'Loin des villes, l'exode des exclus' (1998), in *Le Figaro* du 30 mai 1998.

Lopes, Fernando Farelo (1991), 'Caciquismo e política em Portugal: uma pespectiva sobre a Monarquia e a Primeira República', in *Sociologia – Problemas e Prácticas*, N°. 9, pp. 127-137.

Lowe, P. (1994), 'Social Exclusion in Rural Europe', unpublished paper to conference on Meeting the Challenge of Exclusion in Peripheral Rural Areas, Clifden, Ireland.

Lowe, P. (1997), 'Conceptualisations and representations of rurality in a globalising world', paper at the 48th European Association of Agricultural Economists Seminar 'Rural Restructuring within Developed Economies', 20-21 March, Dijon.

Lowe, P. and Brouwer, F. (2000), 'Agenda 2000: A Wasted Opportunity?' in Brouwer, F. and Lowe, P. (eds), *CAP Regimes and the European Countryside*, Prospects for Integration between Agricultural, Regional and Environmental Policies, CABI Publishing, Wallingford, pp. 321-334.

Lowe, P.; Ray, C.; Ward, N.; Wood, D. and R. Woodward (1999), *Participation in Rural Development*, European Foundation for the Improvement of Living and Working Conditions, Office for Official Publications of the European Communities, Luxembourg.

Lutz, et al. (1993), *Von Ausgrenzung bedroht*, Forschungsberichte aus Sozial- und Arbeitsmarktpolitik Nr.50 des Bundesministeriums fur Arbeit und Soziales, Wien.

MacDonald, R.F. (1988), 'Out of town, out of work; research on post-sixteen experience in two rural areas', In: Coles, B. (ed) *Young Careers*, Milton Keynes, Open University Press.

MacGrath, B.; Canavan, J. and Curtin, C. (2000), *Voices of Rural Youth: Young People's Reflections on Life, Work, Education and Training in North West Connemara*, Department of Political Science and Sociology, National University of Ireland, Galway.

MacNamee, P. et al (1995), *Adult Education, Community Development and Rural Regeneration*, University of Ulster.

Mafalda, (2000), *Jahresbericht 1999*, Graz.

Malinen, P.; Keränen, H.; Niska, J.; Aaltonen, S.; Kataja, J.-P.; Keränen, R.; Luttinen, A.P. and Lumijärri, I. (1997), Interim report of the Mainland Finland Objective 5b programme, Oulu.

Mannila, S. (1993), *Tyohistoria ja syrjaytyminen*. Vaikeasti tyollistyvien terveysongelmaisten elamankulusta. Kuntottussaatio, Tutkimuksia 41/1993. Tyoministerio, tyopoluttinen tutkimus.

Marsden, T.; Murdoch, J.; Lowe, P.; Munton, R. and Flynn, A. (1993), *Constructing the Countryside*, UCL Press, London.

Matthieu, Nicole (1999), 'La campagne renvoie à la solidarité et à une image de dignité', in *Le Monde* du 9 Janvier 1999.

May, M. (1998), 'The role of Comparative Study' in: Alcock P, Erskine A. and May M., *The Student's Companion to Social Policy*, Blackwell: Oxford, Malden, Chapter I.3.

McAvoy, B.R. (1984), 'Trials and Tribulations of closing branch surgeries', *Update*, pp. 50-58.

McLaughlin, B.P. (1986a), 'Local approaches to rural disadvantage-the growing dilemma', *Local Government Studies*, 12.

McLaughlin, B.P. (1986b), 'Rural policy in the 1980s-the revival of the rural idyll', *Journal of Rural Studies*, 2, 81-90.

McLaughlin, B.P. (1986c), 'The rhetoric and the reality of rural disadvantage', *Journal of Rural Studies*, 2, 291-307.

Meert, H. (1999) 'Surviving on the Fringes of Society: Poor Rural Households in Belgium and a Typology of their Strategies', paper to European Society of Rural Sociology XVIII Congress 1999, Lund, Sweden.

Mernagh, M. and Commins, P. (1992), *Europe 2000: Meeting the Challenge of Exclusion in Peripheral Rural Areas*, Poverty 3 RDU, Dublin.

Mernagh, M. and Commins, P. (1997), *In From The Margins: Rural inclusion and rural development in the Europe of the new millenium: some lessons from Poverty 3*, Dublin: SICCDA.

Millar, J. (2000a), *Keeping track of welfare reform: The New Deal programmes*, York: York Publishing Services for the Joseph Rowntree Foundation.

Millar, J. (2000b), *'The new Deals: the experience so far'*, Findings, Joseph Rowntree Foundation, Ref 740; July 2000, UK.
http://www.jrf.org.uk/knowledge/findings/socialpolicy/740.asp

Miller, G. (1994), 'Marshalling Cultural Change for Development: In Search of a Better Way', In: Wiberg, U. (ed.), *Marginal Areas in Developed Countries*, Centre for Regional Science (CERUM), Umeå University, Umeå, Sweden, pp. 101-126.

Mitchell, J.C. (1969), *Social networks in urban situations*, Manchester, England, Manchester University Press.

Mol an Óige Project (2000), *Developing a systemic response to the challenges of educational disadvantage and social exclusion in Co Tipperary,* Final report of the Mol an Óige Project written by Dan Condren, Rose Tully, Mary Slattery, Philip Mudge, Norberta O Gorman. Tipperary: Mol an Óige.

Molm, L.D.; Takahashi, N. and Peterson, G. (2000), 'Risk and trust in social exchange: an experimental test of a classical proposition', *American Journal of Sociology*, 105 (5), 1396-1427.

Monk, S. & Hodge, I. (1995), 'Labour markets and employment opportunities in rural Britain', *Sociologia Ruralis*, 35, 135-172.

Monk, S.; Dunn, J.; Fitzgerald, M. and Hodge, I. (1999), *Finding Work in Rural Areas : Bridges and Barriers*, York Publishing Services, York.

Moray YOUTHSTART Partnership (2000), *Annual Report*.

Moulaert, F. (1995), 'Measuring socio-economic disintegration at the local level in Europe: an analytical framework', in Room, G (ed.) *Beyond the threshold: the measurement and analysis of social exclusion*, the Policy Press, Bristol.

Muilu, T.; Jarmo Rusanen and Arvo Naukkarinen (1999), 'Job development and regional structure: local examples of growing and declining industries in Northern Finland'. Paper presented at the IGU Commission Meeting in Albuquerque, USA, June 21-26, 1999 (in press, will be published in UK by Ashgate).

Muilu, T. and Onkalo, P. (2000), Finnish National Report for PaYPiRD, Oulu.

Nardi, B.; Whittaker, S. and Schwarz, H. (2000), 'It's not what you know, it's who you know: work in the information age', *First Monday* (peer-reviewed journal on the internet, Vol. 5, N°. 5, May 3rd, www.firstmonday.org.

Neuman, W. Lawrence (1994), *Social research methods: qualitative and quantitative approaches*, Allyn & Bacon: Boston.

Newby, H. (1985), *Green and Pleasant Land? Social change in rural England* (2nd Ed) Wildwood House, London.

Newby, H et al. (1978), *Property, Paternalism and Power: Class and Control in Rural England*, London: Hutchinson.

Nex:it (2000), Jugendzukunftsfonds Steiermark', www.nexit.at.

Niittykangas, Hannu (1996), 'Entrepreneurship in Rural Areas', in *Maaseudun uusi aika*, Helsinki, English Supplement, pp. 53-66.

Now@ (1999), *Jahresbericht 1999*, Graz.

Nyysola, K. (1994), Nuoret ja tyomarkkinoiden joustavuus. Koulutussosiologian tutkimuskeskuksen raportteja 20. Turun yliopisto.

O'Reilly, Jacqueline (1996), 'Theoretical Considerations in Cross-National Employment Research', Sociological Research Online, vol. 1, no. 1: http://www.socresonline.org.uk/socresonline/1/1/2.html.

OECD (1993a), *Partnerships: the Key to Job Creation, Experiences from OECD Countries*, Paris.

OECD (1993b), *What Future for Our Countryside*, Paris.

OECD (1994), *Creating rural indicators for shaping territorial policy*, Paris.

OECD (1995), *Education at a glance*, OECD indicators, Paris.

OECD (1996a), *Better Policies for Rural Development*, Paris.

OECD (1996b) *Ireland: Local Partnerships and Social Innovation*, Paris.

OECD (1996c), *Local Partnerships and Social Innovation*, Paris.

OECD (1996d), *Rural Employment Indicators*, Paris.

OECD (1996e), *Territorial Indicators of Employment: Focusing on Rural Development*, Paris.

OECD (1998), *Agricultural Policy Reform and the Rural Economy in OECD Countries*, Paris.

OECD (1998), *Developing predominantly rural regions: A policy challenge*, working document, Paris.

OECD (2000a), *Delivering on Social Exclusion: Lessons from the Local Development Programme*, Draft Report, Paris.

OECD (2000b) *Draft Report on Local Partnerships*, Paris.

OECD (2000c), Information and Communication Technologies and their implications for the development of rural areas, Territorial Development Service, Paris (working document).

OECD-Education, (2000) Employment, Labour and Social Affairs: OECD Ministers Conference on Youth Employment, London, 8-9 February 2000.

Office of Population Censuses and Surveys (1995), *Morbidity Statistics from General Practice. Fourth National Study 1991-1992*, London, HMSO.

Olk, T. (1988) *Jugend im internationalen Vergleich: Sozialhistorische und sozialkulturelle Perspektiven*. München: Juventa.

O'Malley, E. (1992), *The pilot programme for Integrated Rural Development, 1988-1990*, ESRI Broadsheet Series, Paper No. 27, Dublin: UCD Environmental Institute.

ÖROK (1998), *Zwischenevaluation des Ziel 1-Programms Burgenland*, Wien.

ÖROK (1999), *Zwischenbewertung der Ziel 5b- und Leader II-Programme 1995-1999 in Österreich*, Österreichische Raumordnungskonferenz (ÖROK), Schriftenreihe Nr. 144, Wien.

Osler, A. and Starkey, H. (1999), 'Rights, Identities and Inclusion: European action programmes as political education', Oxford Review of Education, Vol. 25, Nos. 1 & 2, 1999, pp. 199-215.

Palttila, Yrjö and Erkki Niemi (1999), Suomen maaseutu EU-kauden alussa-Maaseutuindikaattorit (English summary: Finnish Rural Areas at the Beginning of EU Membership-Rural Indicators), Statistics Finland, Reviews 1999/2, p.184. Helsinki.

Panayiotopoulis, P. I. (1993), 'The International Relocation of Labour and Production: Cypriot Migration to the UK 1950-80', Centre for Development Studies, PhD thesis, University of Wales, Swansea, UK.

Parsons, T. (1966), *Societies : Evolutionary and comparative perspectives*, Prentice Hall, New Jersey.

Pascual, A.S. (2000a), Introduction, in Pascual, A.S. (ed.), *Tackling Youth Unemployment in Europe*, European Trade Union Institute, Brussels, 9-15.

Pascual, A.S. (2000b), 'European strategies to fight youth unemployment: a comparative analysis and critical assessment', in Pascual, A.S. (ed.), *ibid.*

Paugam, S. (1995), 'The spiral of precariousness: a multidimensional approach to the process of social disqualification in France' in Room, G (ed.) *Beyond the threshold: the measurement and analysis of social exclusion*, the Policy Press, Bristol.

Paunikallio, Merja (1997), *Helsingin yliopisto, maaseudun tutkimus-ja koulutuskeskus*, series B: 17, Seinäjoki.

Pavelka, F. and Stefanov, M. (1985), *Rural Youth Yesterday, Today, Tomorrow*, Institute of Youth Studies and European Centre for Social Welfare Training and Research, Sofia (and Vienna), p. 332.

Pavis, S.; Platt, S. and Hubbard, G. (2000), *Social Exclusion and Insertion of Young People in Rural Areas*, York Publishing Services, York.

Peck, J. (1994), Localising labour: neoliberalism and the decentralisation of labour regulation. Paper presented to the Annual Association of American geographers, San Francisco.

Pfaffenberger, H. and Chasse, K. (eds.) (1993), Armut im landlichen Raum. Sozialpolitische und sozialpadagogische Probleme. Lit-verlag, Munster/Hamburg.

Philip, L. and Shucksmith, M. (2000), *Conceptualising social exclusion*. Aberdeen Papers in Land Economy, 00-08, October 2000. University of Aberdeen, Aberdeen.

Philips, M. (1993) *Rural gentrification and the process of class colonisation*, Journal of Rural Studies, 9 (2), 123-140.

Piore, M. and Sabel, C. (1984), *The Second Industrial Divide: Possibilities for Prosperity*, New York, Basic Books.

PIU (1999), Rural Economies, Cabinet Office (London).

Polanyi, K. (1944), The Great Transformation, Boston, Beacon Press.

Portela, J.F.G. (1988), 'Employment Composition and Income Generation in a North-East Portuguese Village', Centre for Development Studies, PhD thesis, University of Wales, Swansea, UK.

Portela J.F.G.; Gerry, C.; António, C.P.; Marques, C.P., and Rebelo, V. (2000), *Young People: from vocational dreams to pragmatism*, National Report, prepared as part of the research project on *Policies and Young People in Rural Development* (FAIR contract N° 6-CT98-4171), Department of Economics and Sociology, University of Trás-os-Montes and Alto Douro, Vila Real, Portugal, July.

Portela J.F.G.; Gerry, C.; Marques, C.P.; Rebelo, V. and António, C.P. (1999), *Santa Marta de Penaguião, Douro Valley, Portugal*, Contextual Report prepared as part of the research project *Policies and Young People in Rural Development* (FAIR contract N° 6-CT98-4171), Department of Economics and Sociology, University of Trás-os-Montes and Alto Douro, Vila Real, Portugal, September.

Porter, M. (1990), *The Competitive Advantage of Nations*, London, Macmillan.

Powell, W.W. (1990), 'Neither market nor hierarchy: network forms of organisation', in *Research in Organisational Behaviour*, Vol. 12, pp. 295-336.

Pratt, A. (1996), 'Discourse of rurality, Loose talk or social struggle?' In: *Journal of Rural Studies* 12 (1), pp. 69-78.

Public and Corporate Economic Consultants - PACEC (1998), 'Synthesis of the intermediate evaluation of objective 5(B) programmes', final report, European Commission DG VI, Cambridge.

Putnam, R.D. (1993), *Making Democracy Work: Civic Traditions in Modern Italy*, Princeton University Press.

Quitter la ville, (1997), 'la campagne est-elle prête à accueillir', in *Territoires et Villages* hors série n°379 bis, de Juin 1997.

Rainbird, H. (1996), 'Negotiating a research agenda for comparisons of vocational training', in: Hantrais L. and Mangen S., In: *Cross-National Research Methods in the Social Sciences*, Pinter: London and New York, Chapter 9.

Reddy, V.M. (1990), 'Training of Rural Youth for Self-Employment programme: a case study in Kurnool Samiti of Andra Pradesh', in: *Journal of rural development*/India, National Institute of Rural Development, 9, no. 2, pp. 435-443.

Regional Trends. (1993), *Office of Population, Census and Surveys*, London, HMSO.

Reimer, W. (1998). Personal communication.

Reinhold, A.J. (1993), *Working with rural communities in Nepal: some principles of non-formal education intervention*, UNESCO, Paris.

Riessman, C.K. (1993), *Narrative Analysis*, London: Sage Publications.

Room, G. (1994), Poverty Studies in the EU: Retrospect and Prospect, paper to conference on 'Understanding Social Exclusion: Lessons from Transnational Research Studies', Policy Studies Institute, London.

Room, G. (1995), 'Poverty and social exclusion: the new European agenda for policy and research', in Room, G (ed.) *Beyond the threshold: the measurement and analysis of social exclusion*, the Policy Press, Bristol.

Rugg, J. and Jones, A. (1999), *Getting a Job, Finding a Home: Rural Youth Transitions*, The Policy Press.

Rychener, F. (2000), 'From Amsterdam to Cologne – the European Union's Employment Policy for Young People', in *INBAS* [Institut für Berufliche Bildung, Arbeitsmarkt- und Sozialpolitik] (ed.), Transition from Initial Vocational Training into Stable Employment. Documentation of a European Conference, 'Berichte und Materialien', Vol. 4, Offenbach am Main.

Saraceno, E. (1999), 'The Evaluation of Local Policy Making in Europe. Learning from the LEADER community Initiative', in: *Evaluation* 5 (1999) 4, pp. 439-457.

Scarborough, E. (1995), 'Materialist - postmaterialist value orientations', in Van Deth, J. and Scarborough, E. (eds) *Beliefs in Government Volume Four: the impact of values*, New York, Oxford University Press.

Scheer, G. (1998), Vom alten zum neuen Regionalismus, in: *RAUM*, Nr. 31, Wien, pp. 20-23.

Schumann, H. (2000), 'Frühe Übung' in: *Der Spiegel*, 45/2000, www.spiegel.de/spiegel/0,1518,102270,00.html

Scott, J. (1995), *Development Dilemmas in the European Community*, Buckingham, Open University Press.

Scottish Office (1998), *Opportunity Scotland – a paper on lifelong learning*, Edinburgh, HMSO, Cm 4048.

Scottish Office (1998), *Towards a development strategy for rural Scotland*, Edinburgh, The Stationery Office.

Scottish Office (1999), *SKILLS for SCOTLAND: A Skills Strategy for a Competitive Scotland*, Edinburgh, HMSO.

Scottish Office (1999), *Social Inclusion: Opening the Door to a Better Scotland*, Edinburgh: The Stationery Office.

Shaw, A. et al. (1995), *Moving off income support? Obstacles, opportunities, choices*, Loughborough: Centre for Research in Social Policy, Working Paper 246.

Shortall, S. (1994), The Irish Rural Development Paradigm - An Exploratory Analysis. *The Economic and Social Review*, Vol. 25, no. 3, pp. 233-260.

Shortall, S. and Shucksmith, M. (1998), 'Integrated Rural Development in Practice : the Scottish experience', *European Planning Studies*, 6, 1, 73-88.

Shucksmith, J. (2000), 'Perfect Parents: do efforts to increase parent participation in education increase social exclusion?' in Ryan H and Bull J (eds) *Changing Families, Changing Communities: researching health and wellbeing among children and young people*, London, Health Development Agency.

Shucksmith, M. (1994), Conceptualising Post-industrial Rurality, pp. 124-132 in Bryden, J. (ed) *Towards Sustainable Rural Communities*, University of Guelph, School of Planning and Rural Development, Ontario, Canada.

Shucksmith, M. (2000a), *Social Exclusion in Rural Areas: A Literature Review and Conceptual Framework*, Scottish Executive, awaiting publication.

Shucksmith, M. (2000b), Endogenous development, social capital and social inclusion, *Sociologia Ruralis*, 40, 2, in press.

Shucksmith, M. and Chapman, P. (1998), Rural Development and Social Exclusion, *Sociologia Ruralis*, 38, 2, 225-242.

Shucksmith, M.; Chapman, P.; Clark, G. with Black, S. and Conway, E. (1994), *Disadvantage in Rural Scotland: A Summary Report*, Perth: Rural Forum.

Shucksmith, M.; Chapman, P.; Clark, G. with Black, S. and Conway, E. (1996), *Rural Scotland Today: The Best of Both Worlds?*, Avebury.

Shucksmith, M.; Henderson, M.; Raybold, S.; Coombes, M. and Wong, C. (1995), *A Classification of Rural Housing Markets in England*, Department of the Environment Housing Research Report, London, HMSO.

Shucksmith, M.; Jentsch, B. and Burnett, J.A. (2000), 'Young People in Angus County', *Scottish National Report, Policies and Young People in Rural Development (PAYPIRD)*, Aberdeen.

Shucksmith, M.; Roberts, D.; Scott, D.; Chapman, P. and Conway, E. (1996), *Disadvantage in Rural Areas*, Rural Development Commission, Rural research report 29, London.

Shucksmith, M.; Watkins, L. and Henderson, M. (1993), Attitudes and Policies towards Residential Development in the Scottish Countryside, *Journal of Rural Studies*, 9, 3, 243-255.

Silander, Mika and Jussi, Välimaa (1999), Tavoite 6-ohjelman ESR-toimenpiteiden vaikuttavuuden arvioinnin kehittäminen (Abstract: Developing the Methods of Assessing the Effectiveness of the ESF-Projects of the Finnish Objective 6 Programme). ESF Publications. 77 p. Ministry of Labour, Helsinki.

Social Exclusion Unit (1998), *Bringing Britain Together: a national strategy for neighbourhood renewal*, Cabinet Office, London.

Social Inclusion Strategy Action Team (1999), *Excluded Young People: Report of the Strategy Action Team*, Edinburgh: The Scottish Executive.

Sperl, L. (2000), *Initiative*, 'Frauen für Frauen'. Geschäftsbericht 1999, Murau.

Stone, M. (1994), *More than child's play: a follow-up study of rural childcare*, Report to the Rural Development Commission.

Storey, P. and Brannen, J. (2000) Young people and transport in rural communities: access and opportunity.

Storper, M. (1995), 'The resurgence of regional economies, ten years later: the region as a nexus of untraded interdependencies', *European Urban and Regional Studies*, 2 (3), pp. 191-221.

Strauss, A. (1987), *Qualitative analysis for social scientists*, Cambridge: Cambridge University Press.

Strauss, A. & Corbin, J. (1990), *Basics of qualitative research: grounded theory, procedures and techniques*, Newbury Park, Calif: Sage Publication.

Struff, R (1992) Regionale Lebensverhaltnisse, Teil 1: Wohnen, Arbeiten und Spzialhilfe in Stadt und Land. Schriftenreihe der Forschungsgesellschaft fur Agrarpolitik und Agrarsoziologie, Heft 293, Bonn.

Suomen kuntaliitto (1998), Keke seuraa - paikallisagendan seuranta indikaattoreiden avulla. Paikallinen agenda 21 - projektin julkaisu. 32 p. Suomen kuntaliitto - Association of Finnish Local and Regional Authorities.

Tarling, R.; Rhodes, J; North, J and Broom, G. (1993), *The Economy and Rural England*, Rural Development Commission, London.

Taylor-Gooby Peter; Hartley, Dean; Munro, Moira and Parker, Gillian (1998), 'Risk and the Welfare State', Discussion Paper, Economic Beliefs and Behaviour ESRC Research Programme, http://www.ukc.ac.uk/ESRC/risk.htm.

Tissen, G. and Schrader, H. (1998), Förderung ländlicher Entwicklung durch die europäischen Strukturfonds in Deutschland, Zwischenbewertung der Ziel 5b Politik in Deutschland 1994 bis 1996, Endbericht, Bundesanstalt für Landwirtschaft, Braunschweig.

Tonge, J. (1999), 'New packaging, old deal? New Labour and employment policy innovation', *Critical Social Policy*, Vol. 19 (2), 217-232.

Tonnies, F. (1887), Gemeinschaft und Gessellschaft – published in UK as *Community and Association*, Routledge, 1955.

Tovey, H. (1996), 'Natural Resource Development and Rural Poverty', in C. Curtin, T. Haase and H. Tovey (eds) *Poverty in Rural Ireland*, Dublin: Oak Tree Press.

Tovey, H. and Share, P. (2000), *A Sociology of Ireland*, Dublin: Gill and Macmillan.

Townsend, A. (1991), 'New forms of employment in rural areas: a national perspective', in Champion and Watkins (eds) *People in the Countryside*, Paul Chapman Publishing.

Townsend, P. (1979), *Poverty in the United Kingdom*, Penguin.

Townsend, P. (1987), 'Disadvantage', *Journal of Social Policy*, 16, 125-146.

Turbin, Jill and Stern, Elliot (1987), 'Rural Youth Labour Markets', in: *Education, Unemployment and Labour Markets*, Lewes: The Falmer Press.

Turok, I. (2000), *Local Partnerships in Ireland*, Draft Report, Paris: OECD.

UK Government Green Paper (March 1998), *New Ambitions for our Country: A NEW CONTRACT FOR WELFARE*, London, HMSO. Cm 3805.

Ungerson, C. (1996), 'Qualitative Methods', in: Hantrais L. and Mangen S., *Cross National Research Methods in the Social Sciences*, Pinter: London and New York, pp. 63-65.

Uphoff, Norman (1984), *Analysing options for local institutional development*, New York, USA, Rural Development Committee.

Uphoff, Norman (1986), *Local institutional development: an analytical sourcebook and cases*, New York, USA, Kumarian Press.

Vala, Jorge (1990), Identidade e participação social dos jovens desempregados, in *Desenvolvimento*, Ano III, N°. 5-6, December, pp. 9-22.

Varley, T. (1988) *Rural Development and Combating Poverty*, Research Report No. 2, Galway: Social Sciences Research Centre, UCG.

Varley, T. (1999), 'More Power to the People. The Politics of Community Action in Late Twentieth-Century Ireland', in S. Healy and B. Reynolds (eds) *Social Policy in Ireland; Principles, Practice and Problems*, Dublin: Oak Tree Press.

Vera-Toscano, E. (2000), *Modelling the Labour Market Behaviour of Women in Rural Canada*, PhD thesis, University of Aberdeen.

Virtanen, P. (1995), 'Jos huominen tuo jotain uuttra...' Tutkimus pitkaaikaistyottomien nuorten tyollistamisesta ja nuoria koskevan syrjaytymisproblematiikan luonteesta. Tyovoimapolittinen tutkimus 96.

Walker, R. (1995), 'The dynamics of poverty and social exclusion' in Room, G (ed) *Beyond the threshold: the measurement and analysis of social exclusion*, the Policy Press, Bristol.

Warwick, D.P. and Osherson, S. (eds) (1973), *Comparative Research Methods*, Englewood Cliffs N.J.: Prentice Hall.

Westholm, E.; Moseley, M. and Stenlas, N. (1999), *Local Partnerships and Rural Development in Europe*, interim findings of PRIDE research project, Dalarna Research Institute, Falun (Sweden) and Cheltenham & Gloucester College (UK).

Wiarda, H.J. (1979), 'The corporatist tradition and the corporative system in Portugal: structured, evolving, transcended, persistent', in L.S. Graham and H.M. Makler (eds) *Contemporary Portugal*, Austin, Texas & London, England, University of Texas Press.

Wiesinger, G. (2001), *Die vielen Gesichter der ländlichen Armut, eine Situationsanalyse zur ländlichen Armut in Österreich*, research report no. 46, Bundesanstalt für Bergbauernfragen, Wien.

Williams, N.; Shuckmith, M.; Edmonds, H. and Gemmell, A. (1996), *Scottish Rural Life Update*, Scottish Office, Edinburgh.

Williamson, H. (1993), ,Youth Policy in the UK and the Marginalisation of Young People', *Youth and Policy*, 40, 33-48.

Wolfe, A. (1978), 'The rise of network thinking in anthropology', *Social Networks*, Volume 1, pp. 53-64.

Woodward, R. (1996), '"Deprivation" and the "rural": an investigation into contradictory discourses', *Journal of Rural Studies*, 12, 1, 55-67.

Woollett, S. (1990), *Counting the Rural Cost: The Case for a Rural Premium*, London, National Council for Voluntary Organisations.

Wright, S. (1990), 'Development Theory and Community Development Practice', in H. Buller and S. Wright (eds) *Rural Development: Problems and Practices*, Hants, England: Avebury.

Wyn, J. and White, R. (1997), *Rethinking Youth*, London: Sage.

Young India Project (1988), *Tryst with destiny: critical essays on governmental development policies and anti-poverty programmes*.

Young people (1997), *Arbeitsmarktpolitisches Selbstorganisationsprojekt für Jugendliche im Bezirk Bruck/Mur*, Abschlussbericht, Big – Bruck/Mur, Kapfenberg.

Zejda, J.E.; McDuffie, H.H. and Dosman, J.A. (1993), 'Epidemiology of health and safety risks in agriculture and related industries: Practical applications for rural physicians', *Western Journal of Medicine*, 158, pp. 56-63.

Zinneker, J. (1990), What does the future hold? Youth and Sociocultural Change in the FRG, in Chisholm L, Buchner P, Kruger H and Brown P (eds) *Childhood, Youth and Social Change: A Comparative Perspective*, London, The Falmer Press.

Appendix 1

Tables 1-13

Table 1. Total Unemployment Rates in PaYPiRD Partner Countries and some Sub-regions in 1991-1998

Country / Region	NUTS code	1991	1992	1993	1994	1995	1996	1997	1998
European Union	*eu15*	*7.9*	*8.9*	*10.5*	*11.2*	*10.7*	*10.8*	*10.7*	*10.1*
United Kingdom	uk	**8.6**	**9.8**	**10.5**	**9.8**	**8.7**	**8.2**	**7.1**	**6.2**
London	uki	:	:	:	:	11.9	11.6	9.5	8.1
Eastern Scotland	ukm2	:	:	:	:	7.6	7.1	7.0	6.4
Angus and Dundee City	ukm21	:	:	:	:	8.5	8.4	8.2	:
Austria	at	:	:	**4.0**	**4.0**	**3.9**	**4.5**	**4.5**	**4.8**
Wien	at13	:	:	5.2	5.0	5.2	5.9	6.1	6.8
Steiermark	at22	:	:	4.7	4.6	4.6	5.1	4.8	5.0
Westliche Obersteiermark	at226	:	:	5.5	5.3	5.0	5.9	5.4	5.7
Finland	fi	**7.0**	**12.2**	**17.9**	**19.4**	**16.2**	**14.8**	**14.3**	**12.7**
Uusimaa	fi161	:	:	:	:	:	11.8	10.9	8.8
Eastern Finland	fi13	9.7	14.7	20.9	22.1	19.2	18.3	18.7	17.0
Kainuu	fi134	12.1	19.7	30.2	24.5	22.8	20.4	22.3	19.4
France	fr	**9.0**	**10.0**	**11.2**	**12.2**	**11.3**	**12.0**	**12.0**	**11.4**
Paris	fr101	10.5	10.3	10.7	11.2	10.6	11.3	11.2	10.9
Pays de la Loire	fr51	9.0	10.2	10.9	12.0	10.8	11.2	11.0	10.4
Mayenne	fr513	5.5	5.9	6.3	7.1	5.7	6.7	6.8	5.5
Germany	de	**5.3**	**6.4**	**7.6**	**8.7**	**8.2**	**8.8**	**9.8**	**9.8**
Berlin	de3	8.1	10.0	10.3	10.7	10.4	11.7	13.4	13.7
Weser-Ems	de94	5.1	5.1	6.8	7.8	7.7	8.4	9.3	8.7
Wesermarsch	de94g	5.4	5.2	6.5	7.2	7.1	9.0	10.7	10.0
Ireland	ie	**14.6**	**15.3**	**15.7**	**14.7**	**12.2**	**11.8**	**10.1**	**7.9**
Dublin	ie002	16.2	15.5	16.0	15.0	13.6	12.2	10.9	7.3
West	ie008	11.4	13.4	15.1	14.2	10.3	11.6	9.6	6.6
Portugal	pt	**3.6**	**3.8**	**5.3**	**6.7**	**7.3**	**7.4**	**6.7**	**4.7**
Grande Lisboa	pt132	:	:	:	:	:	:	:	:
Norte	pt11	2.7	3.1	4.5	5.8	6.5	7.0	6.9	4.8
Douro	pt117	:	:	:	:	:	:	:	:

: = not available

Sources: Eurostat NewCronos REGIO database, Employment statistics (Finland).

Table 2. **Young People's (15-24 years) Unemployment Rates in PaYPiRD Partner Countries and some Sub-regions in 1991-1998**

Country / Region	NUTS code	1991	1992	1993	1994	1995	1996	1997	1998
European Union	*eu15*	*15.5*	*17.0*	*20.6*	*21.6*	*21.1*	*21.6*	*20.9*	*19.3*
United Kingdom	uk	**13.8**	**15.8**	**17.6**	**16.5**	:	**14.9**	**13.6**	**12.4**
London	uki								
Eastern Scotland	ukm2	:	:	:	:	:	13.5	14.2	13.5
Angus and Dundee City	ukm21	:	:	:	:	:	16.9	17.3	:
Austria	at	:	:	**6.8**	**6.3**	**5.6**	**6.4**	**7.0**	**6.8**
Wien	at13	:	:	8.5	7.3	7.3	8.0	8.6	9.3
Steiermark	at22	:	:	8.1	7.3	6.8	7.3	7.5	7.6
Westliche Obersteiermark	at226	:	:	9.1	8.3	7.6	8.6	8.7	8.6
Finland	fi	**22.5**	**32.1**	**42.5**	**46.2**	**39.6**	**35.8**	**32.1**	**30.9**
Uusimaa	fi161	:	:	:	:	:	29.0	23.8	19.4
Eastern Finland	fi13	32.9	45.1	50.6	50.4	48.4	41.6	42.8	41.3
Kainuu	fi134	:	:	:	:	64.0	43.6	59.9	46.8
France	fr	**19.0**	**20.6**	**24.7**	**27.3**	**25.0**	**26.1**	**26.7**	**23.9**
Paris	fr101	15.9	13.3	14.9	15.8	14.4	15.6	14.7	13.6
Pays de la Loire	fr51	21.1	22.0	25.8	29.5	25.9	24.7	25.4	21.5
Mayenne	fr513	14.1	14.0	17.6	20.4	15.5	18.4	19.1	12.4
Germany	de	**5.5**	**6.1**	**7.5**	**8.9**	**8.5**	**9.6**	**10.6**	**9.7**
Berlin	de3	9.3	12.3	12.2	12.1	11.9	12.9	14.9	14.6
Weser-Ems	de94	4.8	5.0	6.6	8.4	9.5	10.7	14.1	9.9
Wesermarsch	de94g	5.6	4.9	6.6	8.2	8.6	:	:	:
Ireland	ie	**21.4**	**23.0**	**25.3**	**23.3**	**19.5**	**18.3**	**15.8**	**11.7**
Dublin	ie002	21.4	22.4	23.8	22.6	21.6	19.2	16.1	10.5
West	ie008	20.3	25.9	30.0	28.1	16.6	16.7	17.2	10.1
Portugal	pt	**7.4**	**9.2**	**12.0**	**14.5**	**16.4**	**17.2**	**14.5**	**9.8**
Grande Lisboa	pt132	:	:	:	:	:	:	:	:
Norte	pt11	4.4	6.6	8.3	10.7	13.2	13.8	11.7	8.5
Douro	pt117	:	:	:	:	:	26.0	23.4	12.2

: = not available

Sources: Eurostat NewCronos REGIO database, Employment statistics (Finland).

Table 3. Young Males' (15-24 years) Unemployment Rates in PaYPiRD Partner Countries and some Sub-regions in 1991-1998

Country / Region	NUTS code	1991	1992	1993	1994	1995	1996	1997	1998
European Union	*eu15*	*14.4*	*16.2*	*20.2*	*21.4*	*20.0*	*20.6*	*19.6*	*17.9*
United Kingdom	uk	**15.9**	**19.2**	**21.0**	**19.4**	:	17.9	15.6	13.8
London	uki	:	:	:	:	:	22.5	17.8	15.2
Eastern Scotland	ukm2	:	:	:	:	:	16.9	17.3	16.0
Angus and Dundee City	ukm21	:	:	:	:	:	20.6	20.8	:
Austria	at	:	:	:	**4.5**	**4.0**	**5.1**	**5.5**	**5.1**
Wien	at13	:	:	:	7.4	6.6	8.0	8.2	8.8
Steiermark	at22	:	:	:	4.9	4.5	5.4	5.6	5.1
Westliche Obersteiermark	at226	:	:	:	4.4	4.2	5.3	5.7	5.1
Finland	fi	:	:	:	:	:	:	:	:
Uusimaa	fi161	:	:	:	:	:	:	:	:
Eastern Finland	fi13	:	:	:	:	:	:	:	:
Kainuu	fi134	:	:	:	:	:	:	:	:
France	fr	**16.2**	**17.5**	**22.6**	**25.2**	**21.5**	**23.5**	**24.5**	**21.8**
Paris	fr101	19.0	14.3	15.5	16.9	14.9	17.5	16.6	15.8
Pays de la Loire	fr51	16.5	17.4	22.0	25.0	20.8	19.6	21.5	17.1
Mayenne	fr513	10.0	10.5	14.3	15.8	11.0	13.6	14.2	8.4
Germany	de	**5.2**	**5.6**	**7.4**	**9.3**	:	:	**11.9**	**10.8**
Berlin	de3	9.4	11.7	12.0	13.2	:	:	16.8	16.0
Weser-Ems	de94	4.8	4.9	6.8	9.1	9.9	12.3	16.0	11.0
Wesermarsch	de94g	:	:	:	:	:	:	:	:
Ireland	ie	**22.8**	**24.6**	**27.2**	**25.6**	**21.0**	**19.3**	**16.7**	**12.1**
Dublin	ie002	24.4	26.0	27.8	27.6	26.4	22.6	19.2	13.1
West	ie008	24.0	29.1	30.6	28.3	17.5	17.0	15.1	9.1
Portugal	pt	**5.5**	**8.8**	**9.9**	**12.5**	**15.4**	**14.8**	**11.4**	**8.5**
Grande Lisboa	pt132	:	:	:	:	:	:	:	:
Norte	pt11	3.9	6.4	7.1	10.1	13.7	12.1	11.5	7.2
Douro	pt117	:	:	:	:	:	:	:	:

: = not available

Sources: Eurostat NewCronos REGIO database, Employment statistics (Finland).

Table 4. Young Females' (15-24 years) Unemployment Rates in PaYPiRD Partner Countries and some Sub-regions in 1991-1998

Country / Region	NUTS code	1991	1992	1993	1994	1995	1996	1997	1998
European Union	*eu15*	*16.7*	*18.0*	*21.0*	*21.9*	*22.4*	*22.8*	*22.5*	*21.0*
United Kingdom	uk	11.2	11.8	13.6	12.9	:	11.3	11.2	10.6
London	uki	:	:	:	:	:	15.5	14.6	13.2
Eastern Scotland	ukm2	:	:	:	:	:	9.4	10.4	10.3
Angus and Dundee City	ukm21	:	:	:	:	:	12.5	12.8	:
Austria	at	:	:	:	8.1	7.3	7.8	8.5	8.6
Wien	at13	:	:	:	7.2	7.2	7.3	8.4	9.0
Steiermark	at22	:	:	:	10.0	9.6	9.7	9.8	10.6
Westliche Obersteiermark	at226	:	:	:	12.7	12.6	13.4	12.6	13.2
Finland	fi	:	:	:	:	:	:	:	:
Uusimaa	fi161	:	:	:	:	:	:	:	:
Eastern Finland	fi13	:	:	:	:	:	:	:	:
Kainuu	fi134	:	:	:	:	:	:	:	:
France	fr	22.0	23.9	26.9	29.5	28.6	29.0	29.2	26.3
Paris	fr101	13.3	12.4	14.4	15.0	13.9	13.9	13.1	11.7
Pays de la Loire	fr51	26.0	27.1	30.0	34.7	31.3	30.9	29.7	26.6
Mayenne	fr513	18.7	18.1	21.2	25.8	20.6	24.3	24.5	17.0
Germany	de	5.8	6.7	7.6	8.4	:	:	9.1	8.5
Berlin	de3	9.2	12.9	12.4	10.9	:	:	12.6	13.1
Weser-Ems	de94	4.9	5.2	6.4	7.6	9.0	9.1	12.0	8.6
Wesermarsch	de94g	:	:	:	:	:	:	:	:
Ireland	ie	19.6	21.0	23.0	20.7	17.6	17.1	14.8	11.2
Dublin	ie002	18.3	18.9	19.8	17.8	16.7	15.8	13.0	8.0
West	ie008	15.3	21.3	29.1	27.7	15.4	16.3	19.2	11.4
Portugal	pt	9.6	9.6	14.6	16.8	17.8	20.2	18.4	11.2
Grande Lisboa	pt132	:	:	:	:	:	:	:	:
Norte	pt11	4.9	6.8	9.6	11.5	12.7	15.8	11.9	9.9
Douro	pt117	:	:	:	:	:	:	:	:

: = not available

Sources: Eurostat NewCronos REGIO database, Employment statistics (Finland).

Table 5. Total (≥15 years) Activity Rates in PaYPiRD Partner Countries and some Sub-regions in 1991-1998

Country / Region	NUTS code	1991	1992	1993	1994	1995	1996	1997	1998
European Union	*eu15*	:	:	:	:	*55.2*	*55.3*	*55.4*	:
United Kingdom	uk	**61.8**	**62.4**	**61.9**	**61.7**	**61.5**	**61.6**	**61.8**	**61.6**
London	uki	:	:	:	:	:	:	:	63.0
Eastern Scotland	ukm2	:	:	:	:	:	:	:	63.4
Austria	at	:	:	:	:	**59.4**	**58.8**	**58.4**	**58.8**
Wien	at13	:	:	:	:	59.4	59.3	59.1	60.7
Steiermark	at22	:	:	:	:	55.8	55.7	55.6	56.4
Finland	fi	:	:	:	:	**61.1**	**59.4**	**60.1**	**60.3**
Uusimaa (suuralue)	fi16	:	:	:	:	:	:	:	:
Eastern Finland	fi13	:	:	:	:	57.1	56.2	53.2	56.5
France	fr	**54.5**	**55.5**	**55.5**	**55.5**	**55.4**	**55.8**	**55.4**	**55.5**
Île de France	fr1	60.7	61.3	61.6	61.3	61.8	61.9	61.0	61.3
Pays de la Loire	fr51	56.5	56.9	56.7	56.6	57.3	56.3	56.9	56.8
Germany	de	**58.7**	**58.7**	**58.3**	**58.2**	**57.7**	**57.6**	**57.7**	**57.7**
Berlin	de3	64.1	64.0	63.2	62.9	62.7	62.0	61.2	:
Weser-Ems	de94	54.0	55.5	54.1	55.8	54.4	55.6	55.5	54.7
Ireland	ie	**51.9**	**52.6**	**53.3**	**53.9**	**53.9**	**54.9**	**55.4**	:
Portugal	pt	**59.5**	**59.4**	**58.8**	**58.5**	**58.1**	**57.7**	**57.7**	**60.9**
Lisboa e Vale do Tejo	pt13	58.7	60.1	60.2	58.7	58.4	57.7	56.9	58.7
Norte	pt11	62.2	60.2	59.2	59.4	58.9	57.4	57.7	62.9

: = not available

Source: Eurostat NewCronos REGIO database.

Table 6. Young People's (15-24 years) Activity Rates in PaYPiRD Partner Countries and some Sub-regions in 1991-1998

Country / Region	NUTS code	1991	1992	1993	1994	1995	1996	1997	1998
European Union	*eu15*	:	:	:	:	*47.2*	*46.3*	*45.9*	:
United Kingdom	uk	**64.9**	**67.9**	**66.0**	**64.6**	**63.7**	**64.5**	**64.4**	**64.0**
London	uki	:	:	:	:	:	:	:	:
Eastern Scotland	ukm2	:	:	:	:	:	:	:	:
Austria	at	:	:	:	:	**61.7**	**59.6**	**58.4**	**58.5**
Wien	at13	:	:	:	:	54.7	52.9	53.3	52.8
Steiermark	at22	:	:	:	:	60.8	59.4	59.1	58.5
Finland	fi	:	:	:	:	**49.6**	**47.5**	**48.4**	**49.7**
Uusimaa (suuralue)	fi16	:	:	:	:	:	:	:	:
Eastern Finland	fi13	:	:	:	:	44.2	49.9	47.7	46.1
France	fr	**36.8**	**39.6**	**38.2**	**36.7**	**35.7**	**35.2**	**34.2**	**34.2**
Île de France	fr1	35.6	37.2	35.3	34.3	34.9	34.1	32.1	32.4
Pays de la Loire	fr51	36.7	42.1	39.3	36.8	38.6	38.4	39.6	40.4
Germany	de	**55.8**	**58.3**	**56.2**	**54.9**	**52.5**	**50.4**	**49.7**	**50.0**
Berlin	de3	56.3	57.2	54.8	51.3	49.4	48.5	46.4	:
Weser-Ems	de94	54.4	58.6	55.7	56.9	51.6	52.7	45.4	50.3
Ireland	ie	**44.3**	**46.0**	**46.7**	**46.4**	**45.0**	**43.5**	**45.6**	:
Portugal	pt	**52.2**	**51.0**	**47.5**	**45.2**	**43.1**	**42.3**	**44.2**	**47.5**
Lisboa e Vale do Tejo	pt13	43.8	43.9	40.2	38.5	38.4	37.3	39.5	42.1
Norte	pt11	60.8	57.9	54.8	53.3	49.2	47.4	49.2	55.7

: = not available

Source: Eurostat NewCronos REGIO database.

Table 7. Young Males' (15-24 years) Activity Rates in PaYPiRD Partner Countries and some Sub-regions in 1991-1998

Country / Region	NUTS code	1991	1992	1993	1994	1995	1996	1997	1998
European Union	*eu15*	:	:	:	:	*50.4*	*49.7*	*49.5*	:
United Kingdom	uk	69.1	72.7	70.4	69.0	67.9	68.4	68.4	68.0
London	uki	:	:	:	:	:	:	:	:
Eastern Scotland	ukm2	:	:	:	:	:	:	:	:
Austria	at	:	:	:	:	64.6	62.9	61.4	61.7
Wien	at13	:	:	:	:	54.9	53.8	55.4	52.5
Steiermark	at22	:	:	:	:	65.9	64.2	61.6	61.0
Finland	fi	:	:	:	:	51.1	49.3	52.2	52.1
Uusimaa (suuralue)	fi16	:	:	:	:	:	:	:	:
Eastern Finland	fi13	:	:	:	:	45.1	54.5	52.2	49.5
France	fr	38.7	42.2	40.2	38.7	37.6	37.7	36.7	36.5
Île de France	fr1	35.8	38.3	36.2	34.8	34.9	34.8	32.4	32.6
Pays de la Loire	fr51	39.2	45.8	42.2	40.9	40.0	40.8	42.9	43.2
Germany	de	57.4	60.1	58.4	56.9	54.6	53.6	53.2	53.5
Berlin	de3	58.3	60.9	58.1	53.5	51.0	50.7	49.1	:
Weser-Ems	de94	55.1	61.1	58.6	59.3	55.0	56.6	48.6	54.1
Ireland	ie	48.2	49.6	49.4	49.3	48.3	46.7	49.1	:
Portugal	pt	57.5	56.2	52.0	48.9	47.2	46.2	48.5	51.0
Lisboa e Vale do Tejo	pt13	48.7	48.1	43.7	41.6	41.8	40.6	44.0	43.6
Norte	pt11	64.5	61.3	57.9	56.0	51.8	50.3	50.7	58.4

: = not available

Source: Eurostat NewCronos REGIO database.

Table 8. **Young Females' (15-24 years) Activity Rates in PaYPiRD Partner Countries and some Sub-regions in 1991-1998**

Country / Region	NUTS code	1991	1992	1993	1994	1995	1996	1997	1998
European Union	*eu15*	:	:	:	:	*44.0*	*42.8*	*42.3*	:
United Kingdom	uk	60.5	63.0	61.4	60.0	59.3	60.3	60.2	59.8
London	uki	:	:	:	:	:	:	:	:
Eastern Scotland	ukm2	:	:	:	:	:	:	:	:
Austria	at	:	:	:	:	58.9	56.4	55.4	55.5
Wien	at13	:	:	:	:	54.5	52.1	51.3	53.0
Steiermark	at22	:	:	:	:	55.6	54.5	56.6	56.0
Finland	fi	:	:	:	:	48.1	45.6	44.8	47.4
Uusimaa (suuralue)	fi16	:	:	:	:	:	:	:	:
Eastern Finland	fi13	:	:	:	:	43.5	45.0	42.8	42.6
France	fr	35.0	37.3	36.2	34.7	34.0	32.9	31.7	31.9
Île de France	fr1	35.3	36.3	34.4	33.8	34.9	33.4	31.7	32.3
Pays de la Loire	fr51	34.4	38.7	36.6	32.9	37.3	35.8	36.5	37.6
Germany	de	54.1	56.3	54.0	52.9	50.3	47.1	46.1	46.4
Berlin	de3	54.3	53.4	51.4	49.1	47.8	46.2	43.9	:
Weser-Ems	de94	53.8	56.3	52.9	54.6	48.2	49.2	42.1	46.6
Ireland	ie	40.2	42.3	43.8	43.3	41.4	40.1	41.9	:
Portugal	pt	46.9	46.0	43.0	41.6	38.9	38.3	39.8	43.9
Lisboa e Vale do Tejo	pt13	39.1	40.3	36.8	35.4	34.6	33.7	35.2	40.7
Norte	pt11	57.0	54.6	51.4	50.6	46.4	44.5	47.6	53.0

: = not available

Source: Eurostat NewCronos REGIO database.

Table 9. Proportion (%) of Agriculture, Forestry and Fishing from Employment in PaYPiRD Partner Countries and some Sub-regions in 1988-1995

Country / Region	NUTS code	1988	1989	1990	1991	1992	1993	1994	1995
European Union	*eu15*	*7.1*	*6.7*	*6.3*	*6.0*	*5.8*	*5.5*	*5.4*	*5.1*
United Kingdom	uk	**2.5**	**2.4**	**2.3**	**2.4**	**2.4**	**2.4**	**2.3**	**2.2**
London	uki	0.0	0.0	0.0	0.0	0.0	0.0	0.0	0.0
Eastern Scotland	ukm2	2.3	2.3	2.3	2.2	2.2	2.2	2.1	2.0
Angus and Dundee City	ukm21	2.3	2.3	2.3	2.2	2.3	2.2	2.2	2.1
Austria	at	**7.4**	**7.0**	**6.6**	**6.3**	**5.9**	**5.5**	**5.2**	**4.9**
Wien	at13	0.5	0.4	0.4	0.4	0.4	0.4	0.4	0.4
Steiermark	at22	11.7	11.1	10.4	9.9	9.3	8.8	8.2	7.7
Westliche Obersteiermark	at226	12.2	11.6	11.0	10.8	10.3	9.7	9.3	8.8
Finland	fi	**9.0**	**8.7**	**8.6**	**8.7**	**8.8**	**8.7**	**8.2**	**7.1**
Uusimaa	fi161	1.4	1.3	1.3	1.3	1.3	1.3	1.1	1.0
Eastern Finland	fi13	16.5	16.3	16.2	16.5	16.3	16.2	15.2	13.6
Kainuu	fi134	16.0	15.4	15.0	15.4	14.6	14.9	14.0	12.7
France	fr	**6.8**	**6.5**	**5.5**	**5.3**	**5.2**	**5.0**	**4.8**	**4.6**
Paris	fr101	0.0	0.0	0.1	0.1	0.1	0.1	0.1	0.1
Pays de la Loire	fr51	11.4	10.8	9.8	9.5	9.2	8.8	8.3	8.0
Mayenne	fr513	21.5	20.5	18.5	17.8	17.2	16.3	15.5	14.9
Germany	de	**3.9**	**3.7**	**3.5**	**3.9**	**3.4**	**3.2**	**3.1**	**2.9**
Berlin	de3	0.6	0.6	0.6	0.7	0.7	0.7	0.7	0.7
Weser-Ems	de94	7.9	7.4	6.8	6.7	6.3	6.0	5.7	5.5
Wesermarsch	de94g	8.6	8.6	8.0	7.9	7.1	6.7	6.9	6.7
Ireland	ie	**15.4**	**15.1**	**15.1**	**13.9**	**13.1**	**12.4**	**11.7**	**11.0**
Dublin	ie002	0.8	0.9	0.9	1.1	1.0	0.9	0.8	0.7
West	ie008	30.4	32.3	27.9	27.0	25.4	23.8	22.3	20.9
Portugal	pt	**20.4**	**19.7**	**17.7**	**16.6**	**15.2**	**14.2**	**14.1**	**14.0**
Grande Lisboa	pt132	1.2	1.1	1.0	0.9	0.9	0.8	0.8	0.7
Norte	pt11	20.9	20.2	18.3	17.1	15.3	15.3	15.2	15.3
Douro	pt117	54.4	53.3	49.9	47.5	43.7	42.6	43.0	42.7

Source: Eurostat NewCronos REGIO database.

Table 10.   **Proportion (%) of Manufacturing from Employment in PaYPiRD Partner Countries and some Sub-regions in 1988-1995**

Country / Region	NUTS code	1988	1989	1990	1991	1992	1993	1994	1995
European Union	*eu15*	*31.9*	*32.1*	*31.7*	*31.3*	*30.4*	*29.4*	*29.0*	*28.7*
United Kingdom	uk	**30.4**	**30.4**	**29.4**	**26.6**	**25.5**	**24.4**	**24.5**	**24.3**
London	uki	19.2	19.6	18.3	16.5	15.5	14.3	13.8	13.8
Eastern Scotland	ukm2	29.7	29.3	29.3	26.0	25.2	24.5	23.8	23.0
Angus and Dundee City	ukm21	30.2	31.0	31.0	29.6	28.7	26.0	25.4	23.6
Austria	at	**32.6**	**32.4**	**32.4**	**32.2**	**31.6**	**30.9**	**30.4**	**30.3**
Wien	at13	26.5	25.7	25.1	24.9	24.6	23.9	23.4	23.2
Steiermark	at22	33.3	33.6	34.1	33.9	33.2	32.5	32.0	32.0
Westliche Obersteiermark	at226	40.9	41.1	42.8	39.5	37.8	35.1	35.5	35.5
Finland	fi	**30.4**	**30.3**	**29.2**	**27.0**	**25.7**	**25.6**	**26.6**	**26.9**
Uusimaa	fi161	25.0	25.0	23.7	21.7	20.5	19.9	20.1	20.2
Eastern Finland	fi13	25.7	25.7	24.8	22.5	21.4	21.7	22.7	23.0
Kainuu	fi134	23.6	24.0	23.5	21.5	21.1	21.8	22.8	22.4
France	fr	**29.9**	**29.7**	**29.4**	**28.4**	**27.9**	**26.3**	**26.0**	**25.8**
Paris	fr101	16.0	15.6	15.2	14.6	14.3	12.6	12.3	12.0
Pays de la Loire	fr51	32.1	32.2	32.5	31.7	31.2	30.3	30.3	30.4
Mayenne	fr513	31.8	32.2	33.5	33.0	32.8	32.5	32.4	32.8
Germany	de	**38.9**	**38.9**	**38.8**	**38.9**	**37.2**	**36.1**	**35.2**	**34.8**
Berlin	de3	30.5	30.3	29.9	28.8	27.4	26.1	25.1	24.7
Weser-Ems	de94	34.4	34.8	35.4	35.3	34.9	34.3	33.7	33.9
Wesermarsch	de94g	45.0	45.4	46.3	45.5	45.9	45.0	44.4	44.0
Ireland	ie	**27.1**	**27.8**	**28.0**	**27.6**	**27.6**	**27.6**	**27.6**	**27.6**
Dublin	ie002	24.9	24.4	24.9	24.7	24.2	23.7	23.2	22.7
West	ie008	23.6	24.5	26.2	24.2	24.6	25.1	25.6	26.1
Portugal	pt	**34.9**	**34.8**	**34.3**	**34.0**	**32.6**	**32.4**	**32.3**	**32.3**
Grande Lisboa	pt132	30.5	30.0	28.2	27.2	24.3	23.6	23.3	23.3
Norte	pt11	44.4	44.3	44.3	44.1	43.0	43.0	43.6	42.8
Douro	pt117	11.9	12.0	12.4	12.3	12.4	13.5	13.6	13.8

Source: Eurostat NewCronos REGIO database.

Table 11. Proportion (%) of Services from Employment in PaYPiRD Partner Countries and some Sub-regions in 1988-1995

Country / Region	NUTS code	1988	1989	1990	1991	1992	1993	1994	1995
European Union	*eu15*	*61.0*	*61.2*	*62.0*	*62.7*	*63.9*	*65.1*	*65.6*	*66.1*
United Kingdom	uk	**67.2**	**67.3**	**68.3**	**71.1**	**72.2**	**73.2**	**73.2**	**73.5**
London	uki	80.8	80.4	81.7	83.5	84.5	85.7	86.2	86.2
Eastern Scotland	ukm2	68.0	68.4	68.5	71.8	72.6	73.4	74.1	75.0
Angus and Dundee City	ukm21	67.5	66.6	66.8	68.2	69.0	71.8	72.4	74.4
Austria	at	**60.0**	**60.6**	**61.0**	**61.6**	**62.6**	**63.6**	**64.4**	**64.8**
Wien	at13	73.0	73.9	74.4	74.7	75.0	75.8	76.2	76.5
Steiermark	at22	55.0	55.3	55.5	56.3	57.6	58.8	59.8	60.3
Westliche Obersteiermark	at226	46.9	47.3	46.5	49.8	51.9	55.2	55.3	56.0
Finland	fi	**60.7**	**61.0**	**62.2**	**64.3**	**65.5**	**65.7**	**65.3**	**66.0**
Uusimaa	fi161	73.6	73.7	75.0	77.0	78.2	78.8	78.7	78.9
Eastern Finland	fi13	57.8	58.0	58.9	61.0	62.2	62.1	62.1	63.4
Kainuu	fi134	60.4	60.4	61.2	63.1	64.3	63.4	63.2	64.9
France	fr	**63.3**	**63.8**	**65.2**	**66.4**	**67.0**	**68.6**	**69.2**	**69.6**
Paris	fr101	84.0	84.4	84.7	85.3	85.6	87.3	87.6	87.9
Pays de la Loire	fr51	56.6	57.0	57.7	58.8	59.7	60.9	61.4	61.6
Mayenne	fr513	46.8	47.3	48.0	49.1	50.0	51.2	52.1	52.3
Germany	de	**57.2**	**57.5**	**57.7**	**57.2**	**59.4**	**60.8**	**61.7**	**62.2**
Berlin	de3	68.9	69.2	69.5	70.5	71.9	73.3	74.2	74.6
Weser-Ems	de94	57.7	57.8	57.8	58.0	58.8	59.7	60.6	60.7
Wesermarsch	de94g	46.4	46.2	46.0	46.3	47.0	48.0	48.8	49.6
Ireland	ie	**57.5**	**57.1**	**57.0**	**58.5**	**59.3**	**60.1**	**60.8**	**61.4**
Dublin	ie002	74.3	74.8	74.2	74.2	74.8	75.4	76.0	76.5
West	ie008	46.0	43.2	45.9	48.9	50.0	51.1	52.0	53.0
Portugal	pt	**44.7**	**45.6**	**48.0**	**49.4**	**52.2**	**53.3**	**53.6**	**53.8**
Grande Lisboa	pt132	68.4	68.9	70.8	72.0	74.8	75.6	75.9	76.0
Norte	pt11	34.7	35.5	37.5	38.9	41.7	41.8	41.3	41.9
Douro	pt117	33.7	34.8	37.6	39.8	44.1	43.9	43.6	43.7

Source: Eurostat NewCronos REGIO database.

Table 12. **Indicators on the Structure of Farming in PaYPiRD Partner Countries and some Sub-regions**

Country / Region	NUTS code	Holdings with a manager under 35 years (%)	Holdings with a manager 35-55 years (%)	Holdings with a manager over 55 years (%)	Holdings in less favoured and mountain areas (%)	Part-time farming with other gainful activities
European Union	*eu15*	:	:	:	:	:
United Kingdom	uk	10.5	45.6	43.9	34.8	24.4
London	uki	:	:	:	:	:
Eastern Scotland	ukm2	:	:	:	:	:
Angus and Dundee City	ukm21	:	:	:	:	:
Austria	at	:	:	:	:	:
Wien	at13	:	:	:	:	:
Steiermark	at22	:	:	:	:	:
Westliche Obersteiermark	at226	:	:	:	:	:
Finland	fi	:	:	:	:	:
Uusimaa	fi161	:	:	:	:	:
Eastern Finland	fi13	:	:	:	:	:
Kainuu	fi134	:	:	:	:	:
France	fr	13.4	42.7	43.9	50.2	23.6
Paris	fr101	:	:	:	:	:
Pays de la Loire	fr51	15.8	44.1	40.1	1.8	20.4
Mayenne	fr513	15.7	42.8	41.7	:	14.6
Germany	de	:	:	:	:	:
Berlin	de3	8.5	53.4	38.1	21.1	25.6
Weser-Ems	de94	19.3	49.0	31.7	76.5	30.9
Wesermarsch	de94g	:	:	:	:	:
Ireland	ie	14.3	42.2	43.5	64.2	25.3
Dublin	ie002	11.9	46.4	41.7	17.9	31.1
West	ie008	10.9	40.4	48.7	100.0	27.9
Portugal	pt	7.0	36.1	56.9	67.9	34.6
Grande Lisboa	pt132	5.3	35.8	59.0	:	37.2
Norte	pt11	8.2	37.7	54.2	80.4	26.4
Douro	pt117	7.4	35.9	56.7	100.0	35.3

: = not available

Source: Eurostat NewCronos REGIO database (different years between 1979-1995).

Table 13. Purchasing Power Parities per Inhabitant in Percentage of the EU Average in PaYPiRD Partner Countries and some Sub-regions in 1995-1997

Country / Region	NUTS code	1995	1996	1997
European Union	*eu15*	*100.0*	*100.0*	*100.0*
United Kingdom	uk	**95.8**	**98.5**	**101.9**
London	uki	141.7	142.2	145.7
Eastern Scotland	ukm2	98.0	100.6	102.2
Angus and Dundee City	ukm21	92.0	91.6	93.1
Austria	at	**110.8**	**112.1**	**111.9**
Wien	at13	165.6	167.1	164.1
Steiermark	at22	88.6	90.6	91.2
Westliche Obersteiermark	at226	81.8	83.8	84.5
Finland	fi	**97.2**	**95.7**	**99.6**
Uusimaa	fi161	129.3	132.7	137.1
Eastern Finland	fi13	75.7	72.5	75.1
Kainuu	fi134	71.8	66.9	69.6
France	fr	**103.7**	**101.7**	**99.1**
Paris	fr101	293.5	289.3	283.7
Pays de la Loire	fr51	89.9	89.1	86.7
Mayenne	fr513	89.6	88.7	87.1
Germany	de	**110.3**	**110.0**	**108.4**
Berlin	de3	113.8	112.1	109.0
Weser-Ems	de94	103.2	104.4	102.2
Wesermarsch	de94g	87.7	85.2	83.4
Ireland	ie	**92.5**	**93.4**	**102.1**
Dublin	ie002	118.3	122.0	135.8
West	ie008	69.6	70.7	73.1
Portugal	pt	**70.3**	**69.9**	**73.2**
Grande Lisboa	pt132	113.4	111.3	115.9
Norte	pt11	62.3	61.6	64.3
Douro	pt117	51.0	54.4	53.6

Source: Eurostat NewCronos REGIO database.

Appendix 2

From Chapter 4 Methodology

Table 14. Occupational Category Distribution of Interviewees

	Austria	Finland	France	Germany	Ireland	Portugal	Scotland	Total
House-keeping	1			1				2
Student	11	6	10	4	7	5	22	65
Unemployed	6	14	11	7	8	10	3	59
Trainee	4	9	2	18	6	2	3	44
Farmer			1				1	2
Fisherman					1			1
Self Employed						1		1
Business	1							1
Employed Professional	2						1	3
Middle Management					1	1		2
Desk Worker	1	1		1	1	5		9
Employed (travelling)		1				1		2
Service Job	2	4	4		6	16	2	34
Skilled Manual Worker	4				4	2	1	11
Unskilled Manual Worker			4	3	7	3	1	18
Total	32	34	33	34	41	46	34	254

Appendix 3

Interview Topic Guide
From Chapter 4 – Methodology

1. Introduction

University Departments in seven countries (Austria, Finland, France, Germany, Ireland, Portugal and Scotland) are currently researching young peoples' experiences of looking for employment. We hope that by asking young people about their experiences, we will be able to recommend to policy-makers policies and programmes which can serve young people in their search for employment, as well as improving the conditions under which they live and work. The fact that we can compare your experiences with those of young people in other countries will help us in this process. Please be assured that any information you give to us will remain completely confidential. Your name and address will only be used for administrative purposes and possibly to invite you to participate in a follow-up focus group discussion.

2. 'Warm-Up'

Have you always lived in this area? Are you happy living here?
Prompts: what things do you like doing here? (access to and quality of leisure facilities).
       General prompts throughout: once an answer has been given concerning the own situation of the participant, the participant can be asked to consider the situation of the opposite sex, and other 'social class' groups where appropriate: is it the same or different?

3. Educational / Occupational Status

How would you describe what you are mainly occupied with at present? Are you a student/in a job/looking for a job….?

4. Education

Where did you go to school?

Can you tell me about your education? Have you done anything in education since you left secondary school [compulsory education]? Did you enjoy that experience?

What or who helped you to decide about your educational plans?
Prompts: labour market situation; parents; friends; school; careers guidance; own decision.

How likely do you think is it for you to pursue those plans?
Prompts: possible barriers: housing; transport; childcare? Should more be done to support people in education?

Have your plans changed? Why?

Do you see yourself spending more time in education in the future?

5. Training

1. Have you ever undergone a period of training?

If yes:
2a. Tell me about the training course you're doing/have done.
Prompt: any experiences of special programmes funded by the national government/local authorities designed for the unemployed or people with few qualifications? How beneficial?

3a. What or who helped you to take decisions with regard to your training? In what way(s)?
Prompts: labour market situation; parents; friends; school; careers guidance; own decision.

4a. Are you happy with your training place? Why (not)?
Prompt: can anything be done to improve the training you have experienced?

5a. When you took the course, where did you think it would lead to?
Prompt: are most people's expectations of their training courses fulfilled?

6a. Would you hope to obtain another training course in the future?

If no:
2b. Did you ever consider undergoing training? Why (not)?

3b. Would you hope to obtain a training place in the future? What would you want from it?
Prompt: is there any role the government could play here, for example, financial support; creating training places?

6. Employment

1. Is it important for you to be in a paid job? Why (not)?

If previously or currently employed:
2a. What are your experiences in employment?
Prompts: are you in the same job you have trained for? Do you feel overqualified? Underqualified? Working conditions? Casual/seasonal? Fulfilling? Well-paid?

3a. What or who helped you to take a decision with regard to your employment options?
Prompts: friends; family; a private or public agency.

4a. What kind of help, if any, did you receive to secure employment?
Prompts: friends; family; a private or public agency; education and training helpful?

5a. What kind of job/work would you like to have in the future?

6a. How likely is it for you to achieve those objectives?
Prompts: possible barriers: housing; transport; childcare; 'staying or leaving' issues; availability of local opportunities.

7a. Have your ideas/plans about work changed, and, if so, why?
Prompt: How realistic were they?

8a. Do you know young people who are unemployed? What do you think are the reasons for this?
Prompts: how could *they* improve their job prospects? Is there a role for the government to help them getting a job?

9a. Do you think you get (got) a fair wage for the work you do (did)?
Prompts: could you live on it? What of your expenses did it cover?

*If previously or currently unemployed: (*If interviewee is a student who has never been in employment, ask only questions 5b and 6b)*

2b. What is it like to be unemployed in this area?
Prompts: can you get some casual work from time to time? Do you do any unpaid work? Pressure from family/friends?

3b. What do you think are the reasons for people being unemployed in this area?
Prompts: lack of the skills; lack of jobs; transport.

4b. What do you think should be done to improve the opportunities for young people in your area to find a job?

Prompt: role of government?

5b. How would you describe your employment objectives in the long-term?

6b. How likely is it for you to achieve those objectives?
Prompts: possible barriers: housing; transport; childcare; 'staying or leaving' issues; availability of local opportunities.

7b. How would you describe your past employment objectives?
Prompt: How realistic were they?

7. Housing

1. Do you live in your parental home?
Prompt: household composition.

If interviewee lives with parents
2a. How do you find this arrangement?

3a Have you lived away from home previously? What was that like?

4a. How would you describe your housing plans in the long-term?

5a. How likely is it for you to fulfil this plan?
Prompts: possible barriers: availability; costs; tenure.

6a. How would you describe your past housing plan?
Prompt: How realistic was it?

If interviewee lives independently:
2b. How long did you live with your parents? How did you find this arrangement?

3b. How did you find your independent accommodation?
Prompts: family; friends; social networks; newspaper; estate agency.

4b. How did you get access to your independent housing?
Prompts: availability; costs; type of tenure (rented; private; owner-occupied); role of family.

5b. How easy is it to get a house in this area?

6b. How would you describe your housing plans in the long-term?

7b. How likely is it for you to fulfil this plan?
Prompts: possible barriers: availability; costs.

8b. How would you describe your past housing plan?
Prompt: How realistic was it?

8. Family, Friends and Social Networks

1. Tell me a bit about your parents and other family.
Prompts: locals or migrants? How well connected is family? What kind of support have you received from family and/or is likely to receive? How important are your personal networks in finding work, housing, etc? Can you always rely on the support of your family, friends and/or social networks?

2. Who do you turn to when you experience problems?

3. Have you yourself started a family?

If yes:
4a. Can you envisage staying here in the long-term with your family?

If no:
4b. Can you see yourself having a family here?

5. What would you do in your free time?
Prompt: local clubs and associations, political groups, music.

6. Why this activity/these activities?

7. What do you like and/or dislike about leisure activities/youth culture in this area?

9. Young People's Participation

1. Do young people have a say in what happens around here?

If yes
2a. How can people participate? Does the participation make a difference?

3a. Are there more areas you would like to be involved in?
Prompt: what kind of involvement?

If no
2b. Who does decide what happens in this area?
Prompt: Why do young people feel unable to join in?

3b. Are these good decisions?

10. Summation

1. Overall, can you sum up the benefits and the drawbacks of living in ..... [your area].

2. If you could 'do it all again', would you decide differently? Why (not)?
Prompts: education, training.

3. What future do you see for this area?

4. What do you think about this interview?
Prompts: anything you wish to add to earlier comments? Were questions asked relevant to your life? Are there areas you would have liked to talk about which were not covered?

Appendix 4

Moray Youthstart Partners

1. The Moray Council	Statutory
2. NCH Action for Children (Scotland)	Voluntary
3. Aberlour Childcare Trust	Charity
4. Children 1st	Charity[1]
5. Scottish Homes	Voluntary
6. Grampian Health Board	Statutory
7. Moray Health Services Trust	Charity
8. Grampian Health Promotions	Statutory
9. Moray, Badenoch and Strathspey Enterprise (Local Enterprise Company)	Private
10. Employment Agency	Statutory
11. Grampian Careers Company	Private
12. Moray, Business and Education Partnership	Voluntary Liaison Group
13. Grampian Housing Association	Voluntary
14. Langstane Housing Association	Voluntary
15. Moray Voluntary Services Organisation	Voluntary
16. Moray Landlords' Assoc.	Private Liaison Group
17. Grampian Police	Statutory
18. Drug Action Team	Statutory Liaison Group
19. Children's Panel	Statutory
20. Who Cares?	Voluntary

[1] Equivalent to the National Society for the Prevention of Cruelty to Children (NSPCC) in England

Index

Notes: page numbers in italics refer to tables & figures. Numbers in brackets preceded by *n* are note numbers.

6, 172, *183*
youth projects in *185*
Suomussalmi 61
    career planning in 248, 252
    criteria of study area 4-5, *5*, 34, *66*
    education in 241, 242, 243
    housing in 95
    labour market in 88, 101, 117-18,
        254-5
        youth unemployment *258*, 259,
        261, 263
    methodology used in 67
    perceptions of local area 82, 86
        concerns for future of 97
    social exclusion in 99
    social networks in 224, 225, *225*
    youth crime in 84
sustainable development 9, 32, 97,
133, 139
Sweden 43, 153
    service sector in 27
    unemployment in 36
Switzerland 43

T
Tarling, R. 44
teachers
    attitude to pupils 242-3
    skills gap in 123
    training of 115
technological development 27
tourism sector 2, 76, 77, 160, 161,
181
    as indicator 79
    jobs in 27, 89, 98, 261
        low pay in 21
    training in 169
Trace programme 113, 119
trade unions 129, 132
training 19, 64, 67, 71
    access to 253-4, 260
    certifying 232-3
    and networks 200, 204-5, 231-2
    partnerships 134, 136, 138, 168
    programmes 104, 107-8, 114-17, 125-6
        and rural development 159, 163, 173
    provision for 125
    in questionnaire 315-16
    of teachers 115

vocational 112, 116, 122-3, 164
work experience 144, 252
and youth rights 16
see also apprenticeships
Training & Enterprise Councils (UK)
125
transition *see* youth transition
transport 21, 64, 75, 87-8
    access to, and rural development
        162, *182*
    and education 123, 221, 278
    public, lack of 87, 126, 252, 253
    and social exclusion 22
    to work 24, 87, 260
        costs 18
        solutions 19
    vehicle ownership 24, 87, 88, 252
Turok, L. 131

U
UN-ECE 32
unemployment 71, 130, 251, 258-63
    benefit 21
    defined 35
    government support for 266
    hidden 20
    long-term 111, 112, 113
        PESP Pilot Initiative on 133
    rates 36-8, *37-8*, 142, 258-9, *300-3*
        as indicator 30, 35-8, 41, *42*
        rural/urban compared 47-8, *47-8*,
        52-3, *53*, 55-7, *55-7*
Ungerson, C. 73
United Kingdom 25, 156, 172, *312*
    activity rates *304-7*
    agricultural sector in 26, *311*
    education in, return to 114
    employment
        initiatives 112, 169-71
        rates, sectoral *308-10*
    micro-data in 42
        sample size *45*
    rural population of 28
    rural poverty in 21
    service sector in 27
    small businesses in 27
    social exclusion in 3, 12
    training in 114
    unemployment in 36, *300*